CRACKS IN AN EARTHEN VESSEL:
An Examination of the Catalogues of Hardships in the Corinthian Correspondence

SOCIETY
OF BIBLICAL
LITERATURE

DISSERTATION SERIES

J. J. M. Roberts, Old Testament Editor
Charles Talbert, New Testament Editor

Number 99

CRACKS IN AN EARTHEN VESSEL:
An Examination of the Catalogues of Hardships
in the Corinthian Correspondence

by

John T. Fitzgerald

John T. Fitzgerald

CRACKS IN AN EARTHEN VESSEL:
An Examination of the Catalogues of Hardships in the Corinthian Correspondence

Scholars Press
Atlanta, Georgia

CRACKS IN AN EARTHEN VESSEL:
An Examination of the Catalogues of Hardships in the Corinthian Correspondence

John T. Fitzgerald

Ph.D., 1984
Yale University

Advisor:
Abraham J. Malherbe

Library of Congress Cataloging-in-Publication Data

Fitzgerald, John T., 1948–
Cracks in an Earthen Vessel.
(Dissertation series / Society of Biblical
Literature ; no. 99)
Bibliography: p.
1. Suffering—Biblical teaching. 2. Paul, the
Apostle, Saint. 3. Bible. N.T. Corinthians—
Criticism, interpretation, etc. I. Title.
II. Title: Hardships in the Corinthian correspondence.
III. Series: Dissertation series (Society of Biblical
Literature) ; no. 99.
BS2655.S8F57 1988 227'.206 86-26164
ISBN 1-55540-087-6 (alk. paper)
ISBN 1-55540-088-4 (pbk. : alk. paper)

Printed in the United States of America

Contents

Preface

The completion of this investigation is a tribute to the constant encouragement and unstinting support of my wife Karol. I dedicate it to her and our daughters, Kirstin and Kimberly. I gratefully acknowledge the debt that I owe professionally to all my teachers at Yale University, especially Nils A. Dahl, Wayne A. Meeks, and Abraham J. Malherbe. It was Professor Malherbe who suggested that I investigate the *peristasis* catalogue, and his careful reading of my work has only heightened my appreciation for his insight and keen exegetical judgment. The blunders from which he could not save me are those that remain, and for these I bear sole responsibility.

This work could not have been completed without the assistance and support of my parents, Mr. & Mrs. J. T. Fitzgerald, and a host of people at the University of Miami. Above all, thanks must go to Arthur W. Brown, Dean of the College of Arts and Sciences, and Daniel L. Pals, Chairman of the Department of Religion. If the present work has any lasting merit, it is only because their confidence and forbearance have allowed me the time to do the necessary research on this subject. Finally for the typing of a most difficult manuscript, my thanks and respect are extended to Mrs. Kathy Kelleher and Ms. Patricia Wilson.

Introduction

In 1 Cor 15:30–31 Paul says that "we are in peril every hour" and "I die daily." As an example of his daily death and danger he mentions his battle with the wild beasts at Ephesus (15:32).[1] Elsewhere in his letters to the Corinthians he refers to other dangers and difficulties that he experienced as an apostle. Sometimes the reference is to a particular episode (2 Cor 1:8–10), while at other times it is to a multiplicity of different but related tribulations. In the latter case the reference takes the form of a list of hardships. Such lists occur in both 1 Corinthians (4:9–13) and 2 Corinthians (4:8–9; 6:4–10; 11:23–28; 12:10).

These lists and others in the Pauline corpus (Rom 8:35–39; Phil 4:11–12; 2 Tim 3:11) are often referred to in modern secondary literature as "*Peristasenkataloge*"[2] or "*peristasis* catalogues."[3] This designation stems from the widespread recognition that Paul's lists are similar to lists of "circumstances" (*peristaseis*) found in numerous ancient documents. In view of this general recognition it is surprising that so little research has been devoted to these lists. As Hans Dieter Betz correctly notes in regard to these *peristasis* catalogues, their literary form, function, and origin have not yet been explained.[4]

This lack of attention to the *peristasis* catalogue as such has had certain consequences. First, the understanding of *peristasis* catalogues in non-Christian authors has been formed on the basis of only a few specimens of this literary

[1] On this *crux interpretum*, cf. esp. Abraham J. Malherbe, "The Beasts at Ephesus," *JBL* 87 (1968) 71–80.

[2] Cf., for instance, Ulrich Luz, *Das Geschichtsverständnis des Paulus* (BEvT 49; Munich: Kaiser, 1968) 376; Ernst Käsemann, *An die Römer* (HNT 8a; 3d rev. ed.; Tübingen: Mohr, 1974) 240, 243; Jacob Jervell, "Der schwache Charismatiker," *Rechtfertigung* (E. Käsemann Festschrift; ed. J. Friedrich et al; Tübingen: Mohr; Göttingen: Vandenhoeck & Ruprecht, 1976) 197 n. 64; Peter Fiedler, "Röm 8:31-39 als Brennpunkt paulinischer Frohbotschaft," *ZNW* 68 (1977) 24; and Erich Fascher, *Der erste Brief des Paulus an die Korinther* (THKNT 7.1; 2d ed.; Berlin: Evangelische Verlagsanstalt, 1980) 151.

[3] Cf., for example, Wayne A. Meeks (ed.), *The Writings of St. Paul* (New York: Norton, 1972) 57 n. 2 and 63 n. 6, and *The First Urban Christians* (New Haven/London: Yale, 1983) 96; Nils A. Dahl, "A Fragment and Its Context: 2 Corinthians 6:14–7:1," in his *Studies in Paul* (Minneapolis: Augsburg, 1977) 67; Malherbe, "Beasts," 72, and "Antisthenes and Odysseus, and Paul at War," *HTR* 76 (1983) 171 n. 156; and R. F. Hock, *The Social Context of Paul's Ministry* (Philadelphia: Fortress, 1980) 28, 35, 60.

[4] H. D. Betz, *Der Apostel Paulus und die sokratische Tradition* (BHT 45; Tübingen: Mohr, 1972) 98.

phenomenon, which are then declared "representative." As a result, neither the popularity of these catalogues nor their diversity in content and function has been recognized. Second, this means that a highly select number of "representative" texts has formed the corpus with which Paul's catalogues have been compared. This has resulted in sweeping conclusions being drawn from a very limited data base.

A more detailed examination with a larger data base for comparison with Pauline catalogues is thus a desideratum, and the following study is presented here in the hope that it will make a contribution toward a greater understanding of this ancient literary convention of compiling lists of *peristaseis.* It is hoped that this investigation will broaden the perspective from which Paul's catalogues may be viewed and thus provide a partial check against the reductionist tendencies of present practice. It should serve as well to undergird various correct observations that have already been made. The insight, for example, that *peristasis* catalogues may function to legitimate a person is correct, and so Paul's use of catalogues of hardships to legitimate his claim to be an apostle of Christ is quite in keeping with this standard use of *peristasis* catalogues.[5] But since this is not the only function that such catalogues have, either in Paul or in other authors, a clarification of the forms and functions of *peristasis* catalogues in general and Paul's in particular is in order. By placing Paul's catalogues within the literary traditions of antiquity certain aspects of those catalogues can be understood more precisely.

The procedure adopted here for executing this task is as follows. The first chapter is devoted to a survey of research on Paul and the *peristasis* catalogue. This survey is primarily descriptive, but it is also partially evaluative. Some scholars have shown keen insight in dealing with issues central to this investigation, and their conclusions are foundational not only for this study but for all future research on this topic as well. But the suggestions of some scholars, while quite provocative and highly influential for the way in which Paul's catalogues are currently understood, are problematic and do not merit the continued support of contemporary scholarship. The survey, therefore, will indicate the areas of research that not only require the most attention but also those that promise to yield the highest dividends. These are the areas that receive greatest attention in the subsequent chapters of this investigation.

The second chapter is devoted to an examination of the key word "*peristasis.*" Since there is no adequate discussion of this word, a somewhat comprehensive treatment is provided. This examination of *peristasis,* moreover, will help the reader understand how *peristasis* catalogues were viewed in the ancient world and how they functioned.

[5] For the recognition that the Corinthian correspondence contains "several lists of the vicissitudes and acts which in Paul's view legitimatize the true apostle . . ." cf. Günther Bornkamm, *Paul* (New York: Harper & Row, 1969) 169.

This line of investigation is continued in chapter three, where a brief survey of the more important types of *peristasis* catalogues is provided at the outset. Following this survey, attention for the rest of the chapter is focused on the figure of the wise man. NT scholars have long recognized that a marked similarity exists between ancient depictions of the sage and Paul's depictions of apostolic existence. The sage was frequently discussed in terms of his hardships, so that the *peristasis* catalogues that occur in these depictions merit very careful attention, as does the figure of the sage himself. The increasing recognition that Paul was acquainted with various traditions about the sage makes this concentration all the more promising.[6]

Chapter four contains an examination of three of the *peristasis* catalogues found in Paul's Corinthian correspondence, viz., 1 Cor 4:9–13, 2 Cor 4:8–9, and 2 Cor 6:4–10. These catalogues usually receive less attention than the ones in 2 Cor 11–12, so that a concentration on these specimens can serve to correct this imbalance as well as lay a foundation for a more nuanced understanding of Paul's other catalogues.[7]

Since a major concern in this examination is with the literary function of these catalogues in Paul's letters, considerable attention is devoted to the letters themselves. The catalogues are discussed both within the framework of the canonical context and in relationship to the material examined in chapter two and especially chapter three. It will be seen that each catalogue is written in a distinct style and has certain specific functions within the material in which it occurs. An enhanced recognition of how Paul's catalogues function within the various sections of his letters will thus serve to enrich our understanding of the Corinthian correspondence as a whole. This study thus represents an attempt to use Hellenistic material to address *literary* rather than theological or history of religions issues. While the focus is not, therefore, on the theme of Paul's sufferings as such,[8] it is hoped that this investigation will contribute new information and a sharpened perspective to the treatment of other issues raised by the catalogues.

[6] Cf. esp. Malherbe, "Beasts," 71–80; "Antisthenes," esp. 172; and above all, " 'Gentle as a Nurse': The Cynic Background to I Thess 2," *NovT* 12 (1970) 203–17. Cf. also Betz, *Der Apostel Paulus,* and Hock, *Social Context,* esp. 18, 41, and 47.

[7] It is with great regret that an analysis of the catalogues in Paul's *Narrenrede* (2 Cor 11:23–28; 12:10) is not directly undertaken in this study. The decisive factor that dictates this exclusion is the space required for an adequate treatment of these important catalogues and the highly complex material in which they occur. Faced with the Scylla of a superficial treatment of these lists and the Charybdis of a radical curtailment of the discussion of other material, it seems expedient to omit here the treatment of 2 Cor 10–13 and to devote a special study to it elsewhere. The perceptive reader will note, however, that certain questions involving this material are addressed at various points in the present investigation.

[8] A treatment of Paul's sufferings as a theological theme is offered by Erhardt Güttgemanns, *Der leidende Apostel und sein Herr* (FRLANT 90; Göttingen: Vandenhoeck

Fundamental to this study is the conviction that Paul's Corinthian catalogues play a vital role in his self-presentation (*Selbstdarstellung*). The discussion of his catalogues, therefore, will simultaneously make a contribution to the larger question of Paul's self-presentation in his letters. This, as Hans Dieter Betz has pointed out, is another "literary problem which needs further investigation."[9] The treatment of Paul's catalogues will make clear that he draws on *sophos*-imagery to a considerable extent in depicting not only himself but the Corinthians as well.[10] And while he frequently employs Stoic traditions in particular, his use of those traditions is still much more modest and subtle than that made by Philo, who "never lets us forget that behind the pious Jew stands the Stoic sage."[11]

Some of the more important conclusions to be drawn from the investigation will be given in chapter five. Other conclusions will be so obvious as not to require comment. On the basis of chapter three, for example, it will already be clear that boasting in regard to one's hardships was extrmely common in the ancient world. It will hardly be necessary to state how untenable the claim is that Paul's boasting in this regard is something unusual, that sufferings are something "about which the naturally boastful person would say nothing."[12] But this is to anticipate what will become clear as the discussion proceeds.

Finally, in keeping with contemporary practice in American NT circles, the translations of ancient Greek and Latin authors in the Loeb Classical Library have been used when available.[13] The abbreviations used for the citation of both primary and secondary texts follow, where possible, the guidelines of the Society of Biblical Literature.[14] Where no abbreviation has been recommended by the

---

& Ruprecht, 1966). On the theme of apostolic sufferings (and an *Auseinandersetzung* with Güttgemanns), cf. also Walter Schmithals, *The Office of Apostle in the Early Church* (Nashville: Abingdon, 1969) 47–50, 222–25, and *Gnosticism in Corinth* (Nashville: Abingdon, 1971) 207, 368–70, 380. For a critique of both Güttgemanns and Schmithals, cf. esp. K. M. Fischer, "Die Bedeutung des Leidens in der Theologie des Paulus," (Ph.D. Diss., Humboldt-Universität zu Berlin, 1967) esp. 71–77, 85–99.

[9] H. D. Betz, "De Laude Ipsius (Moralia 539A–547F)," in H. D. Betz (ed.), *Plutarch's Ethical Writings and Early Christian Literature* (Studia ad Corpus Hellenisticum Novi Testamenti 4; Leiden: Brill, 1978) 379 n. 43.

[10] In addition, he can also use traditions about the sage in order to depict his opponents. Cf. 2 Cor 10:3–6 and the discussion of Malherbe, "Antisthenes," esp. 166–73.

[11] Max Pohlenz, "Paulus und die Stoa," *ZNW* 42 (1949) 81.

[12] The claim is that of R. V. G. Tasker, *The Second Epistle of Paul to the Corinthians* (Tyndale NT Commentaries 8; Grand Rapids: Eerdmans, 1963) 167.

[13] In a few instances the LCL translation has been adapted or slightly modified. Where no LCL translation is available or for some reason could not be used, either another standard translation has been used (and the translator indicated) or I have provided my own translation.

[14] Cf. either *JBL* 95 (1976) 331–46 or the *SBL Member's Handbook* (Chico: Scholars, 1980).

SBL, preference in the citation of ancient authors and texts is given to the abbreviations employed in *The Oxford Classical Dictionary*.[15] For modern periodicals and series a similar preference is accorded the abbreviations listed in *L'Année philologique*.[16] Since other abbreviations are self-explanatory, attention may now turn from these preliminary matters and comments to the *Forschungsbericht* on Paul and the *peristasis* catalogue.

[15] Cf. N. G. L. Hammond and H. H. Scullard (eds.), *The Oxford Classical Dictionary* (2d ed.; Oxford: Clarendon, 1970) ix-xxii. Where the *OCD* lists no abbreviation, one of those used in the following works has normally been adopted: H. G. Liddell and R. Scott, *A Greek-English Lexicon* (rev. H. S. Jones & R. McKenzie; 9th ed.; Oxford: Clarendon, 1940); G. W. H. Lampe (ed.), *A Patristic Greek Lexicon* (Oxford: Clarendon, 1961); C. T. Lewis and C. Short, *A New Latin Dictionary* (New York: American, 1907); P. G. W. Glare (ed.), *Oxford Latin Dictionary* (Oxford: Clarendon, 1982); and Alexander Souter, *A Glossary of Later Latin to 600 A.D.* (Oxford: Clarendon, 1949). For Philo, however, the abbreviations employed by Samuel Sandmel have been adopted. Cf. his *Philo of Alexandria* (New York: Oxford, 1979) xi-xii. Finally, for the sake of clarity, some authors and texts are cited without abbreviation.

[16] For the most current list, cf. 51 (1982) xv-xxxvi.

1
History of Research

The name of Rudolf Bultmann frequently looms large in surveys of NT scholarship on various topics and the present survey does not constitute an exception to this phenomenon.[1] Bultmann, more than anyone else, is responsible for the application of the term *Peristasenkatalog* to Paul's lists of difficulties and for the understanding of the catalogues that is current in many scholarly circles. Yet, as in many other fields of investigation, Bultmann was continuing research on a subject already pursued by his teacher Johannes Weiss.[2]

[1] The following survey does not purport to be either comprehensive or exhaustive. An attempt has been made, however, to include a reference to every substantive discussion of the catalogues in the twentieth century.

[2] By beginning with Weiss I do not imply that he was the first to recognize certain affinities between Paul's catalogues and passages from Graeco-Roman literature. Already in 1620 Abraham Scultetus, *Deliciae evangelicae pragenses* (Hanoviae: Typis Wechelianis, apud D. & D. Aubrios & C. Schleichium, 1620) made the suggestion that 2 Cor 11:23–27 had been inspired by the catalogue of "very difficult labors" in Ps-Heraclitus, *Ep.* 4.3 (190,31–192,5 Malherbe). Two centuries later, Amédée Fleury revived the suggestion that the two passages were intimately connected, but maintained that it was Paul who had inspired ps-Heraclitus, not vice-versa. While Fleury noted that Paul enumerated physical trials and ps-Heraclitus moral ones, this fact did not prevent him from linking the two passages. Indeed, he also suggested that 2 Cor 11:23–27 and 12:7–10 had inspired sections of Sen., *Ep.* 65, esp. 65.20–24, and that Lucian, *Peregr.* 32, was an allusion to 2 Cor 11:23–26. This latter suggestion was part of his hypothesis that Lucian's depiction of Peregrinus is a parody of Paul's character and adventures. Cf. A. Fleury, *Saint Paul et Sénèque* (2 vols.; Paris: Ladrange, 1853) 1.36–39; 2.118, 247–49. Bruno Bauer, *Christus und die Caesaren* (Berlin: Grosser, 1877) 52–54, continued the tradition of linking the ps-Heraclitus passage with 2 Cor 11:23–28 but added a reference to Sen., *Ep.* 85.41, which contains an important catalogue of the sage's hardships. Building on Bauer's work, Rudolf Steck observed that Paul's depiction of his hardships agrees better with the catalogues of his contemporaries than with the hardships recounted in Acts. Comparing Sen., *Ep.* 85.26–27 with Rom 8:35, he argued that "the similarity can hardly be accidental" and that it reflects the dependence of "Paul" (ps-Paul) on Seneca. Cf. R. Steck, *Der Galaterbrief nach seiner Echtheit untersucht, nebst kritischen Bemerkungen zu den paulinischen Hauptbriefen* (Berlin: Reimer, 1888) 256. In the previous year, however, Johannes Kreyher,

In the 1897 *Festschrift* for his father, Weiss examined the rhetorical element in Paul's letters.[3] He pointed to Paul's paratactic, non-periodic style and its striking affinities with the Cynic-Stoic diatribe.[4] Paying special attention to parallelism and antithesis, which he viewed as the fundamental elements of Pauline composition,[5] Weiss adduced 2 Cor 4:7-11 and 6:3-10 as examples of the latter and 2 Cor 11:16-31 as an instance of the former, complete with anaphora, antistrophe, homoioteleuton, homoioptoton, and isocola.[6] 1 Cor 4:6-13, Phil 4:11-13, and Rom 8:31-39 received attention as well,[7] with Epictetus, *Diss.* 1.11.33 and 3.3.18 cited as similar to Rom 8:35-39.[8] Weiss was impressed by the versatility

---

L. Annaeus Seneca und seine Beziehungen zum Urchristentum (Berlin: Gaertner, 1887) 86, had already made the same comparison of Sen., *Ep.* 85.26-27 and Rom 8:35 in support of his contention that Paul had influenced Seneca.

Thus, some work on the *peristasis* catalogues had been done prior to Weiss. Yet, the absence of catalogues in the parallels cited by Edmund Spiess, *Logos Spermaticós: Parallelstellen zum Neuen Testament aus den Schriften der alten Griechen* (Leipzig: Engelmann, 1871) is indicative of the neglect of the catalogues up to this point. Indeed, even J. J. Wettstein, *Novum Testamentum Graecum* (1751; 2 vols.; reprinted, Gras, Oesterreich: Akademische Druck-und Verlagsanstalt, 1962) 2.209, provides only a few references to catalogues *per se* (such as Heliodorus, *Aeth.* 2.4), and these are incidental to his main purpose of clarifying individual words and phrases. As far as the Jewish material is concerned, John Lightfoot passes over the possible parallels in his *A Commentary on the New Testament from the Talmud and Hebraica* (4 vols.; reprint of the 1859 translation of the 1658-1674 Latin original; Grand Rapids: Baker, 1979). In addition to this general neglect of the catalogues, it should be emphasized that the future direction of scholarship was set by Weiss and the influence he exerted on Bultmann.

[3] Johannes Weiss, "Beiträge zur Paulinischen Rhetorik," in *Theologische Studien. B. Weiss zu seinem 70. Geburtstage* (ed. C. R. Gregory; Göttingen: Vandenhoeck & Ruprecht, 1897) 165-247.

[4] Ibid., 167-68. Cf. also J. Weiss, *Die christliche Freiheit nach der Verkündigung des Apostels Paulus* (Göttingen: Vandenhoeck & Ruprecht, 1902) 9, 35-36 n. 78, *Die Aufgaben der neutestamentlichen Wissenschaft in der Gegenwart* (Göttingen: Vandenhoeck & Ruprecht, 1908) 11-13, and J. Weiss and R. Knopf, *The History of Primitive Christianity* (2 vols.; New York: Wilson-Erickson, 1937) 1.417.

[5] *History,* 1. 411.

[6] "Beiträge," 177-78, 185-87. Cf. also *Aufgaben,* 19, and *History,* 1.415-16, 419-20.

[7] "Beiträge," 191, 195-96, 209-10. A more detailed discussion of 1 Cor 4:6-13 is given by Weiss in his commentary on 1 Corinthians. Cf. *Der erste Korintherbrief* (MeyerK 5; 9th ed.; Göttingen: Vandenhoeck & Ruprecht, 1910) 100-15. In *Freiheit,* 28, Weiss compares Phil. 4:11-12 to the Cynic and Stoic ideal of *autarkeia.*

[8] "Beiträge," 196. Weiss calls attention to the similarity of Epict., *Diss.* 1.11.33 and Rom 8:35ff also in his *Aufgaben,* 13, and adds here references to Mar. Ant., *Med.* 2.11 and Philo, *Mos.* 2.16. Cf. also *History,* 1.404, where Weiss refers to "certain stereotyped designations of sorrows and needs, such as we find in Rom. 8:35 and 1 Cor. 4:11, and which also have parallels in Epictetus." For Weiss, then, Paul's catalogues are a "fixed rhetorical *topos*" (*Korintherbrief,* 111).

of Pauline rhetoric as a method of self-presentation and emphasized Paul's ability to express very different moods through similar, antithetic forms.[9]

In the thirteen year interim between Weiss' 1897 essay and the appearance of Bultmann's dissertation in 1910, interest in the *peristasis* catalogues remained primarily stylistic. As one would expect, this is especially true for Eduard Norden's treatment of Paul in his study of ancient literary prose, a work that appeared in 1898.[10] Though judging the style of Paul's letters as non-Hellenic on the whole, Norden nevertheless noted that in a number of instances Paul had made use of the stylistic means current in Greek rhetoric. He was especially impressed by Paul's repeated use of antithesis and called attention to its presence in 1 Cor 4:10ff and 2 Cor 5:6–10.[11] The latter passage, he emphasized, had already in antiquity become famous for its antitheses.[12] Such rhetorical means were not, in Norden's view, an end in themselves but served to give expression to the solemnity of Paul's thought.[13]

In 1908 C. F. Georg Heinrici, who had been castigated by Norden for exaggerating the Greek element in Paul's letters,[14] devoted an entire monograph to the question of the NT's literary character.[15] Convinced that Paul thought and spoke under the influence of Hellenistic culture, Heinrici believed that Paul's style was especially comparable to that of Epictetus and the diatribe.[16] He pointed in

[9] "Beiträge," 178. Cf. also *History*, 1.401, 414–16.

[10] Eduard Norden, *Die antike Kunstprosa* (2 vols.; Leipzig: Teubner, 1898) esp. 2.492–510.

[11] Ibid., 507–08.

[12] Ibid., 505, 508 n. 1. Norden refers in particular to August., *doctr. christ.* 4.20.42; *De civ. D.* 11.18; the scholiast to Persius 1.86; and Jerome's Vulgate.

[13] Ibid., 507.

[14] Ibid., 493–98. The work criticized is Heinrici's *Das zweite Sendschreiben des Apostels Paulus an die Korinther* (Berlin: Hertz, 1887). Heinrici responded to this attack in an appendix ("Zum Hellenismus des Paulus") to the eighth edition of his *Der zweite Brief an die Korinther* (MeyerK 6; Göttingen: Vandenhoeck & Ruprecht, 1900) 436–58. The controversy between them was well-known. Cf., for example, T. Nägeli, *Der Wortschatz des Apostels Paulus* (Göttingen: Vandenhoeck & Ruprecht, 1905) 12–13, who takes a mediating, Deissmannian position. Norden himself later apologized for the vociferousness of his attack on Heinrici. Cf. the *Nachträge* to the 3d ed. (1915) 2.3. Despite Heinrici's emphasis on the importance of Hellenism for understanding the NT, it should be noted that he denied that the fundamental perspectives of the NT could be derived therefrom. Cf. esp. his *Hellenismus und Christentum* (Biblische Zeit-und Streitfragen V. 8; Gr. Lichterfelde-Berlin: Edwin Runge, 1909) 31–45, esp. 44, and the remarks of Hans Windisch, "Literature on the New Testament in Germany, Austria, Switzerland, Holland, and the Scandinavian Countries, 1914–1920," *HTR* 15 (1922) 212–13.

[15] C. F. G. Heinrici, *Der literarische Charakter der neutestamentlichen Schriften* (Leipzig: Dürr'sche Buchhandlung, 1908).

[16] The similarity of Paul's method to that of Epictetus had been affirmed earlier in his *Das zweite Sendschreiben*, 576. On the relevance of Epictetus and the diatribe, cf. also his *Der zweite Brief*, 438 n., 439, 442, 448, 451, 454–55.

particular to the similarity of *Diss.* 3.22.21 and Rom 8.[17] He emphasized that Paul used the same means of expression as found in the Cynic-Stoic diatribe, including antithesis (2 Cor 4:7–12; 6:4–10) and enumeration (Rom 8:35).[18] In regard to 2 Cor 11:16–30, Heinrici not only noted Augustine's stylistic discussion of this passage[19] but also quite astutely recommended a comparison of 2 Cor 10–12 with Plutarch's *On Inoffensive Self-Praise.* As Heinrici already saw, "Its suggestions correspond to what Paul does here."[20]

With the connection between the diatribe and Paul's style now established by Weiss, Heinrici, and Paul Wendland (upon whom both Weiss and Heinrici were heavily dependent for their understanding of the diatribe),[21] Bultmann carried out a comprehensive comparison of the two in his dissertation, *The Style of Paul's Preaching and the Cynic-Stoic Diatribe.*[22] He found in the dialogical aspect of the diatribe a simplicity and brevity of style, a feature that he saw balanced by a corresponding quantitative fullness of expression. As examples of the latter he gave enumeration, exemplification of a main idea by the recitation of particulars,[23] catalogues of virtues and vices, and what he called

[17] Ibid., 65–66, esp. 66., n. 1. In the eighth (1900) edition of his *Der zweite Brief* Heinrici adds a reference to Epict., *Diss.* 1.11.33, a passage that he possibly has drawn from Weiss' article on Pauline rhetoric. He treats this as an example of enumeration, one of "the favorite rhetorical means of ancient admonitory literature" (p. 227, the second footnote). For his treatment of Weiss' article, cf. 457–58.

[18] Ibid., 67–68. On the diatribe, cf. 11–12.

[19] Cf. August., *doctr. christ.* 4.7.12–13.

[20] Ibid., 67, esp. n. 2. In the same vein Heinrici aptly refers also to the exordium of Demosthenes, *De corona.*

[21] Cf. Weiss, "Beiträge," 167–68, *Freiheit,* 36–37 n. 7, and Heinrici, *Charakter,* 12 n. 2. For Wendland's work on the diatribe, cf. *Quaestiones Musonianae* (Berlin: Mayer und Müller, 1886), "Philo und die kynisch-stoische Diatribe," in P. Wendland and O. Kern, *Beiträge zur Geschichte der griechischen Philosophie und Religion* (Berlin: Georg Reimer, 1895), and *Die hellenistisch-römische Kultur in ihren Beziehungen zu Judentum und Christentum* (HNT 1:2; 2d and 3d ed.; Tübingen: Mohr, 1912) esp. 75–81. On the diatribe, and Wendland's contributions to its study, cf. now S. K. Stowers, *The Diatribe and Paul's Letter to the Romans* (SBLDS 57; Chico: Scholars, 1981) esp. 12–14.

[22] *Der Stil der paulinischen Predigt und die kynisch-stoische Diatribe* (FRLANT 13; Göttingen: Vandenhoeck & Ruprecht, 1910). In the preceding year the first edition of Carl Clemen, *Religionsgeschichtliche Erklärung des Neuen Testaments* (Giessen: Töpelmann/Ricker, 1909) appeared. Clemen (49) included the enumeration of apostolic sufferings in 1 Cor 4 among the passages for which Stoic-Cynic parallels had been cited. He also (53) acknowledged with Steck the similarity of Sen., *Ep.* 85.26–27 and Rom 8:35 in tone and rhetorical form, but he insisted on the fundamental difference in perspective between Paul and the Stoics. He was followed in this regard by Percy Gardner, *The Religious Experience of Saint Paul* (Crown Theological Library 34; 2d ed.; London: Williams & Norgate, 1913) 142–43.

[23] Bultmann is relying here in part on H. Weber's discussion of *exemplificatio.* Cf. the latter's *De Senecae philosophi dicendi genere Bioneo* (Marburg: F. Soemmerling, 1895) 25–26, 48–49. For a review of Weber's work, to which Bultmann's description of the

Peristasenkataloge.[24] While subsequent research has focused on the issue of catalogues of virtues and vices and their relationship to Paul and other NT writers,[25] it is important to note that Bultmann himself was more struck by the *peristasis* catalogues. "Perhaps the greatest similarity, however, we find in the *Peristasenkataloge.*"[26]

By *Peristasenkatalog* Bultmann understood those passages "where the speaker enumerates the different strokes of Fate (*Fügungen des Geschicks*), the περιστάσεις, over which he boasts as victor."[27] "As the Greek wise man, so also Paul enumerates the strokes of Fate or of the powers to which man is subjected, and he enthusiastically proclaims his superiority to joys and sorrows, to fears and terrors."[28] Bultmann cited examples of such *Peristasenkataloge* from Epictetus, Musonius Rufus, Horace, and Seneca,[29] and pointed especially to Rom 8:35 as an example in Paul.[30]

---

diatribe was greatly indebted, cf. M. Pohlenz's review in *BPhW* 17 (1897), 1064–66. Cf. also Stowers, *Diatribe,* 9.

[24] Bultmann, *Stil,* 17–19.

[25] Cf. A. Vögtle, *Die Tugend- und Lasterkataloge im Neuen Testament* (NTAbh 16, 4/5; Münster: W. Aschendorff, 1936); S. Wibbing, *Die Tugend- und Lasterkataloge im Neuen Testament und ihre Traditionsgeschichte unter besonderer Berücksichtigung der Qumran-Texte* (BZNW 25; Berlin: Töpelmann, 1959); E. Kamlah, *Die Form der katalogischen Paränese im Neuen Testament* (WUNT 7; Tübingen: Mohr, 1964); R. J. Karris, "The Function and Sitz im Leben of the Paraenetic Elements in the Pastoral Epistles," (Th.D. Diss., Harvard, 1971).

[26] Bultmann, *Stil,* 71.

[27] Ibid., 19.

[28] Ibid., 71.

[29] Ibid., 19. The passages cited are Epict., *Diss.* 1.1.22; 4.24; 11.33; 18.22; 2.1.35; 16.42; 18.30; 3.22.21f, 45; Mus. Ruf. 26, 13ff; 83, 12; Hor., *Sat.* 2.7.84f; Sen., *Prov.* 6.1; *Const.* 6.1, 3; 8.3; *Tranq.* 11.6; *V. B.* 7.3; *Ep.* 82.14. Of these, Weiss had already referred to Epict., *Diss.* 1.11.33 and Heinrici to 3.22.21. Several of the other references are problematic. Bultmann's reference to Sen., *Prov.* 6.1 is apparently to 6.1ff. The reference to *V. B.* 7.3 is either a misprint or a mistake in classification, for it contains a contrast of *virtus* and *voluptas* but no *peristasis* catalogue. Again, Mus. Ruf. 83,12 does not contain a *peristasis* catalogue. Furthermore, Epict., *Diss.* 2.18.30 deals with only one *peristasis,* viz., a storm, and with what happens in it (thunder and lightning). It is thus an example of one *peristasis* treated at length, not a catalogue of various *peristaseis.* Compare the way in which the one *peristasis* of illness serves in *Diss.* 3.26.37 as the basis for composing a catalogue of the adverse circumstances that attend illness. As this already suggests, Bultmann was rather loose in his use of the term "catalogue." Another of his catalogues has only two items (death and exile), viz., Epict., *Diss.* 3.22.21f. The classification of this passage as a "catalogue" is supported, however, by Margarethe Billerbeck, *Epiktet: Von Kynismus* (Leiden: Brill, 1978) 75.

[30] Ibid., 71. In addition, Bultmann makes reference to 1 Cor 3:22; 4:11f; 2 Cor 6:4f; 12:10; Phil 4:11–13. The reference to 1 Cor 3:22 is misguided, whereas the omission of 2 Cor 11 is striking.

Another similarity Bultmann discerned in the rhetorical means used to describe the conqueror of his circumstances. "As the Greek preacher describes in paradoxical antitheses the condition of the perfect wise man, Paul correspondingly describes his own condition as a Christian apostle in powerful series of antitheses."[31] He pointed specifically to Epictetus, *Diss.* 2.19.24 for the picture of the true Stoic and to 2 Cor 4:8-11 and 6:9-10 for Paul's paradoxical self-descriptions.[32] Bultmann differed from many earlier scholars in emphasizing that Paul used rhetorical means unconsciously and without premeditation. "It seems inconceivable to me," he stated, "that so lively and ardent a section as 2 Cor 11:16-12:10, in which the finest arrangement is discernible, rests on previous reflection."[33] Paul's use of rhetorical means like parallelism and antithesis was neither conscious nor designed for oratorical ornamentation. It was rather the result of his use of the diatribe, for such devices appeared in it as accompanying phenomena of the form itself.[34]

With the similarities Bultmann recognized certain differences as well. He noted that Paul 1) named blows of misfortune (*Unglückschläge*) almost exclusively rather than instances of good and ill fortune equally, and that he 2) enumerated different sufferings than those given by Greek preachers.[35] That Bultmann would to a certain extent minimize rather than maximize these recognized differences is natural in view of his thesis about Paul's dependence on the diatribe.[36] Thus, in regard to the first difference Bultmann acknowledged that Paul had a different evaluation of "the good gifts of the world" from that held by Cynics and Stoics. Yet he pointed to the way in which "death" and "life" as well as "things present" and "things to come" are paired in Rom 8:38 and saw this as quite comparable to the diatribe in expression and tone.[37] The second difference he attributed to the differing situations of Paul and the Greek preacher and the particular hazards faced by each. Nakedness was as natural to the one as exile was to the other.[38]

Bultmann's chief merit lies in the attention he called to *peristasis* catalogues as a literary phenomenon similar to catalogues of virtues and vices and in the

[31] Ibid., 80. For Bultmann's own description of the ideal sage, in which he cites 3 of the texts that he listed in *Stil* as *peristasis* catalogues (viz., Epict., *Diss.* 1.11.33 18.22; 2.16.42), cf. his *Primitive Christianity* (Cleveland/New York: World, 1956) 135-45.

[32] Ibid.. 27, 80.

[33] Ibid., 78.

[34] Ibid., 2, 20, 74, 78-79, 85.

[35] Ibid., 71. In examining the differences precisely where the greatest formal similarities occur, Bultmann is carrying out a task laid down by Weiss in *Aufgaben,* 13 (cf. also 50-55).

[36] Ibid. 108. Bultmann by no means always glosses over differences and he can emphasize these where they appear significant to him. Cf. pp. 87, 107.

[37] Ibid., 71.

[38] Ibid., 71-72.

collection of illustrative parallel texts that he compiled. He, moreover, correctly recognized that such catalogues are frequently connected with boasting and the superiority of the sage to his circumstances, and he rightly perceived that Romans 8 bears a certain similarity in form and function to these Hellenistic catalogues. To his credit he stressed that the use of paradoxical antitheses is not unique to Paul's descriptions of apostolic existence but occurs as well in depictions of the ideal sage.[39]

Bultmann's failings are by and large the product of the brevity of his discussion. Since he was only concerned with *peristasis* catalogues as one of many features common to Paul and the diatribe, he could not be expected to discuss the topic with all the nuances and qualifications required in a more detailed discussion. Indeed, he undoubtedly gave as much prominence to the topic as he did because of the paucity of previous discussion of this subject.[40]

The next scholar to contribute to research in this area was Adolf Bonhöffer, who in his 1911 study of Epictetus and the NT made two observations of considerable importance for the study of the *peristasis* catalogue.[41] First, whereas Bultmann had pointed to the *peristasis* catalogue as a striking feature of the Cynic-Stoic diatribe, Bonhöffer correctly pointed out that its occurrence was not restricted to either the Cynics and Stoics or the diatribe. As evidence he cited the catalogue in Plato, *Resp.* 2.361E–362A.[42] For Bonhöffer, such catalogues apparently belong to the *Umgangssprache* of the Hellenistic world.[43] Second, Bonhöffer made the astute observation that περιστάσεις have the same significance

[39] Bultmann's insight here goes beyond the general similarities which various scholars had already noted between the Stoic picture of the ideal sage and Paul's description of the ideal Christian life. Cf., e.g., J. B. Lightfoot, *St. Paul's Epistle to the Philippians* (London: Macmillan, 1891) 304–05, and Paul Feine, "Stoizismus und Christentum. II.: Stoizismus und Neues Testament," *Theologisches Literaturblatt* 26 (1905) 79–80, who also recognizes the similarity of Paul's dialectical manner of argumentation to that of the diatribe. On the latter point, cf. also Feine's *Der Apostel Paulus* (BFCT, 2. Reihe, 12. Band; Gütersloh: Bertelsmann, 1927) 527.

[40] In view of previous work on catalogues of virtues and vices, Bultmann, by contrast, merely indicates their presence in Paul and the authors he discusses, and he refrains from discussing them at length.

[41] Adolf Bonhöffer, *Epiktet und das Neue Testament* (Religionsgeschichtliche Versuche und Vorarbeiten 10; Giessen: Töpelmann, 1911).

[42] Bonhöffer, *Epiktet und das NT,* 392. This point, though indisputable in and of itself, is in keeping with Bonhöffer's excessive minimization of specific Stoic influence on the NT. Bonhöffer completely rejects Bultmann's claim that Paul was dependent on the Cynic-Stoic diatribe and attributes the similarity of Paul's style to that of the diatribe to the general colloquial speech (*Umgangssprache*) from which both Paul and the popular preachers drew. Cf. Bonhöffer, *Epiktet und das NT,* 140–46, 179–80 n. 1. Bonhöffer's explanation is rightly rejected by P. Wendland (*Die hellenistisch-römische Kultur,* 356–57, esp. n. 4).

[43] See note 42 above.

in Epictetus as the πειρασμοί do in the NT, viz., that both serve as tests and opportunities sent or allowed by God for the verifying demonstration of moral power and faith.[44] Yet two differences are discerned even here. In Epictetus the demonstration is one's own deed, whereas in the NT it is simultaneously and more fundamentally the result of divine assistance.[45] Consequently, in the second place, the passing of the test redounds in Epictetus to the credit of the individual, while in the NT to the glory of God or Christ.[46]

While the general topic of Paul and Hellenism continued to be discussed in the decade and a half following the contributions of Bultmann and Bonhöffer,[47] only occasional or peripheral interest seems to have been taken in the specific issue of the *peristasis* catalogue.[48] The next scholar to treat the Pauline

[44] Bonhöffer, *Epiktet und das NT,* 301 (cf. also 232 and 277 n. 4). For the treatment of the hardships of 2 Cor 4:8–9 as *peirasmoi* that are permitted by God for the sake of "exercise" (*gymnasia*), cf. John Chrysostom, *hom. 9.1 in 2 Cor.* (*PG* 10.459). Cf. also Eusebius, *Comm. in Ps.* (on Ps. 4:8) (*PG* 5.109D).

[45] Bonhöffer naturally recognizes that Epictetus occasionally represents humans as the recipients of power from God to bear adversity. Cf., for instance, Epict. *Diss.* 1.6.28, 37 and Bonhöffer, *Die Ethik des Stoikers Epictet* (Stuttgart: F. Enke, 1894) 23–24, and *Epiktet und das NT,* 291. While Epictetus is, of course, grateful for this power, Bonhöffer argues that Epictetus' prayer of thanksgiving is not for any particular divine assistance or benefaction. It is rather only an expression of general gratitude for the fact that God has arranged man in such a way that his true happiness is not dependent on anything external. Man is to expect his happiness from himself, so that his prayer of entreaty to God is ultimately a powerful appeal to himself and his higher nature (cf. *Epiktet und das NT,* 65 n. 1). By opposing his virtue to the "evils" that he encounters, man is using the divinely ordained means of extinguishing these evils. The perspective is thus similar to the one that A. D. Nock attributed to first-century Judaism's view of redemption: "Redemption was self-redemption, under God and with the use of the means which he had provided." Cf. Nock, *St. Paul* (New York: Harper, 1938) 76.

[46] Bonhöffer, *Epiktet und das NT,* 301. For other similarities and differences between the Epictetan and Christian view of evil, cf. Bonhöffer, *Epictet und die Stoa* (Stuttgart: F. Enke, 1890), 36, and *Ethik,* 24–25.

[47] The *Auseinandersetzung* of Bultmann and Bonhöffer in the *ZNW* of 1912 did not, unfortunately, involve a discussion of the *peristasis* catalogue *per se.* Bultmann did, however, mention the theme of *peristaseis* and its relation to the topics of *pronoia* and *anechesthai.* He, moreover, referred to 3 of the passages listed in *Stil* as *peristasis* catalogues (viz., Epict., *Diss.* 1.11.33; 18.22; 2.16.42) and compared them to Rom. 8:31–39 and Phil. 4:11–12. Cf. Bultmann, "Das religiöse Moment in der ethischen Unterweisung des Epiktet und das Neue Testament," *ZNW* 13 (1912) 97–110, 177–91, esp. 108, 177, and 183, and also Bonhöffer, "Epiktet und das Neue Testament," *ZNW* 13 (1912) 281–92, esp. 290, who complains that Bultmann lets recede into the background Epictetus' strong emphasis on the educative and probative functions of adversity.

[48] Among those who do mention the *peristasis* catalogue are Maurice Jones, Constant Toussaint, and Rudolf Liechtenhan. In his "The Style of St. Paul's Preaching," *The Expositor,* Eighth Series, 14 (1917) 241–58, 330–47, esp. 250, 258, Jones provides an extensive summary of Bultmann's dissertation, but he adds nothing new in regard to the

catalogues in any detail and with an eye to similar catalogues in the Graeco-Roman world was Hans Windisch, who did so in his masterful 1924 commentary on 2 Corinthians.[49] Windisch's treatment is as interesting as it is

peristasis catalogue. More substantial are the remarks of Toussaint, whose *L'Hellénisme et l'Apôtre Paul* (Paris: Nourry, 1921) was the most extensive treatment of the question of Paul and Hellenism to appear during this period. Toussaint (283) follows Bultmann in emphasizing Paul's debts to the diatribe. Among these debts is the love of paradox, as seen in passages like 1 Cor 4:10-13 and 2 Cor 6:4-10. Toussaint, moreover, compares 2 Cor 11:25-28 and statements from 1 Cor 9 to the depiction of the ideal Stoic-Cynic missionary by Epictetus (*Diss.* 3.22 and 4.7.30f) and remarks that Paul emerges as one of the most perfect realizations of this ideal (347-48; cf. also 284). Bultmann's argument that Paul was dependent on the diatribe and its *Peristasenkataloge* was accepted also by Liechtenhan, *Die göttliche Vorherbestimmung bei Paulus und in der Posidonianischen Philosophie* (FRLANT 35; Göttingen: Vandenhoeck & Ruprecht, 1922) 10, 126. In Liechtenhan's judgment, 2 Cor 4:8-9 and 6:9-10 are "completely in Stoic style" and most likely derive from Stoic diatribes. He stresses, however, that the idea of freedom from fate was something that Paul had learned from the OT and that he borrowed formulations from the Stoics because he recognized that certain of their ideas and value judgments were related to those that he already held. For Liechtenhan's analysis of similarities and differences in Stoic and Pauline treatments of the triumph over suffering, cf. his "Die Ueberwindung des Leides bei Paulus und in der zeitgenössischen Stoa," *ZTK* 30 (1922) 368-99. Cf. also Kurt Deissner, *Paulus und Seneca* (BFCT 21/2; Gütersloh: Bertelsmann, 1917) 22-23, 30-31, who mentions the Corinthian catalogues and Phil 4:11-13 in connection with a discussion of suffering. Unfortunately, however, he pays no attention to the *peristasis* catalogue as such. The same is true of Adolf Deissmann, *Paul: A Study in Social and Religious History* (1st Ger. ed. 1911; 2d ed.; London: Hodder & Stoughton, 1926) esp. 60-65, 181-83, who emphasizes Paul's sufferings and "passion mysticism," and Otto Schmitz, *Das Lebensgefühl des Paulus* (München: Beck, 1922) 49-53, 68, 105-17, who stresses the place of suffering in the new *Lebensgefühl* that Paul gained at his conversion. Cf. also the latter's comparison of the way in which Paul and Epictetus treat freedom from the powers of fate in his *Der Freiheitsgedanke bei Epiktet und das Freiheitszeugnis des Paulus* (NTF 1; Gütersloh: Bertelsmann, 1923) 25-28, 46-48, 65-66. Finally, in addition to the inescapable references to the Corinthian passages in discussions of suffering, rhetorical features of the catalogues continued to attract attention. Cf., for example, Paul Wendland, *Die urchristlichen Literaturformen* (HNT 1:3; Tübingen: Mohr, 1912) 354-58.

[49] Hans Windisch, *Der zweite Korintherbrief* (MeyerK 6; 9th ed.; Göttingen: Vandenhoeck & Ruprecht, 1924). Windisch follows Heinrici in the sustained use of comparative material for the interpretation of 2 Corinthians. In contrast to this line of inquiry stands the 1915 commentary of Alfred Plummer, *A Critical and Exegetical Commentary on the Second Epistle of St. Paul to the Corinthians* (ICC; Edinburgh: Clark, 1915), who tends to use non-biblical material only for the interpretation of individual words and phrases. Curiously, the 2d edition of C. Clemen, *Religionsgeschichtliche Erklärung des Neuen Testaments* (2d ed.; Giessen: Töpelmann, 1924), omits the references to Paul's catalogues of hardships that were given in the first edition (cf. n. 22 above).

detailed.[50] On the one hand, he continued the Bultmannian connection of the *peristasis* catalogue with the diatribe.

> So we have in our section [2 Cor 6, esp. 6:8b–10] a description of the external appearance and the standard of life of the apostle, which (like the analogous depiction in I 4:9ff) has the greatest affinity with the ideal of the Cynic-Stoic diatribe; all the more so as here that connection with Christ and the Christian hereafter is omitted. The rhetoric is completely that of the diatribe; many of the antitheses are probably Hellenistic loan goods.[51]

In this connection Windisch not only adduced new examples of Stoic *peristasis* catalogues but also called attention to relevant Cynic texts.[52]

While stressing the contact with Stoicism, Windisch, on the other hand, pointed à la Bonhöffer to *peristasis* catalogues in authors who were not Stoics. He noted both the catalogues of calamities in astrological writers like Vettius Valens[53] and the similarities of thought and formulation in authors as diverse as Cicero, Ovid, and Plutarch.[54] More important, he repeatedly referred to passages in Philo of Alexandria.[55] By so doing he clearly demonstrated the existence and employment of *peristasis* catalogues in Hellenistic Judaism. Finally, Windisch even pointed to the presence of a *peristasis* catalogue in an apocalyptic work, the Slavonic Apocalypse of Enoch (2 Enoch).[56]

[50] While Windisch has put generations of scholars in his debt by the wealth of material he gathered, the commentary format of his presentation precluded a systematic and thorough analysis of this material. There is, then, no separate discussion by Windisch of the *peristasis* catalogue outside of the ones in 2 Corinthians. Windisch himself was acutely aware of the limitations imposed by the commentary format (cf. *Korintherbrief*, v-vi).

[51] Windisch, *Korintherbrief*, 209 (cf. also 143–44, 204, 207–08).

[52] Cf. for example, Sen., *Const.* 10.4; Epict., *Diss.* 3.24.28–29; and ps-Crates, *Ep.* 7 (Windisch, *Korintherbrief*, 143, 357, 209, respectively).

[53] Windisch, *Korintherbrief*, 205. Already in 1914 Franz Boll had pointed to the similarity of calamities in Hellenistic astrology to the apocalyptic woes in the Synoptic apocalypse and Revelation. Cf. his *Aus der Offenbarung Johannis: Hellenistische Studien zum Weltbild der Apokalypse* (Stoicheia 1; Leipzig/Berlin: Teubner, 1914) esp. 83, 87, 130–36, and also 21 n. 7, where Boll thanks J. Weiss for pointing out that Rom 8:35, like Rev, contains 7 plagues.

[54] Cf., for instance, Cic., *Arch.* 6.14; *Sen.* 23.82; Ovid, *Tr.* 5.3.12; and Plut., *De exil.* 11 (*Mor.* 603 E). Cf. Windisch, *Korintherbrief*, 360, 357, 359, respectively.

[55] Cf. esp. Philo, *Det.* 34; and *Jos.* 26. Cf. Windisch, *Korintherbrief*, 209, 358, respectively.

[56] 2 Enoch 66:6 (cf. Windisch, *Korintherbrief*, 204, 206). The similarity of this passage to Rom 8:35 and 2 Cor 11:27 had already been noted by R. H. Charles, first in W. R. Morfield and R. H. Charles, *The Book of the Secrets of Enoch* (Oxford: Clarendon, 1896) 82 n. 6, and then in *APOT* 2.468. This passage has continued to be cited by some modern scholars as a parallel to various Pauline texts, but it should be dropped. There are two main recensions of 2 Enoch, and the parallel occurs *only* in recension A. When Charles, Windisch, and also N. Bonwetsch, *Das slavische Henochbuch* (Berlin: Weidmann, 1896) 54, referred to this passage, it was commonly believed that A was the earlier recension and

By his use of the term "*Peristasenkatalog*" in his Meyer commentary and his equation of it with "*Leidenskatalog*" (catalogue of sufferings), Windisch secured the continued use of "*peristasis* catalogue" in NT studies as well as influenced the way in which the term would be understood and used.[57] In addition, Windisch's treatment was somewhat prophetically symptomatic of subsequent work on the *peristasis* catalogue. Like Windisch, most interpreters would continue to look to the Cynic-Stoic diatribe and its series of paradoxical antitheses as the primary or ultimate source of the *peristasis* catalogue. The comment of Jacques Dupont on 2 Cor 4:8–9 is typical: "As for the style, this series of opposites is incontestably allied with the Cynic-Stoic diatribe; this is not the place to insist on this fact, recognized by all."[58] Yet the existence of *peristasis* catalogues in other genres and authors left open the possibility of an alternate explanation. The Jewish materials would not be explored until later, with the Hellenistic-Jewish passages examined first, then the apocalyptic ones.[59] Thus it was to other Graeco-Roman materials that scholars first turned, and it was especially Scandinavian scholars who did so.

In the years 1928–1929 Anton Fridrichsen published two articles on the *peristasis* catalogue in 2 Cor 11. In the first of these articles he advanced the thesis that Paul in 2 Cor 11:23–33 was consciously imitating the style of the *cursus honorum*.[60] Using the Monumentum Ancyranum and other inscriptions

---

that the Greek original dated from the first half of the first century C.E. In 1952, however, A. Vaillant, *Le Livre des Secrets d'Hénoch* (Paris: Institut d'études slaves, 1952), convincingly demonstrated that B, the shorter recension, is the earlier recension, and that A is a late medieval Christian recension. 2 Enoch 66:6 is, therefore, no longer seen as a pre-Christian, Jewish parallel to Paul's catalogues, but as an echo of the latter, esp. 2 Cor 6:4ff. Cf., for instance, Ulrich Fischer, *Eschatologie und Jenseitserwartung im hellenistischen Diasporajudentum* (BZNW 44; Berlin/New York: de Gruyter, 1978) 39. Finally, the authorship and date of composition of the original 2 Enoch continues to be debated. Whereas the majority of scholars continue to regard it as a Jewish work written prior to the destruction of the temple in C.E. 70, J. T. Milik, *The Books of Enoch* (Oxford: Clarendon, 1976) 107–16, esp. 110, argues that it is a Christian work dating from the ninth or tenth century C.E. Cf. also Arie Rubinstein, "Observations on the Slavonic Book of Enoch," *JJS* 13 (1962) 1–21.

[57] Windisch, *Korintherbrief*, 349 ("*ein konkreter Leidens- oder Peristasenkatalog*"), 353, 357. For "*Leidenskatalog*," cf. also 204, 393. Windisch also uses the phrase "*Peristasenreihe*" (cf. 354).

[58] Jacques Dupont, ΣΥΝ ΧΡΙΣΤΩΙ: *L'union avec le Christ suivant Saint Paul* (Bruges, Belgium: Abbaye de Saint-André, 1952) 117. Cf. also E.-B. Allo, *Saint Paul, Seconde Épître aux Corinthiens* (EBib; 2d ed.; Paris: Lecoffre-Gabalda, 1937) 175–78, and Lucien Cerfaux, "L'antinomie paulinienne de la vie apostolique," *RSR* 39 (1951) 227.

[59] See below, pp. 28–30.

[60] Anton Fridrichsen, "Zum Stil des paulinischen Peristasenkatalogs 2 Cor. 11:23ff.," *SO* 7(1928) 25–29.

as representatives of the chronicle of offices and honors attained by an individual, he isolated six basic features that such inscriptions and 2 Cor 11 have in common. These are as follows: 1) the recitation of the events for the purpose of boasting, 2) the use of πολλάκις, 3) the use of the first person singular verb in the aorist tense, 4) the statement of numerical data (e.g., "once," "thrice,"), 5) the *peristaseis* of the person, and 6) the epic chronicle style. The result of this imitation on the part of Paul is a "highly original *cursus honorum*," in which there is a "paradoxical discrepancy between the form and content of the *peristasis* catalogue."[61]

Encouraged by the response given his thesis by Gunnar Rudberg[62] and informed by E. Kornemann's study of the Monumentum Ancyranum,[63] Fridrichsen in a second article sought to refine and strengthen his thesis about an adoption of style on Paul's part.[64] He now saw Paul imitating the *res gestae* (πράξεις, acts, achievements),[65] which contained not only the official offices and honors attained by a person (the *cursus honorum*) but also the deeds done in service of the public. He argued that the "I-form" was the decisive formal feature of the *res gestae* and that the latter as a *Gattung* was modeled on oriental royal inscriptions (such as the inscription on the Behistun Rock by Darius the Great and the inscription of King Antiochus I of Commagene). This *Gattung*, in the view of Fridrichsen, was marked by a combination of deeds and virtues, the use of comparison (*synkrisis*), the absence of order in the enumeration of items, hymnic rhythm, and epic narration. Since Fridrichsen found for most of these features a corresponding item in 2 Cor 11, the latter emerged as Paul's distinctive *res gestae*.[66]

Since the *res gestae* were a recognized form of self-presentation (*Selbstdarstellung*)[67] that easily lent itself to self-glorification, Fridrichsen's thesis has continued to attract attention in scholarly circles.[68] In certain respects,

[61] Fridrichsen, "Stil," 27, 29.

[62] Gunnar Rudberg, *Hellas och Nya Testament* (Stockholm: Uppsala Svensk kyrk. diak. Bokförlag, 1929) 110ff, 117ff.

[63] E. Kornemann, *Mausoleum und Tatenbericht des Augustus* (Leipzig: Teubner, 1921).

[64] Anton Fridrichsen, "Peristasenkatalog und Res Gestae," *SO* 8 (1929) 78–82.

[65] For the equation *res gestae*=πράξεις, cf. the preamble of the *Res Gestae Divi Augusti* and Wendland, *Literaturformen*, 315 n. 2.

[66] Cf. esp Fridrichsen, "Res Gestae," 81–82. The absence of order in enumeration is limited, in Fridrichsen's view, to the sequence of items within the 3 groups that he isolated. The larger 3-fold structure that he saw in the catalogue was attributed to the Greek spirit of order. For *synkrisis*, cf. 11:22–23; for hymnic style, cf. 11:29; for epic narration, cf. 11:32–33.

[67] Wendland, *Literaturformen*, 315 n. 2.

[68] Already in 1936 Bultmann noted that Fridrichsen's explanation would serve to make clearer the paradoxical character of Pauline boasting. Cf. his "Neueste Paulusforschung," *TRu*, N. F. 8 (1936) 14, and the reiteration of this judgment in his *Der zweite Brief an die Korinther* (ed. E. Dinkler; MeyerK 6; Sonderband; Göttingen: Vandenhoeck & Ruprecht, 1976) 217–18. Others who find Fridrichsen's hypothesis attractive include W. G. Kümmel

Fridrichsen's thesis can even be strengthened. Augustus not only recorded his *res gestae* but also his expenditures (*impensae*= δωρεαί) for the state, both of which justified the honors and privileges bestowed on him. Financial considerations, of course, both precede (11:7–10) and follow (12:13–18) Paul's *peristasis* catalogue, and Paul speaks of his willingness to be depleted by the Corinthians (12:15) and complains about the recognition due him that he has not received (12:11). Such similarities in subject matter thus can be added to Fridrichsen's stylistic observations in order to strengthen his position.

In the final analysis, however, Fridrichsen's thesis is beset by severe limitations and insurmountable difficulties. As to its limitations, it can at best explain only the style of the catalogue in 2 Cor 11. Only here are found the first person singular verb in the aorist tense, the use of πολλάκις, the statement of numerical data, and the short narrative at the end of the catalogue. This uniqueness means that other models for the remainder of the Pauline *peristasis* catalogues must be adduced. Unlike Bultmann's diatribe, the *res gestae* thesis does not offer a comprehensive solution to the question of the source of Paul's catalogues. Instead it requires the assumption of at least two stylistic models on the part of Paul for the statement of catalogues of similar content and function. Fridrichsen himself recognized this implication, and he did not hesitate to point to Stoic depictions of the sage as offering the best stylistic parallel to 2 Cor 6 (see below).

In addition to its limited utility, Fridrichsen's thesis has certain difficulties. First, stylistic differences emerge along with the similarities when the *res gestae* of Augustus and 2 Cor 11 are compared. Augustus, for instance, frequently gives temporal data as well as numerical data, so that one can date precisely many of his exploits on the basis of the inscription alone. The only temporal datum in 2 Cor 11 comes in the Aretas episode of 11:32–33, thus falling outside the catalogue proper and still allowing only an approximate dating. An imitation of style by Paul can be only partial at best.

Second, many of the features isolated by Fridrichsen are not unique to the *res gestae*. The first person form of presentation was used by Augustus in his official reports to the senate and people, a fact that led Kornemann to see these reports as a possible model for Augustus' *res gestae*.[69] *Synkrisis*, numerical data, the overcoming of hardships, and the narration of episodes are stock items in encomia and are as old as Pindar's epinician odes. There is no stylistic basis for confining such features to the *res gestae*.[70] Indeed, the style of the *res gestae* is

---

in the appendix to Hans Lietzmann, *An die Korinther I/II* (HNT 9; 5th ed.; Tübingen: Mohr, 1969) 211; E. Kamlah, "Wie beurteilt Paulus sein Leiden?," *ZNW* 54 (1963) 221–22; and C. K. Barrett, *A Commentary on the Second Epistle to the Corinthians* (HNTC; New York: Harper & Row, 1973) 300.

[69] Cf. Excursus 8 in Kornemann, *Mausoleum* (mentioned also by Fridrichsen, "Res Gestae," 80).

[70] The presence of numerical data in the biography and diatribe was conceded by Fridrichsen in "Stil," 28–29.

not *sui generis* but represents a development out of the Roman *elogia* of men's careers and deeds.[71] "The style is that of the Roman texts concerning triumphs."[72]

Third, for his description of the *Gattung* Fridrichsen drew upon oriental royal inscriptions, viewing these as the models for the Roman *res gestae.*[73] In so doing he was following the lead of Mommsen and others.[74] These Eastern royal inscriptions are, however, no longer readily accepted by historians as a sound parallel to the Roman *res gestae.*[75] The reports of oriental rulers about their military campaigns are viewed as more comparable to the emperor's official reports to the senate at their pre-literary stage.[76] This means that the *Gattung* described by Fridrichsen and others on the basis of the oriental inscription is no longer tenable and must not be used for stylistic comparison with 2 Cor 11.

Fourth, as mentioned above, Fridrichsen's procedure quantifies models on stylistic criteria alone. It leads potentially to as many models as there are stylistic variations in the Pauline catalogues. Style should not be investigated apart from content, and Fridrichsen's thesis concerning 2 Cor 11 is possible only as long as the two are kept apart. The *res gestae* are *not* a résumé of hardships borne on behalf of the public. They are an account of services rendered to the state which serves to justify a person's honored position in the state. *Res adversae* play no necessary role in such catalogues of achievements. They appear only incidentally, for example, in Augustus' *res gestae* (14.1; compare Suet., *Tib.* 23), which is Fridrichsen's main specimen of the *Gattung* he claims Paul is imitating. When

[71] P. A. Brunt and J. M. Moore (eds.), *Res Gestae Divi Augusti* (Oxford: University Press, 1967) 3. Cf. also H. Volkmann, "Monumentum Ancyranum," *Kl. Pauly* 3 (1969) 1420.

[72] Arnaldo Momigliano, "Monumentum Ancyranum," *OCD*² (1970) 700. For a discussion, cf. esp. Jean Gagé (ed.), *Res Gestae Divi Augusti* (3d ed.; Paris: Les Belles Lettres, 1977) 29–31, 216, and the summary of his "Le genre littéraire des '*res gestae*' triomphales et ses thèmes" in *REL* 17 (1939) 33–34.

[73] In addition to the Monumentum Ancyranum, Fridrichsen made use of the Monumentum Adulitanum (*OGI* 199), the inscription of King Antiochus I of Commagene (*OGI* 383), and the inscription of the Nubian King Silko (*OGI* 201). Cf. Fridrichsen, "Stil," 28–29.

[74] Cf. Fridrichsen, "Res Gestae," 80.

[75] Brunt & Moore, *Res Gestae,* 4: "The nature of Augustus' position has led some to compare the *Res Gestae* with the great royal inscriptions of the East such as that of Darius at Behistun, but this is not a sound parallel." Cf. also D. R. Stuart, *Epochs of Greek and Roman Biography* (Sather Classical Lectures 4; Berkeley: University of California Press, 1928) 226, and Gagé, *Res Gestae,* 31–34, 216.

[76] E. Täubler, "Die Anfänge der Geschichtschreibung," in his *Tyche. Historische Studien* (Leipzig-Berlin: Teubner, 1926) 42; R. Laqueur, "Formen geschichtlichen Denkens im alten Orient und Okzident," *Neue Jahrbücher für Wissenschaft und Jugendbildung* 7 (1931) 493; and Bertil Albrektson, *History and the Gods* (ConB: OT Series 1; Lund: Gleerup, 1967) 44, to whom I owe the references to Täubler and Laqueur.

they are mentioned, moreover, the reference serves to magnify the particular achievement that is being recounted. They are ancillary items in the *res gestae*, not primary ones.

Fridrichsen's hypothesis, therefore, must be rejected.[77] It serves, however, the useful function of calling attention to the encomiastic features present in Paul's "foolish" self-laudation in 2 Cor 11. Such features are present in both Augustus' *res gestae* and the oriental royal inscriptions, and in this regard they do throw light on Paul's boasting. Two words of caution about their use, however, need to be heeded. First, the element of self-glorification in Augustus' *res gestae* is restrained. As Brunt and Moore note, "none of the bombastic boastfulness which may be seen in some funerary monuments" is present. While Augustus is by no means modest, "the nature of the *Res Gestae* is such that a certain self-glorification is proper, and Augustus keeps it within reasonable limits."[78]

Second, the old oriental royal inscriptions are *not* primarily the specimens of arrogant boasting that they are still popularly understood in NT circles to be. The misconception is undoubtedly perpetuated by Fridrichsen's articles, which represent the older viewpoint of Mowinckel and others that the "I-form" was a mark of egocentricity and that "the purpose of the inscriptions was to glorify the king as much as possible and to represent his services as the greatest possible."[79] More recent study has demonstrated that the older inscriptions serve primarily to glorify, not the ruler's own exploits, but the god who commissioned him as his representative. As Bertil Albrektson states,

> the texts reporting the royal victories and achievements are primarily to be seen as communications from the king to his god. They are not primarily intended to diffuse the rulers' fame far and wide. . . . The king's achievements give cause for the praise of the gods because he has not acted on his own behalf but as their representative and instrument. And it is precisely in their capacity as the representatives of the gods on earth, who have to render account to the real king, that the Oriental rulers speak in their inscriptions. . . . The enumeration of the glorious deeds, then, is not so much self-praise as an account of how the god's commission had been executed. . . . The big words were justified because ultimately the inscriptions served the purpose of glorifying the god, not his representative.[80]

[77] Already in 1935 Jean Gagé had found Fridrichsen's analogy between 2 Cor 11 and the *res gestae* to be "très contestable." Cf. his *Res Gestae,* 32 n. 2. Cf. also the critical remarks of Karl Prümm, *Diakonia Pneumatos: Der zweite Korintherbrief als Zugang zur apostolischen Botschaft* (2 vols. in 3 parts; Rome: Herder, 1960–1967) 1.638–40 and esp. 2/2.115.

[78] Brunt & Moore, *Res Gestae,* 7.

[79] S. Mowinckel, "Die vorderasiatischen Königs- und Fürsteninschriften. Eine stilistische Studie," in H. Schmidt (ed.), ΕΥΧΑΡΙΣΤΗΡΙΟΝ. *Studien zur Religion und Literatur des Alten und Neuen Testaments. Hermann Gunkel . . . dargebracht . . .* (FRLANT N.F. 19; Göttingen: Vandenhoeck & Ruprecht, 1923) 282, 298–300.

[80] Albrektson, *History,* 43–45. This is not to deny completely that some inscriptions,

In a similar way Paul presents himself as the servant and representative of the divine. If his deeds and sufferings redound to his own personal credit, they do so as well *ad maiorem dei gloriam.* Self-laudation and praise of God are in the oriental rulers and Paul correlates, not utter contradictions. Augustus' *res gestae,* though they mention his revival of the old Roman religion, do not redound to the glory of God and stand in marked contrast to Paul and his older oriental counterparts. Paul's distinction from the latter comes in *what* he boasts of, viz., his weaknesses, not in the fact that the execution of his commission serves to magnify God.

Interest in the *peristasis* catalogue seems to have faded after the appearance of Fridrichsen's two articles.[81] Indeed, it was not until 1943 that the next article on the catalogue appeared, and its author was none other than Fridrichsen himself. While not recanting his *res gestae* thesis, he called attention to the presence of *peristasis* catalogues in yet another literary genre, viz., the Greek novel, and he noted certain stylistic parallels that these catalogues offered to the Corinthian catalogues.[82]

In the following year Ragnar Höistad, one of Fridrichsen's students, pointed to Dio Chrysostom's highly Cynic description of the wise man in *Oration* 8.15–16 and compared it to Paul's description of the servants of God in 2 Cor 6:3–10.[83]

---

especially the later ones, "exhibit a growing tendency among the kings to write for human eyes" (Albrektson, *History,* 44 n. 7). Such inscriptions derive at least partially from the old Sumerian "hymn to oneself" and perhaps are reflected in Deutero-Isaiah. Cf. H.-M. Dion, "Le genre littéraire sumérien de l' 'hymne soi-même' et quelques passages du Deutéro-Isaïe," *RB* 74 (1967) 215–34.

[81] No studies of major importance on the *peristasis* catalogue appeared in the decade of the thirties. The eclipse of the catalogue as a topic of investigation is signaled already by the fact that Martin Dibelius, in his 1931 survey of form critical research on Acts-Revelation, discusses both the *Haustafel* and the *Lasterkatalog,* but does not even mention the *Peristasenkatalog.* Cf. his "Zur Formgeschichte des Neuen Testaments (ausserhalb der Evangelien)," *TRu* N.F. 3 (1931) 207–42. In this period of eclipse, perhaps the most astute observation in regard to the catalogue was one made by Kurt Deissner, "Das Sendungsbewusstsein der Urchristenheit," *ZST* 7 (1930) 772–90, esp. 784–86. Building on Bultmann's comparison of Epict., *Diss.* 2.19.24 with 2 Cor 4:8–11 and 6:9–10, Deissner called attention to the presence of λυπούμενοι in 2 Cor 6:10 and pointed out that a similar item is completely absent from Epictetus' catalogue. The latter contains only external misfortunes, for, according to Deissner, it was inconceivable to Stoics that the sage might experience sorrow. In addition to this observation, Deissner pointed to the antithetical descriptions of the sage in Sen., *Ep.* 41.4 and *V.B.* 4.2. For Deissner's earlier work on Seneca and Paul, cf. note 48 above.

[82] Anton Fridrichsen, "Sprachliches und Stilistisches zum Neuen Testament," *Kungliga Humaniska Vetenskapssamfundet I* (Uppsala, *Årsbok,* 1943) 24–36, esp. 31–34 ("Zum Stil des Peristasenkatalogs"). He cited catalogues in Chariton (3.8.9; 4.3.10; 4.4.10; 5.5.2; 6.6.4) and Achilles Tatius (5.18.4).

[83] Ragnar Höistad, "Eine hellenistische Parallele zu 2. Kor. 6.3ff.," *ConNT* 9 (1944) 22–27.

According to Höistad's analysis, the two passages are not only diatribal in style but also share six motifs in common.[84] By stressing both the formal relation of 2 Cor 6 to a Cynic text and the loose connection of Paul's catalogue to its context, Höistad was able to highlight the self-contained nature of Paul's catalogue and to argue that its presence in 2 Cor 6 is "a typical example of the transplantation of an already existent form into a milieu of a different sort."[85]

Höistad's analysis prompted Fridrichsen to devote one final article to the *peristasis* catalogue.[86] Affirming the basic Stoic foundation of 2 Cor 6, he supplemented Höistad's treatment with observations on the three triads of hardships in verses 4 and 5. Interpreting the ἀνάγκαι of 2 Cor 6:4 as meaning "distresses" (*Notlagen*), he suggested that the entire first triad depicted the emotional situation (*Stimmungslage*) of the apostle and the second the *peristaseis* by which he was oppressed. Fridrichsen also pointed to a description of the Stoic sage in Plutarch's *Moralia* (1057D–E), comparing its style to 2 Cor 4:8–9 and its tone to 2 Cor 6:10. He concluded that "in the *peristasis* catalogues Paul is a pronounced Hellenist," who was *formally* dependent on "the Hellenistic scheme with its enumerations, antitheses, paradoxes, and concepts."[87]

Only sporadic and ancillary interest was taken in the *peristasis* catalogue in the two decades that followed the 1944 articles by Höistad and Fridrichsen.[88] While Stoic depictions of the suffering sage were not forgotten,[89] the most significant

[84] The six motifs isolated by Höistad are as follows: the person's characteristics, his activity, perseverance, sufferings, *adoxia,* and paradoxical joy. These six motifs are united by the basic battle motif in which both Paul and Dio's diatribes are grounded.

[85] Höistad, "Parallele," 22. Höistad is careful to make due allowance for the differences between Paul and the Cynics in the motifs that they share. For Höistad's treatment of Cynicism, cf. his *Cynic Hero and Cynic King* (Lund: C. Blom, 1948). The connection of 2 Cor 6:3–10 to its context is not, however, as loose as Höistad assumes. Cf. the treatment of this passage in chapter four.

[86] Anton Fridrichsen, "Zum Thema 'Paulus und die Stoa'. Eine stoische Stilparallele zu 2. Kor. 4,8f.," *ConNT* 9 (1944) 27–31.

[87] Fridrichsen, "Paulus und die Stoa," 28 n. 2, 31. While acknowledging à la Bultmann that Paul's formal dependence on Stoic models attested a certain psychological relation between Paul and the Stoics, he also stressed the differences between them in their outlook and thought.

[88] The continuing interest in the catalogue by Scandanavian scholars was due to Fridrichsen's influence. Cf., for example, the comments on the catalogue by Helge Almquist, *Plutarch und das Neue Testament* (ASNU 15; Uppsala: Appelberg, 1946) 105–06, 108.

[89] Cf. the works of Dupont and Cerfaux cited in note 58 above. Sometimes, however, the sufferings of the *sophos* were recalled only to have their relevance for Paul's catalogues completely denied. For instance, J. N. Sevenster, *Paul and Seneca* (NovTSup 4; Leiden: Brill, 1961) 159, criticized Dupont for connecting 2 Cor 4:8–9 with the depiction of the suffering sage. Cf. also pp. 115–17 (on 1 Cor 4:9) and 229–31. Reservations about the relevance of the *sophos*-material for the understanding of 2 Cor 4 and 6 were expressed also by Prümm, *Diakonia Pneumatos,* 1.234–36, 368–69.

development during this period was the increasing recognition that examples of *peristasis* catalogues occur in the writings of Hellenistic Jews. Hartwig Thyen, for example, following in the path of his teacher Rudolf Bultmann, attempted to show that elements of the Cynic-Stoic diatribe had been adopted for use in the synagogue homily of Hellenistic Judaism. In support of this thesis he collected examples of the features of the diatribe that Bultmann had identified, including *peristasis* catalogues. He did not discuss these at any length, but simply used them in support of his larger thesis that Paul's use of the diatribe was part of his heritage as a child of the Diaspora.[90]

In the decade of the sixties[91] the importance of the *peristasis* catalogue in ancient propaganda was stressed by Dieter Georgi in his treatment of Paul's opponents in 2 Corinthians. Arguing that the word *peristasis* was a *terminus technicus* in the Cynic-Stoic diatribe, he emphasized that *peristaseis* function within the diatribe to prove the presence of divine power in the missionary. Since *peristaseis* thus serve to undergird propaganda, they are recounted in "propaganda style."[92]

In view of Georgi's analysis of *peristaseis*, it is surprising that he does not draw the conclusion that Paul's opponents used *peristasis* catalogues as part of their propaganda. Instead, he argues that they used letters of recommendation that were chronicles of their deeds of pneumatic power. They boasted of their spiritual experiences and mighty acts, and believed that the power of Christ was present in these mighty deeds of his messengers. Paul, by contrast, boasted of

[90] Hartwig Thyen, *Der Stil der Jüdisch-Hellenistischen Homilie* (FRLANT 65; Göttingen: Vandenhoeck & Ruprecht, 1955) 47. Thyen's examples of *peristasis* catalogues come not only from the writings of Hellenistic Jews but also from the writings of Jewish-Christians with a Hellenistic background. As examples of the former he cites *T.Jos.* 1 and Philo, *Det.* 34; *Som.* 2.84. From non-Pauline early Christian literature he cites Heb 11:36–38 and *1 Clem.* 45.4. For a short critique of Thyen's work, cf. Stowers, *Diatribe,* 41. Another scholar to compare Paul's catalogues to Hellenistic-Jewish material was Jean Daniélou, *Philon d' Alexandrie* (Paris: A. Fayard, 1958) 200–01, who compared and contrasted Philo, *Det.* 34, to parts of 2 Cor 6:4–10.

[91] In his *Diakonia Pneumatos* of 1960–1967 Karl Prümm repeatedly used the term *Peristasenkatalog* to refer to the lists of hardships in the Corinthian correspondence. Despite his repeated use of the term, Prümm was extremely reluctant to concede Paul's use of non-canonical models (1.234–36, 368–69, 638–40; 2/2.115; cf. also notes 77 and 89 above) and insisted that the use of the term should not obscure the conceptual differences between Paul and the Stoics (1.232). His chief contribution to the study of the catalogues was his recognition that they have different functions within the Corinthian correspondence (1.368,666; 2/1.11–12, 156; 2/2.277, 344).

[92] Cf. Dieter Georgi, *Die Gegner des Paulus im 2. Korintherbrief* (WMANT 11; Neukirchen-Vluyn: Neukirchener Verlag, 1964) 194–95, 245 n.1. Cf. also 64 n. 4; 150 esp. n. 2; 186–87. Georgi's understanding of the function of *peristaseis* is accepted by many scholars, including Hans Conzelmann, *1 Corinthians* (Hermeneia; Philadelphia: Fortress, 1975) 89 n. 43.

his sufferings and saw the power of God revealed in his weakness. The *Peristasenkataloge* in 2 Corinthians are, in short, Paul's answer to his opponents' lists of mighty deeds, and thus constitute an ironic imitation of their self-presentation.[93]

Georgi is clearly correct in connecting *peristaseis* with demonstrations of power, but his reconstruction of Paul's opponents seems flawed in regard to the issue of suffering. It is far more likely, as Oda Wischmeyer has suggested,[94] that his opponents did boast of their hardships as *diakonoi* of Christ and that their letters of recommendation contained *peristasis* catalogues.[95] For this and other reasons,[96] it is extremely unlikely that Paul's catalogues ironically imitate his

[93] Cf. Georgi, *Gegner*, 241–46 (esp. 244, 245 n. 1), 288 n. 5, 295.

[94] Cf. Oda Wischmeyer, *Der höchste Weg* (SNT 13; Gütersloh: Mohn, 1981) 85–86, esp. n. 218–20.

[95] The shift from κἀγώ to ὑπὲρ ἐγώ in 2 Cor 11:23, followed by adverbs indicating excess, clearly implies that Paul is comparing his own sufferings to those of his opponents and using his greater number of hardships to declare himself superior to them. The logic is crude, and *deliberately* so. Since he has suffered *more* than his opponents, he is *more* a messenger of Christ than they. For this sort of logic used in a *peristasis* catalogue, cf. esp. Arrian, *Anab.* 7.10.1–2. Georgi, *Gegner*, 295, seeks to evade the implication that the superapostles also boasted of their hardships, and he does so by suggesting that Paul means that he is Christ's envoy because he—in contrast to them—can boast of his sufferings. This is most unlikely. First, praise and self-praise for the endurance of hardships were extremely widespread in the ancient world, and it would be surprising if his opponents did *not* refer to hardships in their self-commendation. Even the Stoic and Cynic material cited by Georgi in connection with the term *diakonos* suggests the connection of adversity with this title. Second, it is far more likely that Paul differed from them in his *interpretation* of his hardships, not in the fact that he suffered and they did not. The difference is that he sees his weakness as the primary sphere for the manifestation of divine power, and they "signs, wonders, and mighty works" (12:12). Third, elsewhre in this section Paul is clearly responding to items the opponents boasted of, their Jewishness (11:22), their status as *diakonoi* of Christ (11:23), their "visions and revelations" (12:1), and their miracles (12:12). To view the *peristasis topos* as another item in their list of vaunts is to treat it in continuity with the other items in this section. To deny that they boasted of sufferings for Christ is to make this material *sui generis* within this section. It is preferable to treat it like 12:1–10 and look for the "twist" in Paul's treatment of this subject than it is to see the catalogue with Georgi (245 n. 1) as Paul's ironic imitation of their self-depiction. For other considerations in favor of the view that the opponents did boast of their hardships, cf. Wischmeyer, *Weg*, 86, esp. n. 218. Cf. also Georgi, *Gegner*, 288 n. 5.

[96] Other suggestions in regard to 2 Corinthians are at least compatible with the view adopted here. For example, the interpretation of 2 Cor 11:29 advanced by M. L. Barré clearly implies that Paul's opponents boasted of their struggles. Cf. his "Paul as 'Eschatologic Person': A New Look at 2 Cor 11:29," *CBQ* 37 (1975) 500–26, esp. 518. Also, if one wishes to follow Gerhard Friedrich and connect Paul's opponents with the Hellenistic Jewish circle around Stephen, then it should be recalled that this is above all a group that has experienced severe persecution (Acts 8:1–3)! For Friedrich's reconstruction, cf. his "Die Gegner des Paulus in 2. Korintherbrief," *Abraham unser Vater* (O. Michel Fstschrift; ed. O. Betz et al.; Leiden: Brill, 1963) 181–215.

opponents' *Selbstdarstellung.*[97] Be that as it may, the use of *peristasis* catalogues in early Christian letters of recommendation is virtually certain (cf. esp. Acts 15:25–26).[98]

Following Georgi, the next scholar to call particular attention to Paul's use of the *peristasis* catalogue was Hans Dieter Betz,[99] who noted that Paul's use of the catalogue corresponds to its use in the Cynic-Stoic diatribe. In addition, he recalled that ancient political speeches often made mention of dangers and hardships suffered for the city, and that these had been parodied already in the Old Comedy. More important was the significance he attached to the use of *peristaseis* in self-laudation and the relevance of this practice for the understanding of Paul's *Narrenrede* in 2 Cor 11–12.[100] He saw clearly that boasting about hardships was not unique to Paul, and he called particular attention to Cynic

[97] To see Paul's catalogues in 2 Corinthians as imitations of his opponents' self-presentation is to pay insufficient attention to 1) the stylistic diversity of Paul's catalogues in this letter; 2) the fact that he used a catalogue in dealing with the Corinthians prior to his opponents' arrival in Corinth (1 Cor 4:9–13); 3) the non-polemical character of the catalogues in Rom 8:35 and Phil 4:11–12; and 4) the fact that Paul's self-praise is focused on items for which he commonly praises his associates and churches. In short, it is to attribute too much importance to Paul's opponents in viewing his response to them. Paul is drawing out of his stock of items, not ironically imitating a staple of the superapostles. The situation at Corinth evokes the multiplicity of his catalogues in 2 Corinthians, it does not create them as such. If there is imitation on Paul's part, it seems likely only in 2 Cor 11:23–27, and the imitation would not be ironic, but modeled on the opponents' own *peristasis* catalogues. For this idea, cf. Wischmeyer, *Weg*, 86 n. 220. But the affinities of 2 Cor 11 with Phil 3 suggest that the basic form of 2 Cor 11 ultimately derives from Paul himself, with the catalogue of hardships an inversion of his vaunt as a persecutor of the church (Phil 3:6).

[98] The theme of toil, hardships, and risks certainly does occur in letters that function to commend people (Acts 15:25–26; cf. also Phil 2:19–22; Col 4:12–13). Paul clearly uses this theme in praising various people. He commends people primarily for their service (cf. Rom 16:1–2,6,9,12), and his esteem for this service grows in accordance with the sacrifices and hardships involved in rendering it. To suffer illness (Phil 2:29–30), imprisonment (Rom 16:7), or to risk one's life (Rom 16:3–4) is the highest form of service and therefore worthy of the highest commendation. Such a person is approved (Rom 16:10). While evidence is lacking, the amplification of this theme of toil and suffering by means of a catalogue clearly lies close at hand and it seems very likely to have been done in given instances. At any rate, the theme of one's sufferings is part of the "credentials" section of the letter of recommendation. For an analysis of this letter type, cf. Chan-Hie Kim, *Form and Structure of the Familiar Greek Letter of Recommendation* (SBLDS 4; Missoula: SBL, 1972) sp. 101, 119–42.

[99] H. D. Betz, *Der Apostel Paulus und die sokratische Tradition* (BHT 45; Tübingen: Mohr, 1972) 97–100.

[100] Betz touches on this connection between self-praise and *peristaseis* in his 1978 discussion of Plutarch's treatise on self-praise. Here he states clearly that *peristasis* catalogues are a traditional type of the self-praise that Plutarch commends. Cf. his "De Laude Ipsius (Moralia 539A–547F)," in H. D. Betz (ed.), *Plutarch's Ethical Writings and Early*

boasting about the hardships of poverty and the "power" that is displayed in the Cynic's way of life.[101] The connection that Betz establishes between *peristaseis* and self-praise is indeed a frequent one in Hellenistic literature and is of fundamental importance for the understanding of Paul's Corinthian catalogues.[102]

Betz's work appeared in 1972, and in that same year J.-F. Collange[103] advanced the argument that 2 Cor 6:4-10 was not spontaneously dictated in response to the Corinthian crisis, but that it was more or less a "pre-existent text" inserted by Paul after 6:2 in order to bring to a conclusion the "letter" of 2:14-6:10.[104] He saw this catalogue inspired by similar Stoic *peristasis* catalogues,[105] but suggested that it functioned in Christian circles as "a sort of breviary of the servant of God." Paul himself, he ventured, may have established this account of the qualities of the *diakonos* for his own use and that of his associates. Furthermore, he maintained that 2 Cor 6:5 contained a precise scheme of apostolic *peristaseis*, a scheme which had been elaborated by Paul on the basis of his reflections about his life and apostolic experiences.[106]

In 1974 two scholars discussed the *peristasis* catalogue at considerable length. The first was Daniel Fraikin, who did so in connection with an analysis of Rom 8:31-39.[107] Attentive to the fact that *peristasis* catalogues in the diatribe function in different ways, he isolated two basic levels at which catalogues play a role, the descriptive and the demonstrative. He rightly emphasized the latter function as

---

Christian Literature (Studia ad Corpus Hellenisticum Novi Testamenti 4; Leiden: Brill, 1978) 377–78 (esp. 378), 392.

[101] Cf. also "De Laude Ipsius," 388: "Thus Paul's concept of καυχᾶσθαι ἐν ταῖς ἀσθενείαις (2 Cor 11:30; 12:9; Rom 5:3), although based upon his christology of 'Christ crucified,' was by no means alien to the culture."

[102] Betz mentions but unfortunately does not discuss the *peristasis* catalogue of 2 Cor 12:10 in his "Eine Christus-Aretalogie bei Paulus (2 Kor 12, 7–10)," *ZTK* 66 (1969) 288–305, esp. 303.

[103] J.-F. Collange, *Énigmes de la deuxième épître de Paul aux Corinthiens* (SNTSMS 18; Cambridge: University, 1972) 283, 290–91, 294.

[104] For Collange's literary theory, cf. *Énigmes*, 282–83.

[105] Collange's judgment about the Stoic inspiration of 2 Cor 6:4–10 stands in marked contrast to his minimization of Stoic influence for 4:8–9. Cf. *Énigmes*, 148.

[106] This latter idea is particularly unpersuasive and rests in part on the mistaken assumption that 5 of the 6 items in 2 Cor 6:5 occur in precisely the same order in 2 Cor 11:23,27. This is not the case, as a quick comparison of 2 Cor 6:5a with 11:23 will show. It is better to say that Paul works with a stock number of items and freely adds others. When *all* Paul's catalogues are considered, it is scarcely possible to establish a precise scheme that he in each instance has followed or elaborated. Cf. esp. 1 Cor 4:9–13; 2 Cor 4:8–9 (where the idea of *diakonos* is imparted by 4:1; cf. Georgi, *Gegner*, 244); Rom 8:35; and Phil 4:11–12.

[107] Daniel Fraikin, "Romains 8:31–39. La position des églises de la Gentilité," (Ph.D. Diss., Harvard, 1974) 70–78 and esp. 107–18. I wish to thank Dr. Fraikin for his kindness in supplying me with a copy of his work on the *peristasis* catalogue.

the crucial one in the Stoic treatment of the sage. "The sage is demonstrated as such by his comportment under adverse circumstances."[108] The endurance of *one* hardship would hardly demonstrate either the sage's worth or his invincibility. An enumeration of various ordeals, therefore, is essential for this demonstration. *Peristaseis* thus show the sage and also the power of the principle that inspires him. They offer proof, but the precise nature of what is proved is dependent on the context in which the catalogues occur.

Paul's Corinthian catalogues have this demonstrative function, and in them Paul, like the sage, shows himself as realizing a certain ideal. To be more precise, they function to qualify Paul as an apostle and demonstrate him as a hero in a given order of reality. Furthermore, the hardships that Paul enumerates do not function to show the power of reason (as with the sage) or of piety (as in 4 Maccabees), but rather give the conditions for the manifestation of divine power in the apostle's life. The catalogue in Rom 8 has, according to Fraikin, a similar demonstrative function, for here the *peristaseis* serve to qualify the Christians as beneficiaries of the love of God.

Fraikin thus lays great stress on the function of the catalogue in the demonstration of the sage, and in doing so he is quite correct. Chapters two and three of this investigation will serve to demonstrate the extent to which this is true, and chapters four and five will show the relevance of this for an understanding of Paul's catalogues. But the very relevance of this Stoic material for the understanding of Paul's catalogues was challenged by the other scholar who dealt with the *peristasis* catalogue in 1974. This was Wolfgang Schrage, who emphasized the importance of Jewish apocalyptic for a proper perception of Paul's catalogues.[109]

According to Schrage, it is apocalyptic that provides the primary traditional background for Paul's *peristasis* catalogues.[110] In support of this he adduces a number of Jewish texts that contain lists of various calamities and hardships.[111] While he stresses apocalyptic, he does not, however, exclude direct Stoic influence entirely, for he feels that one must reckon with it in Phil 4:11-12.[112] What he challenges in particular is the notion that the Stoic concept of the endurance of sufferings is quite close to what appears in Paul's catalogues. He insists that it is not Stoicism, and not even Jewish apocalyptic, that provides the all-decisive

[108] Ibid., 115.

[109] Wolfgang Schrage, "Leid, Kreuz und Eschaton. Die Peristasenkataloge als Merkmale paulinischer theologia crucis und Eschatologie," *EvT* 34 (1974) 141–75. Cf. also E. S. Gerstenberger and W. Schrage, *Suffering* (Biblical Encounter Series; Nashville: Abingdon, 1980) esp. 155–57.

[110] Ibid., 143–47. Cf. also p. 165, where Schrage qualifies his assertion of the primacy of apocalyptic as a background by saying that this is "wahrscheinlich."

[111] Ibid., 143–46; cf. esp. the catalogue in *Jub.* 23:13. For a Gnostic *peristasis* catalogue, cf. 172 n. 89.

[112] Ibid., 147, n. 16.

horizon for the understanding of Paul's catalogues. The key, he insists, is Paul's christology. It is this that sets Paul's catalogues off from their background in Jewish apocalyptic.[113]

This survey is not the place to enter into a full discussion of Schrage's important and influential article. In view of the direction that this investigation takes, however, certain comments are necessarily in order. First, there can be no question but that Paul's understanding of suffering in general is incomprehensible apart from his christology, and that his catalogues at certain key points reflect this. But Schrage not only emphasizes christology to the neglect of theology,[114] but he also tends to treat all Paul's catalogues in light of 2 Cor 4:8–11. As a result, the differences between Paul's catalogues do not emerge. It simply is not true that "Paul can and *must* break open the form of the *peristasis* catalogue and speak antithetically."[115] He *can*, but he does not always do so, as a close examination of his catalogues will show.

Second, several of the apocalyptic texts to which Schrage calls attention are clearly important for an understanding of both the *peristasis* catalogue as such and Paul's particular catalogues. But just as many of the Greek texts cited by other scholars often turn out to be either illusory or only partial parallels at best, so, too, with Schrage's catalogues. It is not simply form, but also function that is important, and Schrage does little to show how the various *functions* of the catalogues he cites are relevant to an understanding of Paul's catalogues. Some, indeed, are more important than Schrage himself indicates, and these are cited at appropriate places in chapter four.

Third, Schrage simply does not do justice to the "Hellenistic" elements in Paul's catalogues, whether they derive directly from the Graeco-Roman world or indirectly through Hellenistic influences on Judaism. This is typical of Schrage's work in general, for he tends to see an unbridgeable gap between Stoicism and Jewish apocalypticism. Without question there is a sharp hiatus between the two, but that Paul did accept and use "certain Stoic values, which were indeed in logical tension with other values he held," has been ably demonstrated by David L. Balch, who quite rightly takes Schrage to task for his treatment of material that has both Stoic and apocalyptic parallels.[116]

Paul is fully capable of blending highly heterogeneous material in remarkable ways. 2 Cor 4:16–5:10, for example, is a striking mixture of terms and concepts current in Hellenistic popular philosophy with images drawn from apocalyptic.[117] The contrasts outer/inner man (4:16) and visible-transient/unseen-eternal

[113] Ibid., esp. 142, 150–51, 165–68.

[114] Nils A. Dahl, "The Neglected Factor in New Testament Theology," *Reflection* 73 (1975) 5–8, has pointed out that this neglect is typical of NT scholarship as a whole.

[115] Schrage, "Leid," 168 (emphasis mine).

[116] David L. Balch, "1 Cor 7:32–35 and Stoic Debates about Marriage, Anxiety, and Distraction," *JBL* 102 (1983) 429–39, esp. 430.

[117] Meeks, *Writings*, 55.

(4:17–18) as well as the concept of the body as a tent (5:1) are part of the stock of popular philosophy. These images are interspersed among, and alternate with, those drawn from apocalyptic. These latter include the contrast of present affliction/eternal glory (4:17), the image of a house stored up in heaven (5:1), and the thought of final judgment (5:9–10). Again, the expression "day by day" is a Hebraism, and "weight of glory" is but a Greek translation of a paronomastic Hebrew expression. These Greek and Jewish elements are so interwoven that it is impossible to separate them without destroying the thought complex erected by Paul. The use of "inner man," for example, facilitates the metaphors of putting off, putting on, putting on over, as well as the image of a person doing something good or evil "through the body" (5:10). 2 Cor 4:16–5:10 is thus a hybrid produced by crossing philosophical with apocalyptic strains. The crossing of these strains, while creating certain exegetical difficulties, does not result in hopeless or irreconcilable incongruities. On the contrary, the various terms in this hybrid are used in a coherent way, and, as is frequently the case, the hybrid is stronger and more impressive than either of the strains from which it was taken.

Finally, certain questions may be raised not only about Schrage's exegesis of various passages in Paul,[118] but also about his use of various "apocalyptic" texts. For example, he uses 2 Enoch 66:6 as a prime example of an apocalyptic text. As we have already seen, however, this particular passage stems from a medieval Christian redactor.[119] Whether or not the redactor is imitating one or more of Paul's catalogues is hardly the issue here.[120] The point is simply that the passage does not stem from the Jewish apocalyptic circles of Paul's day, and thus it should not be used as illustrative of the catalogues that those circles produced.

In short, Schrage's article constitutes an important check against the tendency of NT scholars to look only to Stoic sources. Various hardships mentioned in Paul's catalogues, like those in 2 Cor 6:4b, clearly have an important background in Jewish depictions of eschatological tribulations,[121] and some Jewish catalogues do appear to function in a manner similar to Paul's. But, on the whole, the Hellenistic discussions of the sage appear to offer a better means for sharpening our understanding of Paul's catalogues, and it is for this reason that attention in this investigation is focused on the sage. If this concentration proves helpful, then this particular focusing of the analysis will receive a sufficient justification.

[118] For example, the phrase "having nothing" in 2 Cor 6:10 hardly has reference to "nichts Innerliches oder Religiöses." Cf. Schrage, "Leid," 153.

[119] Cf. above, note 56.

[120] Contrast Schrage, "Leid," 144 n. 6.

[121] The relevance of Jewish apocalyptic for the understanding of Paul's catalogues was stressed the following year (1975) by M. L. Barré (cf. note 96 above), who called particular attention to the *Hôdāyôt* and argued that "these Qumran hymns and the trials-lists in Paul (at least 2 Cor 4:7–12 and 11:23–29) belong to the same eschatological universe of discourse" ("Paul as 'Eschatologic Person'," 519). Cf. also his "Qumran and the 'Weakness' of Paul," *CBQ* 42 (1980) 216–27.

Two final treatments of the *peristasis* catalogue merit attention. In 1978 Josef Zmijewski investigated the stylistic form of Paul's *peristasis* catalogues as part of an analysis of the "foolish discourse" in 2 Cor 11:1-12:10. Restricting himself to an analysis of the Corinthian catalogues and Rom 8:35-39, he isolated various stylistic characteristics of Paul's catalogues and then discussed the use of this "*Stilform*" in 2 Cor 11. The strength as well as the weakness of his analysis is obviously its exclusive focus on Paul's catalogues. In view of this focus, however, one can only wonder why he excluded the catalogues in Phil 4:11-13 from his survey![122]

Finally, the most recent study, though brief, is far more valuable than Zmijewski's stylistic analysis. In a 1983 article Robert Hodgson has done NT scholarship the great service of making clear, once and for all, that lists of hardships are not restricted to either the diatribe or apocalyptic writings. They occur as a literary convention in a wide variety of authors and texts, and thus the analysis of "tribulation lists" needs to be placed within a much broader hermeneutical context than has yet been done. Hodgson points in particular to catalogues in Josephus, the Nag Hammadi texts, the Mishnah, Plutarch, and Arrian. He suggests specifically that "the mythological labors of Heracles . . . is a history of religions background which illumines Paul's trial list at 2 Cor 11:23-29 as effectively as Stoic and apocalyptic parallels, and perhaps even more."[123]

This survey of scholarship on the *peristasis* catalogue is now complete. It reveals both the basis and the need for a detailed study addressing this subject. Indeed, Hodgson states explicitly that his article is designed "to promote a much needed monograph on the subject of Paul's tribulation lists."[124] The present investigation can be seen as the response to his call for greater treatment of this widespread literary convention of compiling lists of hardships. The first step in extending the investigation is an examination of the key term "*peristasis.*" This term is used frequently in secondary literature, yet this usage is sometimes either imprecise or uninformed. The chapter that follows is intended to remedy this situation.

[122] Josef Zmijewski, *Der Stil der paulinischen "Narrenrede"* (BBB 52; Köln/Berlin: Hanstein, 1978) 307-23. Given the author's interest in style, it is regrettable that he does not attempt to compare the results of his analysis of Paul's catalogues with non-Pauline examples. Barré, "Paul as 'Eschatolgic Person'," 509-09, and 519-26, provides a stylistic analysis of the Corinthian catalogues and Rom 8:35-39, but, like Zmijewski, fails to discuss Phil 4:11-13.

[123] Robert Hodgson, "Paul the Apostle and First Century Tribulation Lists," *ZNW* 74 (1983) 59-80, esp. 61. I wish to thank Dr. Hodgson for his kindness in furnishing me with a copy of his article prior to its appearance in *ZNW.*

[124] Ibid., 61.

2

The Term *Peristasis*

Περίστασις occurs for the first time in a line from an unnamed play of Telecleides, the Athenian comic poet of the fifth century. In its initial appearance it indicates the gathering of a crowd because of a disturbance.[1] Its next certain occurrence[2] is apparently in Aristotle's *Meteorologica*, where it is used in the plural to indicate the veering of the winds.[3] The first repeated use of the word comes in Epicurus' letter to Pythocles, where it occurs 8 times in the discussion of various celestial phenomena.[4]

In the Hellenistic period the word becomes extraordinarily common. Polybius uses it at least 38 times in his history of Rome's rise to world power,[5] and in a

[1] Fr. 35: "What's all this din and crowd around the house?" (τίς ἥδε κραυγὴ καὶ δόμων περίστασις;). Cf. *CAF* I, 217 = *FAC* I, 190–91. The translation is that of J. M. Edmonds in the *FAC*. On the passage cf. W. G. Rutherford (ed.), *The New Phrynichus* (London: Macmillan, 1881) 473.

[2] The word occurs in ps-Hippocrates, *Praec.* 3 (*CMG* 1:1.31.14) and in a collection of sayings attributed to Democritus (68.B302 = 2.222.9 Diels-Kranz, *Vorsokr.*[7]).

[3] Cf. *Mete.* 2.6.364b14. The word occurs twice in ps-Aristotle, *Problemata* (2.29.869a21; 26.26.942b 27). Aristotle's pupil and successor Theophrastus (*apud* Diomedes, p. 487,12 Keil) used the term in his definition of tragedy (τραγωδία ἐστιν ἡρωϊκῆς τύχης περίστασις), probably in the sense of περιπέτεια ("tragedy is the sudden reversal of heroic fortune"; cf. LSJ, 2099). The occurrence of the term in Theophrastus, *Char.* 8.12, however, is from a late addition to his work. The use of the term by Eudemus, Aristotle's pupil and friend, is possible but uncertain (cf. 1.78.19 Diels-Kranz, *Vorsokr.*[7]). The word also occurs in Dinarchus' Tyrrhenian speech (fr. 12.5 Conomis = Harpocration, s.v. περίστασις: 1.247.14–248.3 Dindorf; also, s.v. Κύκλοι: 186.3–5), apparently in the sense of an encircling crowd (compare Timon *apud* Diog. Laert. 4.42 and the use of περίστατος in Isocrates, *Arch.* 95 and *Antid.* 299).

[4] *Ep.* 2.92 (39,13), 102 (46,7), 104 (47,11), 106 (48,17), 107 (49,13), 109 (50,13), 111 (52,5 and 9). All citations are from Hermann Usener, *Epicurea* (Leipzig: Taubner, 1887) and the references are to the section, page and line numbers of this edition. For a discussion of the term in this writing, cf. Cyril Bailey, *Epicurus: The Extant Remains* (Oxford: Clarendon, 1926) 289, 305, 312, and 319.

[5] Cf. 1.32.3; 35.10; 54.6; 65.7; 82.7; 84.9; 88.5; 2.17.11; 21.2; 41.6; 55.8; 3.31.2; 84.2; 98.2; 112.9; 4.32.2; 33.12; 38.10; 45.10; 67.4; 5.45.1; 6.5.5; 18.1; 31.1, 7, 14; 41.2–3; 9.34.4; 10.14.5; 21.3; 11.18.13; 19.5; 18.53.11; 31.26.3; 28.9. Two additional occurrences are printed in J. Schweighäuser (ed.), *Lexicon Polybianum* (Oxford: Baxter, 1822) 346. This list of occurrences does not purport to be complete.

striking variety of ways.[6] Two senses, however, clearly predominate. These are 1) "circumstances" and 2) "danger"[7] or "difficulty." There are a number of instances in which one of these two meanings is quite clear, but in many others it is difficult to decide which meaning is to be understood.[8]

The use of *peristasis* reflected in Polybius continues through the later Hellenistic and into the Roman period. The word is used in a variety of fields, in meteorology and astronomy[9] as well as in architecture.[10] But the two meanings that predominate in Polybius continue to be the standard ones and it is on these that attention here is to be focused.

Peristasis in the sense of "circumstance(s)" is a neutral term and can indicate both pleasant and unpleasant situations. In this way it is very much like the word συμφορά, another basically neutral term capable of a positive as well as a negative connotation.[11] As a neutral term *peristasis* often has the word "all" (πᾶσα)[12] or "various" (ποικιλία)[13] used with it to indicate the wide range of situations envisioned.[14] And, as one might expect, it frequently occurs in conjunction with some temporal term like καιρός[15] or ὥρα.[16] Athenaeus, for instance, says that

[6] In its treatment of *peristasis* LSJ, e.g., cites Polybius for 6 separate entries (all under the main headings I and II). Unfortunately, the volume containing the treatment of *peristasis* has not yet appeared in Arno Mauersberger (ed.), *Polybios-Lexicon* (Berlin: Akademi, 1956–).

[7] J. L. Strachan-Davidson, *Selections from Polybius* (Oxford: Clarendon, 1888) 11–12.

[8] Ibid., 12. Cf. also F. W. Walbank, *A Historical Commentary on Polybius* (3 vols.; Oxford: Clarendon, 1957–79) 1.132 (on Polyb. 1.65.7).

[9] Cf. LSJ, 1388a (II. 4ab). For its use by an astronomer, cf. Vettius Valens (67,8; 115,5; 117,10; 225,7; 244,2; 286,4 Kroll).

[10] Ibid. (I. 2abc); cf. also H. van Herwerden, *Lexicon Graecum suppletorium et dialecticum* (Leiden: Sijthoff, 1910) 1161.

[11] On *symphora* as a neutral term cf. the scholiast on Aristophanes, *Eq.* 404 (conveniently printed in J. M. Edmonds, *Lyra Graeca* [LCL 142–44; 3 vols; rev. ed.; London: Heinemann, 1931] 2.304) and the *Suda,* s.v. Συμφορά (4.462.3–7, Nr. 1408 Adler). On the various usages of *symphora,* cf. W. Donlan, "Simonides, Fr. 4D and *P. Oxy.* 2432," *TAPhA* 100 (1969) 84–85.

[12] Cf., e.g., Polyb. 3.31.2; 6.18.1; *OGI* 335.15; Epict., *Diss.* 1.15.4; 22.1; Clem. Al., *Str.* 4.6.25.1 (=2.259.15 Stählin). Cf. also Clem. Al., *Str.* 4.5.19.2 (=2.257.4 Stählin).

[13] Cf., e.g., Schweighäuser, *Lexicon,* 346, and Ps-Plut., *Mor.* 103B. Cf. also Polyb. 11.19.5. For διαφόροι περιστάσεως, cf. Sext. Emp., *Math.* 11.65,67.

[14] In Polyb. 4.67.4 both war and peace are termed *peristaseis.* To indicate the multiplicity of circumstances a quantitative word like πολλαί is sometimes used with *peristasis.* Cf., e.g., Polyb. 4.32.2, and Ps-Plut., *Mor.* 103B.

[15] Cf., e.g., Polyb. 1.35.10; Hierocles *ap.* Stob. *Ecl.* 4.25.3 (=4.641.21 Hense). For *kairos* used in connection or combination with *peristasis,* cf. Polyb. 2.55.8; 4.32.2; 9.34.4; *SIG* 569.24; 731.2; 762.39; Josephus, *Ant.* 16.269; Sext. Emp., *Math.* 11.65; Aristides Rhetor (2.524.32 Spengel); cf. also *OGI* 735.10.

[16] Athenaeus 10.430A. Cf. also Plut., *Mor.* 137B.

Alcaeus the lyric poet is found drinking "at all times and in all circumstances" (10.430A). Winter, summer, and spring are then specified as the times at which Alcaeus drank and "disasters" and "cheerful occasions" as the circumstances (430 A-B).

In the sense of "circumstance(s)" the term *peristasis* is common in discussions by both philosophers and rhetoricians.[17] Among philosophers,[18] the older Sceptics termed the fourth of their 10 modes for the suspension of judgment "that based on circumstantial conditions."[19] The Stoics, for whom *peristasis* was a *terminus technicus*,[20] were fond of using it in various ethical discussions. Posidonius' work on duties, for example, included a section, "Duty depending on given circumstances."[21] Some duties were unconditional (ἄνευ περιστάσεως) and therefore always binding, while others were incumbent only in certain circumstances (κατὰ περίστασιν).[22] The latter might dictate something as drastic as the consumption of human flesh.[23] On the other hand, some circumstances might prove a hindrance and lead the sage to forego certain normal obligations, like marriage and procreation.[24] Hence the concept of *peristasis* plays a key role in symbouleutic literature where deliberation and advice are required and where

[17] The use of the term by historians continues as well. Josephus, for example, uses it 3 times (*Ant.* 16.269, 368; 17.331) with a variety of meanings. Cf. K. H. Rengstorf, *A Complete Concordance to Flavius Josphus* (3 vols.; Leiden: Brill, 1973–79) 3.401. For *Ant.* 16.368, cf. L. H. Feldman's review of Rengstorf in *JBL* 100 (1981) 152.

Medical writers were still another group to use the word with some frequency and also in a variety of senses. Cf. Ps-Hippocrates, *Praec.* 3 (= *CMG* 1:1.31.14); Aretaeus of Cappadocia, *SD* 2.9 (= *CMG* 2.77.25–26); Soranus of Ephesus, *On Gynecology* 1.1 (= *CMG* 4.14.25); 1.60 (= *CMG* 4.45.17); 2.10 (= *CMG* 4.57.30); 2.18 (= *CMG* 4.65.14); 2.28 (= *CMG* 4.74.12); 4.36 (= *CMG* 4.149.3) and Ps-Dioscorides, *Alex.* Praef. (p.5, 5 Sprengel). The philosopher-physician Galen also uses the word a number of times, especially in the phrase περίστασις πραγμάτων. This phrase occurs 6 times in Galen's *De sanitate tuenda* (2.1.6, 8 = *CMG* 5:4:2.38.15, 21; 2.3.17 = 44.5; 3.1.5 = 73.12; 4.7.2 = 123.21; 6.1.9 = 168.28; cf. also *Protr.* 2.4 = 1.105.1 Marquardt and *Comm. in Hippocratis de victu auctorum* 4.1.735 = *CMG* 5:9:1.272.19). For other occurrences of *peristasis* in Galen, cf. *Comm. in Hippocratis prognosticum* 3.33.281 (= *CMG* 5:9:2.358.4) and *Protr.* 11.30 (= 1.123.29 Marquardt).

[18] The use of *peristasis* by Epicurus and Aristotle has already been noted.

[19] Sext. Emp., *Pyr.* 1.36 and esp. 100–17. Cf. also *Math.* 7.254.

[20] R. Eucken, *Geschichte der philosophischen Terminologie* (Leipzig: Veit, 1879) 176 n. 3.

[21] Cicero, *Att.* 16.11.4. Posidonius' teacher Panaetius may also have dealt with circumstances as one of the determinants of ethical choice. Cf. Cicero, *Off.* 1.30.107–32.117, esp. 32.115, and the discussion by P. H. De Lacy, "The Four Stoic *Personae*," *ICS* 2 (1977) 163–72.

[22] Diog. Laert. 7.109 (= *SVF* 3.135.8–9). For circumstantial duty, cf. also Mar. Ant., *Med.* 1.12.

[23] Diog. Laert. 7.121 (= *SVF* 3.186.5). Cf. also Diog. Laert. 7.188.

[24] Hierocles *apud* Stob. *Ecl.* 4.22a.22 (= 4.502.11,14 Hense), and 4.24a.14 (= 4.604.10 Hense; cf. also 603.17).

general considerations are adapted to specific situations.[25] For some older Stoics like Herillus of Carthage, the *telos* of action can even change in accordance with changing circumstances.[26]

Among rhetoricians the term *peristasis* is also frequent.[27] The introduction of this term into the field of rhetoric goes back to Hermagoras of Temnos in the second century B.C.E.[28] Hermagoras made what was to be an important distinction between *thesis* (θέσις) and *hypothesis* (ὑπόθεσις). Whereas *theses* deal with general issues and do not mention particular persons, *hypotheses* concern specific individuals and definite occasions.[29] A *thesis* is therefore ἀπερίστατος[30] or ἄνευ περιστάσεως,[31] while the specificity of the *hypothesis* demands that various *peristaseis* be created. These *peristaseis* concern the particulars of a given case,[32] such as the person involved, the deed, the time, place, cause, manner, and starting point.[33] These are the circumstances of a case and comprise what Hermagoras termed the μόρια περιστάσεως[34] and were later called τὰ περιστατικὰ μόρια.[35]

[25] Cf. J. Klek, *Symbouleutici qui dicitur sermonis historiam criticam per quattuor saecula continuatam* (Rhetorische Studien 8; Paderborn, Schöningh., 1919) *passim* (*s.v.* index, 166). For a summary and review of Klek's work, cf. F. Levy in *BPhW* 40 (1920) 577–87.

[26] Diog. Laert. 7.165 (= *SVF* 1.91.28).

[27] Cf. esp. F. Striller, *De Stoicorum studiis rhetoricis* (Breslauer philologische Abhandlungen I. 2; Breslau: Köbner, 1886) 27–31.

[28] On Hermagoras, cf. esp. D. Matthes, "Hermagoras von Temnos 1904–1955," *Lustrum* 3 (1958) 58–214. It seems likely that Hermagoras borrowed the term and concept from the Stoics. Cf. W. Kroll, "Rhetorik," *PWSup* 7 (1940) 1095, citing Sternkopf and Immisch. Cf. also Striller, *Stoicorum*, 27–29, and P. Wendland's review of Striller in *BPhW* 7 (1887) 369.

[29] For the basic distinction and the controversies to which it gave rise, cf. Cic., *Inv.* 1.6.8; *De Or.* 1.45–46, 138–41; 2.41–42, 65.

[30] Aphthonius, *Progym.* 13 (= 2.49.23 Spengel).

[31] H. von Arnim, *Leben und Werke des Dio von Prusa* (Berlin: Weidmann, 1898) 93.

[32] Quint., *Inst.* 5.10.104.

[33] The number and particular items given by rhetoricians differ. Cf. Quint., *Inst.* 3.5.17–18; Hermogenes, *Inv.* 5 (= 2.212.17–21 Spengel); Aphthonius, *Progym.* 13 (= 2.49.24–5 Spengel); Fortunatianus, *Artis rhetoricae* 2.1 (= 103. 1–2 Halm); Augustine, *De rhetorica* 7 (= 141.20–21 Halm); Julius Victor, *Ars rhetorica* 16 (= 424.27–9 Halm); and Thomas Magister, 291.5–6 Ritschl. On these circumstantial points, cf. Richard Volkmann, *Die Rhetorik der Griechen und Römer* (1885; repr. Hildesheim: G. Olms, 1963) 36–37, and Striller, *Stoicorum*, 29–31.

[34] Augustine, *De rhetorica* 7 (= 141.15 Halm).

[35] Menander Rhetor, *Epid.* 3 (3.366.5 Spengel). On this phrase, cf. D. A. Russell and N. G. Wilson, (ed. and trans.), *Menander Rhetor* (Oxford: Clarendon, 1981) 269. For a rhetorical definition of *peristasis*, cf. Hermogenes, *Inv.* 3.5 (= 2.212.17–20 Spengel). Augustine, *De rhetorica* 7 (=141.13–14), declines to give a definition, offering the following explanation: "But that which is *peristasis* is able to be understood more easily by a division into parts than by its definition."

Therefore, the term *peristasis* was well-established in rhetorical circles by the first century, in both Greek and Latin.[36] From its origin it was firmly associated with the *hypothesis*,[37] yet occasionally it was even employed in connection with the *thesis*.[38] From this origin it entered into the definition and/or discussion of other rhetorical categories, such as the narration (διήγησις),[39] the *chreia*,[40] and the *epicheireme*.[41]

The "circumstances" in which philosophers and rhetoricians interested themselves are constantly changing, a fact which they perceived and which is reflected in the conjunction of περίστασις and μεταβολή in certain passages.[42] The many diverse *peristaseis* which occur in life bring about a reversal of human fortunes.[43] *Peristasis* is thus often bound up with the idea of vicissitude, the alternation and fluctuation of human fortune.[44] Given the mutability of human fortune, a common Hellenistic ideal is self-sufficiency in every circumstance of life,[45] no matter how extreme. It is sufficient to note this idea here, for it will appear at several points in chapter three.[46]

Via the notion of vicissitude, the meaning of *peristasis* could easily pass over from mere "circumstance" into "adverse, unfavorable circumstance." Such a circumstance could be simply unpleasant or quite critical and precarious. In either case the circumstance presented itself as a "hardship," a "difficulty," an "adversity." This is the second of the standard meanings of *peristasis* in Polybius and the one that is most germane to this investigation.

[36] Among Latin writers περίστασις is either used or transliterated into Latin. When translated, the Latin *circumstantia* is the most common rendering (cf. Quint., *Inst.* 5.10.104; Augustine, *De rhetorica* 7 [= 141.11–12 Halm]). Other renderings include *compositio circumstantiae* (Victorinus, *Explanationum in rhetoricam M. T. Ciceronis* 2.18 [= 275.12–13 Halm]), *negotium* (Quint., *Inst.* 3.5.17–18), and perhaps *interpositio* (cf. Striller, *Stoicorum*, 28, on Cic., *Inv.* 1.6.8). In Sen., *Q Nat.* 2.7.2, ἀντιπερίστασις is rendered by *circumstantia*.

[37] Sometimes the term *peristasis* is equivalent to *hypothesis*, e.g., in Petronius, *Sat.* 48.4 (cf. LS 1345 and Herwerden, *Lexicon*, 1161).

[38] Theon, *Progym.* 12 (= 2.128.10–11 Spengel). Cf. also Matthes, "Hermagoras," 125–27, esp. p. 127, n. 2.

[39] Cf. the definitions and debates in "Cornutus," *Rh.* 46 and 51 (= 1:2.362.13–16 and 363.6–11 Spengel-Hammer).

[40] Theon, *Progym.* 5 (= 2.97.19 Spengel). Cf. also Lausberg, *Handbuch*, 537 (§ 1118.1aβ).

[41] Hermogenes, *Inv.* 3.6 (= 2.210.11–13 Spengel).

[42] Cf., e.g., Ps-Hippocrates, *Praec.* 3 (= *CMG* 1:1.31.14) and Plut., *Mor.* 137B.

[43] Ps-Plut., *Mor.* 103B.

[44] Cf. Walbank, *Commentary*, 1.259 (on Polyb. 2.55.8) and 2.173 (on Polyb. 9.34.4). Cf. also Polyb. 2.41.6; 11.19.5; Theophrastus, *apud* Diomedes, p. 487,12 Keil; and *OGI* 335.15 (= *fortunae vicissitudo;* s.v. index, vol. 2, p. 693).

[45] The phrase πρὸς πᾶσαν περίστασιν αὐτάρκης occurs already in Polyb. 3.31.2.

[46] Cf., for example, the section on "The Serene and Steadfast Sage."

Epictetus provides a convenient statement concerning the use of *peristasis* in the sense of "hardship."

> Yet no one of us is willing, even when necessity calls, to obey her readily, but what we suffer we suffer with fears and groans, and call it "circumstances" (περιστάσεις). What do you mean by "circumstances," man? If you call "circumstances" your surroundings (τὰ περιεστηκότα), all things are "circumstances"; but if you use the word of hardships (δύσκολα), what hardship (δυσκολία) is involved when that which has come into being is destroyed? (*Diss.* 2.6.16–17).

Though Epictetus is here advising his students to use the term *peristasis* only in its literal sense,[47] it is clear that *peristaseis* are equivalent in the common parlance to *dyskola*, "hardships" and "difficulties." Indeed, even Epictetus himself uses *peristasis* in this sense (*Diss.* 1.24.1) and says that it constitutes a load or burden (φορτίον: *Diss.* 4.13.16).[48] A partial list of such *peristaseis* occurs in John Chrysostom's homilies on Hebrews. Chrysostom is here concerned with the problem that some Christians are not helping the needy because the latter are suspected of being imposters and frauds.

> "What do you say, O man? For the sake of one loaf and a garment do you call him a fraud?" "But he immediately sells it," he replies. "And you, do you manage well all your possessions? What then? Are all in need from idleness? Is no one in need from shipwreck? No one from lawcourts? No one from theft? No one from dangers? No one from sickness? No one from another hardship (*peristasis*)?" (*hom. 11.4 in Heb.* [*PG.* 12.117C]).

The use of "another" (ἄλλη) with *peristasis* clearly indicates that shipwreck, loss of goods from judicial process or theft, dangers, and sickness are viewed as *peristaseis* by John Chrysostom. A similar list occurs in John of Damascus' *On Heresies.* In the passage that follows, John is describing the Massalians (Euchites) and their refusal to assist the destitute.

> What is more, they also avoid manual labor as not befitting Christians. And they are especially inhuman in their treatment of the poor, declaring that it is not proper that they who have renounced all worldly goods or who are entirely devoted to the doing of good should help public beggars, or abandoned widows, or those in straightened circumstances (*peristaseis*), or the mutilated, or the diseased, or those suffering from harsh conditions or from the incursions of thieves or barbarians, or such as have met with any misfortune (*symphora*) of the sort. Rather, they say that they themselves should be furnished with everything, because they are the truly poor in spirit.[49]

[47] Cf. A. Bonhöffer, *Epictet und die Stoa* (Stuttgart: F. Enke, 1890) 36. Cf. also his companion volume, *Die Ethik des Stoikers Epictet* (Stuttgart: F. Enke, 1894).

[48] For Epictetus' comparison of *peristasis* to a load, cf. Bonhöffer, *Epictet und die Stoa,* 306, and *Ethik,* 22.

[49] John of Damascus, *haer.* 80 (*PG* 94.732C). The translation is that of F. H. Chase, Jr. (trans.), *Saint John of Damascus: Writings* (FC 37; New York: Fathers of the Church, 1958) 133.

Peristasis appears here as part of one of the items in this list of destitute persons. The comprehensive term at the end of the list is *symphora,* which in fact is usually synonymous with *peristasis.* Indeed, the second century C.E. lexicographer Phrynichus says that Stoic philosophers use *peristasis* instead of *symphora.*[50] Some writers use both words,[51] while others show a predilection for one or the other.[52] Nor is *symphora* the only word with which *peristasis* is associated.[53] The connection with *dyskolon* has already been seen (Epict., *Diss.* 2.6.16–17). Other words include ἀτύχημα,[54] δεινόν,[55] δυστυχία,[56] κακόν,[57] κακοπάθεια,[58] πειρασμός,[59] πόνος,[60] σύμπτωμα,[61] and especially κίνδυνος.[62] Furthermore, to be in *peristasis* often involves ἀπορία,[63] θλῖψις,[64] λύπη,[65] ταραχή,[66] and φόβος.[67]

In the lists of both John Chrysostom and John of Damascus the basic hardship is poverty. The other items are, in the main, the means by which destitution

[50] Phrynichus, *Epit.* 353 Fischer (= 376 Lobeck = 352 Rutherford). Cf. also *Epit.* familia q 353 Fischer and Thomas Magister 291.1 Ritschl.

[51] Maximus of Tyre uses both *symphora* (*Or.* 10.7f = 123,5 Hobein; 10.9b = 125,6; 13.4d = 162,16; 13.8d = 168,8; 13.9c = 169,11; 14.6c = 177,16; 26.9a = 319,5; 26.9g = 320,7) and *peristasis* (22.6d = 275,14; 34 [title] = 390,10; 36.5b = 420,13; 36.6a = 423,17; 36.6d = 424,9; 36.6i = 425,11).

[52] Epictetus uses *peristasis* 27 times and *symphora* only 3 times. Marcus Aurelius uses *peristasis* 4 times and *symphora* only once. In the Cynic Epistles, however, *symphora* occurs 7 times and *peristasis* only 3 times.

[53] For the occurrence of *peristasis* and *symphora* in the same context, cf. Max. Tyr. *Or.* 22.6d (= 275,14 Hobein) and Porph., *Abst.* 1.55.

[54] Polyb. 4.33.11–12.

[55] Clem. Al. *Str.* 4.7.55.1 (= 2.273.21 Stählin); 6.9.72.3 (= 2.468.11 Stählin).

[56] Porph., *Abst.* 2.9; *Suda,* s.v. Συμφορά (3.500.12, Nr. 110 Adler).

[57] Polyb. 2.21.2.

[58] Porph., *Abst.* 1.55.

[59] Eusebius, *Comm. in Ps.* (on Ps. 4:8) (*PG* 5.109D).

[60] Clem. Al. *Str.* 7.11.62.5 (= 3.45.6 Stählin). Cf. also 7.3.18.1 (= 3.13.21 Stählin). According to von Arnim, *Dio,* 265, however, the Cynics always use *ponos* of bodily strains and pains, so that it is not synonymous with *lypē, symphora,* and *peristasis.*

[61] Schweighäuser, *Lexicon,* 346.

[62] This point deserves emphasis in view of Paul's eight-fold use of *kindynos* in 2 Cor 11:26. Cf. Polyb. 4.32.2; 10.14.5; *SIG* 708.7; Soranus, *Gyn.* 1.60 (= *CMG* 4.45.17); Galen, *Protr.* 2.4 (1.3.16–4.3 Kühn); Clem. Al., *Str.* 4.7.55.1 (= 2.273.21–22 Stählin); and Ps-Dioscorides, *Alex.* Praef. (5.5 Sprengel).

[63] *SIG* 731.2,6.

[64] *SIG* 731.2; Clem. Al., *Str.* 4.9.75.2 (= 2.282.5 Stählin); and Eusebius, *Comm. in Ps.* (on Ps. 4:8) (*PG* 5.109D).

[65] Eusebius, *Comm. in Ps.* (on Ps. 4:8) (*PG* 5.109D). Cf. also Clem. Al., *Str.* 6.9.72.3 (= 2.468.11 Stählin).

[66] Porph., *Abst.* 1.55.

[67] Polyb. 4.32.2 and 10.14.5 (compare with 6.18.2,5).

has been brought about. Elsewhere poverty is also seen as a *peristasis*,[68] with shipwreck[69] and sickness[70] treated as *peristaseis* in their own right. Other evils either defined as or associated with *peristasis* include such things as war,[71] the capture of a city,[72] earthquake,[73] famine,[74] hunger and thirst,[75] journeys,[76] necessities,[77] old age,[78] ill repute,[79] possession by demons,[80] a fall,[81] persecution,[82] bonds,[83] blows,[84] violence,[85] exile,[86] slavery,[87] and, of course, death.[88]

While all such things can be counted as *peristaseis* by various individuals, what a particular person defines as a *peristasis* ultimately involves an inescapably subjective factor. Not everyone will define a particular circumstance as a *peristasis*, a hardship. As Dio Chrysostom (*Or.* 13.3) asks, "May not exile . . . and poverty, yes, and old age too and sickness, and all such things, appear heavy to some and grievous, but to others light and easy?" Whether a given circumstance is a hardship depends ultimately on the attitude that one adopts toward it. What is desired and voluntarily elected is no hardship to the one who chooses it, no matter how burdensome and harsh it appears to others. What makes something a hardship is the fact that it is unwanted and not freely chosen.

Maximus of Tyre makes precisely this point when he asks, "Do we consider hardship (*peristasis*) to be anything else than the use of a condition not

[68] Teles, VI (52,3 Hense); Galen, *De sanitate tuenda* 2.1.6–7 (= *CMG* 5:4:2.38,15–7); and Clem. Al., *Str.* 4.6.38.3 (= 2.265.19 Stählin).

[69] Teles, VI (52,3 Hense) and Galen, *Protrep.* 2.4 (1.3.17–4.4 Kühn).

[70] *SIG* 731.7; Clem. Al., *Str.* 4.6.38.3 (= 2.265.19 Stählin); Origen, *Cels.* 8.58; *In Jer. Hom.* 14 (on Jer 15:10–19) (*PG* 13. 404); and Psellus, *Chronographia* 231.28. Cf. also Clem. Al., *Str.* 7.11.61.5 (= 3.44.27 Stählin).

[71] Polyb. 4.67.4; *SIG* 685.137; Max Tyr., *Or.* 22.6d (= 275,14 Hobein); and Procl., *In Ti.* 56.11, 29–30 Diehl.

[72] *SIG* 708.7. Cf. also *OGI* 194.5–6 and *IG* 2^2.1338.12,27.

[73] Galen, *Protr.* 11.13 (1.30.14–5 Kühn). Cf. also Orph., frg. 285.63 Kern.

[74] *SIG* 731.7 and Porph., *Abst.* 2.9.

[75] Palladius, *h. Laus.* 18.8 (*PG* 34. 1057A).

[76] Ps-Dioscorides, *Alex.* Praef. (5.5 Sprengel).

[77] Clem. Al., *Str.* 7.11.62.5 (= 3.45.6 Stählin). Cf. also 4.6.39.3 (= 2.266.2 Stählin).

[78] Clem. Al., *Str.* 4.6.38.3 (= 2.265.19–20 Stählin). Cf. also Soranus, *Gyn.* 1.21 (= *CMG* 4.14.25).

[79] Teles, VI (52,3 Hense).

[80] Origen, *Cels.* 8.58.

[81] Soranus, *Gyn.* 4.36 (= *CMG* 4.148.29–149.3).

[82] Cf. Clem. Al., *Str.* 4.11.78.1 (= 2.283.3 Stählin).

[83] Porph., *Abst.* 1.55. Cf. also Max. Tyr., *Or.* 36.5b (= 420,23–4 Hobein).

[84] Soranus, *Gyn.* 4.36 (= *CMG* 4.149.1–3) and Galen, *Protr.* 11.13 (1.30, 15–16 Kühn).

[85] Soranus, *Gyn.* 4.36 (= *CMG* 4.148.29–149.3).

[86] Teles, VI (52,3 Hense) and Lucian, *Peregr.* 18.

[87] Galen, *De sanitate tuenda* 2.1.6–7 (= *CMG* 5:4:2.38,15–18).

[88] Cf. Clem. Al., *Str.* 4.11.78.1 (= 2.283.3 Stählin) and 7.11.61.5 (= 3.44.27 Stählin).

voluntarily chosen?"[89] Nor is Maximus alone in this view. Clement of Alexandria speaks of the things that befall the gnostic against his will as "involuntary hardships" (τὰς ἀκουσίους περιστάσεις).[90] These are of the same order as the "involuntary misfortunes" spoken of by Maximus[91] and the "undesired and critical circumstances" mentioned by Plutarch.[92] The following advice offered by Musonius Rufus reflects this same idea:

> And if you choose to hold fast to what is right, do not be irked by difficult circumstances (*peristaseis*), but reflect on how many things have already happened to you in life in ways that you did not wish, and yet they have turned out for the best (frg. 27 Hense; cf. also Epict., *Diss.* 2.6.16; 3.24.104–05).

Musonius shows here the same concern with free choice and desire that we have seen in later writers. And the same contrast between choice and circumstance[93] recurs in the distinction drawn between περιστατικαὶ ἀρεταί and προαιρετικαὶ ἀρεταί. The latter are deliberately chosen whereas the "circumstantial virtues" are involuntary and dependent upon chance.[94] The important point, however, is that *peristaseis* raise the question of the will, and, as we shall see, it is here that many of the solutions to *peristaseis* are sought. In addition, the involuntary element in *peristasis* opens the door to the inclusion of lesser events and experiences than those mentioned above. Even the normal entanglements of living in society can become *peristaseis.*[95]

In addition to the question of human will, a second crucial issue raised by *peristaseis* concerns their origin. Bultmann, as we have seen, treats Fate as the source of *peristaseis.*[96] It is indeed a common Graeco-Roman conception to see Fate or Fortune (Tyche) as the source of *peristaseis.* Teles, for instance, begins his *On Circumstances* with the statement that "Fortune, like some poetess, creates roles of every kind: the shipwrecked man, the poor man, the exile, the man of repute, the man without repute."[97] Yet, as common as this idea is, it is

[89] Max. Tyr., *Or.* 36.6a (423,16–424,1 Hobein) (my translation). Cf. also *Or.* 7.21 (78,19–21 Hobein).

[90] Clem. Al., *Str.* 7.11.62.5 (= 3.45.6 Stählin).

[91] Max. Tyr., *Or.* 36.6g (424,21 Hobein). Cf. also *Or.* 34.5a (396,18 Hobein).

[92] Plut., *Mor.* 169D. Cf. also 167F; 168E; 469A; and Plot., *Enn.* 1.4.5,9 and 1.4.8,28.

[93] Cf. esp. Nemesius, *de nat. hom.* 19 and also Epict., *Diss.* 3.14.7; Clem. Al., *Str.* 1.1.17.3 (= 2.12.23 Stählin); 6.10.83.1 (= 2.473.12 Stählin).

[94] Palladius, *h. Laus.* 15.3 (*PG* 34.1041B) and Marc. Diac., *v. Porph.* 73. The juxtaposition of *peristasis* and *prohairesis* is as old as Polyb. 2.17.11.

[95] Cf. esp. Max. Tyr., *Or.* 36.5b (420,9–421,50, esp. 420,13 Hobein) where *peristaseis* are equated with *desmoi* that tie and bind one to the *polis* with its tyrant and law, to wife and children and to various occupations. Cf. also 36.6d (424,9–11 Hobein) and 36.6i (425,10–11 Hobein).

[96] See the discussion of Bultmann in chapter one above.

[97] Teles, VI, 52,2–3 Hense (= 58,1–3 O'Neil). Cf. also Sen., *Marc.* 10.6.

not the only one. Tyche herself, for example, may be regarded as a *peristasis.*[98] More important for this investigation is the fact that the divine may be seen as the giver of *peristaseis.*[99] This perspective will be discussed in detail in chapter three.[100]

A third crucial issue raised by *peristaseis* concerns their function. Indeed, Epictetus defines *peristaseis* in terms of their function. Αἱ περιστάσεις εἰσὶν αἱ τοὺς ἄνδρας δεικνύουσαι. "It is difficulties that show what men are" (*Diss.* 1.24.1; cf. also 1.6.36). While this particular definition is quintessentially Stoic, the basic notion it represents is both ancient and widespread, viz., that *adversity reveals the character of a person.* The individual who handles hardship well is revealed as educated, virtuous, brave, and free. On the other hand, the person who is overcome by the difficulties and dangers of life is shown thereby to be ignorant, ignoble, craven, and servile.[101]

Already in Isocrates' *Archidamus,* for instance, one finds the argument that good men show their superiority in times of misfortune and crisis, "for prosperity helps to hide the baseness even of inferior men, but adversity speedily reveals every man as he really is" (101–02). The vile man's success, for example, is apt to cover his faults, but "if he trips," says Demosthenes, "then we shall know all about his vices" (*Or.* 2.20). More important for this investigation, however, is the fact that prosperity also tends to hide virtue, so that it is adversity which brings one's virtue into the light. As Ovid expresses it, "the virtue which lies hidden and hangs back unrecognized in times of prosperity, comes to the fore and asserts itself in adversity" (*Tr.* 4.3.79–80).[102]

Therefore, *calamitas virtutis occasio est* (Sen., *Prov.* 4.6). "Disaster is Virtue's opportunity," for true greatness shows itself best in misfortune (*Prov.* 4.2; *Ep.* 120.13). Just as war, storm, and disease provide soldiers, sailors, and physicians with the occasion for displaying their respective skills, so is adversity the occasion for displaying virtue (Ov., *Tr.* 4.3.75–84). According to the Neo-Platonist Proclus,

> War exhibits the magnitude of virtue in a greater degree than peace, just as mighty waves and a tempest show in a stronger light the skill of the pilot's art. And, in short, this is effected by hardships (*peristaseis*), as the Stoics also are accustomed to say,

[98] Metrodorus, frg. 49 Körte=Epicurus, frg. A XLVII Bailey. Cf. also E. Bignone, *Epicuro* (Studia Philologica 4; ed. anast.; Rome: "L'Erma" di Bretschneider, 1964) 156.

[99] Cf., e.g., Epict., *Diss.* 1.6.37; 24.1.

[100] See chapter three below on "Fortune, God, and Free Will."

[101] Cf., for instance, Verg., *Aen.* 4.13: "Fear reveals ignoble spirits" (my translation).

[102] On this passage from Ovid, cf. esp. T. J. De Jonge, *Publii Ovidi Nasonis Tristium Liber IV* (Groningen: De Waal, 1951) 119–20, and Georg Luck (ed./trans.), *P. Ovidius Naso, Tristia* (2 vols.; Heidelberg: C. Winter, 1967–77) 2.248. For adversity serving to make virtue more conspicuous, cf. also Max. Tyr., *Or.* 34.5b (397, 1–3 Hobein). Compare Hor., *Sat.* 2.8.73–74.

"Give a hardship (*peristasis*) and receive the man." For that which is not subdued by things which enslave others, manifests a life in every respect worthy.[103]

Adversity occasions the exhibition of virtue[104] because it functions as a *test* of who and what people are. A *peristasis* serves as "the test of the philosopher" (Epict., *Diss.* 3.10.11) by providing him with the opportunity "to show in deed . . . what sort of person a man is who follows the will of nature" (3.20.13).[105] In adversity there is a demonstration of all that virtue entails, viz., the strength or power of the mind,[106] *paideia*,[107] training and exercise,[108] skill in dealing with externals,[109] and true manhood.[110] The scars that the good man sometimes bears on his body are visible tokens of his virtue, "so that not by hearsay but by the evidence of their own eyes men can judge what manner of man he is."[111] The endurance of hardship is thus the *proof of virtue*,[112] the seal of integrity.

In addition, *peristaseis* provide the opportunity to acquire the glory that belongs to virtue. Lucan has Pompey exhort his wife to show courage at his defeat by telling her, "Here is your opportunity for undying fame" (8.74). Similarly, Ovid tells his wife that his exile has given her an opportunity to make her loyalty and virtue conspicuous and thereby to win praise and acquire fame (*Tr.* 4.3.81–84; 5.14.20–28; cf. also 5.5.49–60). Seneca, moreover, declares that "it is more of an accomplishment to break one's way through difficulties than to keep joy within bounds" and thus reserves his greatest praise for those goods which appear only in adversity, like "equanimity in enduring severe illness or

[103] Proc., *In Ti.* 18C Schneider = 56,29–57, 4 Diehl = *SVF* 3.49.30–34. The translation is a modified version of that offered by T. Taylor, *The Commentaries of Proclus on the Timaeus of Plato* (2 vols.; London: the translator, 1820) 1.48.

[104] Cf. Epict., *Diss.* 3.22.59; Sen., *Prov.* 4.2–3; *B.V.* 18.1; *Ep.* 85.39. Cf. also *Helv.* 17.4; *Tranq.* 5.3–4; and Mar. Ant., *Med.* 5.5; 6.50.

[105] For the idea of testing, cf. also 3.12.11; Sen., *Ep.* 13.1; 4 Macc 17:12; and Pall., *H. Laus.* 18.8 (*PG* 34.1057A).

[106] Sen., *Ep.* 26.6; 71.26; *Prov.* 4.3; Epict., *Diss.* 2.1.39; 3.22.87; Hor., *Sat.* 2.8.73–74; Plot., *Enn.* 1.4.14,27.

[107] Isoc., *Or.* 6.102; Epict., *Diss.* 1.29.33,44; 2.1.35; 4.4.30; Ps-Plut., *Mor.* 102F.

[108] Epict., *Diss.* 3.10.8; 4.4.30.

[109] Epict., *Diss.* 2.5.21; Max. Tyr., *Or.* 26.9a (319,5–6 Hobein).

[110] Accius, *trag.* 460 (= 440 Warmington); Epict., *Diss.* 1.24.1; Clem. Al., *Str.* 7.3.18.1 (3.13.21 Stählin); Proc., *In Ti.* 18C Schneider.

[111] The thought is an adaption of Xen., *Ages.* 6.2.

[112] Dio Chrys., *Or.* 3.3; Sen., *B.V.* 18.1; *Prov.* 4.12. Cf. also Epict., *Diss.* 3.10.11 and 3.24.118. In Jewish and Christian circles this basic idea is expressed in different terms. In 4 Macc 11:12, for example, suffering serves to exhibit endurance for the Torah, whereas in Clem. Al., *Str.* 4.7.55.1 (2.273.20–22 Stählin), hardship functions to demonstrate the true gnostic's love for God. For Clement's prayer to God to send a *peristasis*, compare esp. Epict., *Diss.* 1.6.37.

exile" or "fortitude in resisting torture" (*Ep.* 66.36–37, 49–50). In this way *peristaseis* become a means of self-adornment for the man of virtue.[113] They are a foil for him, so that the more dismal the hardships sustained, the more illustrious the heroic fame that accrues to him.[114] In and through his trials the virtuous man gains a ground for boasting (cf. Sir 31:10).

Peristaseis, therefore, are intimately bound up with virtue.[115] Adversity does not conceal or destroy virtue (Arist., *Eth.Nic.* 1.10.12; Luc. 3.690), but rather reveals and demonstrates it. Indeed, it is in and through adversity that the man of virtue sets himself off from the base, that the true philosopher distinguishes himself from those who merely lay claim to the title.[116] As one would expect, this point is of crucial importance for understanding why Paul in 2 Corinthians so often has recourse to the theme of his sufferings.

Three more observations need to be made before drawing this section to a close. First, it has become clear that *peristaseis* are both logically and etymologically "external things."[117] They may be physical, somatic afflictions, but they remain external to the *psyche.* According to the Stoics, trouble arises when these external circumstances gain entrance into the soul via a false judgment about their true status. Since an external circumstance can and does affect one's internal, mental life, *peristasis* is occasionally applied to the *effect* wrought by the *peristasis* itself. Thus, Marcus Aurelius can say, "This day have I got me out of all trouble (*peristasis*), or rather have cast out all trouble (*peristasis*), for it was not without, but within, in my own imagination."[118] Marcus' statement is intentionally paradoxical: "I cast out my surroundings by expelling the judgment *within* me."[119] As we shall see, occasionally one finds internal items, like

[113] Cf., for example, Epict., *Diss.* 3.20.13–14, and the discussion of this thought in Epictetus by Bonhöffer, *Ethik,* 24–25, and *Epiktet und das Neue Testament* (Religionsgeschichtliche Versuche and Vorarbeiten 10; Giessen: Töpelmann, 1911) 232, 277 n. 4, 291, 300–01.

[114] Cf. B. Bauer, *Christus und die Caesaren* (Berlin: Grosser, 1877) 52. Hardships are thus "grist for his mill," the raw material whereby he becomes better and more praiseworthy. Cf. Mar. Ant., *Med.* 4.1; 7.58; 10.33.4.

[115] Cf also Sen., *Her. F.* 432–36; Ov., *Tr.* 4.3.76.

[116] Cf esp. Epict., *Diss.* 2.8.27–29; 2.19.12–24; and also 4.6.1–3. Furthermore, just as *peristaseis* reveal the true philosopher, he in turn reveals the true nature of *peristaseis* (2.16.43; 3.20.14; 4.7.13).

[117] Etymologically the verb περιίστημι means "to stand around" and a περίστασις is that which "stands around" or "surrounds" one and thus is external to a person. Occasionally one finds either ἔξω or ἔξωθεν used with *peristasis,* usually for emphasis or clarity. Cf. Polyb. 18.53.11; *SIG*² 590.91(?); Galen, *De sanitate tuenda* 2.3.17 (= *CMG* 5:4:2.44.5); Sext. Emp., *Math.* 7.245; Porph., *Abst.* 1.55; *IG* 7.3073.90.

[118] Mar. Ant., *Med.* 9.13. The passage is an example of *epidiorthosis.* Cf. J. Dalfen, "Formgeschichtliche Untersuchungen zu den Selbstbetrachtungen Marc Aurels," (Ph.D. Diss., Ludwig-Maximilians-Universität zu München, 1967) 157.

[119] A. S. L. Farquharson, *The Meditations of the Emperor Marcus Antoninus* (2 vols.; Oxford: Clarendon, 1944) 2.802 (emphasis his).

emotions, mentioned in what are primarily lists of external and/or bodily hardships. In most cases, this is simply the inclusion of an effect within a list of causes, but it serves to indicate that the word *peristasis* is occasionally used in reference to "internal phenomena."[120]

Second, the word *peristasis* occurs in patristic literature in two of the senses that have been proposed for ἐπίστασις in 2 Cor 11:28. *LPGL*[121] gives both "assault, siege,"[122] and "pressure, besieging with importunate requests"[123] for *peristasis.* While it would be going too far to suggest that ἐπίστασις is an ancient error for περίστασις, the proposed meanings for the former are clearly related to those attested for the latter. This fact does not decide the meaning of *epistasis* in 2 Cor 11:28, but it does broaden the perspective from which the passage may be viewed.

Third, the use of the phrase "*peristasis* catalogue" to describe certain Pauline passages seems warranted both by the flexibility of the term *peristasis* and by its use in antiquity. It can be justifiably applied to passages as diverse as Phil 4:12 and 2 Cor 11:22–28. A *peristasis* catalogue is ultimately a "catalogue of circumstances." The circumstances envisiond may be either "good" or "bad" or both. The catalogues that contain several of both kinds of circumstances are the most comprehensive and constitute the basic category. Catalogues that emphasize or concern only one set of circumstances represent subsets of this basic category.

The best example of the basic type in the Pauline corpus is Phil 4:12. An apt description of this passage and one that takes into account the Hellenistic emphasis on the fluctuation of human fortune is "catalogue of vicissitudes." It is a *peristasis* catalogue that lists various circumstances and contemplates the shift from one circumstance to another.

Most of Paul's *peristasis* catalogues, however, emphasize only one set of circumstances, with the other set either not mentioned at all or only in passing. An example of the latter is 2 Cor 6:3–10, where δόξα and εὐφημία are almost

[120] Even when a *peristasis* is explicitly identified as "external," it is sometimes difficult to see in what sense it is such. Cf., for example, Sext. Emp., *Math.* 7.253–57, and the discussion of this passage by Heinrich von Staden, "The Stoic Theory of Perception and Its 'Platonic' Critics," in P. K. Machamer and R. G. Turnbull (eds.), *Studies in Perception* (Columbus: Ohio State, 1978), 108.

[121] *LPGL,* 1072a, nos. 3 and 4.

[122] Compare the "attack, onset" given by BAGD 300a, for Acts 24:12, and the variant ἐπισύστασις that occurs at both Acts 24:12 and 2 Cor 11:28. The idea in the pertinent patristic passages is that of "besetment" for purposes of assault. Cf. John Chrysostom, *hom. 2.7 in 2 Cor.* (*PG* 10.438C); *hom. 3.4 in 1 Thess.* (*PG* 11.446E); and Macarius Aegyptius, *hom.* 50.4 (*PG* 34.820A). This use of *peristasis* is thus closely related to εὐπερίστατος, the adjective that occurs in Heb 12:1 in the phrase often translated "the sin that so easily besets." Cf. BAGD 324a; and the discussions by J. H. Moulton and W. F. Howard, *A Grammar of New Testament Greek* (Edinburgh: Clark, 1929) 282, and B. F. Westcott, *The Epistle to the Hebrews* (3d ed.; London: Macmillan, 1914) 395.

[123] Eustratius, *v. Eutych.* 12 (*PG* 86.2288C).

eclipsed by the major emphasis of the context (6:8). The catalogues found elsewhere in the Corinthian correspondence are examples of the former inasmuch as they deal exclusively with adverse circumstances. In view of this emphasis on suffering, privation, and toil, it seems appropriate to designate these passages and the subtype to which they belong as "catalogues of hardships."[124] They are still *peristasis* catalogues, with *peristasis* understood now in the sense of distress, danger, and difficulty. The other subtype or subset ("catalogues of advantageous circumtances") does not figure in Paul's self-descriptions and thus will not be a major concern in the subsequent discussion. It may be worthwhile, however, to point out that Paul's ironic description of the Corinthians in 1 Cor 4:8,10 contains several of the items usually included in such catalogues (viz., wealth, wisdom, and kingship).

It is in light of this general discussion of "*peristasis*" that particular examples of *peristasis* catalogues are to be seen. The next chapter begins with a survey of some of the major types of catalogues of hardships and then focues on the figure of the sage and his sufferings.

[124] Clem. Al., *Str.* 4.14.96.2 (= 2.290.27 Stählin) refers to Rom 8:38–39 as a συγκεφαλαίωσις, a summary or compendious account of the gnostic martyr. Sen., *Helv.* 3.2, speaks of heaping up (*coacervata*) all of Helvia's misfortunes (*mala*). Cf. also Ovid, *Met.* 8.485.

3
The Hardships of the Sage

Introduction: The Variety of Peristasis Catalogues

Since the idea of vicissitude lies at the heart of Greek anthropology, it is not surprising that hardship and the mutability of fortune are stock subjects in ancient Greek and Roman literature. The cataloguing of vicissitudes and hardships is likewise an ancient phenomenon, one that clearly antedates Homer.[1] Even a cursory examination of the literature will reveal that *peristasis* catalogues are of various kinds, derive from diverse *Sitze im Leben,* appear in several genres, and serve to elucidate numerous themes and *topoi.*

Of the numerous types of catalogues that occur in this literature, seven seem to be the most prominent. First, in terms of content, the most general *peristasis* catalogues are those which enumerate the various ills to which humans qua humans are liable. For the most part, these *catalogues of human hardships* serve to elucidate and illustrate the ineluctability of human suffering, whether it be for consolation, admonition, or some other purpose.[2] Second, more specific are those catalogues that delineate the *hardships of national groups,* such as the Spartans, Cretans, and Germans.[3]

A third type consists of *catalogues of occupational hardships.* Of the various occupations, the ones most famous for their hardships and hazards were the farmer or husbandman, the trader or traveling merchant, the sailor, the hunter, and the soldier.[4] The most grueling and gruesome occupation of all, however, was

[1] J. N. H. Austin, "Catalogues and the Catalogue of Ships in the *Iliad,*" (Ph.D. Diss., Berkeley, 1965) 131–32.

[2] Cf. esp. Epict., *Diss.* 3.24.28–29; Dio Chrys., *Or.* 16.3; Philo, *Virt.* 5; and Sen., *Marc.* 18.8. For other Senecan catalogues of human hardships, cf. *Ep.* 107.2,5; *Ben.* 1.11.2–3; *Helv.* 11.7; *V.B.* 15.6.

[3] Cf. esp. Cic., *Tusc.* 2.14.34; Sen., *Prov.* 4.14–15; Dio Chrys., *Or.* 25.3.

[4] For the theme of the farmer's psychic and physical hardships, his toil and fortitude, cf. Hor., *Ep.* 1.7.86–89; 8.3–6; 2 Tim 2:6; and Max. Tyr., *Or.* 24.6d (294,13–18 Hobein). For the hardships of the farmer, sailor, and esp. the hunter, cf. Dio Chrys., *Or.* 3.56, 64–65, 135–36. For the hardships of the soldier, cf. Aesch. *Ag.* 555–66; Hor., *Carm.* 1.17.17–21; 18.5; Dio Chrys., *Or.* 1.28; and Suet., *Iul.* 68.1–2.

that of the gladiator, whose oath of allegiance to his trainer took the form of a catalogue of hardships.[5]

A fourth type of *peristasis* catalogue appears frequently in discussions of justice and injustice and consists of an enumeration of various punishments. The penalties mentioned in these *catalogues of punishments* are sometimes merited because justice has been violated, and the most shocking examples of this type are drawn from tortures in vogue among the barbarians.[6] At other times, however, an individual is punished for crimes of which he is innocent. Such a person is a "righteous sufferer," and the catalogue of his hardships is thus a catalogue of the punishments to which he unjustly has been subjected. The theme of the "righteous sufferer" and the catalogues connected with it are important and will be treated later in this chapter.[7]

The hardships of the passions constitute a fifth type of catalogue, one in which toils and afflictions that are the consequence of passions like *ira, cupiditas,* and *amor* are enumerated.[8] Catalogues of this kind are often used protreptically by moralists within the *synkrisis* of virtue and passion, as, for instance, by Seneca in *Ep.* 76.20.

A sixth type of catalogue contains *the vicissitudes of particular individuals.* Pliny the Elder, for example, gives a lengthy catalogue of Augustus' hardships in order to support his thesis that Fortune's mutability makes it impossible to declare any mortal truly "happy" (*HN* 7.45.147–50). Again, Demosthenes in his

[5] Cf. esp. Petron., *Sat.* 117: "*Uri, vinciri, verberari, ferroque necari, et quicquid aliud [patior].*" For other instances and adaptions of this oath, cf. Hor., *Sat.* 2.7.58; Sen., *Ep.* 37.1; 71.23; Ps-Sen., *Apocol.* 9; and Tib. 1.9.21–22.

[6] Cf. Hes., *Op.* 238–47; Anacreon of Teos, frg. 388 *PMG* (= frg. 82 Gentilli = frg. 97 Edmonds = Ath. 12.533F-543B); Aesch., *Eum.* 185–90; Pl., *Grg.* 473C; 480C-D; Cic., *Rab. Post.* 5.16; Sen., *Ep.* 24.3; *Ira* 3.19.1; *Ag.* 988–93; and also *Clem.* 1.15.7; *Ep.* 24.14; 26.10; *Ira* 1.16.2–4; 3.3.6; 32.2; 43.4; *Marc.* 20.3; *Tro.* 578–86. Also to be included in this basic category are: 1) catalogues of curses in ANE treaties and plague prayers, wherein calamities are the consequence of a breach of oath or treaty; 2) OT lists of afflictions in which suffering is the punishment for sin (e.g., Lev 26; Deut 28; Sir 39:29–30); and 3) lists of apocalyptic tribulations that befall the wicked (e.g., *Jub.* 23:13). For additional examples of the latter, cf. esp. the texts collected by Klaus Berger, *Die Griechische Daniel-Diegese* (SPB 27; Leiden: Brill, 1976) 42–46.

[7] Cf. the section below on "The Righteous Sufferer as the 'Foolish' Wise Man."

[8] For hardships and anger, cf. esp. Sen., *Ira* 2.36.5 and also 1.2.2–3; 2.14.3–4; 3.27.1. A host of hardships, toils, and dangers are associated with *cupiditas*, especially as they involve the adulterer (Hor., *Sat.* 1.2.37–46; 2.7.46–67), the athlete (Sen., *Ep.* 78.16), the explorer (Sen., *Ot.* 5.2), the ambitious (Sen., *Ep.* 94.66; Hor. *Sat.* 2.3.165–66; Dio Chrys., *Or.* 52.12; 59.1–2), and the avaricious (Hor., *Ep.* 1.1.42–46; *Sat.* 1.1.38–40; Sen., *Ep.* 4.11; 15.9; 87.28; *QNat.* 3 Pref. 17; 1 Tim 6:9; and Nr. 207 in Wachsmuth's *Gnomologium Byzantium* [*Studien zu den griechischen Florilegien Nr.V*], p. 200, cited by R. Heinze, *De Horatio Bionis imitatore* [Diss., Bonn; Leipzig: Fock, 1899] 17). For *amor* and hardships, see Sen., *Ep.* 94.64, and compare Max. Tyr., *Or.* 11.10c (141,1–4 Hobein); 20.2a–e (244,10–245,4 Hobein); and 1 Cor 13:3.

De Corona catalogues both the acts of aggression by Philip of Macedon (71) and the injuries he sustained in the process (67). The two catalogues are complementary and serve to depict Philip as a dangerous and capable man who is prepared to suffer grievously in order to achieve his imperial aims. In addition, the use of the first person singular to recount one's hardships is particularly noteworthy and occurs especially in petitions, prayers, and laments. Such is not restricted to the OT Psalter and the *Hôdāyôt,* but is found also in the Hellenistic novel. Chariton, for example, has Callirhoe give a catalogue of her hardships in a prayer to Aphrodite (3.8.9) and in laments addressed to Tyche (5.5.2) and her own beauty (6.6.4). Again, both Chariton's Chaereas (4.4.10) and Achilles Tatius' Leucippe (5.18.3–6) write letters to their lovers in which the listing of their hardships is central to the petitions that they make.

Finally, there are numerous catalogues that depict *the hardships of various types.* The orphan, for example, is a specific type whose hardships can be catalogued.[9] A more general type is the wanderer, for the "woes of the wanderer" is a theme that applies in part to any ancient traveler or wayfarer. Discomforts and dangers were the lot, for instance, of both the itinerant philosopher and the traveling merchant as they marketed their respective wares. Also subject to these woes were persons displaced by reason of war, exile, or economic necessity. The vagrant, the mendicant, and all those without sufficient financial resources to insulate them from the harsher aspects of nomadic existence were naturally those who found itineracy the most difficult.[10]

For the purposes of this investigation, the most important of the various types is *the wise man.* Hellenistic moralists were fond of discussing the wise man in terms of the hardships that he experienced. This theme of "the suffering sage" is particularly relevant to that of "the suffering apostle," because catalogues of hardships appear in connection with both the *sophos* and the *apostolos.* Implicit in this theme are important questions concerning such matters as the role of reason and free will in dealing with adversity, the relation of Fortune and God to the sage's suffering, the sage's demeanor under duress, and the utility of adversity for the sage and his virtue.

The subsequent discussion in this chapter will focus, therefore, on the figure of the wise man and on those legendary and historical individuals who exhibited the characteristics of the sage. Since the various *peristasis* catalogues should not be examined apart from the themes and concerns with which they are connected, this examination will take the form of an essay in which the catalogues are used primarily to illustrate the points under discussion. It is hoped that this format will do justice to the contexts in which the catalogues appear as well as facilitate

[9] Cf., for example, Hom., *Il.* 22.487–99.

[10] The "woes of the wanderer" is a theme that appears already in the *Iliad* (24.531–33) and occurs repeatedly in the *Odyssey* (cf., for example, 1.49; 2.370; 3.94–95; 4.81,324–25; 7.152; 10.463–65; 14.362; 15.342–45,400; 16.205; 21.284). Cf. also Archil., frg. 58 Diehl (= frg. 56 Edmonds) and Aesch., *Ag.* 1273–74.

the presentation of the material, thereby relieving the reader of the tedium of perusing a catalogue of catalogues. The reader, for his part, must be attentive to the presence of catalogues in the material cited, for only occasionally will their presence be made explicit.

In recognition of the vitality of Stoicism during the first century C.E. and the great influence it exerted on Hellenistic culture in general, special emphasis in the following discussion will be given to Stoics and those whom they influenced.[11] Seneca receives particular attention, for, in the first place, he is a contemporary of Paul, and certain similarities between their thought and/or forms of expression have long been recognized. Second, the sage and his sufferings are central to Seneca's philosophy as a whole, so that a concentration on him is not only useful but also unavoidable. Third, Seneca's views are frequently representative of Hellenistic ideas in general and Stoic perspectives in particular. The footnotes will afford ample illustration of this fact. Fourth, Seneca's idiosyncrasies as a Stoic often provide a helpful entrée into ancient debates about particular topics. Therefore, since a concentration on Seneca will allow both the unity and diversity in ancient thought to emerge more clearly, he will frequently (but not invariably) be used to organize the discussion.[12]

[11] The literature on Stoicism is vast. For a general orientation, cf. Eduard Zeller, *The Stoics, Epicureans, and Sceptics* (rev. ed.; London: Longmans, Green, and Co., 1892); St. George Stock, *Stoicism* (New York: Dodge, 1909); R. D. Hicks, *Stoic and Epicurean* (1910; repr., New York: Russell & Russell, 1962); E. V. Arnold, *Roman Stoicism* (Cambridge: University Press, 1911); E. Bevan, *Stoics and Sceptics* (Oxford: Clarendon, 1913); Paul Barth, *Die Stoa* (3d ed.; Stuttgart: Frommann, 1922); R. M. Wenley, *Stoicism and Its Influence* (Boston: Marshall Jones, 1924); J. Christensen, *An Essay on the Unity of Stoic Philosophy* (Copenhagen: Munksgaard, 1962); Max Pohlenz, *Die Stoa* (2 vols.; 3d ed.; Göttingen: Vandenhoeck & Ruprecht, 1964); A. Bridoux, *Le Stoicisme et son influence* (Paris: Librairie philosophique J. Vrin, 1966); Ludwig Edelstein, *The Meaning of Stoicism* (Cambridge: Harvard, 1966); J. M. Rist, *Stoic Philosophy* (Cambridge: University Press, 1969); A. A. Long (ed.), *Problems in Stoicism* (London: Athlone, 1971); F. H. Sandbach, *The Stoics* (New York: Norton, 1975). For some particular topics, cf. Benson Mates, *Stoic Logic* (Berkeley: University of California Press, 1973); S. Sambursky, *Physics of the Stoics* (London: Routledge and Kegan Paul, 1959); Heinrich von Staden, "The Stoic Theory of Perception and Its 'Platonic Critics,' " in P. K. Machamer & R. G. Turnbull (eds.), *Studies in Perception* (Columbus: Ohio State, 1978) 96–136; D. Tsekourakis, *Studies in the Terminology of Early Stoic Ethics* (Wiesbaden: Steiner, 1974); and Gerard Watson, *Stoic Theory of Knowledge* (Belfast: The Queens University, 1966).

[12] For bibliography and an orientation to Seneca, cf. esp. Gregor Maurach (ed.), *Seneca als Philosoph* (Wege der Forschung 414; Darmstadt: Wissenschaftliche Buchgesellschaft, 1975). For Seneca's fundamental Stoicism, cf. esp. P. Grimal, *Sénèque, sa vie, son oeuvre, sa philosophie* (2d ed.; Paris: Presses universitaires de France, 1957). Especially valuable are the analyses of Winfried Trillitzch, *Senecas Beweisführung* (DAWB; Berlin: Akademie Vlg., 1962); I. Hadot, *Seneca und die griechisch-römische Tradition der Seelenleitung* (Berlin: de Gruyter, 1969); and Hildegard Cancik, *Untersuchungen zu Senecas Epistulae morales* (Spudasmata 18; Hildesheim: Olms, 1976). A convenient collection of Senecan

The discussion will begin with an examination of the way in which Hellenistic philosophy addressed itself to the various problems created by the mutability of fortune and with the crucial role played by reason in dealing with adversity and suffering. After this, the discussion will turn to the figure of the sage and the one who was on the road to wisdom, the *proficiens.* The following section deals with "the serene and steadfast sage," where the wise man's superiority to adversity is established as a commonplace of Graeco-Roman thought. The impact of hardships on the sage—or the lack of it—is discussed in terms of "the struggling sage." In "Fortune, God, and Free Will," the sources of the sage's sufferings are discussed, as well as the role that volition plays in the contest with adversity. In winning this contest the sage exhibits his virtue, especially his courage, and the key to his victory is his *askēsis,* which is the focus of the following section ("The Sage's *Andreia,* Action, and *Askēsis*"). The final sections discuss the wise man as a "fool," his demeanor, the praise that he receives, and the way in which he praises himself in terms of his hardships. A short summary brings the chapter to a close.

The Crucial Role of Philosophy and Reason

The demise of the city-state in the wake of Alexander the Great's conquests contributed greatly to the emergence of a widespread feeling of helplessness and insecurity during the Hellenistic period. The classical city-state, in contrast to its post-Alexandrian successor, had been the presupposition for philosophical discussion and the lives of men and women had been virtually predetermined by its traditions and customs. After Alexander, the *polis,* to be sure, was still there, but its intellectual and emotional walls of protection had crumbled to the ground. The old *polis*-oriented philosophy was decimated, and, as a consequence, the feeling of rootlessness and impotence was rampant. With this came a heightened sense of human frailty, a conviction that man is but "a vessel that the slightest shaking, the slightest toss will break," that his body is "weak and fragile" and "in its natural state defenceless" (Sen., *Marc.* 11.3).

Extricated from the shelter of the closed society and its firm moorings, people felt exposed to the disruptive forces of life, a prey to powers beyond their control. Tyche and Fortuna became the dominant forces in life. In contrast to the archaic period, however, Tyche during the Graeco-Roman period was characterized by

texts on various themes is available in H. B. Timothy, *The Tenets of Stoicism, Assembled and Systematized, from the Works of L. Annaeus Seneca* (Amsterdam: Hakkert, 1973). A helpful older work is that of W. C. Summers, *Select Letters of Seneca* (London: Macmillan, 1910). As to the centrality of the sage in Seneca's works, cf. J. N. Sevenster, *Paul and Seneca* (NovTSup 4; Leiden: Brill, 1961) 165. Sevenster's bibliography on Paul and Seneca, while by no means complete, mentions the most important twentieth century discussions.

caprice.[13] For Pindar and his contemporaries "what comes by τύχα is unforeseeable and mysterious, but it is managed by divine will, not by random chance."[14] The common man of the Graeco-Roman period, by contrast, felt only the flux and lacked the assurance of a benevolent flow to the flux. What he needed was a counterbalance that would neutralize the perniciousness of Fortune's mindless mutability.

Hellenistic philosophy sought to provide the solution to his needs. It was, for example, "the essential purpose of Stoicism . . . to provide protection against the experience of suffering evil."[15] The answer given to the problem of vicissitude was imperturbability, inner tranquility in the midst of external turbulence. This state was seen as indispensable for εὐδαιμονία, happiness or well-being. And this, it was clear, could not "consist in freedom from pain and sickness and ill luck and falling into great misfortunes," for, if it did, "it would be impossible for anyone to be well off when any of these circumstances opposed to well-being was present" (Plot., *Enn.* 1.4.6,1-4). The term used to describe this happy state of stable calmness and contentment varied from school to school and from

[13] Cf. esp. "Cebes," *Tabula* 7.2; 31.1-5; and the discussion by J. T. Fitzgerald and L. M. White, *The Tabula of Cebes* (SBLTT 24; Chico: Scholars, 1983) 141-42. On the more general topic of the collapse of the *polis* and its consequences, cf. esp. Gilbert Murray, *Five Stages of Greek Religion* (3d ed., 1951; repr., Garden City: Doubleday, 1955) 77, 123.

[14] G. M. Kirkwood, "*Nemean* 7 and the Theme of Vicissitude in Pindar," in Kirkwood (ed.), *Poetry and Poetics from Ancient Greece to the Renaissance* (Cornell Studies in Classical Philology 38; Ithaca/London: Cornell, 1975) 71. Hellenistic Tyche's characteristic action of randomly taking back what she has given, for instance, was attributed by Hesiod to the goddess Hecate, who did so according to her will (*Theog.* 442-43).

[15] N. T. Pratt, Jr., "The Stoic Base of Senecan Drama," *TAPhA* 79 (1948) 4. For philosophy in the Hellenistic period, cf. the works cited in notes 11 and 12 above and also Constant Martha, *Les Moralistes sous l'empire romain* (1865; 7th ed.; Paris: Hachette, 1900); Wilhelm Windelband, *History of Ancient Philosophy* (New York: Scribners, 1899); Samuel Dill, *Roman Society from Nero to Marcus Aurelius* (1904; repr., Cleveland/New York: World, 1956) 289-440; E. Bevan, "Hellenistic Popular Philosophy," *The Hellenistic Age* (ed. J. D. Bury; Cambridge: University Press, 1923) 79-107; P. E. More, *Hellenistic Philosophies* (Princeton: University Press, 1923); E. Zeller, *Die Philosophie der Griechen in ihrer geschlichtlichen Entwicklung*, Vol. III.1: *Die nacharistotelische Philosophie* (2 vols.; 6th ed.; Darmstadt: Wissenschaftliche Buchgesellschaft, 1963); F. Ueberweg and K. Praechter, *Grundriss der Geschichte der Philosophie*, Vol. I: *Die Philosophie des Altertums* (12th rev. ed; Berlin: Mittler, 1926); A. H. Chroust, "The Meaning of Philosophy in the Hellenistic Roman World," *Thomist* 17 (1954) 196-253; M. P. Nilsson, *Geschichte der griechischen Religion* (2 vols.; Munich: Beck, 1967) 2.395-466; É. Bréhier, *The History of Philosophy: The Hellenistic and Roman Age* (Chicago: University Press, 1965); A. H. Armstrong, *An Introduction to Ancient Philosophy* (3d ed.; Boston: Beacon, 1967) 114-204; P. Merlan, "Greek Philosophy from Plato to Plotinus," *The Cambridge History of Later Greek and Early Medieval Philosophy* (ed. A. H. Armstrong; Cambridge: University Press, 1967) 11-132; and A. A. Long, *Hellenistic Philosophy: Stoics, Epicureans, Sceptics* (New York: Scribners, 1974).

individual to individual;[16] but the answer was essentially the same.[17] The answer to the problem of external flux had to be an internal one, a mental and emotional state free from disturbance, a condition that was often called ἀταραξία. Differences lay in how one arrived at this state, in how one reached this goal. But reach it one must, for happiness was seen as impossible without doing so.

Stoics, for instance, made virtue alone sufficient for happiness, for they considered virtue "the provider of all goods" (Mus. Ruf., VII, 29, 2–3 Hense = 56,24 Lutz).

> No other sense underlies the word happy, when we use it, except the fulness of combined good and complete separation of evil. Virtue cannot secure [happiness], if there is any good besides itself; for there will come as it were a throng of evils, if we regard them as evils, poverty, obscurity, insignificance, loneliness, loss of property, severe physical pain, ruined health, infirmity, blindness, fall of one's country, exile and, to crown all, slavery: in all these distressing conditions—and more still can happen—the wise man can be involved; for chance occasions them, and chance can assail the wise man; but if these are "evils," who can show that the wise man will be always happy, seeing that he can be involved in all of them at one and the same time? (Cic., *Tusc.* 5.10.29; cf. also *Fin.* 5.28.84).

Accepting the traditional identification of virtue with knowledge, they saw in virtue the perfection of reason (cf. also Plot., *Enn.* 1.4.2, 41–43) and thus shared with others the view that virtue is an intellectual performance or achievement.[18] But virtue itself was made dependent on philosophy. Musonius Rufus is typically Stoic when he argues that the courage to face hardships comes *only* from a firm conviction about their true nature and that this conviction is the product of philosophical instruction *alone* (VIII,35,8–36, 1 Hense = 62,23–31 Lutz).[19]

Philosophy fortifies and arms the mind by enlightening it concerning the true nature of good and evil (Mus. Ruf., VI, 26, 11–17 Hense = 54, 30–35 Lutz). For Stoics, virtue is the only good and vice the only evil. Everything else falls within the category of things indifferent (ἀδιάφορα, *indifferentia, media*), that is, things which are neither good nor bad, but simply neutral in and of themselves. As such, they neither benefit nor harm, and they contribute nothing to happiness.[20] These *adiaphora* are spelled out in catalogues and include "such things as life, death, fame, ignominy, pain, pleasure, wealth, poverty, sickness, health, and the

[16] For an early example of such fluidity in terminology, cf. Democritus A 167 (2.129.15–16 Diels-Kranz).

[17] Cf. esp. Albrecht Dihle, *The Theory of Will in Classical Antiquity* (Sather Classical Lectures 48; Berkeley: University of California, 1982) 41.

[18] Ibid., 37, 45, 49, and 54.

[19] In making the virtue of courage dependent upon philosophy Musonius is following in a tradition long established in philosophical circles, one that appears already in Plato. Cf., for instance, Pl., *Lach.* 199B-C; *Prt.* 349D; 359B; *Resp.* 429B-430B; 442C; and A. E. Taylor, *Plato: The Man and His Work* (1926; reprinted, New York: Meridian, 1956) 63.

[20] Cic., *Fin.* 3.15.50; Diog. Laert. 7.104; Sext. Emp., *Math.* 11.59–61; *Pyr.* 3.177.

like" (*SVF* 1.47.24–26 [§190] = 3.17.20–21 [§70]).[21]

Since the mutability of fortune makes everyone a potential candidate for almost all these *adiaphora,* this evaluation is of crucial importance (Sen., *Ep.* 95.54; Mar. Ant., *Med.* 12.8). The Stoic assumption is that the soul has in it "the power of living ever the noblest of lives" and the key to doing so is the adoption of an indifferent attitude toward things that are indifferent (Mar. Ant., *Med.* 11.16). As long as the correct judgment about good and evil is not formed, it is impossible to act correctly (*Med.* 9.1.4; 11.10; cf. also 2.11 and 8.14). But once philosophy has informed the mind about the true nature of things, it becomes impervious to pleasure and pain alike, enabling a person to do his duty in all circumstances of life. The philosophically informed mind, says Marcus Aurelius, "is a very citadel, for a man has no fortress more impregnable wherein to find refuge and be untaken for ever" (*Med.* 8.48; cf. also Sen., *Const.* 6.8; *Ep.* 74.19; Ps-Plut., *Mor.* 5E). Again, nothing can "thwart the inner purposes of the mind. For it no fire can touch, nor steel, nor tyrant, nor obloquy, nor any thing soever" (8.41; cf. also 4.39; 8.48–49,51). Since he has no Achilles' heel where he is vulnerable (Sen., *Const.* 8.3),

> the wise man is fortified against all inroads; he is alert; he will not retreat before the attack of poverty, or of sorrow, or of disgrace, or of pain. He will walk undaunted (*interritus*) both against them and among them (Sen., *Ep.* 59.8).[22]

Cynics also affirmed the great power of the rational mind and agreed completely with the Stoics that virtue is the only thing of value and that only vice is to be rejected. But whereas Cynics tended to view everything else as utterly insignificant, Stoics made allowances for the human inclination to have desire for certain indifferent things and aversion toward others (cf., for example, Sen., *Ep.* 123.13). They divided the *adiaphora* into three different categories. Natural things with a positive value were judged "preferred" (προηγμένα); negative, unnatural items were placed in the "rejected" (ἀποπροηγμένα) category; and truly neutral items without a positive or negative value were treated as simply "indifferent" (Cic., *Fin.* 3.15.50–16.54; Diog. Laert. 7.105; Sext. Emp., *Math.* 11.62). Both the preferred and the rejected items were frequently enumerated:

> Thus things of the preferred class are those which have positive value, *e.g.* amongst mental qualities, natural ability, skill, moral improvement, and the like; among bodily qualities, life, health, strength, good condition, soundness of organs, beauty, and so forth; and in the sphere of external things, wealth, fame, noble birth, and the

[21] For other catalogues of *adiaphora,* cf. Sen., *Ep.* 82.10, 14; Epict., *Diss.* 2.19.13; and Diog. Laert. 7.102.

[22] This four item catalogue is formed with each of the hardships preceded by *non si:* not if poverty, not if sorrow, not if disgrace, not if pain makes an attack, will he make a retreat. *Interritus* is emphatic, indicating that the sage is fearless in regard to his hardships. Cf. also *Ep.* 109.18: philosophy makes one *intrepidus.* Compare the emphatic position of *impavidum* in Hor., *Carm.* 3.3.8.

like. To the class of things "rejected" belong, of mental qualities, lack of ability, want of skill, and the like; among bodily qualities, death, disease, weakness, being out of condition, mutilation, ugliness, and the like; in the sphere of external things, poverty, ignominy, low birth, and so forth (Diog. Laert. 7.106; cf. also Cic., *Fin.* 3.15.51; Sext. Emp., *Math.* 11.63).

It is clear from the preceding catalogue that hardships belong in Stoic theory to the "rejected" category. They are not "goods," they are not even to be "preferred." This is important, for it shows that Stoicism is not masochistic (cf. also Sen., *Ep.* 85.40). Nevertheless, in discussing hardships Stoics sometimes treat hardships as potential goods because of the benefits that can be derived from adversity.[23] Similarly, they point to situations in which hardships are to be preferred because this is what virtue and duty demand.[24] Such considerations, however, represent refinements rather than contradictions of their basic theory.

In short, philosophy is the key, for it is only from philosophy that one derives the rational capacity to prefer adversity when necessary and turn it to one's advantage. Above all, it is only philosophy that makes the mind impregnable, impervious to adversity's assaults. "Philosophy is your most unfailing safeguard, and she alone (*sola*) can rescue you from the power of Fortune" (Sen., *Helv.* 17.5; cf. also *Ep.* 16.5; 37.3–4; 53.8, 12; 82.5). As one might expect, these mighty powers of philosophy are frequently recounted in catalogues of hardships that specify the "evils" against which it provides protection:

> Would you really know what philosophy offers to humanity? Philosophy offers counsel. Death calls away one man, and poverty chafes another; a third is worried either by his neighbour's wealth or by his own. So-and-so is afraid of bad luck; another desires to get away from his own good fortune. Some are ill-treated by men, others by the gods. . . . You have promised to help those in peril by sea, those in captivity, the sick and the needy, and those whose heads are under the poised axe (Sen., *Ep.* 48.7–8; cf. also 109.18 and contrast 117.31).

The Sapiens and the Proficiens

The person who availed himself of philosophy's precepts and protective power was the sage, a figure whose teaching and example carried immense authority in Stoic circles.[25] By insisting that the distinction between virtue and vice was

[23] Cf. esp. Sen., *Ep.* 71.5; and also *Ep.* 45.9; 66.49–52; 71.5; *V.B.* 25.5. Cf. also T. Schreiner, *Seneca im Gegensatz zu Paulus: Ein Vergleich ihrer Welt-und Lebensanschauung* (Ph.D. Diss., Basel; Tübingen: E. Göbel, 1936) 35. For two full treatments of the idea that it is possible to derive advantage from *peristaseis,* cf. Epict., *Diss.* 3.20, and Max. Tyr., *Or.* 34 Hobein.

[24] Cf. Sen., *Ep.* 66.52, which is to be read in light of *Ep.* 67.3–6.

[25] H. A. Fischel, *Rabbinic Literature and Greco-Roman Philosophy* (SPB 21; Leiden: Brill, 1973) 86, 460–68, emphasizes the extent to which post-Socratic philosophy in general became *sophos*-centered. This was especially true for Roman Stoicism. Cf. R. H. Barrow, *The Romans* (1949; repr., Baltimore: Penguin, 1965) 158. For treatments of the figure of

absolute, members of the Early Stoa placed a great gulf between the sage and everyone else. Allowing no room for an intermediate class between the happy wise man and the miserable fool, they generally either denied the possibility of moral improvement (προκοπή Diog. Laert. 7.127) or, as was more common, denied that such progress was accompanied by a diminution of vice (Cic., *Fin.* 4.24.67; Plut. *Mor.* 1062E–1063A). Everyone was either a *sapiens* or a *stultus,* for "a man that has made some progress towards the state of virtue is none the less in misery than he that has made no progress at all" (Cic., *Fin.* 3.14.48; cf. also 4.9.21). The change from vice to virtue was thus as instantaneous as it was total, with the man who was the very worst in the morning becoming, as it were, the very best by evening (Plut., *Mor.* 75E; cf. also 1057E; 1058A-B).

This absolutism, which was part of Stoicism's inheritance from Early Cynicism, clearly continued in more austere Stoic circles into the period of the Late Stoa and was subjected to a vigorous attack by Plutarch in his essay on "Progress in Virtue." But already in the time of the Middle Stoa a strong mollifying tendency had appeared. Panaetius, for example, ". . . rejected the belief that only the absolutely wise man can be virtuous" and recognized a class of those who were making progress in wisdom and virtue (προκόπτοντες).[26] The one who

---

the sage, cf. Rudolf Hirzel, *Untersuchungen zu Cicero's philosophischen Schriften* (3 vols.; Leipzig: S. Hirzel, 1877–83) 2.271–308; A. Bonhöffer, *Die Ethik des Stoikers Epictet* (Stuttgart: F. Enke, 1894) 147–50; Karl Holl, "Die schriftstellerische Form des griechischen Heiligenlebens," *Neue Jahrbücher für das klassische Altertum* 29 (1912) 407–27, esp. 413–21; Barth, *Stoa,* 131–35; Kurt Deissner, *Das Idealbild des stoischen Weisen* (Greifswalder Universitätsreden 24; Greifswald: Bamberg, 1930); J. Hausleiter's review of Deissner's *Idealbild* in *DLZ* 36 (1930) 1688–91; Johannes Stelzenberger, *Die Beziehungen der frühchristlichen Sittenlehre zur Ethik der Stoa* (Munich: Hueber, 1933) 277–306; Johannes Juhnke, *Das Persönlichkeitsideal in der Stoa im Lichte der paulinischen Erlösungslehre* (Greifswalder Theologische Forschungen 5; Greifswald: Bamberg, 1934); Pohlenz, *Stoa,* 153–58; R. H. Hock, "Simon the Shoemaker as an Ideal Cynic," *GRBS* 17 (1976) 41–53; and also M. Billerbeck, *Epiktet: Von Kynismus* (Leiden: Brill, 1978). For Seneca's portrait of the sage, cf. J. H. L. Wetmore, *Seneca's Conception of the Stoic Sage in his Prose Works* (Alberta, Canada: University of Alberta, 1936); A. Guillemin, "Sénèque directeur d'âmes, I. L'idéal," *REL* 30 (1952) 202–19; and esp. Wilhelm Ganss, *Das Bild des Weisen bei Seneca* (Freiburg, Schweiz: Buchdruckerei Gutenberg, Schaan, 1952). For the sage in Philo's works, cf. Edmund Turowski, *Die Widerspiegelung des stoischen Systems bei Philon von Alexandria* (Borna-Leipzig: Universitätsverlag von R. Norske, 1927) 41–42; and also É. Bréhier, *Les idées philosophiques et religieuses de Philon d'Alexandrie* (Études de philosophie médiévale 8; 3d ed.; Paris: J. Vrin, 1950) 250–71.

[26] Kurt von Fritz, "Stoa," *OCD*[2] 1015. On the term *prokopē,* cf. Hirzel, *Untersuchungen,* 2.291–93 n. 1. The roots of this Middle Stoa development clearly lie in the Early Stoa itself. Indeed, the idea of "progress" may go back to Zeno himself (cf. Plut., *Mor.* 82F). It was probably Chrysippus, however, who first employed *prokopē* as a *terminus technicus* and conceived of a middle group between the wise and the foolish. Cf. esp. Bonhöffer, *Ethik,* 147–48. An intermediate group between the completely righteous and

was making moral progress but had not yet achieved the ideal was the *proficiens.* Milder Stoics continued to acknowledge this intermediate group and even distinguished three different grades of *proficientes.*[27]

The *proficiens* was the product not only of paraenetic necessity but also of discussions about the attainability of the ideal. The existence of the wise man was an old topic of discussion, with people like Protagoras affirming his existence (Pl., *Tht.* 166D). But the ever escalating claims made for the perfect *sapiens* rendered it increasingly difficult to point to anyone who truly deserved the title. One looked more and more to the distant past than to the present for candidates worthy of the designation "sage." Many grew sceptical as to his existence, while others, like Cicero, denied it outright.[28] Cynics and most Stoics, however, continued to believe that the ideal could be realized and denied that the sage was a fiction (Sen., *Const.* 7.1). But there was an important difference between them on this point. As A. J. Malherbe points out,

> The Cynics held to the profound distinction between the wise and the foolish, and confidently assumed that the ideal could be realized as it had been by the ancients. The Stoics, on the other hand, defined the ideal in such a way that its attainability was only an abstract possibility. The ideal sage, Seneca says, may appear like the phoenix, only once in five hundred years (*Moral Epistle* XLII.1). The Stoic philosopher is only a *proficiens* who is making progress toward the ideal.[29]

According to Seneca, the rare individual who attains the ideal does so by winning the battle between reason and the passions. This is a battle that rages in the heart of every individual. Everything for everyone turns on the outcome of this basic battle. A victory by passion leads to rampant evil (*Ep.* 85.10–11),

---

the totally wicked is also found in some rabbinic texts. Cf. *Ber.* 61b; *Ros. Has.* 16b; and H. A. Wolfson, *Philo* (2 vols.; Cambridge: Harvard, 1947) 2.272.

[27] Cf. Sen., *Ep.* 75.8. For Epictetus' recognition and treatment of the *proficiens,* cf. *Diss.* 4.2; *Ench.* 5; and Bonhöffer, *Ethik,* 144–53.

[28] Cic., *Acad. Pr.* 47.145; *Fin.* 4.24.65. Cf. also *Amic.* 2.9; 5.18; 6.21; *Nat.D.* 3.32.79; *Off.* 1.15.46; Philo, *Mut.* 36; Plut., *Mor.* 1076B; Quint., *Inst.* 12.1.18; and Sext. Emp., *Math.* 7.432–33; 9.133.

[29] A. J. Malherbe, "Cynics," *IDBSup* 202. Cf. also Malherbe, "Pseudo-Heraclitus, Epistle 4: The Divinization of the Wise Man," *JAC* 21 (1978) 42–64, esp. 54–58. Stoic belief in the actual attainability of the ideal declined markedly after Panaetius and Posidonius. Cf. esp. Sen., *Tranq.* 7.4; Epict., *Diss.* 2.19.25; 4.1.151–52, 159; *Ench.* 15; 51.3; *SVF* 3.159.25 (§619); 16ɔ.23–25 (§658); 167.34–36 (§668); Philo, *Mut.* 34, 37; Sext. Emp., *Math.* 9.90 (compare Philo, *Her.* 307; Sen., *Ep.* 124.12); and Cic., *Amic.* 2.7; *Nat.D.* 2.13.36. Compare Ps-Pl., *Epin.* 973C; 992C; and Juv., *Sat.* 13.60–67. For denials that one has attained the ideal, cf. Pythagoras, *apud* Diog. Laert. 1.12; Chrysippus, *apud* Plut., *Mor.* 1048E; Panaetius, frg. 56 Fowler (= Sen., *Ep.* 116.5); Sen., *Ep.* 6.1; 7.1; 57.3; 71.30; *V.B.* 17.3; 18.1–2; Epict., *Diss.* 1.8.14; 2.8.24; 4.1.151,167; 8.43; Mar. Ant., *Med.* 8.1. Epicurus, on the other hand, did claim to be a sage. Cf. frg. 146 Usener; frg. 65.29–40 Arrighetti; Cic., *Fin.* 2.3.7; Plut., *Mor.* 1100A; Sen., *Ep.* 18.9.

whereas a victory by reason leads to good. All good and all evil in the world are thus reducible to the preeminence of reason or passion, to the qualities of virtue and vice.[30] To the extent that reason is preeminent a person is making progress. If a person becomes a sage, that is, if once the reason in him triumphs over the passions and their concomitant vices, the victory is total and permanent (*Helv.* 13.3). Virtue once gained cannot be lost (*Ep.* 50.9), for "wisdom never slips back into folly" (*Ep.* 76.19). The wise man is forever healed, "healed for good and all," and thus he "cannot slip back, or slip into any more illness at all" (*Ep.* 72.6).[31]

Correlative to a person's progress toward wisdom are his self-confidence (*fiducia*) and attitude toward Fortune. Some are momentarily able to look Fortune in the face, while others can even match glances with her. But the sage is the only one who is full of self-confidence (*Ep.* 71.34). Indeed, "so great is his confidence in himself that he does not hesitate to go against Fortune, and will never retreat before her" (*Tranq.* 11.1). It is this *fiducia* that is the decisive difference between the wise man and the *proficiens* who is closest to achieving the ideal. The most advanced of the *proficientes* "have already arrived at a point from which there is no slipping back" into the various faults from which they have escaped. They have gained a place near wisdom and "have already laid aside all passions and vices." Yet, decisively, "their assurance (*fiducia*) is not yet tested," and they do not even realize their impregnable position (*Ep.* 75.9).[32]

This emphasis on the sage's self-reliance is one that Seneca shares with other philosophers and moralists.[33] Since the Stoic philosopher is only a *proficiens,* however, this means that he has only a certain degree of confidence, not full self-assurance. This fact is reflected, for example, in the idea that one is to beware of Fortune (Sen., *Ep.* 98.7). The Cynic, on the other hand, is in practice much more self-confident than the Stoic, for he is unabashedly confident that the attainment of the ideal is an actual possibility for him or that he himself already has realized it (cf., for example, Ps-Heraclitus, *Ep.* 4). For the Hellenistic Stoic, such self-confidence tends to be self-deception and the mark of immaturity rather than perfection (Sen., *Ep.* 16.1–2; 27.4; 42.2; 71.30; Epict., *Diss.* 4.8; cf. also Cic., *Fin.* 2.3.7).

Unshaken *fiducia* is the key to *securitas,* the freedom from care and anxiety that is the sum and substance of happiness (Sen., *Ep.* 31.3; 44.7; 92.2–3; *Helv.*

[30] Cf. Pratt, "The Stoic Base of Senecan Drama," 5.

[31] One of the issues at debate within Stoic circles was whether virtue could be lost. Seneca sides with Cleanthes against Chrysippus (Diog. Laert. 7.127–28), as had Cicero before him (*Tusc.* 2.14.32). Cynics, following Antisthenes (Diog. Laert. 6.12,105), generally maintained that virtue was permanent, whereas Socrates, Plato, Xenophon, and others argued that virtue could be lost if it was not exercised (Xen., *Cyr.* 7.5.75; *Mem.* 1.2.19–23; and cf. Dihle, *Will,* 51). For the perspective of Epicurus on the attainment of wisdom, cf. *Vit.Epicur.* 117.6–8; 121b.3–4 = Diog. Lart. 10.117, 120.

[32] See also Philo, *Agr.* 160–61; Plut., *Mor.* 75D-E; 1042F; 1062B. Compare Plot., *Enn.* 1.4.9 and Eubulides, frg. 64 Döring.

[33] Cf. for example, Plot., *Enn.* 1.4.15,12ff and "Cebes," *Tabula* 18.4; 23.4.

5.1).[34] Seneca's *proficiens* has not achieved *securitas,* for this "is the peculiar blessing of the wise man" (*Const.* 13.5). Joy (*gaudium*) can be attained only by the sage (*Ep.* 59.2, 17), so that it is he alone who is "elate with constant joy" (*Const.* 9.3) and is completely, supremely happy (*Ep.* 92.14–24). Since the Senecan sage cannot lose the virtue he has attained, it is impossible for him at any time to fall back into non-happiness and forfeit his joy (*Ep.* 59.16; 92.23). His happiness and tranquility, which he owes to philosophy (*Ep.* 30.3), not only relate him to the gods (*Ep.* 59.14, 16) but also distinguish him from every *proficiens* (*Ep.* 72.4; cf. also *Clem.* 2.4.4–5).

In summary, then, reason and virtue have reached perfection only in the sage. His perfect reason and virtue separate him from the most mature *proficiens,* as do his unshaken self-confidence and undiminished joy. These *theoretical* differences between the *sapiens* and the *proficiens* are consistently maintained by milder Stoics. In *practice,* however, the distinction between them almost seems to vanish, especially where moral instruction and exhortation are concerned. Those who do not see themselves as wise men, for instance, still point to themselves as models for those in adversity.

The Serene and Steadfast Sage

One of the products of the sage's *securitas* and *tranquillitas* is his *constantia* (cf. Cic., *Off.* 1.20.69). Extolled in Seneca's *De Constantia Sapientis,* it is an old Roman military virtue (Livy 30.7.6) and one of the chief characteristics of the suffering sage. As Lactantius observes,

> this is the true virtue, which the vaunting philosophers also boast of, not in deed, but with empty words, saying that nothing is so befitting the gravity and constancy (*constantia*) of a wise man as to be able to be driven away from his sentiment and purpose by no torturers, but that it is worth his while to suffer torture and death rather than betray a trust or depart from his duty, or overcome by fear of death or severity of pain, commit any injustice (*Div. Inst.* 5.14).

Ancient moralists repeatedly use both individual calamities and *peristasis* catalogues in describing the sage in order to demonstrate that he not only endures adversity commendably but also that he is relatively or absolutely unaffected by it. In general, therefore, *the sage's hardships serve as literary foils in the depiction of his serenity and endurance.* This is characteristic of the whole Graeco-Roman tradition, for to endure adversity with sangfroid was universally taken as a mark of real character.

Already in the *Phaedo,* for instance, Socrates argues not only that it is irrational to be frightened and troubled at the prospect of dying but also that

[34] Cf. also Cicero, who equates or links *securitas* with *animi tranquillitas, euthumia,* and the *beata vita,* lack of anxiety (*anxius*), *vacuitas aegritudinis,* and *vacuitas ab angoribus* (*Fin.* 5.8.23; *Off.* 1.21.69–73; *Tusc.* 5.14.42). It is also typically Epicurean to see *securitas* as a component of the *beata vita* (Cic., *Nat.D.* 1.20.53). Cf. also Cic., *Amic.* 13.45.

it is philosophers who find death least alarming (67E). Indeed, it is in the confrontation with death that the true philosopher is revealed, for the man who is troubled at the prospect of dying reveals himself thereby as a φιλοσώματος ("lover of the body") rather than a true philosopher, a φιλόσοφος (68B). Of all mortals, the genuine philosopher is the most αὐτάρκης for living well. "Least of all then to him is it a terrible thing to lose son or brother or his wealth or anything of the sort." As a result, "he makes the least lament and bears it most moderately when any such misfortune overtakes him" (*Resp.* 387D–E; cf. also 603E and *Cri.* 43B). Such statements reflect Plato's conviction that the true sage is no less happy even if he is without such advantages as health, strength, wealth, good birth, and reputation (Diog. Laert. 3.78).

The Early Academics, such as Speusippus and Xenocrates, continued this emphasis and exalted virtue as indispensable for happiness (Cic., *Tusc.* 5.18.51). Indeed, they held that the sage was relatively happy even when tortured (Sen., *Ep.* 71.18; cf. also Cic., *Tusc.* 5.26.75). Polemo, moreover, demonstrated in his own life the unruffled calm that he acquired from philosophy, not even turning pale when bitten by a mad dog (Diog. Laert. 4.17).

Aristotle, likewise, stressed that the sage "endures repeated and severe misfortune with patience," and that he cannot be dislodged from his happiness easily or "by ordinary misfortunes, but only by severe and frequent disasters."[35] But the security and serenity of the Peripatetic sage was negligible in comparison with that enjoyed by his Epicurean counterpart. Arguing that injuries are tolerable (Sen., *Const.* 16.1), Epicurus asserted that the wise man is always happy (Cic., *Fin.* 5.27.80; *Tusc.* 3.20.49; 5.10.31; 26.73,75; 41.119; Lactant., *Div. Inst.* 3.27.5). Although the Epicurean sage gives pleasure the priority, he is deemed happy even when suffering excruciating pain (Plut., *Mor.* 1090A; Lactant., *Div. Inst.* 3.17.5), for, according to Epicurus' famous and influential paradox, "even if the wise man be put on the rack, he is happy" (*Vit. Epicur.* 118.1 = Diog. Laert. 10.118 = frg. 601 Usener).[36] Similarly, Pyrrho, the founder of Greek scepticism, remained calm during a storm at sea and told his fearful companions that it was necessary in such circumstances for the wise man to remain unperturbed (Diog. Laert. 9.68; Plut., *Mor.* 82F).

The Stoics, affirming that "many who appear to be the sport of adverse circumstances are happy" (Tac., *Ann.* 6.22), readily accepted Epicurus' paradox about the racked but happy sage (Cic., *Fin.* 3.13.42) and added that he remained happy even when he suffered the disasters of Priam (*SVF* 3.153.39–40 [§585]) or

[35] Arist., *Eth.Nic.* 1.10.11–14. It is Aristotle, however, who makes the most concessions to the power of adversity to destroy the sage's happiness. Though denying that the happy man ever becomes miserable, Aristotle does concede that the sage can lose his blessedness and happiness. See esp. 1.10.14 and also Diog. Laert. 5.30; Cic., *Fin.* 3.13.42.

[36] On this paradox and the formulations it inspired, cf. the passages assembled by Hermann Usener (ed.), *Epicurea* (Leipzig: Teubner, 1887) 338–39, and compare Epicurus, frg. A LVI Bailey.

was roasted in the bull of Phalaris (*SVF* 3.154.1-4 [§586]). He, moreover, "remains fearless and undistressed and invincible and unconstrained while wounded, in pain, on the rack, in the midst of his country's destruction, in the midst of his own private calamities" (Plut., *Mor.* 1057D).

Teles, a major representative of the hedonistic wing of Cynicism,[37] advocated the ancient ideal of αὐτάρκεια,[38] arguing that the person who is αὐτάρκης is content with his present lot (IVA, 38,10-11 Hense = 38,84-85 O'Neil; 41,12 Hense = 42,130 O'Neil). This contentment is a product of his independence and self-sufficiency as a person, and the good man, Teles insisted, does not try to change his circumstances but performs and makes use of whatever role Fortune assigns him.[39] Since he is content, he remains happy in the midst of tragedy, "so that he is not pained over the death either of a friend or a child, nor even over his own death" (VII,56,14-57,1 Hense = 64,38-40 O'Neil). He thus is living proof that such things as old age, poverty, and lack of citizenship are not evils in and of themselves (II,11,4-12,8 Hense = 10,83-12,103 O'Neil).

The New Academician Cicero, always eclectic, makes repeated use of the old Epicurean paradox in order to show "that there is no time when the wise man, even if burnt, racked, cut in pieces, cannot cry out: 'I count it all as nothing!' " (*Tusc.* 5.26.73).[40] For him it is a vivid demonstration that "the power of virtue is so great that the good man can never be otherwise than happy" (*Pis.* 18.42). "Suppose," he says, "a man to be at once blind, infirm, afflicted by dire disease, in exile, childless, destitute, and tortured on the rack." If he is virtuous, he will be nonetheless happy, for "the virtuous man will be happy even in the bull of Phalaris" (*Fin.* 5.28.84-85). In short, Cicero concurs with the Stoics that "the wise man is not susceptible of distress (*aegritudo*)" and "will always be free from it" (*Tusc.* 3.7.14-15; cf. also 3.8.18; 34.82; 5.10.30; 15.43; 16.48). Similarly, "no one can be just who fears death or pain or exile or poverty" (*Off.* 2.11.38). The sage, finally, bears every hardship with aplomb (*Tusc.* 2.18.43; 20.46; 24.58; *Verr.* 2.2.84), in a way that befits his status as both man (*Tusc.* 2.24.57-58) and philosopher (*Off.* 1.20.67; *Tusc.* 5.31.89).

[37] On hedonistic Cynicism, cf. G. A. Gerhard, "Zur Legende vom Kyniker Diogenes," *ARW* 15 (1912) 388-408; Hock, "Simon the Shoemaker," 48-53; and A. J. Malherbe, "Self-Definition among Epicureans and Cynics," in B. F. Meyer and E. P. Sanders (eds.), *Jewish and Christian Self-Definition,* Vol. III: *Self-Definition in the Greco-Roman World* (Philadelphia: Fortress, 1982) 51.

[38] For the understanding of this term in Cynic circles, cf. esp. A. N. M. Rich, "The Cynic Conception of ΑΥΤΑΡΚΕΙΑ," *Mnemosyne,* Ser. IV. 9 (1956) 23-29.

[39] For the idea of performing well the role assigned by Tyche, cf. Teles, II,5,3 Hense = 6,3 O'Neil; VI,52,2-4 Hense = 58,1-4 O'Neil. For the idea that one should not try to change circumstances, cf. II,9,8-10,2 Hense (=10,65-68 O'Neil). On making use of one's circumstances, cf. II,10,6 Hense (=10,73 O'Neil); 13,12 Hense (=12,122 O'Neil); VI,53,16 Hense (=58,27 O'Neil).

[40] See also Cic., *Fin.* 2.27.88; 5.27.80; 28.85; *Pis.* 18.42; *Tusc.* 2.7.17; 5.10.31; 26.75. Cf. *Fin.* 3.13.42.

The poet Horace reflects this philosophic tradition when he polemicizes against avarice and extols the ideal of contentment. By embracing the conviction that "the ideal of αὐτάρκεια implies necessarily the fight against μεμψιμοιρία" (discontent) and by establishing a causal nexus between discontent and avarice,[41] he is able to make discontentment a mark of πλεονεξία and contentment the proof that one is without avarice. Whereas the avaricious man is palpably discontent, the self-sufficient man is content with what he needs and thus is not troubled by hardships:

> He who longs for only what he needs is troubled (*sollicitat*) not by stormy seas, not by the fierce onslaught of setting Arcturus or rising Haedus—not by the lashing of his vineyards with the hail, nor by the treachery of his farm, the trees complaining now of too much rain, now of the dog-star parching the fields, now of the cruel winters (Hor., *Carm.* 3.1.25-32).[42]

Again, the eclectic moralist "Cebes" argues that the person who has reached Happiness is henceforth immune from anything that might cause him distress. "He will not be troubled in the least either by Pain or by Grief, Incontinence, Avarice, Poverty, or any other Ill" (*Tabula* 26.2; cf. also 23.2; 24.2). Similarly, Dio Chrysostom argues that "the intelligent man ought not to feel pain about anything whatever," whether it be "loss of reputation, a financial reverse, complete or partial failure in some undertaking, danger," or another hardship like death or illness (*Or.* 16.2-3; cf. also 34.33).

Among later Platonists the same thoughts recur. The Platonist orator Maximus of Tyre, for example, depicts Pherecydes "lying in Syros, his flesh corrupting but his soul standing erect" (*Or.* 7.4k = 81, 9-11 Hobein; my transl.). Again, the Neo-Platonist Plotinus stresses that the suffering sage is always happy and thus is not to be pitied for his pain; "his light burns within, like the light in a lantern when it is blowing hard outside with a great fury of wind and storm" (*Enn.* 1.4.8, 3-6).[43]

From Plato to Plotinus, therefore, the basic sentiment remains the same, viz., that adversity has little or no effect on the calmness and joy of the wise man. No group, however, celebrated the sage's firmness and imperturbability more enthusiastically than did the Stoics, whose statements thus merit closer analysis. Seneca, for instance, stresses that the sage's deportment under duress is truly

[41] Eduard Fränkel, *Horace* (Oxford: Clarendon, 1957) 90-94. Cf. esp. *Sat.* 1.1.108ff and the discussions by Walter Wimmel, *Zur Form der horazischen Diatribensatire* (Frankfurt am Main: Klostermann, 1962) 8, and H. Herter, "Zur ersten Satire des Horaz," *RhM* 94 (1951) 1-42.

[42] For Horace's commitment to the ideal of the simple life in accordance with the "golden mean," cf. esp. *Carm.* 2.3.1-8; 10.13-15, 21-24; and also Rüdiger Vischer, *Das einfache Leben* (Göttingen: Vandenhoeck & Ruprecht, 1965) 147-52. Cf. also *Carm.* 1.31.16; 4.9.45-52; *Ep.* 1.16.20.

[43] On the happiness and endurance of Plotinus' sage, cf. esp. *Enn.* 1.4.12 and 1.4.5,9 and also 1.4.4,31ff; 1.4.14,27ff. Cf. also Ps-Plut., *Mor.* 102E-103A.

remarkable. In keeping with his *constantia* and *firmitas* the sage bears adversity *aequo animo, facile, magno animo, moderate,* and *placide.*[44] He stands erect under any load, for his mind does not sag, bend, or collapse under the great pressure exerted by his various hardships. "The wise man," for example, "is not distressed (*adfligitur*) by the loss of children or of friends" (Sen., *Ep.* 74.30). It is he "who, when he sees death at hand, is not so disturbed as though he saw a fresh object; who, whether torments are to be suffered by his whole body, or a flame is to be seized by his mouth, or his hands are to be stretched out on the cross, does not inquire what he suffers, but how well" (*apud* Lactant., *Div. Inst.* 6.17). Not merely is he "happy in adversity" but even "unterrified in the midst of dangers" and "peaceful amid the storm" (*Ep.* 41.4). Since no hardship even displeases him, he refuses to complain about his difficulties (*Ep.* 71.26). Content with whatever his lot may be (*V.B.* 6.2), he is even content when he loses a hand or his eyesight (*Ep.* 9.4), and he "can without concern (*securus*) hear talk of chains, or of exile, or of all the idle fears that stir men's minds" (*Ep.* 76.33).[45]

The Senecan sage remains unperturbed because he is "not harmed by poverty, or by pain, or by any other of life's storms" (*Ep.* 85.37), nor by any injury or insult. People, to be sure, try to hurt the sage by injury or insult, but the effort is in vain. Injuries and insults are *offered,* but the sage does not *receive* them as such (Sen., *Const.* 7.3).[46] In view of the fact that "the wise man can receive neither injury nor insult," Seneca insists that the sceptic should desist from his doubts about the sage's capacities:

> Therefore leave off saying: "Will the wise man, then, receive no injury if he is given a lashing, if he has an eye gouged out? Will he receive no insult if he is hooted through the forum by the vile words of a foul-mouthed crowd? If at a king's banquet he is ordered to take a place beneath the table and to eat with the slaves assigned to the most disreputable service? If he is forced to bear whatever else can be thought of that will offend his freeborn pride?" (*Const.* 15.1; cf. also Pl., *Ap.* 41D; *Grg.* 527C-D).

[44] Cf., for example, *Const.* 6.2–3; 8.3; *Ep.* 76.23; *Ira* 3.43.5; and *Prov.* 4.16.

[45] For the idea that the sage is *securus* in the most stressful and dangerous situations, cf. esp. *Ep.* 76.33; 85.25; 109.18; 113.27; *Const.* 6.3. For the manifestation of *securitas* in the face of death, cf. also Pliny, *Ep.* 6.16.12; and Tac., *Ann.* 11.3 *fin.*

[46] Cf. also Sen., *Ben.* 2.35.2, and compare *Ira* 2.26.4. Seneca's thesis is an old one among Stoics, with the basic idea involved here appearing already in Chrysippus (*SVF* 3.152.8–10 [§574]). Cf. also *SVF* 3.152.28–41 (§§578–79). Epictetus expresses the same thought when he says of the Cynic that "nobody reviles him, nobody beats him, nobody insults him" (*Diss.* 3.22.100; cf. also 4.1.127; *Ench.* 20). Compare the formulations in Cass. Dio 62.15.4 and Ps-Dio Chrys., *Or.* 37.45. In the view of Epicurus, on the other hand, the sage is injured but his injuries are viewed as tolerable (Sen., *Const.* 16.1). The Epicurean sage bears them and overcomes them by means of reason. Cf. *Vit.Epicur.* 117.4–6 = Diog. Laert. 10.117.

The Stoic sage is thus radically different from the common people. Musonius Rufus notes that whereas the latter "think that they are insulted if someone gives them a malignant glance or laughs or strikes them or reviles them," "the wise and sensible man, such as the philosopher ought to be, is not disturbed by any of these things" (X,53,11-54, 2 Hense = 76,30-78,4 Lutz). To flare up in anger at some slight abuse (X,55,1 Hense = 78,15 Lutz) or "to be annoyed or racked" about insults is the mark of a petty person (X,54,9 Hense = 78,9-10 Lutz). Such is not the magnanimous philosopher, who unlike the masses, does not view insults as intolerable and is not driven mad by them (X,53,6-9 Hense = 76,27-29 Lutz) or by death and hardships (VIII,35,12 Hense = 62,26 Lutz). He knows full well that exile is no cause for feeling grief or despondency or for being weighed down in discontent (IX,49,15-50,5 Hense = 74,17-20 Lutz). He knows, moreover, that the sensible man bears exile "easily" (IX,51,7 Hense = 76,4 Lutz), injustice "very meekly" (X,55,14 Hense = 78,26 Lutz), hardships on behalf of virtue "cheerfully" (VII,28,4 Hense = 56,15 Lutz), and whatever happens "easily and silently" (X,54,10-12 Hense = 78,10-11 Lutz). This knowledge he also inculcates, insisting that even children "must be accustomed to endure hardship, not to fear death, not to be disheartened in the face of any misfortune" (IV,18,10-11 Hense = 48,5-7 Lutz).[47]

The same basic sentiments are found in Epictetus, who argues strongly that external things like a tyrant, disease, poverty, or an obstacle are not legitimate grounds for being disturbed (*Diss.* 4.12.9). He laments the fact that ". . . where death, or exile, or hardship, or ignominy faces us, there we show the spirit of running away, there we show violent agitation" (2.1.10). A person who is afraid "of death, exile, loss of property, prison, disfranchisement" has over him "masters in the form of circumstances" (4.1.59-60; cf. also Ps-Diog., *Ep.* 12 = 106,10-11 Malherbe). It is children and fools who believe imprisonment, decapitation, and lack of burial are terrifying (4.7.31-32). The body is necessarily "a slave of fever, gout, ophthalmia, dysentery, a tyrant, fire, iron, everything that is stronger" (3.22.40), but the mind of a fearful person is a slave to these things as well. After enumerating a host of hardships, Epictetus in bitter sarcasm tells one of his students, "Sit down, therefore, and get all wrought up at each one of these events, mourning, unfortunate, miserable, depend on something other than yourself . . .!" (3.24.30). The sage, in contrast to this wretch, is free and totally self-reliant, and he exhibits none of these reactions to suffering. He "suffers no harm, even though he is soundly flogged, or imprisoned, or beheaded," and he bears all this nobly and with personal profit (4.1.127), for this is the mark of a good man (frg. 2).[48] The true Stoic is he "who though

[47] For the bearing of adversity, cf. also VII,29,16 Hense = 58,6 Lutz; XVII,91,7-9, 20 Hense = 108,26-28, 37 Lutz; and esp. XVIIIB,104,11-12 Hense = 120,4-5 Lutz: "enduring more cheerfully cold, heat, lack of sleep, and every such hardship."

[48] On the manner of enduring various hardships, cf. also *Diss.* 2.1.38-39; 8.28; 3.10.6,8; 26.5; 4.1.30,154; 4.21. Cf. also 3.12.10, where instructions are given to endure when reviled

sick is happy, though in danger is happy, though dying is happy, though condemned to exile is happy, though in disrepute is happy" (2.19.24). Likewise, the true Cynic proclaims in the midst of all his hardships, "Make trial of me, and . . . see that I am free from turmoil" (4.8.31).[49] Indeed, by dying or bearing disease unperturbed he shows to others "the sinews of the philosopher" (2.8.27–29).

The failure of adversity to have its customary impact testifies to the extent to which the Stoic sage has insulated himself from pressures and tribulations. The ideal is thus, as Marcus Aurelius learned from the Stoic philosopher Apollonius of Chalcedon, "to remain ever the same, in the throes of pain, on the loss of a child, during a lingering illness" (*Med.* 1.8).[50] As Cicero affirms, "it is a fine thing to keep an unruffled temper, an unchanging mien, and the same cast of countenance in every condition of life" (*Off.* 1.26.90).[51] This is the essence of virtue, which is "so steeled against the blows of chance that she cannot be bent, much less broken. Facing the instruments of torture she holds her gaze unflinching, her expression changes not at all, whether a hard or a happy lot is shown her" (Sen., *Const.* 5.4–5). The expression on one's face is thus especially important, for it is the external sign of a deep inner equilibrium. The countenance always unchanged is "that look of the wise man—that look ever the same." It is "a calm and sunny look" no matter what happens, for "the mind from which the countenance receives its mould undergoes no change."[52] It is, moreover, proof that one is a good man who is devoid of all pretense (Cass. Dio 72.34.5), and the absence of pretense is one of the signs of the sage (Diog. Laert. 7.118).

The Struggling Sage

As the preceding section has demonstrated, the consensus in philosophical circles was that the ideal philosopher was revealed as such by his steadfast refusal to be bowed down under affliction.[53] There were important differences, however,

---

and not to be depressed when insulted.

[49] The translation modifies the form but not the import of Epictetus' statement.

[50] Cf. also the *Suda,* s.v. 'Αεί (§607, p. 61,10 Adler): "And the wise man must always be the same, in the throes of pain, on the loss of a child, during a lingering illness. Such was Apollonius of Tyana." Cited by Joachim Dalfen, *Marci Aurelii Antonini, Ad se ipsum libri XII* (Leipzig: Teubner, 1979) 3. Cf. also Sen., *Ep.* 104.30, cited by A. S. L. Farquharson, *The Meditations of the Emperor Marcus Antoninus* (2 vols.; Oxford: Clarendon: 1944) 2.448, and Pliny, *HN* 7.19.79.

[51] Cited by Farquharson, *Meditations,* 2.448. Cf. also Cic., *Tusc.* 2.17.41. Tacitus links an unchanging countenance with *securitas* (*Ann.* 3.44; cf. also 15.55). Cf. also Plut., *Phoc.* 36.1, where the same countenance is seen as a sign of *apatheia* and *megalopsychia.*

[52] Cic. *Tusc.* 3.15.31. The tense has been altered to conform to the context.

[53] Even outside the philosophical tradition the ability to face calamity with as little distress as possible was seen as the mark of true strength. Cf., for instance, Thuc. 2.64.2,6; Suet., *Vesp.* 13.

in how the various schools viewed the role of the emotions and passions (πάθη) in the life of the sage. Three basic positions were developed, with individual philosophers making modifications or taking intermediate positions.

Platonists, Peripatetics, Epicureans, and Cyrenaics generally espoused μετριοπάθεια, arguing that the emotions were to be moderated and kept in check.[54] They were to be neither obliterated nor indulged, simply restrained. In this view an emotion like grief has its origin in nature. To grieve and suffer at the loss of a friend is natural, and it is perfectly appropriate to shed tears to a moderate degree. The ideal sage in these traditions is thus *imperturbatus* only in the sense that he is "one who is rarely perturbed and only to a moderate degree, and not one who is never perturbed" (Sen., *Ep.* 85.3).[55]

A second position in regard to the emotions was taken by Stoics and Cynics, who characteristically argued that the emotions do not originate in nature but are the result of an act of judgment or opinion. Emotions and passions are not natural but against nature and irrational. Consequently, they advocated ἀπάθεια, freedom from passion and its concomitant indifference to external circumstances.[56] The sage, in their view, simply was not susceptible to either grief or fear (Sen., *Ep.* 74.30).[57] To read Cynic and Stoic literature is to realize with Seneca that it was both Cynic and "Stoic fashion to speak of all those things, which provoke cries and groans, as unimportant and beneath notice" (*Ep.* 13.4).

A third basic position involved a more radical understanding of the term ἀπάθεια by certain austere Stoics and Cynics. These so extolled the sage's freedom

[54] For Platonic *metriopatheia*, cf. Pl., *Leg.* 732C; 960A; *Resp.* 603E; Cic., *Tusc.* 3.6.12; Ps-Plut., *Mor.* 102C–103B, 112E–113B. For Peripatetic *metriopatheia*, cf. Diog. Laert. 5.31; Sen., *Ep.* 85.3–4; 116.1–4; *Ira* 1.7.1; 3.3.1. The Epicurean sage's greater susceptibility to emotion (Diog. Laert. 10.117) made this position obligatory for adherents of the Garden. Cf. Cyril Bailey, *Epicurus: The Extant Remains* (Oxford: Clarendon, 1926) 417. For the Cyrenaic position, cf. Diog. Laert. 2.91.

[55] For the susceptibility of the sage to grief and fear, cf. Arist., *Eth.Eud.* 3.1.5 (1228b4–8); Cic., *Fin.* 5.11.31–32; Diog. Laert. 2.91; 10.117–18,120; Epicurus, frg. A. LVII Bailey; Ps-Arist., *Mag.Mor.* 1.20.11 (1191a29f); Sen., *Ep.* 85.24. In view of this position, courage becomes a matter of "feeling and controlling fear." Cf. David Pears, "Courage as a Mean," in *Essays on Aristotle's Ethics* (ed. A. O. Rorty; Berkeley: University of California, 1980) 171–87.

[56] For Stoic *apatheia*, cf. *SVF* 3.108–10 (§§443–55); Diog. Laert. 7.117–18; Sen. *Ep.* 9; 85; Epict., *Diss.* 1.4.1–3,28–29; 2.8.23; 17.31; 3.2.4; 13.11; 15.12; 21.9; 24.24; 26.13; 4.3.7; 4.9,36; 6.34; 8.27; 10.13,22,26; *Ench.* 12.2; 29.7. Cf. also Pliny, *HN* 7.19.79–80. For *apatheia* in hedonistic Cynicism, cf. Teles, frg. VII. Panaetius (frg. 14 Fowler; Gell. 12.5.10) may form an exception to the Stoic defence of *apatheia*, though he may simply have denied *apatheia* in the sense of *analgesia*.

[57] Fear and grief are related passions in Stoicism, with fear being concerned with future evil and grief with present evil (Cic., *Tusc.* 4.6.11). For Seneca and the Stoics in general, the sage is literally fearless, not feeling this emotion even on rare occasions or to a slight degree (Cic., *Tusc.* 3.7.14–15; Sen., *Ep.* 85.16).

from passion that it amounted to ἀναλγησία ("insensibility") and ἀνωδυνία ("freedom from pain").[58] As Stoicism became more humane and developed the theory of the rational dispositions of feeling (εὐπάθειαι) by way of contrast to the irrational emotions,[59] this more radical position came to be popularly identified with Cynicism.[60] This is unfortunate, for the Cynics themselves did not necessarily hold to this view. Lucian, who often had only a very superficial view of what he satirized,[61] reflects the popular prejudice when he depicts the Cynic being flogged and twisted on the rack, yet feeling no pain (*Vit. Auct.* 9). It is in keeping with this only partially correct identification of Cynicism with insensibility that Seneca distinguishes Stoics from Cynics as follows: "There is this difference between ourselves and the other school: our ideal wise man feels his troubles, but overcomes them (*vincit . . . sed sentit*); their wise man does not even feel them" (*ne sentit quidem: Ep.* 9.3; cf. also *SVF* 3.152.8–10 [§574]).

For the purposes of this investigation it is the second of these positions that is the most interesting, especially as it was developed by milder Stoics. Seneca, for example, attempts to present the dogma of ἀπάθεια (*impatientia*) as an honorable middle course between μετριοπάθεια and ἀναλγησία, taking the strengths yet avoiding the weaknesses of each. He wants, on the one hand, to maintain of the sage that "all these feelings, which I prefer to call rather annoyances (*molestias*) than distresses (*miserias*) of the mind, he does not have to overcome—nay, he does not even have them" (*non vincit sed ne sentit quidem: Const.* 10.3; contrast Cic., *Fin.* 5.31.93). Again, he firmly rejects μετριοπάθεια in regard to both grief (*Ep.* 116.3-4) and anger (*Ira* 1.7.2–8.7), maintaining that they are more easily forestalled initially than later foregone and that they are best not indulged in by the average person.

Yet, on the other hand, Seneca makes some significant concessions to human weakness by not excluding tears entirely. These concessions are part of an

58 This idea is clearly attacked by Aristotle, *Eth.Nic.* 1.10.12 (1100b30ff; cf. also 3.7.7 [1115b26f]), Crantor (cf. Cic., *Tusc.* 3.6.12 and Ps-Plut., *Mor.* 102C-D), Cicero (*Tusc.* 2.14.33), and Calvisius Taurus in Gell. 12.5.10. According to Joël, Plato is attacking this conception of Antisthenes in *Resp.* 603E. Cf. Paul Shorey (trans.), *Plato: The Republic* (LCL 237/276; 2 vols.; London: Heinemann, 1930–35) 2.453. The language of painlessness occurs also in hedonistic Cynicism; cf. Teles, II,9,4–8 Hense (= 8,59–10,63 O'Neil); 11,10 Hense (= 10,91 O'Neil). For *apatheia* in austere Cynicism, cf. Ps-Crates, *Ep.* 34.4 (86,3 Malherbe); Ps-Diogenes, *Ep.* 12 (106,7 Malherbe); 47 (178,7); and esp. 21 (114,8), where the author has Diogenes describe himself as "the prophet of *apatheia*."

59 Cf. Cic., *Tusc.* 4.5.10–7.15; Diog. Laert. 7.116; August., *De civ. D.* 14.8. The theory may, however, go back to Zeno himself. Cf. Rist, *Stoic Philosophy,* 31–32.

60 As part of his Stoicizing treatment of the ideal Cynic, Epictetus, for example, attributes the view that the Cynic is "insensate and a stone" to "the common people" (*Diss.* 3.22.100). Cf. also 1.25.29 and 3.2.4.

61 Cf., for example, the way in which Lucian confuses Jews and Christians in *Peregr.* 11. On Lucian's treatment of the various philosophical schools, cf. Rudolf Helm, *Lucian und Menipp* (Leipzig/Berlin: Teubner, 1906) 371–86.

apologia necessitated by the critique of the Stoic position by men like the Epicurean Metrodorus, "men who accuse us of too great strictness, slandering our precepts because of supposed harshness—because (say they) we declare that grief should either not be given place in the soul at all, or else should be driven out forthwith" (*Ep.* 99.26). Over against this representation of the Stoic position, Seneca argues that "that which we Stoics advise, is honourable; when emotion has prompted a moderate flow of tears, and has, so to speak, ceased to effervesce, the soul should not be surrendered to grief" (*Ep.* 99.27).

Seneca's claim notwithstanding, it is clear that not all Stoics would subscribe to this view of grief and tears. Seneca is speaking here in his "milder style," wherein he recognizes the truth of the "great-sounding words" which treat hardships as "unimportant and beneath notice" (*Ep.* 13.4), but personally maintains a less harsh position. Unlike the more austere Stoics, Seneca clearly and emphatically argues that even the sage will experience grief and shed tears, and wishes for a mean between indifference and madness (*Polyb.* 18.5–6).

In the matter of one's personal misfortunes "the right way to act is to bestow on them the measure of sorrow that Nature, not custom, demands" (*Tranq.* 15.6). This applies to the wise man as well, who, able to halt his tears at will, "can safely control himself without becoming over-anxious" (*Ep.* 116.4). The tears that the wise man can control at will are those in which he can safely indulge, for he knows how to do so properly and beneficially. Other tears are shed as an involuntary physiological reaction (*Ep.* 99.18–20). These tears are like blushes, which no amount of wisdom can remove. "That which is implanted and inborn can be toned down by training, but not overcome" (*Ep.* 11.1). It is a simple fact that "bad news makes the hair stand on end. . . . Because none of these things lies within our control, no reasoning can keep them from happening" (*Ira* 2.2.1).

Seneca maintains his Stoic self-understanding by refusing to term these involuntary physiological reactions and initial emotional responses "passions." "They are not passions, but the beginnings that are preliminary to passions" (*Ira* 2.2.5; cf. also 2.3.1). The sage is as subject to these "pre-passions" as anyone else. "He will experience . . . certain suggestion and shadows of passion, but from passion itself he will be free" (*Ira* 1.16.7; cf. also *Ep.* 57.4). This *apatheia* is decisive in distinguishing the *sapiens* from the most advanced *proficiens,* for the latter still feels the passions "even when very near perfection" (*Ep.* 75.11–12).

It is in this way, therefore, that Seneca defends Stoicism's insistence on the *apatheia* of the sage and distinguishes it from the *metriopatheia* practiced by the *sapiens* in other traditions.[62] The Senecan sage is even further removed from the

[62] The judgment of Ganss, *Das Bild des Weisen,* 29, is correct: "Durch die Scheidung der 'natürlichen Affektionen' und 'Vorafekte' von den eigentlichen Affekten ist die völlige Apathie dogmatisch auch zu verteidigen." It should be stressed, however, that the *practical* result of these theoretical distinctions was a narrowing of the gap between Stoics and the proponents of *metriopatheia.* Platonists, too, narrowed the gap by adopting a position that approximated *apatheia.* Cf. esp. Plot., *Enn.* 1.4.4,34ff and 1.4.15,15ff. As Rist, *Stoic*

image of the insensible sage. Although Seneca affirms, for example, that "the assaults of adversity do not weaken the spirit of a brave man," he quickly adds the caveat that "I do not mean to say that the brave man is insensible to these, but that he overcomes them" (*Prov.* 2.1–2).

Seneca's sage is thus still a man (*Ep.* 71.27; *Const.* 16.2). Since virtue does not transcend nature, "the wise man will tremble, will feel pain, will turn pale" (*Ep.* 71.29; cf. also 74.30–31; 99.15; and esp. 85.28–29). In the sage's case, "sometimes an external happening reminds him of his mortality, but it is a light blow, and merely grazes the surface of his skin" (*Ep.* 72.5). The conviction is that "the mind ought to be schooled by hardship to feel none but a crushing blow" (*Ira* 2.25.4). Mighty blows may indeed graze the sage, but lesser blows are to have all the impact of a feather on an armor-clad warrior (*Ep.* 45.9; cf. *Const.* 19.3).

It may be true, then, on the one hand, that "the invulnerable thing is not that which is not struck, but that which is not hurt" (*Const.* 3.3). But there are things that can indeed cause wounds of the sort that require healing. These heavy blows and the damage they cause vis-à-vis other things are indicated in *Const.* 10.4:

> Quite different are the things that do buffet the wise man, even though they do not overthrow him, such as bodily pain and infirmity, or the loss of friends and children, and the ruin that befalls his country amid the flames of war. I do not deny that the wise man feels these things; for we do not claim for him the hardness of stone or of steel. There is no virtue that fails to realize that it does endure. What, then, is the case? The wise man does receive some wounds, but those that he receives he overcomes, arrests, and heals; these lesser things he does not even feel, nor does he employ against them his accustomed virtue of bearing hardship, but he either fails to notice them, or counts them worthy of a smile.

Seneca's treatment of *apatheia* shows, therefore, that he seeks to maintain the thesis that the sage has "the weakness of a man and the serenity of a god" (*Ep.* 53.12; cf. also *Const.* 8.2). His security is the basis of his serenity, and his sensibility as a human exposes him to the harshest vicissitudes of life.

The position taken by Seneca is clearly in line with that adopted by other Graeco-Roman Stoics. Epictetus, for example, condemns lamentation but adds that "I am not saying that it is not permissible to groan, only do not groan in the centre of your being" (*Diss.* 1.18.19). Again, it is significant that Calvisius Taurus, who says of himself that "I am no great friend of the Stoics," argues that Stoicism defends unavoidable groans (Gell. 12.5.5). In reference to a Stoic philosopher who was seen in intense physical agony, Taurus gives what he believes a Stoic would say in defense of groaning:

> Hence you saw the philosopher, relying upon the efficacy of his system, wrestling with the insolent violence of disease and pain, yielding nothing, admitting nothing; not, as sufferers commonly do, shrieking, lamenting and calling himself wretched

---

Philosophy, 26–27, points out, what separated the schools was primarily a different understanding of *pathos.*

and unhappy, but giving vent only to panting, breathing and deep sighs, which are signs and indications, not that he is overcome or subdued with pain, but that he is struggling to overcome and subdue it (Gell. 12.5.9; cf. also 12.5.3, 11–12; cf. also Cic., *Tusc.* 2.24.57; Aesch., *Sept.* 50–53).

Fortune, God, and Free Will

Whether relatively or absolutely unaffected by adversity, the sage was by no means immune from it. The wise man's hardships were, in general, attributed to two sources: Fortune and God. While the discussion naturally varied according to which of these sources was in view, the key element in both cases was that of *the will.*

Virtuous action was viewed by ancient philosophers not simply as rational but also as voluntary.[63] According to Seneca, "virtue does nothing under compulsion" (*Ep.* 82.17; cf. also 66.16). Yet in Graeco-Roman thought volition or intentionality was not unrelated to the intellect. In this period the "will" was not a separate category but was conceptually linked to its origin in emotion or thought.[64] In either case, volition was intimately tied to intellectual activity. In the one case, the impulse originating in emotion was to be guided by the intellect so that the action would be rational as well as voluntary. In the other, the intellect was itself the source of human intentionality. This latter view was extremely widespread,[65] but nowhere was it more central than in Stoicism. "Conduct," says Seneca, "will not be right unless the will (*voluntas*) to act is right; for this is the source of conduct. Nor, again, can the will be right without a right attitude of mind; for this is the source of the will" (*Ep.* 95.57).[66]

The issue of volition was central to the ancient discussion of hardship. As we have seen, a *peristasis* is a circumstance that is not voluntarily chosen.[67] An early *peristasis* catalogue by Bacchylides contains this very point.

[63] Cf. esp. Arist., *Eth.Eud.* 2.11.1-13 (1227b12–1228a21); *Eth.Nic.* 3.5.1-20 (1113b3–1114b30); and R. W. Browne, *The Nicomachean Ethics of Aristotle* (Bohn's Classical Library; London: Bohn, 1850) 66. Cf. also Dio Chrys., *Or.* 3.123. The voluntary nature of courage is especially emphasized. Cf. Hdt. 7.99; Thuc. 2.39.4; 4.120.3; (and also 2.64.2a); Pl., *Prt.* 359E; Xen., *Symp.* 8.43; Arist., *Eth.Nic.* 3.8.4–5 (1116a30–1116b3), 12 (1117a5–6).

[64] Cf. esp. Dihle, *Will,* 20, 24–25.

[65] Ibid., 30, 32, 34, 43, 59: Thucydides, Antiphon, Greek legal theory, Theophrastus, Aristotle.

[66] It should not be forgotten that the standard Greek word for "good will" was *eunoia.* Cf. Dihle, *Will,* 34. On Stoicism's constant appeal to the will and the power of the will to achieve the highest of ideals, cf. Deissner, *Idealbild,* 5–6, who stresses that this appeal is part of a developed *Seelentechnik.* For the latter, cf. esp. Paul Rabbow, *Seelenführung: Methodik der Exerzitien in der Antike* (München: Kösel, 1954).

[67] See the discussion of *peristasis* in chapter two above.

> Not by their own choice comes prosperity to mortals, nor stubborn war, nor civil strife, the all-destroying; but Destiny, who gives all things, brings down a cloud, now on this land, now on that (frg. 24 Snell).[68]

The challenge that a *peristasis* presented was its undesired character. The task was to treat the *peristasis* in such a way as to remove this element of undesirability. By accepting a hardship one robbed it of its most pernicious aspect. Even in circles where fatalism and determinism were accepted as axiomatic, this was the basic approach to the problem of *peristaseis*. Where events were fated, one was at least still free to *assent* to what was already decreed. Thus, where compliance was inevitable, the possibility of *willing* compliance remained.[69]

Philosophers were naturally concerned with providing a rationale for volitional suffering. According to Xenophon, Socrates himself debated the relative merits of voluntary suffering with Aristippus. Whereas the latter argued that the voluntary acceptance of "hunger, thirst, cold, [and] sleeplessness" was utter folly, Socrates recounted the advantages of voluntarily undergoing toil and hardship, including the boon that "he who endures hardship willingly enjoys his toils because he is comforted by good hope" (*Mem.* 2.1.17–18).[70]

Furthermore, the Socratic notion that "philosophers ought to be ready and willing to die" was strongly ingrained in subsequent Greek thought (Pl., *Phd.* 62C). It influenced all, but the idea of volition was especially emphasized by the Stoics. Stoicism's contention that death and sickness are not evils but *adiaphora* was advanced as the rational premise that made the willing acceptance of them possible.[71]

Seneca emphasizes, accordingly, that the man of complete virtue "welcomes (*amplexatur*) that which all other men regard with fear" (*Ep.* 71.28; cf. also 30.9; *Ira* 1.5.2) and undergoes them *libens* and *volens*.[72] In Frg. VII Musonius Rufus

[68] In other editions, cf. frg. 36 Bergk = frg. 20 Jebb = frg. 48 Edmonds. The translation is that of R. C. Jebb, *Bacchylides: The Poems and Fragments* (Cambridge: University Press, 1905; reprinted, Hildesheim: Olms, 1967) 420.

[69] On the topic of fate and free will in general, cf. David Amand, *Fatalisme et liberté dans l'antiquité grecque* (Louvain: 1945; reprinted, Amsterdam: Hakkert, 1973). On unrestricted intellectual activity as the standard Greek presupposition for human freedom, cf. also Dihle, *Will,* 39, 42, 45. Even in an author like Aristotle, the terms *hekōn* and *hekousion* essentially have to do with a person's consent to perform a particular deed, no matter whether that consent is expressed in "passive acquiescence" or "intentional and deliberate conduct." Cf. Martin Ostwald, *Aristotle, Nicomachean Ethics* (Indianapolis/-New York: Bobbs-Merrill 1962) 308. Cf. also Joseph., *AJ* 18.13.

[70] The LCL translation of Marchant has been modified here.

[71] The source of this insight is clearly Socratic-Platonic. Cf. esp. Pl., *Prt.* 358B–E, and also F. M. Cornford (trans.), *The Republic of Plato* (New York/London: Oxford, 1966) 12, 119.

[72] Cf. Sen., *Clem.* 1.13.1; *Ep.* 37.2–3; *Prov.* 3.1; 4.3; 5.4,8; *V.B.* 15.5. For Seneca, then, the man of virtue "triumphs over his fate by willingly surrendering to it." See Berthe Marti, "Seneca's Tragedies. A New Interpretation," *TAPhA* 76 (1945) 237.

argues that the worthy man is ready to bear hardship for the sake of the ideal good and complete happiness, whereas "the man who is unwilling to exert himself almost always convicts himself as unworthy of good."[73] According to Marcus Aurelius, one is to accept (δέχεσθαι) and welcome (ἀσπάζεσθαι) hardships with all one's heart.[74] One is to be both content (ἀρκεῖσθαι) and pleased (ἀρέσκεσθαι / εὐαρεστεῖν) with one's lot, fraught though it be with difficulties, even taking delight (στέργειν / φιλεῖν / χαίρειν) in it.[75] Indeed, it is "the characteristic of the good man to delight in and to welcome what befalls and what is spun for him by destiny" (*Med.* 3.16.2).

That endurance of adversity must be both rational and voluntary appears in one of Epictetus' *peristasis* catalogues. The response to the first four items indicates volition, and the elaborate response to exile and death show reason in action. The latter makes clear that the endurance of adversity must spring from reason, not insanity or habit (*Diss.* 4.7.6; cf. also Mar. Ant., *Med.* 11.3). There is to be a noetic quality in one's perseverance, a sense in one's stamina (cf. also Sen., *Ep.* 74.21). A person is not simply to "hang in there" with the invincible obstinancy of an ass (*Diss.* 1.18.20).

> "Would you have me bear poverty?"
> Bring it on and you shall see what poverty is when it finds a good actor to play the part.
> "Would you have me hold office?"
> Bring it on.
> "Would you have me suffer deprivation of office?"
> Bring it on.
> "Well, and would you have me bear troubles?"
> Bring them on too.
> "Well, and exile?"

[73] Mus. Ruf., VII,31,9–11 Hense (= 58,27–28 Lutz). Cf. also VII,28,4–29,3 Hense (= 56,15–25 Lutz); 30,7–8 Hense (= 58,13 Lutz); and XX,112,15 Hense (= 126,8 Lutz).

[74] For the acceptance of an often hard lot (such as "sickness or maim or loss or what not of the same kind": Mar. Ant., *Med.* 5.8.1), cf. 2.17; 7.66; 8.23,43; 11.13; 12.11. For the welcoming of everything, no matter how severe, cf. 3.4.3; 3.16.2; 4.33; 5.8.1–2; 6.44; 8.7; 10.6.2. Cf. also 4.34; 10.8.1; 10.28. This attitude is based in part on the fact that everything is seen as humanly bearable: 5.18; 8.46; 10.3.

[75] For the idea in Marcus Aurelius of being content and (well-) pleased with hardships, be it a hindrance (*Med.* 8.32), death (9.3), or little in the way of "lodging or bed, dress, food or attendance" (6.30.2), cf. 3.6.1; 4.25; 5.27; 6.50; 7.54; 8.45; 9.6; 10.1; 10.6.2; 10.11. Cf. also 2.2,5,13,16; 3.7; 4.3.1–2; 4.29; 5.8.3; 7.64; 8.46–47; 9.40; 10.3; 10.6.1; 10.7.2; 10.25,28; 11.13; 11.18.10; 11.20.2; 12.27. For the idea of taking delight in one's harsh lot, cf. 3.16.2; 5.8.3; 6.44,49; 7.57; 10.11; 11.16; 12.1.1. Compare the use of *agapan* in other moralists; cf., for example, Dio Chrys., *Or.* 11.139; 31.2; and also 8.15. Cf. also Hor., *Carm.* 3.2.1.

> Wherever I go it will be well with me, for here where I am it was well with me, not because of my location, but because of my judgments, and these I shall carry away with me; nor, indeed, can any man take these away from me, but they are the only things that are mine, and they cannot be taken away, and with the possession of them I am content, wherever I be and whatever I do.
> "But it is now time to die."
> Why say "die"? Make no tragic parade of the matter, but speak of it as it is: "It is now time for the material of which you are constituted to be restored to those elements from which it came." And what is there terrible about that? (*Diss.* 4.7.13–15).[76]

Since the Stoic sage knows that hardships are not evils and consents to their part in his life, he has an effective carapace against the onset of *Fortune.* His battle with her is a *Blitzkrieg* in which hardships serve as the missiles with which she bombards the sage. It is a savage attack that severely damages the sage's body, yet leaves his mind intact. Through reason and consent he can easily withstand her fierce assault, for, as Seneca affirms,

> if it is realized that death is not an evil and therefore not an injury either, we shall much more easily bear all other things—losses and pains, disgrace, changes of abode, bereavements, and separations. These things cannot overwhelm the wise man, even though they all encompass him at once; still less does he grieve when they assault him singly. And if he bears composedly the injuries of Fortune, how much more will he bear those of powerful men, whom he knows to be merely the instruments of Fortune! (*Const.* 8.3).[77]

[76] My arrangement of Oldfather's LCL translation. For the use of a question-and-answer *peristasis* catalogue in a rabbinic text to express readiness to suffer and die for the sake of the Torah, cf. *Mek. Bahodesh* 6 (Lauterbach 2.247):

"Why are you being led out to be decapitated?"
"Because I circumcised my son to be an Israelite."
"Why are you being led out to be burned?"
"Because I read the Torah."
"Why are you being led out to be crucified?"
"Because I ate the unleavened bread."
"Why are you getting a hundred lashes?"
"Because I performed the ceremony of the Lulab."

[77] The catalogue of hardships given here by Seneca is, to be precise, a catalogue of the injuries inflicted by Fortune. As Pierre Grimal notes, these *iniuriae* correspond to the three categories of injury distinguished at *Const.* 5.4. Losses and pains (*damna et dolores*) concern injury done to the body (cf. also 6.3), disgrace and changes of abode (= exile; cf. *Helv.* 6.1) concern a person's position (*dignitas*), and bereavements and separations deal with the death of loved ones, who are among those things external to man. Cf. his *Sénèque, De Constantia Sapientis, Commentaire* (Paris: Société d'Édition "Les Belles Lettres," 1953) 67–68. In accord with this judgment is Francesca Minissale, *L. Annaei Senecae, De Constantia Sapientis* (Messina: EDAS, 1977) 125–26. For other catalogues of hardships inflicted by Fortune, cf. Sen., *Marc.* 10.6; Plut., *Mor.* 498F–499D; and Apul., *Met.* 11.15. For a catalogue of hardships inflicted by an Erinys, cf. Heliodorus, *Aeth.* 2.4.1.

The Stoic sage bears the injuries of Fortune with composure because he is not afraid of what she can inflict. Owing to his self-reliance, he realizes that Fortune has lost all control over his true self (Sen., *Ep.* 51.9; 57.3; 110.20) and thus he faces her free and undaunted, crying out, "You have to deal with a *man;* seek someone whom you can conquer" (*Ep.* 98.14).[78]

> Who then is free? The wise man, who is lord over himself, whom neither poverty nor death nor bonds affright, who bravely defies his passions, and scorns ambition, who in himself is a whole, smoothed and rounded, so that nothing from outside can rest on the polished surface, and against whom Fortune in her onset is ever maimed (Hor., *Sat.* 2.7.83–87).

The Stoic sage's fearlessness in the face of Fortune is made clear by Seneca in the following exchange between himself and his interlocutor, an exchange in which both "speakers" use a catalogue of hardships:

> "What then? Is he not to fear death, imprisonment, burning, and all the other missiles of Fortune?" Not at all; for he knows that they are not evils, but only seem to be. He reckons all these things as the bugbears of man's existence. Paint him a picture of slavery, lashes, chains, want, mutilation by disease or by torture,—or anything else you may care to mention; he will count all such things as terrors caused by the derangement of the mind (*Ep.* 85.26–27; cf. also Plot., *Enn.* 1.4.7,21ff; 8,27).

His attitude toward Fortune and her hardships is thus one, not of fear, but of utter contempt. Fear is servile, but contempt is the attitude of a superior to an inferior (Quint., *Inst.* 12.8.14), and the sage's disdain for Fortune is a sign that he feels himself superior to her and what she is able to inflict. He overcomes her (cf. also Pliny, *HN* 7.27.106) in and through philosophy, and in triumph gloats over his fallen foe. His bravery also surfaces in this attitude, for *fortitudo* "is the virtue that scorns (*contemnens*) legitimate dangers" (Sen., *Ben.* 2.34.3; cf. also *Ep.* 88.29; *Prov.* 4.12–13). Hence, the Senecan sage despises what other men fear (*Ep.* 85.25), ills such as toil (*Ep.* 31.3–4), pain (*Ep.* 70.18), grief, care, illness, old age (*Ep.* 107.3), losses, wrongs, abuse, and taunts (*Ira* 3.43.5), even death itself (*Ep.* 23.4; 36.8). In the following catalogue Seneca has God himself recommend this attitude toward hardships and Fortune:

> 'Yet,' you say, 'many sorrows, things dreadful and hard to bear, do befall us.' Yes, because I [=God] could not withdraw you from their path, I have armed your minds to withstand them all; endure with fortitude (*ferte fortiter*). In this you may outstrip God; he is exempt from enduring evil, while you are superior to it.
> Scorn (*contemnite*) poverty; no one lives as poor as he was born.
> Scorn pain; it will either be relieved or relieve you.

[78] For the thought, cf. Teles, VII, 62,3–4 Hense = 70,146–47 O'Neil. On the practice of addressing Tyche and various hardships, cf. Rabbow, *Seelenführung,* 198–200, 349–51. For Fortune and the Epicurean sage, cf. Cic., *Fin.* 2.27.89; *Tusc.* 3.20.49; and Diog. Laert. 10.120,131.

Scorn death, which either ends you or transfers you.
Scorn Fortune; I have given her no weapon with which she may strike your soul (*Prov.* 6.6).[79]

Whereas the sage despises Fortune, she sees in him a worthy opponent. Fortune ignores and disdains those whom she views as unworthy cowards, so that to be bypassed by her is no boon but a disgrace. Fortune "seeks out the bravest men to match with her; some she passes by in disdain. Those that are most stubborn and unbending she assails, men against whom she may assert all her strength." The person who is being assailed by Fortune is thus being paid a compliment, and the more violently a person is assailed, the greater Fortune's esteem for him (*Prov.* 3.3–4; cf. also *Polyb.* 2.7).

The initiative in this fray, however, does not always lie with Fortune, for when she has been slow to attack, "some men have presented themselves voluntarily to laggard misfortune" (*Prov.* 4.3). The man who aspires to wisdom should engage her willingly, for his contest with Fortune will strengthen him (*Prov.* 4.12–13). Even the *proficiens,* then, finds in his adversary Fortune a means of using her for his own advantage.

Whereas the sage is Fortune's foe, he is God's true friend. This relationship means that the perspective from which the sage's hardships are treated changes radically once *God,* not Fortune, is seen as their source. The idea that banes as well as blessings emanate from the gods is one that appears already in early Greek thought,[80] with both "goods" and "evils" being termed

[79] The arrangement of Basore's LCL translation is mine. The idea that one is to have unmitigated contempt for hardship and Fortune occurs elsewhere in Seneca (*Ep.* 9.13; 16.5; 24.6; 76.21; 93.4; *Prov.* 6.1,5) and represents an old and established conviction that this is the proper attitude to have toward adversity. Cf. Pl., *Ap.* 28C; Cic., *Sest.* 21.48; *Tusc.* 2.1.2; 16.38; 18.43; 26.64; 5.1.4; Mus. Ruf., VII (title); 31,13 Hense (= 58,30 Lutz); X,53,2–4 Hense (= 76,23–24 Lutz); Plut., *Brut.* 12.1; frg. 32 Sandbach; Epict., *Ench.* 19.2; Mar. Ant., *Med.* 2.2; 4.50; 9.28.2; 12.24,34; Max. Tyr., *Or.* 7.4k (81,7–9 Hobein); *Soc.Ep.* 14.8 (256,35 Malherbe); Plot., *Enn.* 1.4.7,15–18; and the catalogues that appear in Ps-Diog., *Ep.* 31.4 (136,10–11 Malherbe: despise "poverty, disrepute, lowly birth, and exile") and Strabo 10.4.16 ("scorn heat, cold marches over rugged and steep roads, and blows received in gymnasiums or regular battles").

[80] For the gods as givers of both blessings and banes, especially prosperity and adversity, cf. Hom., *Il.* 24.527–51; *Od.* 4.236–37; 6.188–90; 18.133–35; Archil., frg. 58 Diehl (= frg. 56 Edmonds); Theog. 157–58, 441–46, 591–92; Pind., *Pyth.* 3.80–83; Stob., *Fl.* 51.8. Cf. also Archil., frg. 8 Diehl (= frg. 16 Edmonds); Sol., frg. 1.63–64 Diehl (= frg. 13.64–65 Edmonds); Theog. 171–72, 355–56; Pind., *Nem.* 7.53–58. For the gods as the source of banes, cf. Hom., *Od.* 6.172–74; 7.242; 14.198; 19.80; 20.195–96; Ps-Hom. *Epigr.* 4.13–14 White; *Hymn.Hom.Dem.* 147–48, 216–17; Hes., *Theog.* 570, 585, 600; *Op.* 57, 82, 88–89, 95, 100–03, 178; Theog. 1029–36; Simon., frg. 527 *PMG* (= frg. 33 Edmonds); and esp. the catalogue of ills in Mimn., frg. 2.11-16 Diehl/Edmonds. Cf. also Hom., *Od.* 24.306; Hes., *Op.* 91–92; Bacchyl., frg. 13 Snell (= frg. 23 Edmonds); and Eur., *Andr.* 851–52. For additional references and discussion, cf. N. J. Richardson, *The Homeric Hymn to Demeter* (Oxford: Clarendon, 1974) 192–94. On the whole issue of the gods and evil in early Greek

"gifts."[81] Since one cannot choose which of the god's gifts to accept nor rid oneself of a gift once it is accepted,[82] fluctuation in fortune is inevitable. Thus "it is the part of the wise man to accept the vicissitudes of human life and concentrate on the good."[83] The good man refuses either to blame the gods for his sufferings or to attribute his hardships to any envy on the part of the divine at his prosperity. He knows a respite will come from the turbulence of his present misfortune, and it is to God that he looks for this relief.[84]

In the Graeco-Roman period several moralists exploited the ancient idea of adversity as a gift. A lofty conception of deity as well as a refusal to call hardships "evils" opened the way in Stoic circles for the treatment of hardship as a benefaction bestowed out of the divine's love for humanity. In this tradition, which has a clear Platonic basis (*Resp.* 379C-380C), God is not the author of evil, but of adversity, and hardships are part of the divine's designs for the sage. Seneca, for example, explicates these ideas in his *De Providentia,* the relevant sections of which form the basis for the following treatment.

According to Seneca, hardship is the sign, not of God's hostility or negligence, but of his *love* for the sage. The sage is God's friend, his pupil, imitator, and

---

thought, cf. esp. W. C. Greene, *Moira* (Cambridge: Harvard, 1944). Cf. also Job 2:10; Lam 3:38; Sir 11:14.

[81] It is striking that the verb *didōmi* is often used by early Greek authors in order to indicate the bestowal of ills and that the ills themselves are frequently termed *dōra,* "gifts." Cf., for example, Hom., *Il.* 24.528–29, 531; *Od.* 4.237; 6.190; 7.242; 18.142; *Hymn.Hom.Dem.* 147,216; Hes., *Op.* 57, 82, 92, 178; Mimn., frg. 2.16 Diehl/Edmonds; Solon frg. 1.64 Diehl (= frg. 13.64 Edmonds); Theog. 444, 446, 591, 1033. Cf. also Archil.. frg. 8 Diehl (= frg. 16 Edmonds) and Pind., frg. 42 Schroeder. The most famous use of this idea is probably in the Pandora story of Hesiod, where the idea of a gift is central to the deception of Epimetheus by Zeus. For Hesiod's use of this concept, cf. esp. Pietro Pucci, *Hesiod and the Language of Poetry* (Baltimore: Johns Hopkins, 1977) 2–3, 82, 85–86, 97–98.

[82] For the idea that a divine donation can be neither refused nor returned, cf. Hom., *Il.* 3.64–65; *Od.* 18.142; *Hymn.Hom.Dem.* 147–48, 216–17; Solon, frg. 1.63–64 Diehl = frg. 13.63–64 Edmonds); Theog. 444–46, 1033–36.

[83] Kirkwood, "The Theme of Vicissitude," 72. Cf. esp. Pind., *Pyth.* 3.81–83, and also Theog. 155–58, 591–92, 441–46, 657–58, 1029–32. The good man accepts and endures the unending oscillation between good and bad fortune because he *understands* that life has this ebb and flow. Cf. Archil., frgs. 7 and 67 Diehl (= frgs. 9 and 66 Edmonds) and Bruno Snell, *The Discovery of the Mind* (Cambridge: Harvard, 1953) 53–62, esp. 56.

[84] On the idea of not blaming God for human sufferings, cf. Hom., *Od.* 1.32–34; Bacchyl. 15.51–55 Snell (= 10.51–55 Edmonds); Pl., *Resp.* 617E; *Tim.* 42D. (The passage from Bacchylides is quoted by Clem. Al., *Str.* 5.14, whereas the *Republic* passage is quoted by Justin Martyr, *1 Apol.* 44.8). Cf. also note 95 below. The primitive idea of the "envy of the gods" is rejected already by Solon, frgs. 1.9–32 and 5.9–10 Diehl (= frg. 13.9–32 and frg. 6 Edmonds), and it is vigorously combatted by Aeschylus, *Agam.* 750–81. For the hope that the divine will respond to prayer and remove misfortune, cf. Theog. 171–72, 355–60.

true offspring (1.5). God is thus the father of the good and rears his progeny as befits a good father, that is, "as strict fathers do, with much severity" (1.5; cf. also *Clem.* 1.14.1). Good men are seen laboring and sweating as they climb a difficult road, and this indicates the sterner discipline that God uses with the good. God "does not make a spoiled pet of a good man; he tests (*experitur*) him, hardens (*indurat*) him, and fits him for his own service" (1.6). Severe discipline is the sign that one is a son, not a slave (1.6; cf. also Heb 12:5–11).

Just as Lacedaemonian fathers do not hate their sons when they have them lashed in public and exhort them to submit to further flogging (4.11), God does not hate the man of virtue when he sends him hardships as spurs to his soul (4.6; 5.11) and encourages him to endure. God, quite simply, is no mother who coddles and pampers children (2.5). "Toward good men God has the mind of a father, he cherishes for them a manly love, and he says, 'Let them be harassed by toil, by suffering, by losses, in order that they may gather true strength' " (2.6).

> Unimpaired prosperity cannot withstand a single blow; but he who has struggled constantly with his ills becomes hardened through suffering, and yields to no misfortune; nay, even if he falls, he still fights upon his knees. Do you wonder if that God, who most dearly loves (*amantissimus*) the good, who wishes them to become supremely good and virtuous, allots to them a fortune that will make them struggle (*exerceantur*)? For my part, I do not wonder if sometimes the gods are moved by the desire to behold great men wrestle with some calamity (2.6–7).

Hardship is thus a sign of God's love, and divine providence is an expression of the divine's concern for man, a concern that is grounded ultimately in the fact that the human soul is one with the divine soul that penetrates the universe. But hardship is more than a sign of God's loving concern. It is also a mark of God's *approval* and *esteem.* It shows that God has recognized an individual's true worth:

> God, I say, is showing favour to those whom he desires to achieve the highest possible virtue whenever he gives them the means of doing a courageous and brave deed, and to this end they must encounter some difficulty in life. . . . God hardens, reviews, and disciplines (*exercet*) those whom he approves, whom he loves (*quos probat, quos amat*). . . . Why is it that God afflicts the best men with ill health, or sorrow, or some other misfortune? For the same reason that in the army the bravest men are assigned to the hazardous tasks; it is the picked soldier that a general sends to surprise the enemy by a night attack, or to reconnoitre the road, or to dislodge a garrison. Not a man of these will say as he goes, "My commander has done me an ill turn," but instead, "He has paid me a compliment." In like manner, all those who are called to suffer what would make cowards and poltroons weep may say, "God has deemed us worthy (*digni*) instruments of his purpose to discover how much human nature can endure." . . . Why, then, is it strange if God tries (*temptat*) noble spirits with severity? No proof (*documentum*) of virtue is ever mild. . . . It is, therefore, to the advantage even of good men, to the end that they may be unafraid, to live constantly amidst alarms and to bear with patience the happenings which are ills to him only who ill supports them (4.5,7–8,12,16).

The worthy man thus views his hardships and scars as tokens of God's loving esteem for him and accepts them as a divine donation that is in his own best interest. The man who has experienced no hardships, by contrast, is deemed neither happy nor worthy, for "the gods have passed an adverse judgment upon him. He was deemed unworthy (*indignus*) ever to gain the victory over Fortune" (3.3). God is doing such a man no favor by withholding hardship from him; on the contrary, "he is really keeping [him] soft against ills to come" (4.7).

Since these Stoic views are not self-evident but must be established by philosophical argument, Seneca has his interlocutor raise various objections to these assertions, objections which are sometimes cast in the form of catalogues of hardships:

> "Is it," you ask, "for their own good that men are driven into exile, reduced to want, that they bear to the grave wife or children, that they suffer public disgrace, and are broken in health?" (3.2).
> "But," you say, "it is unjust that a good man be broken in health or transfixed or fettered, while the wicked are pampered and stalk at large with whole skins" (5.3).
> "Why, however," do you ask, "was God so unjust in his allotment of destiny as to assign to good men poverty, wounds, and painful death?" (5.9; cf. also *Ep.* 74.10; *Ira* 2.27.2).

Seneca responds to such objections by delineating the advantages of adversity and by rejecting the claim that the suffering of the sage involves injustice on God's part. As part of his theodicy Seneca argues that God would be unjust only if he were to harm the good man. But not only is God unwilling to harm the good man, he is incapable of doing so (*Ep.* 95.49; *Ira* 2.27.1). God does not allow evil to touch the good man. Evil does not befall good men, adversity does. "The good man himself he protects and delivers: does any one require of God that he should also guard the good man's luggage? Nay, the good man himself relieves God of this concern; he despises externals" (*Prov.* 6.1). God does not change the decrees of Fate which he himself wrote, but always obeys them (*Prov.* 5.8). Nor would he do so, even in response to prayer, for what he has decreed is advantageous for the good man, and any change would only be for the worse.[85]

[85] As Dihle, *Will*, 3, points out, not only Stoics but also Platonists "explicitly rejected the idea that prayer could influence or change the intention of God. Such a change could only lead to something worse, since God could not possibly improve on his own perfect rationality." In the philosophical tradition prayer is not an act in which one tries to influence or change the divine will. It is rather an attempt at the cognition of God. That is, it is the process or dialogue by which one seeks to understand the divine's intention so that one can concur with it and consent to what its perfect rationality dictates. Moreover, "the basic belief that the divine order is immutable and that, consequently, the gods cannot possibly change their mind (for this could only restrict their perfection) is as firmly established in Herodotus' Histories as in Platonic philosophy" (Dihle, *Will*, 161). As far as Seneca is concerned, this statement needs one minor qualification. He says in *QNat.* 2.37.2 that certain things have been left in suspense by the gods as a part of fate. It is in regard to these few indeterminate things that prayers and vows can influence the outcome.

The good man, for his part, does not ultimately *obey* God, for that would be the mark of a slave. It is rather the case that he *agrees* with God as to his allotment.[86] This is why he is God's friend, and in certain respects is even superior to God.[87] And God, for his part, only bestows on good men what they sometimes voluntarily choose for themselves, and what he bestows has a didactic purpose (*Prov.* 6.2–3).

The suffering of the sage thus plays a role in the divine plan. Not only is the sage's suffering personally advantageous to him, it also has value for others. First of all, by testing the sage through adversity God establishes him as a worthy model to whom others may look for guidance in living the life of virtue and enduring hardships.[88] God treats good men as teachers do their pupils, in that "they require most effort from those of whom they have the surest hopes" (*Prov.* 4.11). Through being thoroughly tested by the divine the sage discovers and exhibits what human nature is capable of enduring (*Prov.* 4.8), and becomes thereby a great exemplar of endurance.

Second, the fact that the sage as a good man experiences "evils" while evil men enjoy "goods" is part of God's plan to discredit the common understanding of what constitutes good and evil (*Prov.* 5.2). "It is God's purpose, and the wise man's as well, to show that those things which the ordinary man desires and those which he dreads are really neither goods nor evils" (*Prov.* 5.1). Not only

---

Seneca's main emphasis, however, is that one is to accept adversities and turn them to one's advantage, not beg the gods to deliver one from them. Needless to say, the philosophical conception of God and prayer stands in vivid contrast to both popular Greek piety and the ancient Israelite conception. Cf. Dihle, *Will,* 3, 160–62.

[86] Seneca, it is true, can speak of "obeying God" and receiving in a good spirit whatever happens (cf., for instance, *Ep.* 16.5; *V.B.* 15.4,7: *deo parere*). But for him it is more fundamentally a matter of *agreeing* with God. Cf. esp. *Ep.* 96.2: "I do not obey God; rather I agree with him (*non pareo deo, sed adsentior*). I follow Him because my soul wills it, and not because I must." Cf. also *Prov.* 5.6: "I am under no compulsion, I suffer nothing against my will, and I am not God's slave but his follower (*nec servio deo sed assentior*). (The translation of the first sentence of *Ep.* 96.2 is that of Dihle, *Will,* 18). These statements are, of course, expressions of the Stoic doctrine of "resignation." This doctrine is based on the immutability of Fate (*Polyb.* 4.1; *Oed.* 980–92; *Ben.* 6.23.1) and is advised by *prudentia* (*Ep.* 67.10). For the statement of this concept in "God-language," cf. *Ep.* 16.4–5; 74.20; 76.23; 90.34; 98.4–5; 107.9–11; and *QNat.* 3. Pref. 12. Cf. also *Ep.* 54.7; 94.7; 107.7–11; 120.12; *Tranq.* 10.1–4; and *Ira* 2.28.4; 3.16.1.

[87] Cf. esp. *Prov.* 6.6; *Ep.* 53.11; 73.12–15. On the sage and the divine in Seneca, cf. also *Ep.* 41.4; 87.19; 92.3; 93.10; 124.23; *Const.* 8.2; Ganss, *Das Bild des Weisen,* 38–47; Barth, *Stoa,* 132; and Pierre Thévenaz, "L'intériorité chez Sénèque," in *Mélanges offerts à M. Niedermann* (Neuchâtel: Univ. de Neuchâtel, 1944) 192–94.

[88] On the human need for a model in Seneca, cf. esp. *Ep.* 11.8–10 and 52.2,7–8. For the sage as the one who teaches men to know and follow the gods and "to welcome the gifts of chance precisely as if they were divine commands," cf. *Ep.* 90.34. Cf. also Schreiner, *Seneca,* 116–18.

does the sage demonstrate the true nature of that over which he triumphs, but he also "domesticates" the "wild beasts" that terrify man. A veritable animal trainer, the *sapiens* "is a skilled hand at taming evils. Pain, want, disgrace, imprisonment, exile,—these are universally to be feared; but when they encounter the wise man, they are tamed" (*Ep.* 85.41).[89] "Much that is hard, much that is rough will befall him, but he himself will soften the one, and make the other smooth" (*Prov.* 5.9).

The suffering sage, loved and esteemed by the divine, is clearly an exemplar of virtue and thus is worthy of the highest praise and glory. Not all, of course, accord him the recognition that he deserves, yet he uses that failure of others to adorn himself further. By remaining superior to others' disrespect he reveals again and again who he is, and that revelation only augments the praise that is his due.

The victory is clearly the sage's, and yet there is a sense in which the Senecan sage owes to the divine his triumph over adversity as well as his attainment of virtue.[90] If the divine had not exercised him, had not hardened him, there would have been no victory. Were there no providence, there would be no sage. God, moreover, has not merely trained the sage and provided the opportunity for his development. He also has helped the sage in that he has armed his mind for the battle with adversity (*Prov.* 6.6). For Seneca, "no man can be good without the help of God. Can one rise superior to fortune unless God helps him to rise?" (*Ep.* 41.2). "The gods are not disdainful or envious; they open the door to you; they lend a hand as you climb. Do you marvel that man goes to the gods? God comes to men; nay, he comes nearer,—he comes into men. No mind that has not God, is good" (*Ep.* 73.15–16).

At the sight of someone "who is unterrified in the midst of dangers . . . , happy in adversity, peaceful amid the storm," an observer should be prompted to say, "A divine power (*vis divina*) has descended upon that man" (*Ep.* 41.4; cf. also 41.5). Yet the divine power or force (*potentia*) that has descended upon man and enables his conduct is no special "supernatural" power.[91] Indeed, since "God" is identical with "Nature" (cf. esp. *Ben.* 4.8.2–3), this power can be seen from one perspective as a "natural" one. But, from another perspective, the power is truly divine. The God who dwells within man is that part of the human soul that is one with the divine soul that permeates the universe. It is the divine seed that has been implanted in every human soul (*Ep.* 73.16).[92] To triumph over adversity by the power of God is to triumph by means of that part of man which is divine. The victory is nothing more and nothing less than that of *reason.*

[89] For the imagery of hardships as "wild beasts," cf. "Cebes," *Tabula* 22.1–23.2; 26.2–3.

[90] Cf., among others, Johannes Kreyher, *L. Annaeus Seneca und seine Beziehungen zum Urchristentum* (Berlin: Gaertner, 1887) 106, and Schreiner, *Seneca,* 33, 110.

[91] Cf. Kurt Deissner, *Paulus und Seneca* (BFCT 21.2; Gütersloh: Bertelsmann, 1917) 43 n. 30.

[92] Cf. Sen., *Ep.* 31.11; 41.1; 120.14; and also 80.3. For the idea of the divine within, cf. also Epict., *Diss.* 2.8.9–14.

"Reason, however, is nothing else than a portion of the divine spirit set in a human body" (*Ep.* 66.12; cf. also 92.2). God is entirely reason; there is no part of God other than the mind (*QNat.* 1. Pref. 14). As matter is subject to God as mind, so is the material body to be subject to the divine soul in man. That means concretely: "Let us be brave in the face of hazards. Let us not fear wrongs, or wounds, or bonds, or poverty" (*Ep.* 65.23–24). No man overcomes these things *sine deo* because they can be conquered only by the mind which is one with God. To stand unmoved in the face of adversity is thus simultaneouly to "body forth God" (*deum effingas: V.B.* 16.1) and to win the gods' approval as they witness the feat (*Ep.* 102.29).

The Senecan sage thus owes his victory and virtue not only to philosophy, but also to God. The role that God plays is crucial, but it must not be forgotten that the divine is Stoically conceived. The role that God plays in the matter of hardship is also crucially important for other Stoics, especially Epictetus. He, like Seneca, stresses that hardship is no sign of divine hostility or negligence (cf. also Pl., *Ap.* 41D), but that it is rather God's recognition of an individual's worth (ἄξιος).[93] God is like a physical trainer who knows that sweat is the price of victory, and he uses *peristaseis* to exercise a person so that victory may be won.[94] When a person has been sufficiently trained, God sends him forth as his servant, witness, and model.

> These are the terms upon which now He brings me here, and again He sends me there; to mankind exhibits me in poverty, without office, in sickness; sends me away to Gyara, brings me into prison. Not because He hates me—perish the thought! And who hates the best of his servants? Nor because He neglects me, for He does not neglect any even of the least of His creatures; but because He is training me, and making use of me as a witness to the rest of men (*Diss.* 3.24.113).

The witness that the sage bears as a paradigm has to do with things which lie outside the realm of the *prohairesis* and it consists in the message that true goods reside within, not in externals (1.29.47; 3.24.112). "That you may see yourselves, O men, to be looking for happiness and serenity, not where it is, but where it is not, behold God has sent me to you as an example," says the worthy Cynic. "I have neither property, nor house, nor wife, nor children, no, not even so much as a bed, or a shirt, or a piece of furniture, and yet you see how healthy I am" (4.8.30–31). This testimony "in behalf of virtue and against externals," comments Epictetus, is "the work of Zeus or of him whom Zeus deems worthy of this service" (4.8.32).

> And how is it possible for a man who has nothing, who is naked, without home or hearth, in squalor, without a slave, without a city, to live serenely? Behold, God has sent you the man who will show in practice that it is possible. "Look at me," he says,

[93] Cf. esp. Epict., *Diss.* 1.29.47 and also 1.29.49; 2.1.39; 4.8.30,32; *Ench.* 15.

[94] Cf. esp. Epict., *Diss.* 1.24.1–2 and also 3.22.56; 26.31. For the proof of training that God demands, cf. 3.10.8 and 4.4.30.

"I am without a home, without a city, without property, without a slave; I sleep on the ground; I have neither wife nor children, no miserable governor's mansion, but only earth, and sky, and one rough cloak. Yet what do I lack? Am I not free from pain and fear, am I not free? When has anyone among you seen me failing to get what I desire, or falling into what I would avoid? When have I ever found fault with either God or man? When have I ever blamed anyone? Has anyone among you seen me with a gloomy face? And how do I face those persons before whom you stand in fear and awe? Do I not face them as slaves? Who, when he lays his eyes upon me, does not feel that he is seeing his king and his master?" (3.22.45–49).[95]

The person whom God calls (1.29.46; 2.1.39; 3.22.2–8, 23, 53; *Ench.* 22) and sends forth to bear this sort of witness and to set this kind of example does not go out to face hardships unprepared. Epictetus stresses that God has endowed us with the requisite resources and powers "to enable us to bear all that happens without being degraded or crushed thereby" (1.6.40; cf. also 1.6.28; 2.16.13–14; 3.8.6). Since God has provided the proper equipment and training, a person should be eager for an opportunity to use it. He should be like the highly-trained gladiators who "pray to God and go to their managers, begging to fight in single combat" (1.29.37). One is to look at one's faculties and pray, "Bring now, O Zeus, what difficulty (*peristasis*) Thou wilt; for I have an equipment given to me by Thee, and resources wherewith to distinguish myself by making use of the things that come to pass" (1.6.37).

Such a prayer expresses the attitude of one who has been set free by God (4.7.17), who knows God's commands and is attentive to them (3.24.110; 4.7.17), who trusts in God (2.1.39)[96] and makes it his aim to please God rather than man (1.30.1), and who, regarding God's will as better than his own, stands ready to conform his will to that of the divine (4.7.20). His prayer is not a request for external blessings but either a call for God to be his helper and comrade-in-arms (2.18.29) or an expression of gratitude. He thanks God for placing his *prohairesis* under his own control so that he is able to derive what is truly good from himself.[97] Grateful for what externals God does bestow, he is ready to return to

[95] The term "having nothing" (cf. 2 Cor 6:10) is placed at the beginning of the catalogue as a summary item for what follows. The inordinate number of alpha-privative items that follow serves to confirm and specify this initial item. Many of the items are drawn from the traditional depiction of Diogenes the Cynic (cf. Diog. Laert. 6.38). The catalogue as a whole functions in part to establish the kingship of the Cynic, who has entrusted his desire and aversion to Zeus (2.17.22–25). On the idea of not blaming God for what he bestows, cf. also 1.14.16; 2.16.13; 19.26; 3.8.6; 10.13; 22.13; *Ench.* 31.1; and note 84 above.

[96] Cf. also Dio Chrys., *Or.* 45.2. The Stoic's trust in God and/or providence is grounded in his belief in the perfect rationality of the divine. Cf. R. Liechtenhan, "Die Ueberwindung des Leides bei Paulus und in der zeitgenössischen Stoa," *ZTK* 30 (1922) 392. For faith in divine providence as the keystone of Stoic thought, cf. Guillemin, "Sénèque," 207.

[97] Cf. Epict., *Diss.* 1.17.27; 25.1–3; 29.4; 4.4.18; 12.12. See also 3.24.96–97. Adolf Bonhöffer, *Epiktet und das Neue Testament* (Religionsgeschichtliche Versuche und Vorarbeiten 10; Giessen: Töpelmann, 1911) 65 n. 1, emphasizes (following Kuiper) that Epictetus' prayer is a *Dankgebet* rather than a *Bittgebet.* "Gratitude," notes B. L. Hijmans,

God all he has received (4.1.172; *Ench.* 7), whether it be a farm, a child, or a wife (*Ench.* 11).

As an example of how Epictetus wants his students to pray, he offers the following "model prayer" that takes the form of a catalogue of hardships:

> Lift up your neck at last like a man escaped from bondage, be bold to look towards God and say,
> "Use me henceforward for whatever Thou wilt;
> I am of one mind with Thee; I am Thine;
> I crave exemption from nothing that seems good in Thy sight;
> where Thou wilt, lead me;
> in what raiment Thou wilt, clothe me;
> Wouldst Thou have me
> to hold office, or remain in private life;
> to remain here or go into exile;
> to be poor or to be rich?
> I will defend all these Thy acts before men;
> I will show what the true nature of each thing is"
> (*Diss.* 2.16.42–43; my arrangement of Oldfather's LCL transl.).

Whereas the preceding catalogue is prospective, the following one is retrospective. Immediately prior to death a person ideally should be able to say to God that he has not transgressed His commands, that he has not misused the resources, senses and preconceptions He gave him, and that he has not blamed Him or His governance (3.5.8). The backing for these assertions comes in the form of a catalogue of hardships:

> I fell sick, when it was Thy will;
> so did other men, but I willingly.
> I became poor, it being Thy will,
> but with joy.
> I have held no office, because Thou didst not will it,
> and I never set my heart upon office.
> Hast Thou ever seen me for that reason greatly dejected?
> Have I not ever come before Thee with a radiant countenance,
> ready for any injunctions or orders Thou mightest give?
> (*Diss.* 3.5.9; my arrangement of Oldfather's LCL transl.; cf. also 4.1.89–90).

The catalogue attests and confirms the denials of any improprieties on the speaker's part, showing that even adversity did not keep the speaker from heeding God's commands or accepting the divine will. There is a dual emphasis in the speech on God's will and the speaker's willing response to it. His reaction to these hardships *proves* that he has conformed his will to that of the divine, and since God now wills his death, he departs with complete gratitude (3.5.10).

Jr., ῎ΑΣΚΗΣΙΣ: *Notes on Epictetus' Educational System* (Assen: Van Gorcum, 1959), 16, "is Epictetus' strongest feeling toward God, and he often urges his pupils to it."

Whether stated prospectively or retrospectively, these catalogues indicate the stress that Epictetus places on God as the source of human hardships[98] and the necessity of humans completely identifying their own will with that of the divine.[99] It is God who as playwright assigns the roles that each is to play in life, and the roles include poverty and rags, office, lack of office, lameness, exile, death (1.29.44–45; 4.7.13–15; *Ench.* 17; frg. 11), and, of course, the mission as God's representative and witness, a role which may embrace all of the above and more (3.22). Whatever the particular role assigned and however demanding the part, the task of each is that of "playing the part of the good and excellent man, not ostensibly but in reality" (3.24.110), confident that the script of his life has been drafted by a beneficent divine providence (1.6) that deems him worthy of his assigned role.

The vital role that hardships play within the divine plan is emphasized, therefore, by both Seneca and Epictetus. This seems to be the viewpoint of imperial Stoicism in general.[100] This emphasis is also found among Platonists like Plutarch and Maximus of Tyre. Both insist that virtue is not attained without suffering and divine assistance. Plutarch, for example, recounts through the Pythagorean Theanor the divinely authorized assistance that daemons give to those who are struggling valiantly and nearing the goal of virtue and the end of the cycle of births (*Mor.* 593D-594A).

[98] The fact that Tyche does not play a significant role in the Epictetan corpus indicates the extent to which Epictetus has utilized religious imagery to express his philosophical convictions. Whereas Teles (frg. VI), for instance, depicts Tyche as the one who assigns what role each is to play in the human drama, Epictetus makes this the task of God (*Diss.* 3.22.2–8; *Ench.* 17; frg. 11; cf. also Otto Halbauer, *De Diatribis Epicteti* [Leipzig: Robert Norske Bornen, 1911] 40). Again, with only one apparent exception (frg. 2), it is God, not Tyche, who gives and takes back. For Tyche's slight role in Epictetus' thought, cf. the index in Schenkl's edition (p. 696). Similarly, Tyche's role in Marcus Aurelius is also slight (cf. Dalfen's index, p. 172).

[99] For the necessity of making the divine will one's own and thus keeping one's will in harmony with what happens, cf. also Epict., *Diss.* 1.12.16–17; 17.28; 3.22.95; 24.95–102; 4.1.89–90; 3.9; and the following related passages: *Diss.* 1.26.2; 2.2.21; 23.42; 4.1.131; *Ench.* 8; 53; frg. 8; 23.

[100] Cf. esp. Marcus Aurelius, who argues that what betides is from the gods (*Med.* 3.11.3; 10.1; 12.11). It is folly to blame them (8.17) or Providence (12.24), for they do no wrong (12.12) and "all that befalls befalleth justly" (4.10). To blame the gods is but to reveal that one has not understood the *adiaphora* (6.41). One is to follow God (7.31; 12.27), which is tantamount to following reason (12.31) and nature (7.11), and this commitment is revealed in the fact that one takes delight in whatever is one's present lot (10.11). Furthermore, the gods "co-operate with us *even in the things that are in our own power,*" so that prayers to them for freedom from fear and grief are not inappropriate (9.40; cf. also 6.42). Musonius Rufus also relates the divine to hardships, but the connection tends to be by way of philosophy. Since it is philosophy that deals with hardships and makes virtue possible, it is the will of Zeus that one should study philosophy. Cf. Mus. Ruf., XV1,86,18–87,10 Hense = 104,30–106,1 Lutz.

Maximus devotes one of his orations (*Or.* 38) to the question of how one becomes good and achieves virtue. He argues that virtue is not the result of an individual and his *technē*.[101] Virtue is the most perfect good and "there is not any thing good to men which is not derived from the gods" (6e–f = 444,18–445,4 Hobein; cf. also Pl., *Resp.* 379C). God is both willing and able to bestow this good on men, so that virtue is really the "work of Zeus" (1b = 437,12–13; cf. also Epict., *Diss.* 4.8.32). It is thus only by divine allotment that one becomes good.[102] The means by which virtue is effected is that of hardships, for out of his *philia* God allots hardships to those with an aptitude for virtue and these function as exercises through which virtue is ultimately achieved (7d,f = 447, 6–7, 17). These hardships come as a result of God's commands, and the divine surrounds those it loves with antagonists, making their life an *agōn* (7e–f = 448,3–8). On those who are victorious in this contest the gods bestow virtue as a reward (8.7b = 94,9–13).

Yet the deity does not observe this contest as an interested spectator. On the contrary, the divine lends active aid and becomes "the fellow-combatant and ally" that even the best natures require for the attainment of virtue (38.6k = 445,11–446,1). To those of a good mind and robust nature "divinity is willing to be present, to be the defender of their life, and to protect them with his hand" (8.7c = 94,13–15). This aid is necessary, for "what man is so worthy as to pass through life securely and without blame, . . . what man . . . is so good as not to require the piloting, and medical skill, and helping hand of divinity?" (8.7h = 95,8–12). Since Fortune is the antagonist of virtue and threatens to cut it off from view, it is necessary for God to come to the aid of virtue as its ally, fellow-combatant, and comrade-in-arms.[103]

In short, the attainment of virtue is ultimately the result of the divine, who has provided both the means and the assistance that are indispensable for this accomplishment. God, of course, is able to spare humans these gymnastic hardships, but his desire for what is most beautiful and his loving concern for them makes him unwilling to do so (38.7h = 448,11–12).

Such a perspective is clearly absent among the Epicureans, who saw the prosperity enjoyed by the wicked and the adversity suffered by the good as a proof of the gods' total unconcern for human affairs.[104] Again, there is little

[101] Max. Tyr., *Or.* 38.1b (437,12 Hobein), 3a (439,12), 4l (442,20), 5b (443,14–15), 7i–k (448,16–19).

[102] Max. Tyr., *Or.* 38.4i (442,15 Hobein), 7c (446,17–18), 7d (447,6). Cf. also 38.3a (439,13), 4g (442,7), 5a (443,9), 7i–k (448,16–20). Maximus' thesis appears to derive from Pl., *Meno* 99E; 100B.

[103] Max. Tyr., *Or.* 8.7k (96,6–7 Hobein). For Maximus, given his view of God, this divine aid for human *astheneia* appears to come largely through the daemons. Cf. 8.8b–c (96,9–97,6); 38.7e (447,8). Cf. also Philo, *Som.* 1.147.

[104] Cf. Tac., *Ann.* 6.22, and esp. Lactant., *Div.Inst.* 3.17: Epicurus denied providence because he "saw that the good are always subject to adversities, poverty, labours, exile, loss of dear friends," whereas the wicked are honored and happy.

indication that Cynics sought to connect the divine to their virtue and the sufferings that their way of life imposed and invited.[105] In fact, very few seem to have made the connection between virtue and God that is observable in the Stoic and Platonic authors just examined.[106] Although the connection between God and the attainment of virtue was quite old,[107] Cotta seems to speak for the majority when he says that

[105] There is, to be sure, an occasional connection between personal excellence and God in Cynic thought. Cf., for example, *Soc.Ep.* 32.3 (300,2–6 Malherbe) where Ps-Xenocrates says that "I used to reflect on how I might become, to the degree that it was possible, a more excellent person than I myself was or other men were. It should, then, be clear that I am what I say, especially since, with God's help it is easy." The Cynic sage is, moreover, both the friend of God (Ps-Crates, *Ep.* 26 [76,11 Mal.]; Ps-Diog., *Ep.* 10.2 [104,6–7 Mal.]) and the fellow-citizen of the gods, since he dwells with them through virtue (Ps-Heraclitus, *Ep.* 9.3 [212,1–2 Mal.]). Under Zeus he is free (Ps-Diog., *Ep.* 34.3 [144,10 Mal.]), and it is to Zeus that he owes his good (Ps-Diog., *Ep.* 7 [98,10–11 Mal.]). His cloak and wallet are the weapons of the gods (Ps-Crates, *Ep.* 16 [66,5–6 Mal.]; cf. also Ps-Diog., *Ep.* 22 [114,15–16 Mal.]), and he stands under the gods' protection (Ps-Diog., *Ep.* 7 [98,23 Mal.]). Finally, a certain connection between God and Cynic philosophy was assured through Socrates' daemon and experience at Delphi (cf. esp. Ps-Socrates, *Ep.* 1 = *Soc.Ep.* 1).

And yet, in contrast to Stoics like Seneca and Epictetus, the divine has only a minor importance in Cynicism. Most of the items mentioned above are either traditional or peripheral. The idea of the Cynics' hardships as originating in the design of the divine is one that grows out of the religious perspective of a Stoic like Epictetus (*Diss.* 3.22) and not out of Cynicism itself. In general, Cynicism was hostile toward the popular cult and any idea of real dependence upon the divine. Ps-Crates, *Ep.* 19, for example, reproaches Odysseus because "he never did anything without God and fortune" (68,16–17 Malherbe). With undying confidence in the capacity of humans to free themselves from vice and realize the highest ideals of virtue, they emphasized the individual and the power of the will. "The Cynic rejects all supra-individual points of view. He shows no interest in providence, but stresses his own free will and his own accomplishment" (Malherbe, "Cynics," 202). When all else fails, the Cynic's recourse is to himself, not to God.

[106] A connection between God and virtue is also found among Pythagoreans, as the speech of Theanor in Plut., *Mor.* 593D–594A indicates. Cf. also Philost., *VA* 8.7.7: man's "virtues come to him from God."

[107] Cf., for instance Simon., frg. 526 *PMG* (= frg. 32 Edmonds): "No man has ever won *aretē*, no city, no mortal, without the gods." The translation is that of H. Fränkel, *Early Greek Poetry and Philosophy* (Oxford: Blackwell, 1975) 314. Cf. also the interpretation of Simon., frg. 542 *PMG* (= frg. 19 Edmonds) and Hes., *Op.* 289–92, by Kevin Crotty, *Song and Action: The Victory Odes of Pindar* (Baltimore/London: Johns Hopkins, 1982) 33–35: "if *arete* is 'easy,' this is a sign of the gods' benevolent participation in human striving, by which the striving is brought to its goal." The more general idea of divine aid is also quite old. Cf. Hom., *Od.* 13.300–01,318–23; 16.170–71; 19.36–40,52,479; 20.47–48; 24.182,443–44,479. Both ideas occur in Pindar; for his belief in the dependence of man on the gods and the divine origin of human *aretai*, cf. esp. *Isthm.* 3.4–5; *Nem.* 7.6; *Ol.* 9.28; 11.10; *Pyth.* 1.42. For God as the source of virtue, cf. also the texts collected by R. Schneider, *Christliche Klänge aus den griechischen und römischen Klassikern* (Gotha: F. A. Perthes, 1865) 141–43, 185–86, 337, and the discussion by P. Montée, *Le stoïcisme*

virtue no one ever imputed to a god's bounty. And doubtless with good reason; for our virtue is a just ground for others' praise and a right reason for our own pride, and this would not be so if the gift of virtue came to us from a god and not from ourselves![108] . . . Did anyone ever render thanks to the gods because he was a good man? No, but because he was rich, honoured, secure. The reason why men give Jupiter the titles of Best and Greatest is not that they think that he makes us just, temperate or wise, but safe, secure, wealthy, and opulent! (Cic., *Nat.D.* 3.36.87; contrast 2.66.165,167).

Of course, none of the Hellenistic moralists here examined thinks of virtue coming to a person like a sack of money dropped from heaven (cf. esp. Sen., *Ep.* 31.5). What they do argue, however, is that the divine makes it possible for a person to attain virtue and achieve his potential as a human being. That, they are convinced, occurs through the suffering that is experienced at the divine's behest. The intimate connection that they establish between virtue by means of hardships and the divine is what distinguishes them from their peers and relates them to one another. It is not that they all have the same conception of God—for they obviously do not. It is rather that they all seek to relate the sage's suffering to the divine will and purpose. As we shall see, Paul clearly does the same, though his own understanding of God differs in crucial points from that of all the moralists here surveyed.

The Sage's Andreia, Action and Askēsis

The ideal philosopher or sage possesses all the virtues, and he uses them all in meeting adversity, whatever its source. Both popularly and historically, however, it is especially ἀνδρεία that is manifested in the midst of hazards and hardships.[109] *Andreia* means "courage," or, to be more precise,

à Rome (Paris: A. Durand, 1865) 85–98.

[108] Cf. also Alcinous, *Didasc.* 30, who, in arguing that virtue is voluntary, within our power, and without a master, comments that "what is honourable would not be an object of praise, if it were from nature or a *divine lot*" (emphasis mine). The translation is that of Henry Cary, *The Works of Plato* (Bohn's Classical Library 6; London: Bell, 1881) 304. Dio Chrysostom, moreover, says that most men scorn and deem as useless the power and aid that comes from the gods (*Or.* 45.1).

[109] For Seneca on "bravery," cf. Sevenster, *Paul and Seneca,* 157–64. The intimate connection of *andreia* and adversity is also a presupposition in philosophical discussions of this cardinal virtue. The concern here is to define more precisely the arena(s) in which courage is exhibited and to show how adversity demands the use of capacities and virtues other than courage. The relation of adversity and *dikaiosynē* is particularly important, with one aspect of this relation discussed in the subsequent section. In addition, both *phronēsis* and *sōphrosynē* are also connected with hardships. In Stoic circles they are revealed in the judgment that hardships are not evils and in the fact that adversity is not shunned. Cf. Mus. Ruf., IX,51,5–8 and X,53,9–54,3 Hense (= 76,2–4 and 76,29–78,5 Lutz); *SVF* 2.50.16–18 (§174) and 3.63–69 (esp. §§262,265–66,268,274,280). For *sōphrosynē* and hardships in Xenophon (*Ages.* 5.1–7; *Mem.* 1.2.1; 2.1.1,6; etc.) and Diogenes the Cynic

"manliness."[110] In ancient thought it is axiomatic that courage and manly worth are exhibited most clearly in dangerous circumstances. As the *Iliad* amply attests and Aristotle affirms,[111] it is preeminently in war that this quality is seen, with a man's battle scars being the tokens of his valour (cf. Xen., *Ages.* 6.2; Pliny, *HN* 7.28.102–04). But any difficult or hazardous situation, such as sailing, demands it (Strabo 3.1.8; Pl., *Lach.* 191D), for "courage minimizes difficulties" (Democritus B 213 [II,188,14–15 Diels-Kranz]). Courage, moreover, is needed even in times of peace, for then it may be seen "in relation to accidents of fate—earthquakes, famines, plagues, droughts, and so on" (Men. Rh., I,364,18–20). As the quintessential virtue,[112] courage is deemed worthy of honor[113] and gives rise to self-reliance, confident boldness, pride, and boasting.[114]

Andreia (= *fortitudo*) and its allied virtues[115] are manifested in both word and deed. Verbally, a clear sign of courage is παρρησία, frankness and boldness of

---

(Diog. Laert. 6.68), cf. Helen North, *Sophrosyne: Self-Knowledge and Self-Restraint in Greek Literature* (Cornell Studies in Classical Philology 35; Ithaca: Cornell, 1966) 125, 130, 133, 169. For later Cynicism's connection between disciplinary hardships and *sōphrosynē*, cf. Ps-Diog., *Ep.* 44 (174,2–3 Malherbe: bread, water, a bed of straw, and a coarse cloak teach *sōphrosynē* and *karteria*) and *Soc.Ep.* 12 (250,10–12 Malherbe: hunger and thirst are of great help to those who pursue *sōphrosynē*). Cf. also Ps-Diog., *Ep.* 33.4 (142,5–7 Malherbe).

[110] *Andreia* is, above all, the quality that constitutes one a man, so that to act *andreiōs* is to act "like a man," "in a manly way." When Epictetus says that *peristaseis* show "the man" (*Diss.* 1.24.1), he thus is affirming that they bring to light his manliness, his *andreia*. Similarly in Latin, *virtus* is manliness, the quality that makes one a *vir.* Cf. Cic., *Tusc.* 2.18.43.

[111] Arist., *Eth.Nic.* 3.6.8–10, 11–12 (1115a30–35; 1115b1–6). Cf. also 3.9.1–2 (1117a29–36); Hdt. 1.136; 4.65; 7.99; Thuc. *passim;* Pl., *Lach.* 190E; Xen., *Ages.* 6.1–3; Men. Rh., II,372,25–373,15; 422,20–27.

[112] Already for Simonides, to reach *aretē* situated on a lofty peak is to arrive at the summit of *andreia* (frg. 579 *PMG* = frg. 65 Edmonds). In Latin, of course, *virtus* means both virtue and manliness. Cf. also note 110 above.

[113] Protagoras B 9 (II,268,5–11 Diels-Kranz); Soph., *El.* 983; Thuc. 2.64.3; 4.120.3; Xen., *An.* 6.5.14; Arist., *Rh.* 1.9 (1366b1ff); *Eth.Nic.* 3.8.1–3 (1116a17–30); 3.9.2 (1117a34–35); Teles, I,4,8 Hense (= 4,3 O'Neil). Also, it should be recalled that Marcellus' famous temples to *Honos* and *Virtus* were constructed in such a way that access to the former was only by way of the latter. For the disgrace of cowardice, on the other hand, cf. esp. Xen., *Lac.* 9.3–6.

[114] Thuc. 2.39.1; 89.2; 6.72.4; Pl., *Lach.* 182C; *Prt.* 349E–350C; 351A; 360B; Xen., *Ages.* 11.9–10; *Hell.* 2.4.40 (comp. Eur., *HF* 475); Arist., *Eth.Nic.* 3.7.13 (1116a12); 3.8.13 (1117a12); Ps-Arist., *VV* 4.4 (1250a44–1250b7); Cic., *Inv.Rhet.* 2.54.163; *Tusc.* 2.14.33.

[115] The allied virtues include καρτερία, θαρσαλεότης, μεγαλοψυχία, εὐψυχία, φιλοπονία, ὑπομονή, *fides, patientia, perpessio, perseverantia, tolerantia, constantia, fidentia, magnitudo animi, magnificientia, gravitas,* and *despicientia rerum humanarum. Fides,* for example, cries "Burn me, slay me, kill me!" and refuses to betray a trust (Sen., *Ep.* 88.29). Cf. also Sen., *Agam.* 934; *Ben.* 4.21.5–6; and Cic., *Tusc.* 3.7.14 (*fidens*) and 4.37.80

speech.[116] Whereas the common view, for instance, is that exiles lack boldness, the courageous man will speak his mind in all situations, both at home and in exile, and bear whatever the consequences may be.[117]

Courage is exhibited as well in a person's staunch endurance. The poet Horace is but one who extols the tenacity and perseverance of men engaged in honorable causes. As he makes clear in the following catalogue, the just man not only perseveres but also remains undismayed (*impavidum*) through all that would deter lesser men:

> the man tenacious of his purpose in a righteous cause is not shaken from his firm resolve by the frenzy of his fellow-citizens bidding what is wrong, not by the face of threatening tyrant, not by Auster, stormy master of the restless Adriatic, not by the mighty hand of thundering Jove. Were the vault of heaven to break and fall upon him, its ruins would smite him undismayed (*Carm.* 3.3.1–8).[118]

But courage is not simply bold speech and staunch but passive endurance of hardships. Courage is also active, for it is "the thoroughly considered undertaking of perils" (Cic., *Tusc.* 4.54.163; my transl.). According to Cicero, one of the two main characteristics of courage is that "one should do deeds not only great and in the highest degree useful but extremely arduous and laborious and fraught with danger both to life and to many things that make life worth living" (*Off.* 1.20.66). Precisely because reason is inextricably bound up with courage and justice, the deeds in which courage engages are noble rather than vicious. On this point, there is complete unanimity of philosophical thought,[119] and the logic involved is as simple as it is protreptic: since base men are willing to suffer

---

(*fidentia*). For the other allied virtues, cf. esp. *SVF* 3.64.17–18, 23–24 (§264); 67.39–42 (§275); Cic., *Inv.Rhet.* 2.54.163; *Tusc.* 2.13.32–14.33; Ps-Arist., *VV* 4.4 (1250a44–1250b7); Sen., *Ep.* 67.10; *V.B.* 25.6. For *karteria* and *andreia,* cf. also Pl., *Lach.* 192B–194B; Xen., *Ages.* 10.1; *Symp.* 8.8; and Teles, I,4,16–17 Hense (= 4,43–46 O'Neil). The connection between high-mindedness and courage is found already in Protagoras B 9 (II,268,5–11 Diels-Kranz). Stoic texts often connect courage and *hypomonē*. Cf. *SVF* 1.49.25 (§200), 32–33 (§201); 129.1 (§563); 3.64.6–7 (§263), 18 (§264); 69.14–15 (§280); 70.24–25 (§286); 73.3 (§295); 159.31 (§620). Mention may also be made of the somewhat related virtues *assiduitas* (Cic., *Balb.* 2.6; *Fin.* 1.15.49; *Fam.* 7.6.1); *firmitas* (Cic., *Fam.* 9.11.1; *Tusc.* 5.26.74; Sen., *Helv.* 5.5; *Polyb.* 17.1), *firmitudo* (Tac., *Ann.* 6.46), *pertinacia* (Sen., *Ira* 2.12.5; Suet., *Iul.* 68.2), *temperantia* (Sen., *Ep.* 66.5), and *pervicacia* (Frontin., *Str.* 2.13.17).

[116] Cf., for instance, Men. Rh.,II,386,6–10; 416,23–26; and also II,379,24–28.

[117] Cf. Teles, III,23,5 (= 22,37–38 O'Neil) and esp. Mus. Ruf., IX,48,15–49,2 Hense (= 72,35–74,7 Lutz).

[118] For the tortures to which the "courageous" man may be subjected, cf. Teles, I, 4, 9–17 Hense = 4,34–46 O'Neil. Cf. also Arist., *Eth.Nic.* 3.7.8–9 (1115b29–1116a1).

[119] Cf. esp. Cic., *Off.* 1.19.62–63 (citing both Plato and the Stoics) and Arist., *Rh.* 1.9 [1366b11]); *Eth.Nic.* 3.7.6 (1115b23–24). Cf. also *Eth.Nic.* 3.7.2,13; 8.5,14; 9.4; and note 3.1.7.

for ignoble purposes and still others experience affliction as a result of mindless passions, it is valour's part to endure hardship for what is right![120]

Thus, just as Herodotus says that the Persian couriers "are stayed neither by snow nor rain nor heat nor darkness from accomplishing their appointed course" (8.98), so also Seneca stresses that no obstacle, however great, is to stand in courage's path in such a way as to impede its action. All things are to be endured in behalf of what is honorable (*Ep.* 76.26). Disasters, losses, wrongs, vexation, and pain are to be of no consequence to virtue; they are no more to inhibit virtue than clouds do the sun (*Ep.* 66.20; 92.18). It must necessarily be this way, for "it is ever a dishonour for a man to be troubled and fretted, to be numbed when there is any call for activity" (*Ep.* 74.30). No *peristasis* prevents the good man from acting nobly:

> A good man will do what he thinks it will be honourable for him to do, even if it involves toil; he will do it even if it involves harm to him; he will do it even if it involves peril; again, he will not do that which will be base, even if it brings him money, or pleasure, or power. Nothing will deter him from that which is honourable, and nothing will tempt him into baseness (*Ep.* 76.18).

Indeed, the proof that "no fortune, no external circumstance, can shut off the wise man from action" (*Ep.* 85.38), is seen in his conduct, for

> the good man will hasten unhesitatingly (*sine ulla cunctatione*) to any noble deed; even though he be confronted by the hangman, the torturer, and the stake, he will persist, regarding not what he must suffer, but what he must do (*Ep.* 66.21)![121]

The key to the sage's action and his immense success in meeting adversity was his *askēsis*, his preparatory training and practice. In the view of both ancient Greeks and Romans, "exercise and practice provide the basis of any achievement,"[122] and this was particularly true for virtue as an intellectual

[120] Cf. esp. Mus. Ruf., VII. For the idea of suffering to help and protect family, friends, and city, cf. also XVI,86,9–11 Hense (= 104,23–24 Lutz) and contrast XX,113,16–114,2 Hense (= 126,22–25 Lutz). The general idea of undergoing toil and peril in order to secure benefits is common; cf., for instance, Isoc., *Nicocles* 64.

[121] The brave man's lack of hesitation is a sign of his full and willing consent to what virtue demands of him. For this characteristic, cf. Sen., *Ep.* 76.27,29; Mus. Ruf., III,11,13–14 Hense = 40,35 Lutz; III,12,1–2 Hense = 42,8–9 Lutz; XVI,86,9–11 Hense = 104,24–25 Lutz; and contrast XX,113,16–114,2 Hense = 126,22–26 Lutz. Cf. also Soph., *Phil.* 887, and Xen., *Cyr.* 1.4.2.

[122] Dihle, *Will*, 55. To the references that Dihle supplies in support of this assertion, cf. also Protagoras B 3 (2.264.23–24 Diels-Kranz) and the assertion attributed to him in Pl., *Prt.* 323D. On the history of *askēsis*, cf. H. Dressler, *The Usage of* Ἀσκέω *and its Cognates in Greek Documents to 100 A.D.* (Washington, D.C.: The Catholic Univ. of America Press, 1947). Cf. also E. Hatch, *The Influence of Greek Ideas on Christianity* (1889; reprinted, New York: Harper & Row, 1957) 148–50.

accomplishment![123] "More people become virtuous by training than by nature" was an idea as old as Democritus![124] and it was in response to the need for "training in virtue"[125] that Aristotle "put forward the first comprehensive theory of ἔθος (exercise or practice) with reference to all aspects of moral conduct."[126] To become a τέλειος ἀνήρ was scarcely possible without lifelong *askēsis*.[127]

It is in keeping with the traditional value attached to *askēsis* that Hellenistic moralists emphasize the vital role that it plays in overcoming adversity and hardship. Plato's insistence that true philosophers are concerned with μελέτη θανάτου (*Phd.* 81A)[128] made this emphasis inescapable in Platonic circles![129] Training was so important for Cynics that Lucian can refer to the "Cynic *askēsis*" (*Tox.* 27) and the *askēsis* that the Cynic proclaims (*Vit.Auct.* 7)![130] But even Cyrenaics insisted that ills could be softened by adequate preparation (Cic., *Tusc.* 3.13.28–15.31; 22.52–54.)![131]

123 For virtue as an intellectual achievement, cf. above on "The Crucial Role of Philosophy and Reason," and also Ps-Crates, *Ep.* 19 (68,26 Malherbe), where the author affirms that virtue "is something acquired by practice and does not spontaneously enter the soul as evil does." Cf. also Pl., *Grg.* 509E; *Lach.* 184E; Dihle, *Will,* 56; and Bonhöffer, *Ethik,* 129–30.

124 Democritus B 242 (2.193.14–15 Diels-Kranz). The translation is that of Dihle, *Will,* 191 n. 28. On the topic of *askēsis* in Democritus, cf. Hijmans, ῎ΑΣΚΗΣΙΣ, 55–57 and 63 n. 2. The precise relationship between natural endowment and practice or habituation was a topic of debate. Cf. Xen., *Mem.* 3.9.1–3; Arist., *Eth.Nic.* 2.1.1–3 (1103a14–26); *SVF* 3.51.18–23 (§214); Sen., *Ep.* 90.46 (comp. 108.8); Mus. Ruf., IV,15,18–19 Hense (= 44,34–35 Lutz); Fronto, *Ep.* (Vol. I, p. 72 Haines, who refers also to Cass. Dio 72.35.6 and Zonaras ii); Max. Tyr., *Or.* 1.5d (8,16–9,4 Hobein) and *Or.* 38 *passim.*

125 The phrase is taken from Xen., *Mem.* 1.2.20 and Arist., *Eth.Nic.* 9.9.7 (1170a11).

126 Dihle, *Will,* 55. For Dihle's discussion of Aristotle's theory, cf. pp. 54–60. Aristotle's statement that "no one is a wise man by nature" (*Eth.Nic.* 6.11.5 [1143b6]) reflects the importance that he attached to practice. The Aristotelian insistence that the moral virtues are the product of habit (*Eth.Nic.* 2.1.1 [1103a14–17]) has, of course, a Platonic basis (*Resp.* 518D–E), as Shorey, *Republic,* 2.136, points out.

127 Cf. Galen V.14, cited by Farquharson, *Meditations,* 2.751. Cf. also Bonhöffer, *Ethik,* 147.

128 Cf. also Pl., *Phd.* 64A, 67E, and esp. 83B, and also E. J. Price, "Paul and Plato," *HibJ* 16 (1917–18) 276.

129 Cf. Arcesilaus, *apud* Plut., frg. 152 Sandbach; Cic., *Tusc.* 2.14.34–20.46; Plut., *Mor.* 584E–585D, 593D–594A; Ps-Plut., *Mor.* 112D–E; 118D–E; and "On Training" (in *RhM* 27 [1872] 520–38); Max. Tyr., *Or.* 1.5d,h (8,16–17; 10,15 Hobein); 19.5e (242,19–22); 23.2d (280,19–21); 37.3a–b (428,10–17); Plot., *Enn.* 1.4.8,24–27. For Alcinous (Albinus) and *askēsis,* cf. Dihle, *Will,* 63, 194 n. 61. For Plutarch and *askēsis,* cf. Rabbow, *Seelenführung,* 340–42.

130 For Lucian's description of the Cynic course of training, cf. *Vit.Auct.* 9. For Cynic *askēsis,* cf. also Diog. Laert. 6.70–71; Ps-Crates, *Ep.* 11 (62,14 Malherbe); 12 (62,23–24); 19 (68,26); Ps-Diog., *Ep.* 12 (106.10–13 Mal.); 27 (118,16–17); 31 (136,7–12); 37.6 (156,28–33; 158,5–7).

131 For Epicurean *askēsis,* cf. Dihle, *Will,* 60, and W. Schmid, "Epikur," *RAC* 5 (1962)

The importance of *askēsis* for Stoics was immense. Two members of the Old Stoa, Herillus of Carthage and Dionysius, wrote books on *askēsis* (Diog. Laert. 7.166–67). Another, Ariston of Chius, said that "against the whole tetrachord of pleasure, pain, fear, and lust, there is need of much exercise and struggle."[132] Seneca, Musonius, and Epictetus continue this traditional emphasis.

Seneca argues that *askēsis* is of fundamental importance in regard to adversity because the impact of a calamity is intimately tied to one's preparation for it. Lack of preparation compounds a calamity and makes it more difficult to bear, for "it is the unexpected that puts the heaviest load upon us. Strangeness adds to the weight of calamities, and every mortal feels the greater pain as a result of that which also brings surprise" (*Ep.* 91.3). "All misfortune will fall more lightly," on the other hand, "on those who expect it" (*Const.* 19.3; cf. also *Ep.* 107.4).

Preparatory training, therefore, is crucial, and it must occur daily (*Ep.* 2.4). It consists primarily of mental exercises that serve to toughen the mind, with the focus of these exercises on death, the one sure thing that lies in the future (*Ep.* 70.17–18; cf. also 30.12,18). Poverty provides another focus of this *askēsis,* and preparation for this often requires actual physical training.[133] But whatever precise form this training takes, it must be rigorous, tantamount to torture (*Ep.* 78.16). Inadequate training leads only to catastrophe. The war with Fortune is lost if boot camp is too easy (cf. *Ep.* 91; 18.6). Again, this training must be total, lest Fortune find a corridor of vulnerability and race through it to the unprotected area. The constant alertness of a soldier on guard duty is necessary (*Helv.* 5.2–3), for every possible *peristasis* must be expected.

> We should therefore reflect upon all contingencies and should fortify our minds against the evils which may possibly come. Exile, the torture of disease, wars, shipwreck,—we must think on these![134] Chance may tear you from your country or your country from you, or may banish you to the desert; this very place, where throngs are stifling, may become a desert. Let us place before our eyes in its entirety the nature of man's lot, and if we would not be overwhelmed, or even dazed, by those unwonted evils, as if they were novel, let us summon to our minds beforehand, not as great an evil as oftentimes happens, but the very greatest evil that possibly can happen. We must therefore reflect upon fortune fully and completely (*Ep.* 91.7–8).

743ff. For Pythagorean *askēsis*, cf. Hijmans, ʼΑΣΚΗΣΙΣ, 57–58.

[132] *SVF* 1.85.18–19 (§370) = Clem. Al., *Str.* 2.20. Since Stoics saw the soul's health and strength as the result of *askēsis* (*SVF* 3.68.25 [§278]), they could even define philosophy in terms of *askēsis* (*SVF* 2.15.5 [§35]). For the general Stoic emphasis on practice, cf. also *SVF* 3.33.27–35 (§138); 3.51.18–23 (§214); 3.120–21 (§471); 3.133.19 (§490).

[133] Cf Sen., *Ep.* 18.5–11; 20.13; 51.10–11; 56.15; and contrast *Helv.* 12.3. For the monthly regimen advocated by Epicureans, cf. *Ep.* 18.6,9 and Epicurus, frg. 158 Usener.

[134] As R. M. Gummere, *Seneca: Ad Lucilium Epistulae Morales* (LCL 76; London: Heinemann, 1920) 436, notes, this short catalogue appears to rest ultimately on Eur., frg. 964 Nauck. Cf. also *Marc.* 9.4 with the note of J. W. Basore, *Seneca: Moral Essays* (LCL 254; London: Heinemann, 1932) 26; Cic., *Tusc.* 3.14.29; Ps-Plut., *Mor.* 112D; Anaxagoras A 33 (2.14.5ff Diels-Kranz).

What, have you only at this moment learned that death is hanging over your head, at this moment exile, at this moment grief? You were born to these perils. Let us think of everything that can happen as something which will happen. . . .

I may become a poor man;
  I shall then be one among many.
I may be exiled;
  I shall then regard myself as born in the
    place to which I shall be sent.
They may put me in chains.
  What then? Am I free from bonds now?
  Behold this clogging burden of a body,
    to which nature has fettered me!
"I shall die," you say; you mean to say
  "I shall cease to run the risk of sickness;
  I shall cease to run the risk of imprisonment;
  I shall cease to run the risk of death" (*Ep.* 24.15,17).[135]

It is the fool who is continually caught off guard by the machinations of the Fortune in whom he trusts. Because he is unprepared, the novelty of his hardship adds to its crushing weight (*Ep.* 76.34). The wise man, on the other hand, has prepared himself totally for any and every contingency. In his militant defense against adversity "the wise man knows that all things are in store for him. Whatever happens, he says: 'I knew it' " (*Ep.* 76.35).[136]

The trained sage is thus totally prepared, and as such he is like the trained athlete, eager and ready for the *agōn* (*Ep.* 78.16; 80.3).[137] Adversities are like adversaries in wrestling, extremely useful for the *proficiens* and the *sapiens* alike (*Prov.* 2.2–4). The former uses hardships to increase his strength, while the latter keeps himself in peak condition by means of the exercise that adversity provides. In addition to this requisite exercise, *peristaseis* also provide both with the opportunity to display their power and prowess.[138]

[135] This arrangement of Gummere's LCL translation is mine. For the necessity of preparation in general, cf. esp. *Ep.* 74.19; 78.29; 88.17; 91.15; 99.32; 101.10; *Helv.* 5.2–3; *Ira* 2.31.4–5; *Polyb.* 11.3; and *V.B.* 3.3. For calls for preparation with specific hardships mentioned, cf. *Ep.* 2.4; 70.17–18; 91.4–5; 98.5–7; *Ira* 3.37.3; and esp. *Marc.* 9.1–5 and *Tranq.* 11.6–12.

[136] For the sage's total preparation, cf. *Const.* 9.5; *Ep.* 59.7; 70.27; 76.33; 113.27. Cf. also *Ep.* 98.3.

[137] The training of the soul as analogous to the training of the body is Socratic; cf. Xen., *Mem.* 1.2.19–20. For the *agōn* motif, cf. V. C. Pfitzner, *Paul and the Agon Motif* (NovTSup 16; Leiden: Brill, 1967).

[138] It has not been sufficiently recognized that *askēsis* is still important for one who already has become a sage. The typical view is that expressed by P. Grimal, *Sénèque, De Constantia Sapientis,* 42: "En théorie, le Sage parfait n'a pas besoin d'ascèse; celle-ci concerne l'aspiration à la sagesse." Three responses may be offered to this comment. First, whatever barrier Stoic theory presented to the sage's need for training was usually dropped once exhortation became the concern. Second, even at the theoretical level many Stoics

For his part, Musonius Rufus stresses that ἄσκησις must follow μάθησις if there is to be any true benefit realized from one's philosophical instruction (VI,23,14–17 Hense = 52,23–25 Lutz). To become good one must both master the precepts of philosophy and exercise oneself zealously and laboriously in their application.[139] "How could we acquire courage if we had merely learned that the things which seem dreadful to the average person are not to be feared, but had no practice in showing courage in the face of such things?"[140] Training for Musonius is of two types. One pertains only to the soul and inculcates the distinction between evils real and apparent. The other, physical training, does not pertain only to the body, but to both body and soul:

> We use the training common to both when we discipline ourselves to cold, heat, thirst, hunger, meagre rations, hard beds, avoidance of pleasures, and patience under suffering. For by these things and others like them the body is strengthened and becomes capable of enduring hardship, sturdy and ready for any task; the soul too is strengthened since it is trained for courage by patience under hardship and for self-control by abstinence from pleasures (VI,25,6–14 Hense = 54,11–18 Lutz).[141]

Epictetus, even more than his teacher Musonius, emphasizes that practice and training must follow learning (*Diss.* 2.9.13).[142] Epictetan training for hardships involves *askēsis* primarily in the area of desire and aversion,[143] for this

---

clearly insisted that *askēsis* continued to have a vital role in the life of the sage. According to Diogenes Laertius, for instance, the Stoic sage "will submit to training to augment his powers of bodily endurance" (Diog. Laert. 7.123). Third, the person who had just become a sage and was still unconscious of this fact was believed to need "constant practice and continual exercise" (Philo, *Agr.* 160).

Seneca makes *askēsis* important for both the sage and the one who aspires to wisdom. The *proficiens,* on the one hand, clearly ought to test his progress by his deeds (*experimentum profectus tui capias: Ep.* 20.1) inasmuch as virtue tests its progress by its deeds (*Ot.* 6.2). While the sage, on the other hand, no longer needs to test his progress, he still "needs to have his virtues kept in action," just as "skilled wrestlers are kept up to the mark by practice" (*Ep.* 109.2). He stays in shape by means of exercise, and through injury "he finds a means of putting himself to the proof (*experimentum sui capit*) and makes trial of his virtue" (*virtutem temptat: Const.* 9.3). For sage and *proficiens* alike, then, hardship and *askēsis* constitute a test and exhibition of who and what they are.

[139] VI,23,1–3 Hense = 52,12–15 Lutz. Cf. also III,11,16–20 Hense = 42,2–5 Lutz and VI,27,11–15 Hense = 56,7–11 Lutz.

[140] VI,23,8–11 Hense = 52,18–21 Lutz. The translation of Lutz has been modified slightly. Cf. also IV,15,18–19 Hense (= 44,34–35 Lutz).

[141] For the importance Musonius attaches to training and habituation in regard to hardship, cf. also IV,18,7–11 Hense (= 48,4–8 Lutz) and esp. XX,112,16–113,5 Hense (= 128,8–13 Lutz).

[142] For the terms "practice" (*meletē*) and "training" (*askēsis*) used together in Epictetus, cf. *Diss.* 1.25.31; 2.16.3,6. For "learning" and "practice," cf. 1.4.23–24; 29.52; 2.13.3–4; 16.8. For Epictetus' general treatment of *askēsis,* cf. Hijmans, ῎ΑΣΚΗΣΙΣ, esp. 64–91.

[143] This is the first of 3 areas into which Epictetus divides *askēsis.* The second involves

"introduces to us confusions, tumults, misfortunes and calamities; and sorrows, lamentations, envies" (3.2.3). Desire and aversion are to be restricted to things which lie within the province of a person's moral choice (προαίρεσις)[144] and over which one has control, for only these have to do with virtue![145] This task is not easy and can be accomplished only by means of great and constant training (3.12.5–6)![146] One must continually practice how to apply one's judgments about things good and evil (2.16) and thus how to make a proper use of one's external impressions (φαντασίαι)![147] treating the fear of death, not death itself, as the epitome of all ills that befall man (3.26.38–39; cf. also 2.1.13; 16.19; *Ench.* 5; 21).

Askēsis means that one must not only "learn the meaning of death, exile, prison, hemlock," but also "study how a man may rid his life of sorrows and lamentations, and of such cries as 'Woe is me!' and 'Wretch that I am!' and of misfortune and failure" (1.4.23–24). Toward this end one should practice doing such things as living the life of an invalid (3.13.21). To seek to evade hardships is futile, for "if you try to avoid disease, or death, or poverty, you will experience misfortune" (*Ench.* 2.1). One should strive instead to be like the true Cynic, fully prepared for any contingency (3.22.19–23), for thorough preparation is of inestimable value:

---

duty and social obligations, while the third concerns intellectual assent. Cf. esp. *Diss.* 2.17.15–16,31–33; 3.2.1–6; 12.1–17; and also 1.4.11; 21.2; 2.14.7–8; 3.22.31; 4.11.6.

[144] *Prohairesis* is an old moral term which literally means "fore-choice," "a choosing beforehand," "preference," "predilection." Aristotle emphasizes that it is both voluntary and intimately connected with virtue. Above all, it is rational, for it involves both *logos* and *dianoia*. It is closely related to deliberation (*bouleusis*) and defined by Aristotle as "a deliberate desire of things in our power." Cf. *Eth.Nic.* 3.2–3 (1111b4–1113a14) and the discussion of Aristotelian *prohairesis* by Richard Sorabji, "Aristotle on the Role of Intellect in Virtue," *Essays on Aristotle's Ethics* (ed. A. O. Rorty; Berkeley: University of California, 1980) 201–19, esp. 201–05. That *prohairesis* is the act of the intellect in Greek moral philosophy, Greek legal theory, and Greek thought generally is emphasized by Dihle, *Will*, 21, 32, 187 n. 90. Epictetus' use of *prohairesis* as a term for one's moral nature and attitude (in both choice and purpose) follows in this intellectual understanding of the term. Hijmans, ˇΑΣΚΗΣΙΣ, 24 n. 1, notes that the Aristotelian understanding "is in principle adopted by Epictetus," whose stress on the *prohairesis* sets him apart from other Stoics. For discussions of the term, cf. esp. A. Bonhöffer, *Epictet und die Stoa* (Stuttgart: Enke, 1890) 118–19, 259–61, and Hijmans, ˇΑΣΚΗΣΙΣ, 15, 23–27.

[145] Epict., *Diss.* 1.12.32. Cf. also A. J. Malherbe, "Epictetus," *IDBSup*, 271.

[146] For the necessity of practice and training to keep one's desire and aversion restricted to things that pertain to the *prohairesis*, cf. esp. *Diss.* 2.1.29; 3.3.14–19; 12.7–8; 24.84–85; 4.1.81–83,132; *Ench.* 1.5; 14.1; 47. For the failure to practice and its disastrous results, cf. 1.8.3–5; 25.31; 2.16 *passim*, esp. 18–21; 3.3.16–17; 24.5; 4.6.16.

[147] To make a correct use of one's external impressions involves, among other things, examining them to ensure that they are in accordance with nature and the divine will. Cf. 1.1.5,7,12; 7.33; 12.34; 20.5,7; 26.10; 27.1; 28.10; 2.1.4; 8.4,20; 18.20–21,27; 19.32; 22.25; 23.40; 3.1.25; 3.1; 22.20; 24.69; 4.3.7; frg. 9; etc. For exercise in dealing with impressions, cf. esp. 3.8.1–5 and also 2.18.27; 3.12.7; 4.4.26; and *Ench.* 1.5.

> For in every case it is a great help to be able to say, "I knew that the son whom I had begotten was mortal." For that is what you will say, and again, "I knew that I was mortal," "I knew that I was likely to leave home," "I knew that I was liable to banishment," "I knew that I might be sent off to prison" (3.24.105).

For the good man it is better to be overprepared than underprepared, to "expect worse and harsher treatment from the wicked than actually befalls him" (4.5.8). In this way he can count it as gain when his opponents fail to go to the limit with him:

> "So-and-so reviled you."
> I am greatly obliged to him for not striking me.
> "Yes, but he struck you too."
> I am greatly obliged to him for not wounding me.
> "Yes, but he wounded you too."
> I am greatly obliged to him for not killing me
> (4.5.8–9; my arrangement of Oldfather's LCL transl.).

When adversity arises, the philosopher is, first of all, to recall his training (1.30.7; 3.10.7; 4.4.12). Recalling what lies within his power and what not (1.1.11,21), he then is to respond to hardships accordingly:

> I must die: must I, then, die groaning too?
> I must be fettered: and wailing too?
> I must go into exile: does anyone, then, keep me from going with a smile and cheerful and serene?
> "Tell me your secrets." I say not a word; for this is under my control.
> "But I will fetter you." What is that you say, man?
> fetter *me?* My leg you will fetter, but my moral
> purpose not even Zeus himself has power to overcome.
> "I will throw you into prison." My paltry body, rather!
> "I will behead you." Well, when did I ever tell you that mine was the only neck that could not be severed?
> These are the lessons that philosophers ought to rehearse,
> these they ought to write down daily,
> in these they ought to exercise themselves (1.1.22–25; my arrangement of Oldfather's LCL transl.; cf. also 1.1.27,31).

As both the preceding and the following catalogues show, the secret of success in dealing with adversity involves a sharp distinction betwen one's self and one's body or parts thereof:

> When the tyrant threatens and summons me, I answer
> "Whom are you threatening?"
> If he says, "I will put you in chains," I reply,
> "He is threatening my hands, and my feet."
> If he says, "I will behead you," I answer,
> "He is threatening my neck."
> If he says, "I will throw you into prison," I say,
> "He is threatening my whole paltry body";

> and if he threatens me with exile,
> I give the same answer (1.29.5–6; my arrangement of Oldfather's LCL transl.; cf. also 1.29.7–8,10,12,14,22,24).

Training for adversity is what philosophy essentially concerns. "Let others practise lawsuits, others problems, others syllogisms; . . . you practise how to die, how to be enchained, how to be racked, how to be exiled" (2.1.38). "Will you not, as Plato says, study not merely to die, but even to be tortured on the rack, and to go into exile, and to be severely flogged, and, in a word, to give up everything that is not your own?" (4.1.172)![148] Furthermore, this applies not only to injuries but also to insults (3.12.10).

The training of the philosopher is arduous, analogous to the severity of training for the Olympics (3.15.2–4; *Ench.* 29.1–2). The man who would be a philosopher must first consider the demands of the life and then his own natural capacity to endure such demands. To become a philosopher is to begin training camp:

> Do you suppose that you can do the things you do now, and yet be a philosopher? Do you suppose that you can eat in the same fashion, drink in the same fashion, give way to anger and to irritation, just as you do now? You must keep vigils, work hard, overcome certain desires, abandon your own people, be despised by a paltry slave, be laughed to scorn by those who meet you, in everything get the worst of it, in office, in honour, in court. Look these drawbacks over carefully, and then, if you think best, approach philosophy, that is, if you are willing at the price of these things to secure tranquillity, freedom, and calm. Otherwise, do not approach (*Diss.* 3.15.10–12; cf. *Ench.* 29.6–7).

In this passage Epictetus is clearly stressing the rigors of the philosopher's life over against the tendency of many to take it up unmindful of its demands. As he warns in *Ench.* 22, "If you yearn for philosophy, prepare at once to be met with ridicule, to have many people jeer at you, and say, 'Here he is again, turned philosopher all of a sudden,' and 'Where do you suppose he got that high brow?' " (cf. 1 Pet 4:4). It takes an adult, not a child, to live in the way that Epictetus describes (3.15.5,12). The *Sitz im Leben* of this kind of speech is the school and it takes place at the beginning of a student's training. To be a philosopher, Epictetus emphasizes, demands suffering, and so this is stressed at the outset. This suffering begins in the training itself and never ceases, just as the athlete suffers both during training and in the contest itself (3.15.3–4; *Ench.* 29.2). Such warnings serve both to deter the non-serious student and to prepare the serious one for what lies ahead (1.2.32; 4.8.34–39; cf. 1 Thess 3:3–4).

The student who practices as he ought soon surpasses himself (2.16.4). Great power comes from exercise (1.8.7), especially when one does as one should and practices every day (1.1.25; 3.3.16; 8.1; 4.1.113), all day long (2.16.27), from dawn

[148] Cf. the discussion of Pl., *Resp.* 361E–362A in the following section of this chapter, and *Phd.* 64A.

till dusk (3.3.16; 4.1.111). Hardships, by exercising a person (1.6.34–36; 3.20.9–11; 4.4.18), make him stronger, thus helping him to make progress. The harder the exercise, the weightier the burden placed on his back, the greater the profit derived from the exercise (3.20.10). As one progresses, exercises that formerly were formidable become too easy, demanding too little exercise (1.29.34). The contrast between one who has practiced and one who has not becomes blatantly obvious (1.30.5; 2.13.22; 16.4). For "if you form the habit of taking such exercises, you will see what mighty shoulders you develop, what sinews, what vigour" (2.18.26). The proof of an athlete's training is seen in the change in his shoulders, that of the philosopher-athlete in the change in his governing principle (3.21.3). The adversary of each prepares him for the *agōn,* which in turn becomes a showcase for exhibiting both training and proficiency.

Severe, superior training is thus the key to the philosopher's victory and invincibility![149] Although he suffers in his *agōn,* he cannot be "upset" in either sense of the term, that is, he can be neither "conquered" nor "distressed." Epictetus has the sage proclaim his invincibility and its basis by means of a catalogue of hardships:

> The good man is invincible; naturally, for he enters no contest where he is not superior. "If you want my property in the country," says he, "take it; take my servants, take my office, take my paltry body. But you will not make my desire fail to get what I will, nor my aversion fall into what I would avoid." This is the only contest into which the good man enters, one, namely, that is concerned with the things which belong in the province of the moral purpose; how, then, can he help but be invincible? (3.6.5–7; cf. 1.29.10).

The sage is thus the invincible athlete, the undefeated champion who has no fear of losing. As such, in the contest of his choosing he wants a worthy opponent. He is like the athletes who "are displeased with youths of light weight: 'He cannot lift me,' says one. 'Yonder is a sturdy young man' " (1.29.34), viz., one who will give him a good workout and exercise him. He is like those gladiators "who complain because no one brings them out, or matches them with an antagonist," who "pray to God and go to their managers, begging to fight in single combat" (1.29.37) so that they will be tested sufficiently. Yet nothing is a match for him:

> Who, then, is the invincible man? He whom nothing that is outside the sphere of his moral purpose can dismay. I then proceed to consider the circumstances (*peristaseis*) one by one, as I would do in the case of the athlete. "This fellow has won the first round. What, then, will he do in the second? What if it be scorching

[149] Marcus Aurelius also stresses readiness and training. On readiness, especially for adversity, cf. *Med.* 4.12; 7.61,68; 10.35; 11.3,13,19. This readiness entails having at one's disposal various reflections (3.13.1), such as the thought that everything that happens "is a familiar sight" (7.1), including "disease and death and slander and treachery" (4.44). Cf. also 7.64; 8.49; 12.1.2. For training, practice, and exercise, cf. 5.5; 6.53; 10.11; 12.3,6; for the results of training, cf. esp. 10.14. For *askēsis* in rabbinic Judaism, cf. *'Abot* 6.4; *'Abot R. Nat.* 5; and Fischel, *Rabbinic Literature,* 460, 464.

hot? And what will he do at Olympia?" It is the same way with the case under consideration.

If you put a bit of silver coin in a man's way he will despise it.
Yes, but if you put a bit of a wench in his way, what then?
Or, if it be in the dark, what then?
Or if you throw a bit of reputation in his way, what then?
Or abuse, what then?
Or praise, what then?
Or death, what then?
All these he can overcome.
What, then, if it be scorching hot—that is,
What if he be drunk?
What if he be melancholy-mad?
What if asleep?
The man who passes all these tests is what I mean by the invincible athlete (1.18.21–23).[150]

The sage's victory in the *agōn* of life is also extolled by Dio Chrysostom, who has Diogenes the Cynic give the following depiction of the "noble" and "perfect" man:

> The noble man holds his hardships to be his greatest antagonists, and with them he is ever wont to do battle day and night. . . . He is afraid of none of those opponents nor does he pray to draw another antagonist, but challenges them one after another, grappling with hunger and cold, withstanding thirst, and disclosing no weakness even though he must endure the lash or give his body to be cut or burned. Hunger, exile, loss of reputation, and the like have no terrors for him; nay, he holds them as mere trifles, and while in their very grip the perfect man is often as sportive as boys with their dice and their coloured balls (*Or.* 8.15–16).[151]

Dio's Diogenes, moreover, claims the laurel of victory for himself and enumerates the opponents he has defeated:

> Many and mighty antagonists have I vanquished, not like these slaves who are now wrestling here, hurling the discus and running, but more difficult in every way—I mean poverty, exile, and disrepute; yes, and anger, pain, desire, fear, and the most redoubtable beast of all, treacherous and cowardly, I mean pleasure. . . . (*Or.* 9.11–12; cf. also 8.11–13,26).

It must not be forgotten, however, that the sage's victory was a paradoxical one. He *was* defeated in matters pertaining to the body, but *never* in regard to

150 The arrangement of Oldfather's LCL translation is mine. For the first part of the catalogue, compare the similar sequence in 2.22.11. For the items in the second part, cf. 2.17.33; 3.2.5; and also Plut., *Mor.* 82F. The truly invincible person is thus a veritable god (2.17.33) who is not even taken unawares by an unexamined impression, an accomplishment that an interlocutor finds "beyond us," that is, beyond our power (3.2.5).

151 On this passage, cf. esp. R. Höistad, "Eine hellenistische Parallele zu 2. Kor. 6.3ff," *ConNT* 9 (1944) 22–27. The perfect man discloses no weakness because of his rigorous training; cf. Dio Chrys., *Or.* 60.5; 68.2; and also 18.6; 22.2; 28.7; 29.9.

matters of the mind. This paradoxical invincibility was often celebrated in *peristasis* catalogues, and the following example may serve to conclude and summarize this section:

The sage of the Stoics
is not impeded when confined
and under no compulsion when flung down a precipice
and not in torture when on the rack
and not injured when mutilated
and is invincible when thrown in wrestling
and is impregnable when besieged
and is uncaptured while his enemies are selling him
into slavery (Plut., *Mor.* 1057D–E)![152]

The Righteous Sufferer as the "Foolish" Wise Man

In the material examined thus far, the good man and the wise man are one and the same. Since the experience of suffering does not alter this fact, the suffering sage is identical with the righteous sufferer. This is the standard perspective in philosophical circles, but it is not unopposed. In strong opposition to it stands another view, according to which the truly good man is a fool. The *locus classicus* for the foolish righteous sufferer[153] appears in book two of Plato's *Republic*, where it occurs as part of Glaucon's presentation of the common understanding of justice (357A–362C).

As to the nature and origin of justice, the common view is that it is "a compromise between the best, which is to do wrong with impunity, and the worst, which is to be wronged and be impotent to get one's revenge" (359A). Injustice is then the intrinsic good, and justice is only an instrumental good. Men practice justice out of powerlessness and do so with reluctance (359B–360D). Given the opportunity every man would be a Gyges, for each prefers πλεονεξία to ἰσότης (359C–D). The man who had ἐξουσία and failed to employ it to his own advantage would be viewed by men of discernment as an utter fool (360D), for he would be mad to refuse to do so (359B). The wise, of course, praise in public such a fool and thereby encourage the just man in his folly, for by so doing they protect themselves from suffering at his hands (360D; cf. also 348D–349D).

Glaucon concludes his depiction of the common view of justice and its rationale by giving a *synkrisis* of the perfectly just and the perfectly unjust man (360E–362C). The perfectly unjust man is one who is completely adept at acting unjustly, yet has the greatest reputation for justice. To *seem* just but to *be* unjust

[152] The LCL translation of Cherniss has been modified slightly. On this passage, cf. esp. A. Fridrichsen, "Zum Thema 'Paulus und die Stoa'. Eine stoische Stilparallele zu 2. Kor. 4,8f.," *ConNT* 9 (1944) 27–31.

[153] The motif of the "righteous sufferer" is an old one in Greek literature, one which appears already in both Homer (*Od.* 4.695; 22.319; cf. also *Il.* 9.316; 17.147) and Hesiod (*Op.* 190–92; cf. also 202–24).

is the best of both worlds, as the catalogue of his blessings makes clear (362B–C).

The perfectly just man, on the other hand, has the worst possible situation. He *is* just, but to all concerned he *seems* unjust. As a consequence he suffers all the penalties that the unjust man deserves, yet he enjoys none of the blessings that are reserved for the just man. It is here that Glaucon gives a catalogue of the sufferings that the perfectly just man who seems unjust will experience. Having apologized for the coarseness of the catalogue, he gives it as follows:

> Since he is so disposed, the just man will be scourged,
> he will be racked,
> he will be bound in chains,
> he will have both eyes burned out,
> and, finally, after suffering every kind of evil,
> he will be crucified,
> and he will know that one ought to wish, not to be just,
> but only to seem so (361E–362A)![154]

Socrates' (Plato's) rebuttal to these arguments can be seen most clearly toward the end of book 10, where the discussion returns to points raised at the beginning of book 2. Having already established justice as an intrinsic good, Socrates here seeks to complete his argument for justice by showing that it is an instrumental good as well. Whereas the masses think that the unjust are loved by the gods (362C), he maintains that it is the just man who is so loved, and "all things that come from the gods work together for the best for him that is dear to the gods" (612E–613A; cf. also *Ap.* 41D).

> This, then, must be our conviction about the just man, that whether he fall into poverty or disease or any other supposed evil, for him all these things will finally prove good, both in life and in death (613A).

Furthermore, the man loved by the gods, says Socrates, cannot fail to obtain favor in the human community. In most cases the just man ends his life in honor (613C) and with the sort of blessings that the masses claim for the unjust (613D). The opposite is generally true of the unjust. In most cases they suffer the

[154] The translation is mine. According to Ernst Benz, "Der gekreuzigte Gerechte bei Plato, im Neuen Testament und in der alten Kirche," *Akademie der Wissenschaften und der Literatur* (Abhandl. d. Geistes- u. Sozialwiss. Klasse; Mainz: Verlag d. Akademie d. Wissensch. u.d. Lit., 1950) 1029–74, this catalogue represents Plato's re-working of a "passion prediction" made by Socrates about himself. Benz's thesis has been satisfactorily refuted by Hildebrecht Hommel, *Schöpfer und Erhalter* (Berlin: Lettner, 1956) 23–32; and J. Rouwet, "De Lijdende Rechtvaardige bij Plato," *Studia Catholica* 30 (1955) 105–18. For additional criticisms, cf. also W. G. Kümmel's review in *TLZ* 77 (1952) 423–25, and A. Oepke, "Plato Resp II 5,361e eine unbewusste Weissagung auf Christi Passion?," *TLZ* 78 (1953) 639–40. As Hommel in particular points out, the source of this catalogue of punishments (363E) is not a passion prediction by Socrates but rather the list of non-Athenian penalties found in *Grg.* 473C. Th catalogue is thus another example of the barbarian catalogues of tortures mentioned in note 6 above.

unpleasant fate of being derided. To them, moreover, falls the catalogue of punishments that Glaucon gave for the unknown just man:

> They are lashed and suffer all things which you truly said are unfit for ears polite; [then they will be racked and branded.] Suppose yourself to have heard from me a repetition of all they suffer (613D).[155]

As this sketch of the argument shows, the Socrates of the *Republic* utterly repudiates the idea that Glaucon advanced in Book 2.[156] This fact was sometimes forgotten, but Glaucon's *synkrisis* of the perfectly just and unjust men was remembered and became extremely popular in the Graeco-Roman period. Not only was the catalogue of the just man's sufferings adapted and reproduced, in whole or in part,[157] but it also inspired new formulations.

Glaucon's *synkrisis* inspired and informed, for example, Carneades' famous speech against justice, delivered in Rome in 155 B.C.E. This speech in turn inspired sections of Cicero's *De Republica,* which contains in the third book one of the most extensive Hellenistic depictions of the righteous sufferer. Philus, who plays the role of Glaucon and presents the case for injustice, tries to demonstrate that justice is equivalent to folly. His argument, complete with contrasting catalogues, is as follows:

> I put the question to you: Let us suppose that there are two men, one of whom is thoroughly upright and honorable, a man of consummate justice and unique integrity, while the other is a man of extraordinary depravity and shamelessness. And let us assume that the state in which they live is so misguided as to believe the good man a monster of unspeakable criminality, while, on the other hand, it considers the scoundrel to be a model of uprightness and good faith. Let us suppose further that, in conformity with this error on the part of all the citizens, the good man is persecuted, harassed, has his hands cut off and his eyes gouged out, is condemned, cast into chains, tortured by fire, exiled and reduced to destitution. Finally, let us assume that he is universally regarded as justly meriting his wretched condition. On the other hand, let us suppose that the evil man is praised, honored, and esteemed by all; that all sorts of offices, civil and military, and every form of influence and

[155] The translation is that of Shorey, but I have inserted his translation of the bracketed material into his translation of the text. The material enclosed in the brackets may well be an interpolation. Ast, Hermann, and Stallbaum omit it from their editions, but Jowett-Campbell and Burnett retain it. Although I incline to the view that it is an interpolation, I have retained it for the translation.

[156] Cf. esp. the discussion by Rouwet, "De Lijdende Rechtvaardige bij Plato," 105–18.

[157] The catalogue of the just man's sufferings was extremely popular in Christian circles. Cf. *Acta Apollonii* 40; Clem. Al., *Str.* 4.7.52.1 (2.272.11–12 Stählin); 5.14.108–203 (2.398.18–23 Stählin); Eus., *Praep.Evang.* 12.10 (583c–d); and Theod., *Gr.aff.cur.* 8.50 (*PG* 83.1012). Cf. also the applications in Clem. Al., *Str.* 4.7.52.3 (2.272.15–19 Stählin) and Eus., *Praep.Evang.* 12.10 (584b–c). In non-Christian circles it is adapted by Epictetus, *Diss.* 4.1.172, and, as Martin Hengel, *Crucifixion* (Philadelphia: Fortress, 1977) 28, 83, tentatively suggests, Glaucon's catalogue lies back of Lucian, *Pisc.* 2.

> wealth are conferred upon him; and that he is universally held to be an excellent man, fully deserving the best gifts fortune can bestow. I ask you then: Who under these circumstances will be so mad (*tam demeans*) as to doubt which of the two lots he would prefer? (3.17.27)![158]

The disparate experiences of the just and unjust man are used here to argue that enlightened self-interest dictates that injustice is to be pursued rather than justice. In support of this Philus catalogues 10 hardships that the just man will experience, and not all of them are punishments. How the just man appears to the world is now one of the hardships that he suffers. Indeed, it is the climactic one (*postremo . . . omnibus misserimus esse videatur*). This hardship, which is contrasted with the universal esteem that the unjust man receives, compounds the just man's duress and thus gives special impetus to the question generated by the comparison: who is so demented as to choose the life of justice? From this perspective, then, the righteous sufferer is a fool, not a sage.

The Philosopher's Demeanor

Whether derided as a fool or acknowledged as a sage the ideal philosopher reveals his sagacity in the way that he responds to his adversaries. Injury and insult[159] provide the perfect situation for this demonstration, for "the power of wisdom is better shown by a display of calmness in the midst of provocation" (Sen., *Const.* 4.3; cf. also *Ep.* 94.74).

According to Seneca, "it is a petty and sorry person who will bite back when he is bitten" (*Ira* 2.34.1; cf. also Arist., *De An.* 403). Even Philip did not retaliate when cursed (*Ira* 3.24.1). At the very least the good man does not become angry with the ungrateful, but rather pardons them (*Ben.* 5.17.3), for he is "mild and indulgent" to his enemies (*V.B.* 20.5) and even with the vilest of men his sword is sheathed and his mercy is "ever ready at hand" (*Clem.* 1.1.3–4; cf. also Suet., *Vesp.* 14). Indeed, since "the wise man . . . enjoys the giving more than the recipient enjoys the receiving" (*Ep.* 81.10; cf. also Acts 20:35), he is ready to give aid even to his enemies (*Ot.* 1.4; *Ben.* 7.31.5). More fundamental, however, is the conviction that "the mark of true greatness is not to notice that you have received a blow" (*Ira* 3.25.3; cf. also 2.32.2), for it shows more character to refuse to acknowledge that an insult has been offered than to acknowledge and pardon it (*Const.* 13.5; 14.3). It is, moreover, to respond in a manner that is commensurate

[158] The translation is that of G. H. Sabine and S. B. Smith, *On the Commonwealth: Marcus Tullius Cicero* (Columbus: Ohio State University, 1929) 212–13. Lactantius quotes Cic., *Resp.* 3.17.27 in full in his *Div.Inst.* 5.12.5–6 and applies it to Christians (5.12.7–8). He also gives the catalogue of hardships a second time in 5.18.9, this time without its companion catalogue of the unjust's blessings.

[159] Seneca regards injuries as more serious than insults (*Const.* 5.1), whereas Caecilius (*com.* 47 = 43–44 Warmington) reverses this judgment, as Nonius (430,10) correctly observes. For Musonius Rufus, being struck is harder to bear than being verbally reviled or spit upon (X,52,9–10 Hense = 76,19–20 Lutz). In this regard, cf. also Dem., *Meid.* 72.

with the failure of insults and injuries to have an impact on the true self. Thus, "let some men think you even a fool. Allow any man who so desires to insult you and work you wrong; for if virtue dwells in you, you will suffer nothing" (*Ep.* 71.7)![160]

In giving specific recommendations for how one should react to abuse and thus indicating how the sage rsponds in various circumstances, Seneca notes that Augustus was a good "father" inasmuch as "he did not avenge with cruelty even the personal insults which usually sting a prince even more than wrongs, [and] because when he was the victim of lampoons he smiled" (*Clem.* 1.10.3). This smile or laugh can be scornful, as when a person laughs while being flogged (*Ep.* 13.5). An example of scornful smiling was given by "Aristides" (Phocion)[161] when he smiled in response to someone spitting in his face (*Helv.* 13.7; cf. also *Ep.* 76.4).

Best of all, Seneca advises, "if someone strikes you, step back; for by striking back you will give him both the opportunity and the excuse to repeat his blow" (*Ira* 2.34.5). Besides, vengeance is foolish. "How much better it is to take the opposite course and not to match fault with fault . . . How much better it is to heal than to avenge an injury!" (*Ira* 3.27.1; cf. also 1.14.3). The philosopher's "aim is to bear with an ungrateful man so long that he will in the end become grateful" (*Ben.* 5.1.5; cf. also 7.31.1).

Finally, while the sage typically either ignores an offense due to its lack of internal impact or responds to it derisively with a smile or a laugh (*Const.* 10.4), there are times when he will respond more actively to insult and injury. But when he does so, it is for the benefit of those who maltreat him:

> And so the wise man not improperly considers insult from such men as a farce, and sometimes, just as if they were children, he will admonish them and inflict suffering and punishment, not because he has received an injury, but because they have committed one, and in order that they may desist from so doing. . . . For he is not avenging himself, but correcting them (*Const.* 12.3)![162]

Seneca's portrait of the sage's response to his adversaries has clearly been influenced by the Platonic conviction that doing a wrong is far worse than suffering one (Pl., *Grg.* 509C; Sen., *Ep.* 95.52). It is wrong to requite evil with evil, no

[160] The LCL translation of Gummere has been slightly modified. Seneca's thought derives ultimately from Pl., *Grg.* 527C–D.

[161] As Basore, *Seneca: Moral Essays,* 2.464, correctly observes, Plutarch tells this same story of Phocion (*Phoc.* 36.1–2). For Phocion as an example of how to respond to abuse, cf. Ael., *VH* 2.16; 12.49; Mar. Ant., *Med.* 11.13; Mus. Ruf., X,55,2–9 Hense (= 78,16–22 Lutz).

[162] Cf. also *Ira* 1.16.1. If Bailey is correct, the text of *Vit.Epicur.* 121^{b},5–6, says the Epicurean sage "will rejoice at another's misfortune, but only for his correction." For admonition as the proper response to abuse, cf. Plut., frg. 40 Sandbach. On admonition and reproof as the philosopher's task, cf. Dio Chrys., *Or.* 8.5; 33.10; 77/78.38,42; and Plut., *Mor.* 168C.

matter how severe the sufferings one may endure in consequence of the refusal to retaliate in kind (Pl., *Cri.* 49A–D; *Theat.* 173A; cf. also *Grg.* 479E). The conventional morality of helping friends and harming enemies is totally to be rejected![163]

It is clear that Plato's scathing criticism of conventional morality led most philosophers to reject retaliation as the appropriate response to abuse (cf. Juv., *Sat.* 13.174–92, esp. 181–87). Despite different perspectives on the relation of anger to virtue, it was widely held that a disposition devoid of anger "is certainly the mark of a wise man" (Ps-Plut., *Mor.* 10B–C). "I will be kindly and good-natured to everyone," says Marcus Aurelius, "and ready to show even my enemy where he has seen amiss [by scorning or hating me], not by way of rebuke nor with a parade of forbearance, but genuinely and chivalrously" (*Med.* 11.13; cf. also 6.26; 7.22).

This is clearly the view of Musonius Rufus, who fully accepts the Platonic thesis that doing a wrong is worse than suffering one (III,11,7 Hense = 40,30 Lutz; X,54,2–3 Hense = 78,4–5 Lutz). In keeping with this view, in Frg. X he argues strongly against retaliation. For him, the philosopher "would never prosecute anyone for personal injury . . . such as being reviled or struck or spit upon" (52,5–10 Hense = 76,16–20 Lutz; cf. also 53,5–6 Hense = 76,26 Lutz), for "the sensible man would not go to law nor bring indictments, since he would not even consider that he had been insulted" (54,7–8 Hense = 78,7–9 Lutz). Instead of proceeding with lawsuits (as would an Epicurean: Diog. Laert. 10.120), the philosopher should "deem worthy of forgiveness anyone who wrongs him" (56,10–11 Hense = 78,34–80,1 Lutz). Musonius praises Phocion for his refusal to acknowledge that his wife was reviled (55,2–9 Hense = 78,16–22 Lutz) and proceeds to say that

> I might mention many other men who have experienced insult, some wronged by word, others by violence and bodily harm, who do not appear to have defended their rights against their assailants nor to have proceeded against them in any other way, but very meekly bore their wrong. And in this they were quite right. For to scheme how to bite back the biter and to return evil for evil is the act not of a human being but of a wild beast, which is incapable of reasoning that the majority of wrongs are done to men through ignorance and misunderstanding, from which man will cease

[163] For the conventional morality, cf. Solon, frg. 1.5–6 Diehl (= frg. 13.5–6 Edmonds); Theog. 869–72; Aesch., *Cho.* 123, 145–46; Pind., *Pyth.* 2.82–85; Isoc., *Demonicus* 26; Xen., *An.* 1.9.11; *Mem.* 2.3.14; 2.6.35; Pl., *Meno* 71E; *Resp.* 332D; 334B; 362B; and also Matt 5:43. Whether or to what extent the historical Socrates rejected the conventional morality depends in part on one's assessment of Xen., *Mem.* 2.6.35. For a lapse by Seneca into the conventional morality, cf. *Ep.* 81.7. On non-retaliation in the philosophical tradition, cf. esp. Albrecht Dihle, *Die goldene Regel: Eine Einführung in die Geschichte der antiken und frühchristlichen Vulgärethik* (Göttingen: Vandenhoeck & Ruprecht, 1962) 61–71. Cf. also Schneider, *Christliche Klänge*, 323–25, and the praise of non-retaliation in *b. Sabb.* 88b.

> as soon as he has been taught. But to accept injury not in a spirit of savage resentment and to show ourselves not implacable toward those who wrong us, but rather to be a source of good hope to them is characteristic of a benevolent and civilized way of life (55,9–56,9 Hense = 78,22–33 Lutz).

The teachings of Musonius find an echo in his student Epictetus. One of his discourses carries the title "That we ought not to be angry with men" (*Diss.* 1.28), and another "That we ought not to be angry with the erring" (1.18). Instead of growing angry, "when someone treats you ill or speaks ill of you, remember that he acts or speaks thus because he thinks it is incumbent upon him." By bringing this to mind, "you will be gentle with the man who reviles you" (*Ench.* 42). The sage, accordingly, "will be always straightforward to one who is like himself, while to one who is unlike he will be tolerant, gentle, kindly, forgiving, as to one who is ignorant or is making a mistake in things of the greatest importance; he will not be harsh with anybody" (*Diss.* 2.22.36). His gentleness is indicative of the sage's unique affection for all, for "the power to love belongs to the wise man and to him alone" (2.22.3). This love is seen most clearly in the true Cynic sage, for "he must needs be flogged like an ass, and while he is being flogged he must love the men who flog him, as though he were the father or brother of them all" (3.22.54). When he himself is finally forced to revile someone, he does so in this spirit and capacity (3.22.82).[164]

Finally, in the view of the Platonist orator Maximus of Tyre, anger, indignation, vengeance, disgust, and vexation are all inappropriate responses to abuse.[165] By no means, moreover, does the just man return an injury, for the avenger is more unjust than the one who inflicted the harm initially (*Or.* 12.9b = 155,10 Hobein). The good man who attempts to return an injury will only suffer defeat and become ridiculous (12.9f–g = 156,8–16). This refusal by the just man to engage in retribution means that he may suffer severely as a consquence:

> But as a result, some on may say, the just man is treated with indignity, slandered, persecuted, deprived of his possessions, cast into prison, goes into exile, is dishonored, and dies (12.10a = 156,17–20 Hobein; my transl.).

If such is his lot, the just man will accept it and regard the attack on his person and property as puerile. Indeed, for Maximus, the proper response is basically derisive laughter, accompanied by disdain and despite (3.2b = 31,21–32,1; cf. also 36.5c = 421,6). He sees this as Socrates' response to the Athenians and argues that

> in like manner every other good and just man will laugh with utter derision when he sees the unjust eagerly rushing against him, viz., those who think they can

[164] For a positive example of a philosopher (Cleanthes) responding to abuse, cf. Diog. Laert. 7.173. For the failure of philosophers to respond in the appropriate manner, cf. Plut., frg. 40 Sandbach, and esp. Hor., *Sat.* 1.3.133–36. Cf. also Julian, *Misopogon* 337a–b.

[165] For the first 3 terms, cf. *Or.* 12.8a (154,8–9 Hobein). For the fourth and fifth, cf. 3.2b (32,6) and 12.10e (157,16).

accomplish something, yet accomplish nothing. But if they dishonor him, he will utter the saying of Achilles, "I deem I have been honored by the ordinance of Zeus." And if they deprive him of his possessions, he will permit it as if playthings and dice were being taken away, and he will die as if by a fever or stone, without any vexation toward his killers (*Or.* 12.10d–e = 157,8–17 Hobein; my transl.; cf. also Pl., *Ap.* 41D).

Praise and Self-Praise

The suffering sage is clearly worthy of the highest praise. According to Aristotle, "praise is an utterance making manifest the greatness of a virtue" (*Rh.* 1.9).[166] To praise someone is to recognize his worth as an individual and to bestow on him the honor that is his due.[167] Genuine praise grows out of admiration and fondness,[168] and it testifies that a person is worthy of being imitated.[169] While praise can serve to increase virtue (Dio Chrys., *Or.* 21.2), the value of praise depends ultimately on the one who gives it. The praise of the ignorant masses is illusory and irrelevant; it is the testimony and commendation of the expert that is both desirable and decisive (Dio Chrys., *Or.* 77/78.17–25; Epict., *Diss.* 2.5.23).

It is, moreover, crucial that praise be bestowed appropriately (Pind., *Pyth.* 1.42–45; Aesch., *Ag.* 785–87). During the Graeco-Roman period the basic orientation to the topics and techniques of proper laudation was provided in the secondary school, for the encomium was one of the introductory exercises (*progymnasmata*) in which students received training.[170] While a person obviously could be praised for many things (such as health or wealth), it was especially his virtue that commended him.[171] Furthermore, it was the exhibition

[166] The translation is that of Lane Cooper (trans.), *The Rhetoric of Aristotle* (New York: Appleton-Century-Crofts, 1960) 52. For the intimate and ubiquitous connection between virtue and its praise, cf. Dio Chrys., *Or.* 69.1. For *gloria* as the constant shadow of virtue, cf. Sen., *Ep.* 79.13.

[167] Cf. Dem., *Or.* 2.27; Sen., *Ep.* 77.6; *Tranq.* 16.3; Dio Chrys., *Or.* 31.111; and also Pind., *Nem.* 8.39. For the idea that praise and the acknowledgement of achievement is a social obligation basic to the existence of a community, cf. Georges Dumézil, *Servius et la Fortune: Essai sur la fonction sociale de louange et de blâme sur les éléments indo-européens du cens romain* (Paris: Gallimard, 1943), and Crotty, *Song and Action*, 55–62.

[168] Cf. Dio Chrys., *Or.* 18.1,3; 47.4; 51.2; 69.1; Sen., *Ep.* 66.29.

[169] Cf. Sen., *Ep.* 54.7: *lauda et imitare.* Cf. also Max. Tyr., *Or.* 1.7a (11,16–17 Hobein).

[170] Cf. H. I. Marrou, *A History of Education in Antiquity* (Mentor Books; New York: The New American Library, 1964) 272–73.

[171] Virtue was universally acknowledged as a legitimate basis for pride; the dispute among philosophers centered on whether it was the *only* thing of which one might legitimately be proud. Cf. Cic., *Fin.* 4.18.50–51 and also Epict., *Diss.* 2.1.35–36, who limits praise and pride to accomplishments in regard to desire and aversion. Compare Sen., *Ep.* 41.7–8.

of virtue in situations of danger and difficulty that was traditionally accorded the greatest praise.[172] And in this regard the ancient rule of thumb was quite simple: "the greater the difficulty, the greater the glory" (Cic., *Off.* 1.19.64).[173]

As a corollary to the idea that virtue becomes most conspicuous in times of adversity, the conviction is frequently voiced that praise and glory depend on adversity for their very existence. Seneca, for example, says of "sickness, pain, poverty, exile, death," that "nothing can be glorious without them" (*Ep.* 82.10–11; cf. also *Prov.* 3.4). Ovid, in exhorting his wife to endure his exile, provides her with a catalogue of wives whose fame is totally dependent on their husbands' misfortunes. The experiences of Penelope, Euadne, Alcestis, and Laodamia illustrate for him the thesis that "uprightness schooled by adversity in time of sorrow affords a theme for praise" (*Tr.* 5.549–60).

The same sentiments occur in *Oration* 34 of Maximus of Tyre, who says with reference to Socrates, Plato, Xenophon, and Diogenes, that "if you take from them the struggle for good, you deprive the men of their crowns and stop the proclamation of their victory" (34.9f = 401,5–6 Hobein). In support of this contention he provides a catalogue of hardships suffered by the Athenians at Marathon:

> Take from the Athenians the course to Marathon,
> the death there,
> the hand of Cynaegirus,
> the calamity of Polyzelus,
> the wounds of Callimachus,
> and you leave to the Athenians nothing venerable,
> except the incredible fable of Erichthonius and Cecrops![174]

It must be emphasized that it is the exercise and display of virtue that is praiseworthy, *not* adversity itself![175] For Stoics in particular, difficult circumstances elicit the virtues and provide them with a field for action, but are in and of themselves indifferent. Speaking in regard to sickness, pain, poverty, exile, and

[172] Cic., *Off.* 1.18.61; cf. also Sen., *Ep.* 82.17; *Clem.* 1.5.3; *Helv.* 13.6. This is one of the reasons why hardships are a typical topic in the ancient encomium. Theon, for example, includes "braving risks and dangers" among the things for which a person may be eulogized. Cf. Marrou, *History of Education,* 273. For the topic of hardships in the athletic encomium, cf. Dio Chrys., *Or.* 29.11–12 and the discussion by C. P. Jones, *The Roman World of Dio Chrysostom* (Cambridge: Harvard, 1978) 17.

[173] Cf. also Sen., *Ben.* 6.25.4; 36.2; 38.2. On the basic idea of deriving honor from adversity, cf. Epict., *Diss.* 3.20.13; 21.9.

[174] Max. Tyr., *Or.* 34.9g = 401,6–11 Hobein. Taylor's translation of 34.9f–g has been modified, and the arrangement of the translation of 34.9g is mine.

[175] Even in the encomium on hardships (cf., for example Epict., frg. 21) the praise is directed at the utility of hardships in regard to virtue, not at the hardships themselves.

death, Seneca makes precisely this point and illustrates it with a catalogue of hardships:

> None of these things is intrinsically glorious; but nothing can be glorious apart from them. For it is not poverty that we praise, it is the man whom poverty cannot humble or bend. Nor is it exile that we praise, it is the man who withdraws into exile in the spirit in which he would have sent another into exile. It is not pain that we praise, it is the man whom pain has not coerced. One praises not death, but the man whose soul death takes away before it can confound it. All these things are in themselves neither honourable nor glorious; but any one of them that virtue has visited and touched is made honourable and glorious by virtue; they merely lie in between, and the decisive question is only whether wickedness or virtue has laid hold upon them (*Ep.* 82.11–12).

The praise accorded others for their triumph over adversity and for other achievements could naturally be directed to oneself for the same or similar accomplishments. Despite the fact that speech about oneself (περιαυτολογία) was generally viewed as offensive and excitative of envy and hatred, self-laudation was a frequent practice in the Greek and Roman worlds. Precisely because of its frequency and the odium attached to it, rhetoricians and ethicists gave particular attention to the situations in which it was permissible to praise oneself and the methods for doing so inoffensively.[176]

The most extensive treatment of self-praise is that given by Plutarch in his *De laude ipsius* (*Mor.* 539A–547F), who lists a variety of "antidotes" that serve to render self-glorification not only palatable but even beneficial.[177] The situation par excellence in which self-praise is justified is that of defending oneself against slander or an accusation (540C–541A).[178] This *Sitz im Leben* clearly requires one to speak the truth about oneself (539D), so that one boasts from necessity and not for glory (541A; 542E).[179] In this setting one may even "confess" to the

[176] For rhetorical discussions of inoffensive self-praise, cf. esp. Quint., *Inst.* 11.1.15–28; Alexander Rhetor, *On Rhetorical Means* (3.4.9–14 Spengel); Ps-Aristides, *Concerning Civil and Simple Speech* 12.2.7 (2.506.8–20 Spengel); and Ps-Hermogenes, *On Aids for a Vigorous Style* 25 (441,15–442,21 Rabe). Cf. also the commentary of Gregory of Corinth on the latter in Walz, *Rhetores Graeci,* 7.1298–1301.

[177] For bibliography and an excellent analysis of this treatise, cf. H. D. Betz, "De laude ipsius (Moralia 539A–547F)," in H. D. Betz (ed.), *Plutarch's Ethical Writings and Early Christian Literature* (Studia ad Corpus Hellenisticum Novi Testamenti 4; Leiden: Brill, 1978) 367–93.

[178] For self-praise as part of an *apologia,* cf. Gorgias, B 11a.27–32 (2.301.3–302.16 Diels-Kranz); Dem., *Or.* 18 (= *De Cor.*) *passim* (in regard to which, cf. also Aeschin., *Or.* 3. [= *In Ctes.*] 241; Quint., *Inst.* 11.1.18,22–23).

[179] For *anagkē* as the justification for self-praise, cf. also Gorgias B 11a.28,32 (2.301.12; 302.15 Diels-Kranz), where it forms an *inclusio* for the self-laudation; Dem., *Or.* 18.4; Quint., *Inst.* 11.1.18,22–23; Ps-Aristides, *Concerning Civil and Simple Speech* 12.2.7 (2.506.10–12 Spengel); and Ps-Hermogenes, *On Aids for a Vigorous Style* 25 (441,27; 442,6–11 Rabe). Cf. also Plut., *Comp. Dem. et Cic.* 2.1. Related to this is the idea that even

charges but claim that they are really triumphs in which one may glory (541E–F), and demonstrate this by contrasting one's own deeds with what is truly shameful (541F–542A).[180] Again, as long as self-praise is part of the boldness that is shown in calling for justice when one has been wronged, it is appropriate (541C–E).

Another basic situation in which self-praise is legitimate is that of adversity or peril (541A–C). In this case, "the man cast down by fortune, when he stands upright in fighting posture . . ., using self-glorification to pass from a humbled and piteous state to an attitude of triumph and pride, strikes us not as offensive or bold, but as great and indomitable" (541B). Indeed, to point to the hardships and perils undertaken for the benefit of others and to the neglect of one's own affairs is one of the best subjects of self-laudation (544C–D).[181]

Whatever the situation, however, it is as appropriate as it is modest to credit one's success either to luck or to God (542E–543A; 543C), giving the glory to the divine (541C; cf. also Quint., *Inst.* 11.1.23; Cic., *Fam.* 15.5.2).[182] Modesty is also shown in refusing to lay claim to the attainment of wisdom and restricting oneself to the status of a *proficiens* enamoured of wisdom. Self-praise is thus to be tempered by the confession of minor shortcomings, failures, and faults (543E–544C);[183] and mixed with the praise of others (542B–C; cf. also Cic., *Inv.* 1.16.22).

Self-aggrandizement is, moreover, to have the good of others as one of its goals.[184] It is much easier for a speaker to make use of his virtue and do others good where there is affection for him and confidence in him rather than dislike

---

the most arrogant of assertions may be made without offending others, provided that one is speaking toward one's adversaries.

[180] On this point, cf. esp. L. Radermacher, "Plutarchs Schrift de ipso citra invidiam laudando," *RhM* 52 (1897) 422.

[181] Self-laudation in regard to hardships is quite common. One finds boasting, for example, in regard to working day and night (Cic., *Sen.* 23.82; cf. 1 Thess 2:9), the meagerness of one's diet (Sen., *Ep.* 18.9), the simplicity of one's life (Ps-Diog., *Ep.* 27 =118,16–17 Malherbe), and one's patient endurance, be it *patientia* (Cic., *Tusc.* 2.14.33), *constantia* under torture, pain, and death (Lactant., *Div.Inst.* 5.14) or *hypomonē* under frightful circumstances (Ps-Diog., *Ep.* 27 (118,17–18 Malherbe). For boasting in regard to poverty, cf. esp. Apul., *Apol.* 17–23 and the discussion by Paul Vallette, *L'Apologie d'Apulée* (Paris: C. Klincksieck, 1908) 129–57. On exile and boasting, cf. Dio Chrys., *Or.* 45.1–2.

[182] Cf. also Plut., *Per.* 38.4. In addition, compare the way in which Horace in *Sat.* 1.7.45–88 tempers his self-praise by praising his father and acknowledging his debt to him for the blamelessness of his life.

[183] Cf. also Quint., *Inst.* 11.1.28 and the treatment of modesty by Hermogenes in his *On Issues* (pp. 345–52 Rabe), where willingly showing oneself as deficient in a matter is one of the devices by which modesty may be expressed. According to Plut., *Mor.* 82D, it is a sign of progress in virtue to admit one's faults.

[184] For boasting for the sake of others, cf. Max. Tyr., *Or.* 1.7d (12,11–15 Hobein). According to Dio Chrys., *Or.* 57.4–5, "it is the mark of a foolish person to be ashamed to praise himself when by praise he is likely to confer the greatest benefits."

and distrust. Self-praise may serve to create this confidence so that he will be able to confer benefits on those who otherwise would shun them (539F).[185] Again, self-praise may prove extremely helpful as a pedagogical device for giving hope to the despairing, admonition to the overconfident,[186] and instruction to the ignorant (544D–546A).

For Epictetus, it is precisely this desire to benefit others that lies at the heart of proper self-glorification. Indeed, it is what justifies the true Cynic's speech about himself and distinguishes him from the braggarts who merely and too hastily assume the guise of the philosopher (*Diss.* 4.8). The latter are prone to speak as follows:

> I am tranquil and serene; be not ignorant, O men, that while you are tossed about and are in turmoil over worthless things, I alone am free from every perturbation. . . . Come together, all you who are suffering from gout, headaches, and fever, the halt, and the blind, and see how sound I am, and free from every disorder (27–28).

The true Cynic, on the other hand, says:

> That you may see yourselves, O men, to be looking for happiness and serenity, not where it is, but where it is not, behold, God has sent me to you as an example; I have neither property, nor house, nor wife, nor children, no, not even so much as a bed, or a shirt, or a piece of furniture, and yet you see how healthy I am. Make trial of me, and if you see that I am free from turmoil, hear my remedies and the treatment which cured me (30–31).

Both the "philosopher" and the Cynic set themselves apart as examples. Both lay claim to *ataraxia.* Both call attention to their health. But whereas the "philosopher" is content to catalogue the diseases of mankind and invite them to behold his health, the Cynic's ultimate purpose in referring to his health is to offer to others the drugs that cured him. It is out of the Cynic's desire to function as a physician that he points to himself and his health. Since the "philosopher" is concerned only with his own self-exhibition, he is speaking as a fool and a braggart (27), and what he says is both vain and vulgar (29). Such self-praise is inexcusable "unless, like Aesclepius, you are able at once to show by what treatment those others will also become well again, and for this end are producing

[185] According to Aristotle, the encomiast's character and the attitude produced by him in the hearer are the means by which he will make others accept him as a person who is "trustworthy in respect of virtue" (*Rh.* 1.9). Cf. also Dio Chrys., *Or.* 57.4,10.

[186] According to Dio Chrysostom, Nestor's self-praise in Hom., *Il.* 1.260–68, 273–74, functions as admonition directed at the *hybris* and *megalauchia* of Agamemnon and Achilles. Since they were puffed up through reputation and power, "Nestor wished to humble them, and if possible, reduce their pride . . . in the hope that they might abate somewhat their folly and madness" (*Or.* 57.6–8). On this oration, cf. H. von Arnim, "Entstehung und Anordnung der Schriftensammelung Dios von Prusa," *Hermes* 26 (1891) 392, and *Leben und Werke des Dio von Prusa* (Berlin: Weidmann, 1898) 410–11.

your own good health as an example" (29). The Cynic's speech has this character, and as a result it is noble as well as philanthropic (32).

The Cynic's catalogue of hardships and non-possessions has a vital function within his speech. It shows that the Cynic's health is not the product of the "good things" of life but exists despite every adverse circumstance. There can be no other explanation for his health but the drugs with which he was cured. That is, his adverse style of life serves the purposes of the message that he announces. Or, as Epictetus' Cynic puts it, it serves the purposes for which God sent him. His hardships make his message both credible and compelling, and, unlike the pompous "philosophers" who discredit philosophy by failing to live according to its precepts (5, 9, 13), at no time or place does he ever do anything which might "invalidate the testimony which it is his to give in behalf of virtue, and against externals" (32).

Such a person does not brag about the office that Zeus has given him; he proves it by the way that he conducts himself (3.24.118). And the true proof of one's God-ordained training and education is not a diploma or the ability to compose dialogues, but the proper response to adversity (3.10.8,10–11; 24.112; 4.4.30). It is in regard to adversity that one should boast:

> And now, when the crisis calls, will you go off and make an exhibition of your compositions, and give a reading from them, and boast, "See, how I write dialogues"? Do not so, man, but rather boast as follows: "See how in my desire I do not fail to get what I wish. See how in my aversions I do not fall into things that I would avoid. Bring on death and you shall know; bring on hardships, bring on imprisonment, bring on disrepute, bring on condemnation." This is the proper exhibition of a young man come from school (*Diss.* 2.1.34–35).

An example of proper self-laudation in which hardships are prominent is also provided by Seneca. In a lengthy but remarkable passage, Seneca gives the following counsel to Lucilius, who is beset with flatterers:

> When you want to be praised sincerely, why be indebted to someone else for it? Praise yourself (*Ipse te lauda*). Say: "I devoted myself to the liberal arts. Although my poverty urged me to do otherwise and tempted my talents towards a field where there is an immediate profit from study, I turned aside to unremunerative poetry and dedicated myself to the wholesome study of philosophy. I have shown that virtue applies to every heart and, overcoming the limitations of my birth and measuring myself not by my lot but by my soul, I stood equal to the most important men. The Emperor Gaius did not rob me of my loyalty in my friendship with Gaetulicus. Messallina and Narcissus, long enemies of the state before they became enemies of each other, were not able to overturn my resolve in my allegiance to other people also whom it was unlucky to like. I risked my neck for my loyalty. No word was wrung from me which did not come unreservedly from a clear conscience. I feared everything for my friends, nothing at all for myself, except the fear that I had not been a good friend. No womanly tears flowed from me, nor did I cling as a suppliant to anybody's hand. I did nothing a good man, or merely a man, should not do. Rising above my own danger and ready to meet the dangers that threatened, I was grateful to fortune because she was willing to test how much value I placed on loyalty.

> Such a great test could not stand for something of insignificant value to me. I did not even weigh matters very long, for the values did not balance: whether it were better for me to perish for loyalty or loyalty to perish for me. I did not rush headlong into the final decision in order to rescue myself from the rage of rulers. In the time of Gaius I saw tortures, I saw burnings, and under him I knew that men who were merely killed were considered among examples of mercy. Yet I did not fall upon my sword or leap open-mouthed into the sea, lest I seem only able to die for loyalty" (*QNat.* 4A, Pref. 14–17).[187]

In conclusion, it seems possible to distinguish three basic levels of perception in the boasting and self-praise that occurs in regard to adversity and the victory over it.[188] According to the first level, the victory over hardship is a purely personal accomplishment. It is the result of one's own virtue, and the one who has conquered is entitled to boast of his power and performance.[189] Such pride and self-praise are the product of the individual's self-esteem and have no other end in view than the glorification of the person himself. This is the crudest and most offensive form of self-praise and the object of the moralists' polemic.[190]

[187] Cf. also *QNat.* 4A, Pref. 18. Self-praise for loyalty to friends despite the dangers involved is in keeping with the fact that one has friends in order to help them and suffer with them. Cf. *Ep.* 9.8,10; 85.29; *Ben.* 6.35.1; and also *Ep.* 95.51 and *Clem.* 2.6.2–3. For boasting and self-praise in Seneca, cf. also *Ep.* 18.9; *Ben.* 5.7.6; 11.2.

[188] Self-praise, however, is not always restricted to an announcement of victory over adversity and of readiness to meet it. Sometimes it is intertwined with a confession of grief and despair. A particularly interesting example of a "letter of tears" replete with self-praise is a letter that the rhetorician Marcus Cornelius Fronto writes to Marcus Aurelius (Vol. II, pp. 222–32 Haines). It is a letter that combines self-laudation and lamentation, insistence on the probity of life with a confession of despondency. In this way it truly conveys all of Fronto's thoughts (10) and constitutes a testimony prior to his imminent death (8).

On the one hand, he praises himself for the utter blamelessness of his life (8–9) and the fortitude he showed on each of the five occasions when he lost an only child (1–2). He mentions his many acts of generosity and loyalty that were undertaken at risk to his life (*cum periculo*). Since, moreover, he esteemed education more than wealth, he "preferred to be poor (*pauperem*) rather than indebted to another's help, at the worst to be in want (*egere*) rather than to beg" (9).

Yet, on the other hand, he confesses that the recent deaths of his wife and especially of his three-year old grandson have completely devastated him, leading him to fault the gods and to question providence (2–6). He concludes the letter by cataloguing some of his hardships and their present impact on him, with the latter being a veiled plea for pity: "I have suffered from constant and serious ill-health, my dearest Marcus. Then afflicted by the most distressing calamities I have further lost my wife, I have lost my grandson in Germany—woe is me!—I have lost my Decimanus. If I were of iron I could write no more just now" (10).

[189] For the propriety of good men boasting, cf. Chrysippus, *apud* Plut., *Mor.* 1038C.

[190] For examples of offensive self-praise, cf. Epict., *Diss.* 4.8.27–28, and esp. Ps-Diog., *Ep.* 27 (118,14–18 Malherbe). Cf. also the attack of Sext. Emp., *Pyrr.* 1.62 on "those conceited braggarts, the Dogmatists."

According to the second level, the victory over hardship is a personal achievement, but it is one that has been made possible only by the teaching of philosophy. Through its teachings and the practice that it demands, facility in virtue is finally achieved and adversity is conquered. One may legitimately boast, but it is appropriate to acknowledge the magnitude of one's debt by glorifying philosophy and vaunting onself *in its name* (Cic., *Tusc.* 2.14.33).[191]

Finally, in terms of the third level of perception, the victory over hardship is a human act made possible by philosophy, but it is also one in which the divine plays a part. It is "a mixture of human effort and divine benevolence,"[192] in which the accent falls on the contribution of the divine. Indeed, inasmuch as God out of love sends hardships so that worthy individuals may achieve their potential as persons and himself provides the assistance that enables the accomplishment, the victory depends ultimately on the divine. It is, then, an act not only of modesty but also of genuine perception to credit the victory to God and to give him the glory.

The second and third levels of perception overlap to a considerable degree and are found in the same moralists.[193] From both perspectives, proper self-praise acknowledges a debt outside itself and aims at a benefit beyond itself. Yet these levels of perception can be logically distinguished. The second is humanistic in orientation and sees hardships as the weapons of a capricious Tyche. It therefore boasts of its triumph over her and her weapons in terms of the philosophy that has enabled and facilitated the victory. The third level of perception is religious, incorporating Tyche within the divine plan so that her caprice is only apparent and seeing the ultimate source of hardships in the love and benevolence of God. Since not only adversity itself but also the means for enduring and conquering it come from the divine, the religious person deems it appropriate to glorify God and vaunt himself, when necessary, in God's name. Self-glorification thus finds a proper role within the framework of the glorification of God.

Conclusion

The intimate connection between virtue and adversity has been thoroughly documented in the preceding pages. Since *peristaseis* constitute a test of human

[191] To be included in this second level of perception are those instances where the credit for success is attributed to luck, another person, etc.

[192] Crotty, *Song and Action,* 33.

[193] Cicero, for example, clearly reflects both the second and third levels of perception in his self-praises. Cf. Cic., *Tusc.* 2.14.33 and Quint., *Inst.* 11.1.23. Unfortunately, however, he frequently fails to temper his self-praise at all and engages in gratuitous braggadocio (the first level of perception). He is a perfect demonstration of the fact that one can know and use the rhetoric of humility without being at all modest. For criticisms of Cicero's boasting, cf. Plut., *Cic.* 24.1–2; *Comp. Dem. et Cic.* 2.1–3; *Mor.* 540F. On Cicero's self-praise, cf. Jürgen Graff, *Ciceros Selbstdarstellung* (Heidelberg: C. Winter, 1963) esp. 77–80.

character, they have both a revelatory and a demonstrative function. The man with little or no integrity collapses under the weight of his burdens. His *peristaseis* reveal and prove his deficiencies as a person. The *proficiens,* by contrast, shows greater strength of character in dealing with his hardships, so that his *peristaseis* reveal his progress, what he is *becoming.* Since they help to form his character, they play a crucial role in his *paideia.* For the *sapiens,* however, *peristaseis* no longer have this educative character. They provide instead the proof that he is educated. Consequently, they exhibit who he *is,* what he *has become.* His serene endurance of the greatest possible calamities is the definitive proof of his virtue and serves to distinguish him from every charlatan who merely claims to be "wise."

Peristasis catalogues frequently serve as rhetorical and literary foils for the depiction of various aspects of the wise man's existence and character. As the preceding discussion has indicated, they serve to depict such characteristics as 1) the sage's serenity despite the direst calamities of life, 2) his virtue, especially his courage, 3) his endurance of the greatest and most demanding hardships, 4) his perseverence in doing noble deeds despite the dangers involved and his refusal, at any cost, to depart from what justice dictates, 5) his contempt for Fortune, 6) his victory over adversity, 7) his *askēsis* and the role it plays in his victory, 8) his invincibility and invulnerability as a person, 9) his perfect rationality, 10) his demeanor and his response to his adversaries, 11) his consent to the hardships of his life and the volitional character of his suffering, and 12) his conformity to the will of God and the place of his suffering within the divine plan. In short, the catalogues depict and celebrate the greatness of his invincible virtue, the power and tranquility of his philosophically informed mind.

The cataloguing of an individual's *peristaseis* is, moreover, crucial to the claims that are advanced about him. By accumulating and juxtaposing the hardships that a person has faced, a speaker or author seeks to magnify those hardships and lend them importance and grandeur. This amplification (*auxēsis*) of a subject is the traditional function of catalogues, and its use in regard to *peristaseis* is particularly important. By amplifying the hardships that a person has overcome as well as comparing his feat with that of others, a speaker makes the achievement of his hero all the more impressive. In short, he magnifies a person by amplifying his hardships, and "the greater the man, the greater the misfortune" (Hdt. 7.203) that he surmounts. This is one of the reasons why *auxēsis* and *synkrisis* are central to the ancient theory and practice of the encomium. Furthermore, the objective form of the catalogue as such lends an air of facticity and objectivity to the account, so that catalogues often have a probative function as well. In the case of *peristasis* catalogues this verifying function is quite pronounced, because the probative function of adversity in regard to virtue is reinforced by the objective form of the catalogue itself.

In the case of the sage, then, the catalogue of his *peristaseis* not only depicts him but also verifies who he is and justifies the praise he is accorded. It depicts him as a model that not only exemplifies the ideal toward which the *proficiens* is to aspire but also exhorts and admonishes the latter in so far as he fails to attain this goal. The *peristaseis* of the sage thus belong to the pedagogy as well as the propaganda of philosophy. Particular *peristasis* catalogues have additional functions within the contexts where they occur. Some of these have been indicated in this chapter and still others will be mentioned in the next. The focus in this chapter has been on the wise man as a figure, not on particular individuals who either claimed that they had attained the ideal or were said by others to have done so. Epicurus and Cynics such as Ps-Heraclitus are examples of the former, whereas those most often adduced by others as examples of wise men are legendary figures like Heracles and Odysseus as well as historical ones like Socrates, Diogenes the Cynic, and Cato the Younger. Such individuals and their *peristaseis* are important, but they have not been the focus of this investigation because they represent instantiations of the ideal sage. The latter is the basic category, and the importance of these individuals derives from the fact that they claimed to embody the ideal or were believed to do so.

It is thus the figure of the ideal sage and his sufferings that provides the backdrop for the analysis of Paul's Corinthian catalogues in the following chapter, and it is to this analysis that we now turn.

4
The Corinthian Catalogues

There are five times in the extant Corinthian correspondence that Paul compiles a catalogue of his sufferings (1 Cor 4:9–13; 2 Cor 4:8–9; 6:3–10; 11:23–29; 12:10). Paul's statements in these catalogues and elsewhere correspond in part to the picture of the ideal philosopher sketched in the preceding chapter. In lieu of discussing Paul in terms of the rubrics of chapter three, the following treatment approaches the catalogues of 1 Cor 4, 2 Cor 4, and 2 Cor 6 from the literary contexts in which they occur. These catalogues will be examined according to their canonical sequence, beginning with 1 Cor 4:9–13.

The Catalogue in 1 Cor 4:9–13

The Hortatory Character of 1 Cor 1–4

1 Cor 1–4 in general and 1 Cor 4:6–13 in particular are to be interpreted in light of Paul's statements in 4:6 and 4:14. In these two verses Paul makes explicit statements about his purpose and procedure in addressing himself to the Corinthians, and these indicate that 1 Cor 1:10–4:21 is primarily a *letter of admonition.*

The clearest statement of this occurs in 4:14, where Paul says that his purpose in penning the preceding was that of admonition (νουθετῶν).[1] It is in his capacity as the Corinthians' spiritual father (4:15) that he gives this admonition, and it is directed to them as his beloved children (4:14). Paul emphasizes this role and relationship, for admonition coupled with instruction is an established paternal function.[2] Admonition is the proper response to insolence and arrogance, and,

[1] *Contra* H. Lietzmann, *An die Korinther I/II* (HNT 9; 5th ed.; Tübingen: Mohr, 1969) 21, and C. T. Craig, "The First Epistle to the Corinthians," *IB* 10.57, Paul has not been deliberately attempting to shame the Corinthians. The οὐ . . . ἀλλά antithesis of 4:14 is similar to that of 1:17. Paul may have baptized certain ones (1:14–16), but this was not his real purpose in Corinth. Similarly, Paul's words may have caused shame, but in 4:14 he is assuring them that ridicule was not his real intention. Paul has no hesitancy about shaming the Corinthians (6:5; 15:34; cf. also 2 Thess 3:14; Titus 2:8), but that is not what he is about in chapters 1–4. The clarification of one's motives after the use of strong words is a common practice. Cf., for instance, Dio, *Or.* 73.10. The ταῦτα of 4:14 is retrospective, and although it refers specifically to 4:6–13, it also points beyond that section to previous admonitions (such as 3:1–4). See note 13 below.

[2] Cf. 1 Sam 3:13 LXX; Prov 2:2 LXX; Joseph., *BJ* 1.481; *AJ* 3.311; Eph 6:4; *Herm.*

while a good father naturally prefers to reprove his children verbally, he is prepared in cases of recalcitrance to adopt a corporeal form of admonition. In so doing a father acts in the same manner as God, who responds to arrogance with punishment and paternal admonition (Joseph., *AJ* 3.311) and does not refrain from using even the scourge for admonitory purposes (Jdt 8:27).[3]

While it is his children's growing arrogance (4:6, 18–19; 5:2; 8:1) that prompts Paul's paternal admonition, he does so because he loves them (τέκνα μου ἀγαπητά) and in a manner commensurate with that love. He even sends his beloved child Timothy to the Corinthians with instructions to remind his brothers and sisters of their father's ways (4:17). Should his children's arrogance continue, however, Paul is prepared to resort to admonition by a switch (ῥάβδῳ: 4:21).[4] By this means, if by no other, his foolish children may at last acquire the wisdom they naively think is theirs already (cf. Prov 22:15).[5]

Paul understands himself as the Corinthians' father by virtue of the fact that their faith in Christ came to life through his preaching (4:15). Paul's discussion in 1 Cor 1:10–4:21 thus begins (1:13–17) and ends with a reference to his establishment of the church at Corinth, a fact that he understands as the "fathering" of the Corinthians.[6] The image of the parent occurs again in the discussion of the founding of the church in 3:1–4. Here he shifts to maternal imagery, affirming that he fed the Corinthians with milk, not solid food, because they were but babies. He goes on to admonish them by affirming that they have not progressed beyond that stage, as their continuing inability to eat solid food indicates (3:2–3).[7] He thus is continuing, even in 1 Corinthians, to give them milk. The

---

Vis. 1.3.2. For admonition coupled with instruction, cf. Pl., *Leg.* 845B; Philo, *Decal.* 87; Col 1:28; 3:16; and esp. Ps-Demetrius, *Typoi Epistolikoi* 7: "admonition is the instilling of sense in the person who is being admonished, and teaching him what should and should not be done." All translations of this work are those of A. J. Malherbe, "Ancient Epistolary Theorists," *Ohio Journal of Religious Studies* 5 (1977) 3–77.

[3] For the fatherly admonition of God, cf. also Wis 11:10; 12:25–26; *Pss. Sol.* 13:9. For God's use of the rod and scourge, cf. also Ps 89:32.

[4] For paternal discipline by the rod, cf. 2 Sam 7:14; Prov 13:24; 23:13–14; 29:15, 17. Compare also Pl., *Leg.* 700C. For the use of the rod (and scourge) by both parents and teachers, cf. David Daube, "Paul a Hellenistic Schoolmaster?" in *Studies in Rationalism, Judaism and Universalism* (L. Roth Festschrift; ed. R. Loewe; London: Routledge and Kegan Paul, 1966) 67–71.

[5] C. R. Holladay, *The First Letter of Paul to the Corinthians* (The Living Word Commentary 8; Austin: Sweet, 1979) 68–69, astutely notes the role of the rod in the OT wisdom tradition and the appropriateness of the rod-metaphor for the wisdom theme of 1 Cor 1–4.

[6] It should also be noted that the two instances of *parakalō* (1:10; 4:16) serve to frame the discussion in chapters 1–4.

[7] The specific image that underlies Paul's statement in 3:2 is, to be sure, probably that of the wet-nurse, and this represents another use of the simile found in 1 Thess 2:7. But the nurse is a substitute for the mother, so that the imagery is ultimately parental in nature.

repetition of 1:12 at 3:4 is deliberate, for it provides a link between the image of the admonishing parent and the issue raised at the beginning of the discussion. When, therefore, Paul presents himself in 4:14–15 as a parent engaged in admonition, he is not introducing an entirely new concept but rather making explicit what his procedure has been from the beginning. Indeed, as the discussion later will make clear, a statement by Paul already in 4:6 is intended to remind the Corinthians of what was said explicitly in 3:1–3, that they are still children.

Paul's second explicit statement about his procedure also indicates that he has been both admonishing and instructing the Corinthians. This is not only indicated in the two purpose clauses of 4:6, but it is suggested already by the term μετασχηματίζειν. While it is generally recognized that Paul is using this term in a literary, stylistic sense,[8] the precise import of this rhetorical term has largely eluded modern scholarship.[9] Yet the path to the correct understanding of the term was opened long ago by J. B. Lightfoot, who recognized that Paul was using the term to indicate a "covert allusion."[10] This meaning of the term *schema* was the standard one in the first century C.E. (Quint., *Inst.* 9.1.14; 2.65), and so it is not at all surprising to find this technical meaning of the term underlying Paul's use of the compound verb. He is saying, "I have made these covert allusions with respect to myself and Apollos for your sake."

For the use of "nurse" imagery by Paul and various philosophers, cf. A. J. Malherbe, " 'Gentle as a Nurse': The Cynic Background to I Thess ii," *NovT* 12 (1970) 203–17, esp. 211–14.

[8] Cf., for example, J. Weiss, *Der erste Korintherbrief* (MeyerK 5; 9th ed.; Göttingen: Vandenhoeck & Ruprecht, 1910) 101, and J. Schneider, *TDNT* 7.958.

[9] The failure to discern the meaning of the term has resulted in the claim that Paul's use of the term is catachrestic and that it means only "to illustrate," "to exemplify." Cf. the note of A. Dihle to Schneider, *TDNT* 7.958 n. 10, and H. Conzelmann, *1 Corinthians* (Hermeneia; Philadelphia: Fortress, 1975) 85–86.

[10] J. B. Lightfoot, *Notes on the Epistles of St. Paul* (1895; repr., Grand Rapids: Zondervan, 1957) 199. Lightfoot erred, however, by suggesting that the allusion was to the Judaizing factions. Subsequent scholars who have adopted some form of the "covert allusion" interpretation include G. G. Findlay, "St. Paul's First Epistle to the Corinthians," *The Expositor's Greek Testament* (ed. W. R. Nicoll; 5 vols.; 1897–1910; repr., Grand Rapids: Eerdmans, 1980) 2.799; J. Massie, *Corinthians* (The New-Century Bible; New York: Frowde, 1902) 159; A. Robertson and A. Plummer, *A Critical and Exegetical Commentary on the First Epistle of St. Paul to the Corinthians* (ICC; 2d ed.; Edinburgh: Clark, 1914) 81; F. H. Colson, "Μετεσχημάτισα: I Cor. IV.6," *JTS* 17 (1916) 379–84; A. T. Robertson, *Word Pictures in the New Testament* (1930–33; 6 vols.; repr., Grand Rapids: Baker, 1980) 4.104. In all these cases, however, the precise import of the term was not discerned, a judgment that applies also to BAGD 513. An exception is the private, unpublished paper of Benjamin Fiore, "Covert Allusion and Apostolic Example" (1975), which was brought to my attention only after I had completed my own initial investigation of the phenomenon. His emphasis is different, but our conclusions are complementary. His data and the skillful manner in which he treats it have saved me from several blunders. Much of Fiore's paper appears now in "The Function of Personal Example in the Socratic and Pastoral Epistles," (Ph.D. Diss., Yale, 1982) 312–44.

The discussions of covert allusions by Hellenistic rhetoricians are helpful in illuminating Paul's use of the term. Their treatments show that the situation par excellence for employing such covert allusions was the speech before the king. Here it was as impolite as it was dangerous to rebuke the king openly, so that the safest and most appropriate form in which to offer both counsel and censure was that of the veiled allusion.[11]

Ps-Demetrius observes that this device is an effective way in which to chide a king or any overbearing person for his haughty pride (*Eloc.* 289).[12] Along with the rebuke of the ruler's inappropriate attitude and behavior, he argues that a speaker should also present examples of proper conduct and praise them accordingly. These exemplary individuals are like fathers who provide the proper role model for imitation. Through this combination of covert criticism and exemplification a "hearer is admonished without hearing himself censured" (292; cf. also 298). By this indirect method a person is not only admonished by having his ignorance revealed but also exhorted to get instruction (297). The form of these allusions varied, with precepts serving as one of the standard ways by which speakers sought to benefit their audience (296).

The relevance of these discussions for 1 Cor 4 is obvious. Paul is addressing himself to those who not only feel that they are powerful kings (4:8,10) but also display the typical royal vice of arrogant pride (4:6, 18–19; 5:2). Furthermore, though ignorant, they imagine themselves to be wise (3:18; 4:10). In resorting to covert allusions Paul is thus adopting the standard Hellenistic form for admonishing potentates. "So, you think you are kings. Very well, I shall admonish and instruct you in the manner appropriate to your exalted status!" This covert approach commences in 3:5 and includes several indirect, third-person admonitions (3:10,12–15,17–18,21; 4:1) as well as references to himself and Apollos as counter-examples of harmony and humility, and it concludes in 4:6 with the quotation of a relevant precept.[13] In addition, the example of Paul and Apollos

[11] Cf. Quint., *Inst.* 9.2.66–67; Ps-Demetr., *Eloc.* 289, 292–93; and also Philostr., *VS* 2.1 (p. 561 Olearius); Suet., *Dom.* 10.1. On veiled arguments and covert allusions, cf. esp. W. C. Wright (trans.), *Philostratus and Eunapius* (LCL 134; Cambridge: Harvard, 1968) 570.

[12] For an orientation to this work, cf. G. M. A. Grube, *A Greek Critic: Demetrius on Style* (Phoenix Supplementary Volumes 4; Toronto: University Press, 1961).

[13] While it is certain that the ταῦτα of 4:6 is retrospective, there is considerable debate about the scope of Paul's reference. The majority opinion is that 3:5–4:5 as a whole or a pericope within this section is in view. The minority view regards all of 1:10–4:5, or at least 1:18–4:5, as the antecedent of ταῦτα. That Paul has 3:5–4:5 *specifically* in mind seems clear not only from the covert criticism in which he engages but also from the way in which he commences to treat himself and Apollos *by name* at 3:5. The application in 4:1–5 still has both in view, for the "us" of 4:1 and the "each" of 4:5 (like that of 3:5) refer not only to Paul but also to Apollos. While the specific antecedent of "these things" is thus 3:5–4:5, it should not be overlooked that 1:18–3:4 lays the foundation for 3:5–4:5. 1:18–31 deals with the initial phase of missionary activity, where the topics are kerygma (1:21,23) and call

provides not only a positive paradigm for the Corinthians' appropriation but at the same time also an admonishing critique of their lack of harmony and surplus of self-esteem.

In keeping with the rhetorical axiom that hints should be given in order to make one's allusions intelligible (Philostr., *VS* 2.25), Paul's procedure is not entirely covert. Immediately prior to 3:5–4:5 he admonishes them directly (3:1–4) and toward the end of 3:5–4:5 he becomes increasingly direct (4:3–5). In 4:6 he lifts the veil completely and reveals what he has been doing. Normally, of course, a speaker would not do this, but Paul does so to make sure that the import of his allusions will not be lost![14] It is, after all, for their sake that he has made the allusions in the first place (4:6). His method now unveiled, he is free to move from the route of covert allusions to an open *ad hominem* approach in 4:7 and to the closely related approach of irony in 4:8![15]

Before he does so, however, Paul summarizes in 4:6 the two-fold purpose of his μετασχηματισμός.[16] This summary-conclusion only makes explicit what we

(1:26). 2:6–16 takes up the second phase, the post-conversion period of teaching (2:13) and its concern for maturation and perfection (2:6). The repetition of the slogans of 1:12 at 3:4 signals the way in which Paul will begin to rehearse the subject matter of 1:12–3:3 with particular reference to himself and Apollos. Thus, 3:5–17 treats both the first and the second phases together, with Paul constituting the first and Apollos typifying the second phase.

[14] In addition, it is precisely because Paul knows the Corinthians are really not royalty that he becomes explicit about his procedure as a prelude to his ironic treatment of their self-assessment. This disclosure of his procedure is not the only atypical feature of Paul's use of this device. The fact that he refers to himself as a model for the Corinthians is also a striking departure from standard rhetorical practice in such speeches. In fact, the use of the device in a letter is already unusual (cf. Malherbe, "Ancient Epistolary Theorists," 40). At the same time, however, there is a splendid irony in Paul's announcement that he has been using what was considered a very difficult and eloquent rhetorical device (cf. Quint., *Inst.* 9.2.66,96; Philostr., *VS* 2.17; Wright, *Philostratus and Eunapius,* 570). It is ironical because he had not used rhetorical eloquence in his initial preaching in Corinth (1:17; 2:1–5), but now suddenly announces that he has been writing to them employing a sophisticated rhetorical device! In addition, he has used several other rhetorical devices, such as anthropomorphism (3:6–7), metaphor and allegory (3:6–17), contrast (3:14–15), hyperbole (3:22), and simile (4:1). Paul thus has been debunking rhetorical eloquence with the devices of that eloquence itself. He debunks it, not because he is incapable of it (at least on paper), but because it leads to faith in men rather than in God (2:5).

[15] For the close relation of covert allusions to irony, cf. Quint., *Inst.* 9.2.65; Dion. Hal., *Rhet.* 9.323.1 Usener; and Ps-Demetr., *Eloc.* 291. The closeness of the two "figures" made the transition from the one to the other both natural and rhetorically easy. Weiss, *Korintherbrief,* 101–02, and J. Héring, *The First Epistle of St. Paul to the Corinthians* (London: Epworth, 1962) 28, are therefore wrong to emphasize the change of tone between 3:5–4:5 and 4:6ff and to suggest that 4:6ff must have been written a day or two after 3:5ff.

[16] Unlike most exegetes, I take both *hina*-clauses to be dependent on the verb. The resultant meaning is hardly affected, however, if the first *hina*-clause is understood as giving

have seen as typical components of covert speeches to kings that are present in 3:5–4:5, viz., instruction by means of exemplification (ἐν ἡμῖν μάθητε) and admonition in regard to haughty pride (μὴ φυσιοῦσθε). Since both exemplification (4:16) and admonition (4:13) continue to be Paul's concern in the remainder of the chapter, it is clear that only the method of achieving these ends has changed, not the ends themselves.

Therefore, in 4:7–21, as in 3:5–4:5, Paul is concerned with admonishing the Corinthians and presenting himself as a counter-example to them. The catalogue of hardships that occurs in 4:9–13 is intended to achieve these two goals of admonition in regard to what is wrong and of exhortation to commendable conduct. The catalogue both specifies some of the ways of Paul that the Corinthians are to imitate (4:16–17) and illustrates the life that receives praise from God (4:5). In giving the life that is praised by God and the paradigm for the Corinthians' own lives, the catalogue presents the suffering apostolic existence as the praiseworthy paradigm for Christian existence.[17] It does so, for it is only through suffering that true perfection is attained (cf. Heb 5:8–9), and if the Corinthians follow the apostolic model, they, too, will become, like the Thessalonians, sufficiently mature to serve as models for others (1 Thess 1:6–7; 2:14). In addition, the catalogue also provides a rebuke and admonition to human presumption, however theologically founded that presumption may be. Therefore, the purpose statement of 4:6, while relating directly to 3:5–4:5, also provides an apt summary of the two-fold purpose of 4:7–21. A unity of purpose underlies 3:5–4:21, and indeed, all of the first four chapters.

An additional indication that Paul has been concerned with admonition and exemplification is contained in the first *hina*-clause of 4:6. As is generally recognized, the phrase ἐν ἡμῖν points to Paul and Apollos as the models by which the Corinthians are to learn a crucial lesson.[18] It is the nature of the admonition

---

the means by which the second is realized. For the latter interpretation, cf., for example, C. F. G. Heinrici, *Kritisch exegetisches Handbuch über den ersten Brief an die Korinther* (MeyerK 5; 7th ed; Göttingen: Vandenhoeck & Ruprecht, 1888) 123. For the Pauline double *hina,* cf. Rom 7:13; Gal 3:14; 4:5; and esp. 2 Cor 9:3; 11:12. On the last of these, cf. esp. R. F. Hock, *The Social Context of Paul's Ministry* (Philadelphia: Fortress, 1980) 100–01 n. 118, who argues similarly that both *hina*-clauses are dependent on the main clause. Cf. also 2 Cor 12:7 and Gal 6:12–13.

[17] On this point, cf. H.-D. Wendland, *Die Briefe an die Korinther* (NTD 7; 12th ed.; Göttingen: Vandenhoeck & Ruprecht, 1968) 40. For an early application of parts of the apostolic *peristasis* catalogues to Christians in general, cf. *Diogn.* 5.12–15.

[18] The ἐν ἡμῖν is an instrumental dative of means. For this use of the dative case with ἐν, cf. H. W. Smyth & G. M. Messing, *Greek Grammar* (Harvard: Cambridge, 1956) sect. 1511. This construction is very common with verbs of knowing (Thuc. 7.11; Gen 42:33 LXX; Sir 4:24; 11:28; 26:9; John 13:35; 1 John 3:19) to indicate the means by which knowledge is gained. The use here with a verb of learning is simply a variant of this basic form of expression. Cf. esp. Phil 4:9 ἐμάθετε . . . ἐν ἡμῖν, and compare 1 Cor 6:2. C. F. D.

contained in the remainder of the clause that has baffled scholars. It is commonly recognized that the τό serves to identify the words μὴ ὑπὲρ ἃ γέγραπται as a quotation of some sort.[19] Debate has centered on the meaning of the quotation and its background. The *communis opinio,* at least among those who do not resort to emendation, is that the words refer in some way to the OT, and the recent tendency has been to view them as a response to a Gnostic belief that one was free to go "beyond Scripture."[20] The belief that the quotation refers to

---

Moule, *An Idiom-Book of New Testament Greek* (2d ed.; Cambridge: University, 1959) 77, terms this an "exemplary" dative and classifies it as an extension of the instrumental use. This is to recognize that the dative here is paradigmatic as well as instrumental. For Paul's use of ἐν with a personal pronoun to indicate "in the case of," cf. Rom 9:17 (= Exod 9:16); 1 Cor 9:15; Phil 1:30; and also 1 Tim 1:16. Compare 1 Cor 4:2. The claim of H. A. A. Kennedy and N. Turner that the dative here is causal is probably a misprint in both cases for 1 Cor 4:4. Cf. J. H. Moulton, W. F. Howard, and N. Turner, *A Grammar of New Testament Greek* (4 vols.; Edinburgh: Clark, 1906–76) 2.463; 4.93.

Holladay's (*Corinthians,* 61) comprehensive understanding of what the example of Paul and Apollos here entails is to be preferred to the restricted interpretation of P. W. Schmiedel, who limits it to their objective relationship as mere servants. Cf. the latter's "Die Briefe an die Thessalonicher und an die Korinther," *Hand-Commentar zum Neuen Testament* (ed. H. J. Holtzmann, et al.; 2d ed.; Freiburg/Leipzig: Mohr, 1893) 2.112.

[19] Cf., for example, L. Morris, *The First Epistle of Paul to the Corinthians* (Tyndale Bible Commentaries; NT Series 7; Grand Rapids: Eerdmans, 1958) 77, and C. K. Barrett, *A Commentary on the First Epistle to the Corinthians* (HNTC; New York: Harper & Row, 1968) 106. For the use of the neuter definite article to introduce a quotation, cf. Rom 13:9; Gal 5:14; and the examples collected by Turner in his treatment of syntax in *A Grammar of NT Greek,* 3.182.

[20] In addition to the treatment of this well known crux in the standard commentaries, cf. esp. W. F. Howard, "I Corinthians IV.6 (Exegesis or Emendation?)," *ExpTim* 33 (1921–22) 479–80; O. Linton, " 'Nicht über das hinaus, was geschrieben steht' (1 Kor. 4,6)," *TSK* 102 (1930) 425–37; L. Brun, "Noch einmal die Schriftnorm I Kor. 4,6," *TSK* 103 (1931) 453–56; P. Wallis, "Ein neuer Auslegungsversuch der Stelle I.Kor. 4,6," *TLZ* 75 (1950) 506–08; K. L. Schmidt, "Nicht über das hinaus, was geschrieben steht!," *In Memoriam E. Lohmeyer* (ed. W. Schmauch; Stuttgart: Evangelisches Verlag., 1951) 101–09; M. D. Hooker, " 'Beyond the Things Which Are Written': An Examination of I Cor. IV.6," *NTS* 10 (1963–64) 127–32; J. M. Ross, "Not Above What is Written: A Note on 1 Cor 4:6," *ExpTim* 82 (1970–71) 215–17; W. Schmithals, *Gnosticism in Corinth* (Nashville: Abingdon, 1971) 122; A. Legault, " 'Beyond the Things Which are Written' (I Cor. IV.6)," *NTS* 18 (1971–72) 227–31; and J. Strugnell, "A Plea for Conjectural Emendation in the New Testament, with a Coda on 1 Cor 4:6," *CBQ* 36 (1974) 543–58, esp. 555–58. For the claim that this saying belongs to the confrontation of Paul and the enthusiasts at Corinth, cf. W. Lütgert, *Freiheitspredigt und Schwarmgeister in Korinth* (BFCT 12.3; Gütersloh: Bertelsmann, 1908) 97–99; A. Schlatter, *Die Korinthische Theologie* (BFCT 18.2; Gütersloh: Bertelsmann, 1914) 7–33, esp. 7–9, and *Paulus der Bote Jesu* (1934; Stuttgart: Calwer, 1962) 154; J. Moffatt, *The First Epistle of Paul to the Corinthians* (MNTC; London: Hodder & Stoughton, 1938) 47; Craig, *IB* 10.54.

Scripture is anchored in the word γέγραπται, which Paul often uses to introduce an OT quotation (1 Cor 1:19,31; 3:19; etc.). But this anchor will not hold, for the word here is *part* of Paul's quotation, not what he uses to introduce the quotation.

The ellipsis of the verb in the quotation marks it as a proverb, maxim, or precept. Some have suggested that it is a (Jewish) proverb dealing with moderation, like the Greek μηδὲν ἄγαν or Latin *ne quid nimis.*[21] The notion of excess suggested by the ὑπέρ of the quotation, the language of satiety in 4:8, and the concern for moderation in boasting found elsewhere in the Corinthian correspondence (2 Cor 10:13–18) may lend some support to this suggestion. Indeed, the way in which Paul turns in 4:7 to examine their self-knowledge could be taken as indicating that he has moved from "Nothing overmuch" to "Know yourself," thoughts which were inseparably linked as proverbs due to their joint inscription on the walls of the Temple of Apollos at Delphi (Pl., *Prt.* 343B).[22] While this interpretation is attractive, there is a more compelling alternative that not only explains the γέγραπται of 4:6 but also better fits the larger context of 1 Cor 3–4.

The background for the proverb of 4:6 is to be found in the instruction given young children in how to write. Protagoras in Plato, *Prt.* 326D, notes that "writing-masters first draw letters in faint outline with the pen for their less advanced pupils, and then give them the copy-book and make them write according to the guidance of their lines."[23] In this way children are given a model by which they may learn how to draw or write correctly. This method of teaching penmanship was current in the first century C.E. Seneca (*Ep.* 94.51), for example, notes, "Boys study according to direction. Their fingers are held and guided by others so that they may follow the outlines of the letters; next they are ordered to imitate a copy and base thereon a style of penmanship."[24] The point of having a model is naturally that one should follow it, making the letters neither too small nor too large, so that one neither falls short of the model nor exceeds it.

This background dovetails with certain features of 1 Cor 3 and 4. The Corinthians are presented as children (3:1–3) and Paul has characterized his teaching by a rhetorical term, thereby suggesting the schoolboy setting in which elementary training is given. The principle "Not beyond what is written" is identified as a lesson that is to be learned. That the need for solid food (3:1–3) and elementary instruction (4:6) are related and complement each other is surprising to no

[21] The ellipsis of verbs in proverbial statements and precepts is common. The idea that Paul is making use of a rabbinic maxim goes back to Ewald and Godet. The comparison of the proverb to Greek or Latin ones is found, for example, in Lightfoot, *Notes,* 199; Findlay, "Corinthians," 800; and Robertson & Plummer, *Corinthians,* 81.

[22] On the maxim "Know yourself," cf. now H. D. Betz, "The Delphic Maxim 'ΓΝΩΘΙ ΣΑΥΤΟΝ' in Hermetic Interpretation," *HTR* 63 (1970) 465–84.

[23] On this passage, cf. H. I. Marrou, *A History of Education in Antiquity* (New York: New American Library, 1964) 217.

[24] For the practice envisaged here, cf. also Max. Tyr., *Or.* 2.2e (20,13–16 Hobein); Quint., *Inst.* 1.1.27; and perhaps also Clem. Al., *Str.* 5.8.49.1.

one who recalls Heb 5:11-14. Here one finds a rhetorical term (δυσερμήνευτος), a reference to the need for instruction (διδάσκειν) in the alphabet, the ABC's (στοιχεῖα), and a description of the readers as children (νήπιος) in need of milk (γάλακτος) rather than solid food. Such are by no means τέλιοι (cf. 1 Cor 2:6). Both Paul and the author of Hebrews mix their images in treating their audiences as children, treating them as both nurslings and schoolboys. If anything, Paul's mixing of his metaphors is less jarring than that of the more "rhetorical" author of Hebrews, for the latter places them together while Paul separates them. In both cases, however, such mixing is justified by the fact that each is engaged in exhortation (1 Cor 1:10; 4:16; Heb 6:18; 12:5; 13:22) and admonition.

The appropriateness of the proverb in this context can be seen even more clearly when the contexts of the passages in Plato and Seneca are examined. In *Prt.* 320C-328D Plato has the great sophist deliver a speech on behalf of the claim that virtue can be taught. Protagoras argues that children are taught and admonished from earliest childhood, by the nurse, the mother, the pedagogue, and the father (325C). A good moral education is above all what is sought (325D-E). Once under a teacher the children read and memorize works that will provide them with many admonitions and praises of good men who can serve as models for the children (326A). The purpose is "that the boy in envy may imitate (μιμῆται) them and yearn to become even as they are." Even when their schooling comes to an end, young people are not left without guidance, for they are compelled to learn the laws and live in accordance with them (326C). The laws are thus like a pattern.

It is at this point in the speech of Protagoras that the reference to schoolboys copying their ABC's is mentioned. It serves as an analogy to the moral model provided by the laws of the city:

> And when they are released from their schooling the city next compels them to learn the laws and to live according to them as after a pattern, that their conduct may not be swayed by their own light fancies, but just as writing-masters first draw letters in faint outline with the pen for their less advanced pupils, and then give them the copy-book and make them write according to the guidance of their lines, so the city sketches out for them the laws devised by good lawgivers of yore, and constrains them to govern and be governed according to these (326D).

Immediately following this analogy comes the important statement: ὃς δ' ἂν ἐκτὸς βαίνῃ τούτων, κολάζει: "And whoever goes beyond these (laws), (the city) punishes" (my translation).

There are important points of contact between Paul and the speech of Protagoras. The images of the various admonishers mentioned by Protagoras appear also in Paul—that of mother-nurse (1 Cor 3:1-2), father (4:14-15), and pedagogue (4:15). Education of children is a matter of instruction and admonition (4:14). In 3:5-4:5 models of conduct are presented and admonition occurs (cf. also 4:14-16). Here, too, the oblique reference to children learning to draw their letters (4:6) occurs in conjunction with the depiction of a moral model. And, significantly, there is a reference in both texts to going beyond the model.

Seneca's *Ep.* 94 is also helpful in showing the appropriateness of this image for the context of 1 Cor 4. In this epistle Seneca is concerned to show the necessity of admonitory precepts for the philosopher and the student. He insists, among other things, that admonition (*admonitio*) checks vice, causes shame (*pudorem*), makes clear right actions (*rectas . . . actiones admonitio demonstrat*), and gives trust in the truth and confidence. As such it is not superfluous but necessary (44–46), and the testimony of those helped by proverbs (*sententiae*) reflects this fact (46–47).

At this point (48) Seneca raises the question of whether precepts are needed by the sage, since he already has undergone a metamorphosis of the mind (*animus eius transfiguratus est*) and has attained the height of human happiness (*est ac summam consecuti felicitatis humanae*). Some of Seneca's contemporaries claim that precepts are superfluous because the wise man does not need them. Be that as it may, says Seneca, that possibility does not obviate the need for precepts by those who are not already wise (49–50). That is, the already perfect man (*iam perfecti viri*) may not need precepts, but the imperfect (*inperfecto*) individual still needs to have the way (*via*) pointed out to him. Weaker (*inbecillioribus*) folk still need a preceptor, for otherwise they will go astray and not reach the point where self-contentment is possible. "The soul should accordingly be guided at the very moment when it is becoming able to guide itself." It is through guidance by others and imitation of a model that boys learn to write. "Similarly, the mind is helped if it is taught according to direction" (50–51).

Again, as in the case of Plato and Paul, the imagery of children learning to draw by means of a model occurs in the context of moral guidance. Seneca's contrast between the already perfect wise man and the imperfect, weaker individual is, moreover, especially appropriate to the situation addressed in 1 Cor 1–4. The Corinthians think they are σοφοί (3:18; 6:5 = *sapiens:* 48), τέλειοι (2:6 = *perfecti viri:* 50), and ἰσχυροί (4:10 =not *inbecillioribus:* 50), believing that they already (ἤδη: 4:8 = *iam:* 50) have attained the goal of their journey (4:8 = *ac summam consecuti felicitatis humanae:* 50; *possit se esse contentus:* 51). But the mind of the Corinthians has not truly undergone a metamorphosis (cf. Rom 12:2) and they need Timothy to remind them of Paul's ways (ὁδούς: 4:17 = *demonstranda . . . via:* 50). They are not yet πνευματικοί, only ἄνθρωποι, indeed σαρκικοί and νήπιοι (= *inperfecto:* 50). Real progress is possible only if there is admonition (νουθετῶν: 4:14 = *admonito:* 44–46, 50), and possibly the shame that belongs to admonition (ἐντρέπων: 4:14; cf. 6:5; 15:34 = *pudorem:* 44). There must also be a model to guide action. Thus, just as Seneca argues that the mind, like boys, learns *ad prescriptum* (51), so Paul alludes to this schoolboy practice precisely before he begins in the following chapter to prescribe certain kinds of proper behavior. As boys are to imitate (*imitari:* 51) the written model, so are the Corinthians to imitate the model provided by Paul and Apollos (4:6,16).

Seneca's weak, imperfect men still need a preceptor, and Paul's Corinthian children still need a father. The Corinthians are behaving like adolescents, cocky and free and kicking up their heels. They are acting as though their father were not returning. "As though I were not returning to you, some are puffed up" (4:18). This statement, so often misinterpreted, has absolutely nothing to do with any "charge" or "accusation" by the Corinthians that Paul, fearfully conscious of his inferiority, did not dare return to Corinth.[25] On the contrary, it is an image adduced by Paul as part of his depiction of himself in the role of an admonishing father. "You're puffed up like arrogant adolescents who think they are already adults who have outgrown the need for a father. My departure from Corinth was no sign of your maturity, so do not think that your father is not coming home. I shall return, and soon. Mend your ways, or you'll find out how mean a switch a gentle father can wield."

Within such a context the proverb, or better, precept, of 4:6 takes on a vital and quite clear meaning. "By our example in attitude and action Apollos and I provide you with a model for your imitation. Copy us, learn how to write 'not over the lines.' By so doing you will cease being puffed up, neither attributing to us an importance in excess of what is proper (cf. 2 Cor 12:6) nor denying us our due (4:6: κατὰ τοῦ ἑτέρου) as faithful servants and stewards of God" (4:1–2).[26] The Corinthians, so fond of weighty slogans (cf. 1 Cor 6:12, etc.), are thus given one that truly suits them, one that admonishes them by treating them like children. Because they are still immature, Paul exhorts them to become his imitators (4:16), even as he imitates the ultimate model of Christ (11:1). Because Paul himself has not yet attained to full perfection (Phil 3:12–14), he too still needs the model of Christ and the precepts that come from him. To follow that model and those precepts and to spread them is to be God's co-worker and humble servant. The model, therefore, excludes arrogance, whether it is of the sort engendered in favor of one minister at another's expense or is directed at one member of the community over against another (4:6).[27]

[25] For this common line of interpretation, cf., for example, Lietzmann, *Korinther,* 22, and Héring, *The First Epistle to the Corinthians,* 32–33.

[26] It should be recalled that ὑπογράφω, the verb used for the drawing of the lines by the elementary teacher, came to mean "to give an example." Cf. esp. the way in which Plato (*Leg.* 711B) uses the verb to refer to the moral example that the king is to set or "trace out" for his citizens: "by his personal example he should first trace out the right lines, giving praise and honor to these things, blame to those." Cf. also 1 Pet 2:21 and the texts collected and discussed by Schrenk, *TDNT* 1.772–73. Thus Paul and Apollos, like the Lord (Clem. Al., *Paed.* 1.9.84.2), are ὑπογραμμοί for the Corinthian "children."

[27] The prepositions ὑπέρ and κατά, in view of their antithetic correlation, can only mean here "for" and "against." Cf. Rom 8:31; 2 Cor 13:8; Mark 9:40; Luke 9:50. For boasting in behalf of (ὑπέρ) someone, cf. 2 Cor 5:12; 7:4,14; 8:24; 9:2–3; 12:5; and 2 Thess 1:4. Exegetically, the εἷς is one of the "you" who is puffed up (φυσιοῦσθε). While the ἑνός and the ἑτέρου must both refer specifically to the missionaries as the objects of praise and denigration, the attitude adopted toward these would certainly have extended to their adherents.

In conclusion, this analysis of 4:6 and 4:14 supports the suggestion that 1 Cor 1:10–4:21 should be classified as "a letter of admonition." In it Paul presents himself as a model worthy of imitation, as a good father who would rear his children to follow him as he follows his Lord (4:16; 11:1). Exhortation (1:10; 4:16), admonition, and exemplification are Paul's dominant concerns in these chapters, *not* self-defense. The widespread view that 1:10–4:21 is primarily an apology by Paul is, quite simply, wrong.[28] Paul is concerned here with admonishing the Corinthians, with resolving the problem of their intra-mural strife (1:10–12), not with defending himself. He is as much concerned with those who *overestimate* him and other missionaries as he is with those who would rob any of them of their proper recognition as *God's* collaborators. In the first four chapters he is, to be sure, laying the basis for the advice, paraenesis, exhortation, and commands he will give later in the letter, but this basis is itself already hortatory, with the παρακαλῶ-section beginning already in 1:10. 1 Cor 1–4 is thus more similar to 1 Thess 1–3 than to either Galatians or 2 Corinthians.[29]

[28] The interpretation of 1 Cor 1–4 primarily in terms of an apology cannot be sustained. That Paul has been "judged" by certain persons is, of course, clear from the ironical contrast between 4:3–5 and 5:1–2. That is, while the Corinthians are judging Paul (4:3–5), they are *not* judging the sexual offender in their midst (5:1–2). And yet, the *main* problem Paul is addressing in 1 Cor 1–4 is intra-communal strife, not tension between himself and the community. Some of his sharpest words, moreover, are directed toward those who *exalted* him as their mystagogue (1:13–14), and the "judging" section in 4:3–5 is as much concerned with praise (4:5) as with censure. The tension at Corinth is based in part on a misconception of the role of missionaries, and it is this issue that he is addressing throughout chapters 1–4. Again, the procedure and terminology employed in 1 Cor 1–4 and that found in clearly apologetic letters (such as Galatians and 2 Cor 10–13) are quite different. If 1 Cor 1–4 is an apology, it is a very weak one and directed at "charges" that Paul does not consider serious challenges to his ministry. These points are conceded by Nils A. Dahl in a new note to his important and influential article, "Paul and the Church at Corinth according to 1 Corinthians 1:10–4:21," in his *Studies in Paul* (Minneapolis: Augburg, 1977) 61 n. 50. Dahl refuses, however, to abandon the concept of apology entirely. What he labels "apologetic elements" are, in my view, primarily admonitory in function, and any "apology" by Paul is incidental to his admonitory (4:14) and hortatory (1:10; 4:16) concerns.

[29] Cf. also the argument of C. J. Bjerkelund, *Parakalô: Form, Funktion und Sinn der parakalô-Sätzen in den paulinischen Briefen* (Oslo: Universitetsforlaget, 1967) 141–46, that 1 Cor 1:10 and 4:16 form an *inclusio*, which makes the entire intervening section a *parakalô* period. Paul introduces it so early in the letter because he thinks it is necessary to settle the issue of his relationship to the Corinthians before he turns to particular items. For the argument that 1 Thessalonians, including 2:1–12, is paraenetic rather than apologetic, cf. esp. A. J. Malherbe, "1 Thessalonians as a Paraenetic Letter" (Paper delivered at the 1972 SBL Seminar on the Form and Function of the Pauline Letters), incorporated in his article on "Hellenistic Moralists and the New Testament," *Aufstieg und Niedergang der römischen Welt* (ed. H. Temporini; Berlin: forthcoming) Vol. 2, Pt. 3.

The Structure of 1 Cor 4:7–13

Of all Paul's Corinthian catalogues, it is the one in 1 Cor 4 whose structure is the most debated and the least appreciated. For this reason it seems advisable to devote a separate section to the structure of 1 Cor 4:7–13, and to let this serve as a propaedeutic to the exegetical section that follows. As a section, 1 Cor 4:7–13 is highly stylized and contains four sub-sections: vv. 7–8, v. 9, v. 10, and vv. 11–13. The first sub-section (7–8) is tied to the preceding comment in 4:6 by the use of γάρ and the second sub-section (9) is linked with the first by another γάρ. The Corinthians are the main subject of the first sub-section and the apostles are the focus of attention in the second sub-section. In the third sub-section these two groups are contrasted with each other (10). The fourth sub-section (11–13) is devoted solely to the apostles and elaborates the description of the apostles found in the preceding sub-sections.

The first sub-section (7–8) breaks into three units. The first unit (7) contains three short incisive questions, while the second unit (8a–c) has three brief exclamations.[30] The third unit (8d–e) is an unfulfilled wish about the past, which brings the first sub-section to a close. The three questions all employ the second person singular, while the exclamations revert to the second person plural.[31] The apostles, who are not mentioned in the rhetorical questions and the first two exclamations, reenter the discussion by means of the third exclamation. The wish that follows is based on this third exclamation, as the use of the verb βασιλεύω and the connective καί make clear. Both the apostles and the Corinthians are therefore mentioned in the wish, and the concluding ἡμεῖς ὑμῖν συμβασιλεύσωμεν is a conscious contrast to the emphatic χωρὶς ἡμῶν of the final exclamation.[32] The

[30] The text and punctuation printed in the latest edition of Nestle-Aland, *Novum Testamentum Graece* (26th ed.; Stuttgart: Deutsche Bibelstiftung, 1979) are assumed throughout this investigation. Divergences from this edition are explicitly noted. In regard to 4:7–8, the absence of connectives from the exclamations serves to set them off from the preceding questions, which were joined by δέ. The third question and the third exclamation both break the pattern established by the first two questions and exclamations. The εἰ κτλ. breaks the pattern of τίς/τί and the χωρὶς ἡμῶν breaks the pattern of the ἤδη. Such breaks in form are typical devices for ending a series and are used effectively by Paul here.

[31] The shift from plural to singular is facilitated by the εἷς of 4:6. On the shift in Paul's letters from plural to singular, cf. Rom 12:16–20; Gal 4:6–7; 6:1; and G. B. Winer and G. Lünemann, *A Grammar of the Idiom of the New Testament* (7th ed.; Andover: Draper, 1893) 580.

[32] This is to be affirmed in opposition to Weiss, *Korintherbrief*, 108, and others, who deny this contrast by understanding χωρὶς ἡμῶν to mean "without our help" and relating it to the puffed up attitude "against the other" of 4:6. This is to prefer the remote to the obvious. The statement χωρὶς ἡμῶν ἐβασιλεύσατε is, moreover, equivalent to the χωρὶς ἡμῶν τελειωθῶσιν of Heb 11:40. The basic meaning of the prepositional phrase is thus "apart from us," "without us," and stands in contrast to the "with us" of the *hina*-clause.

contrasts that will dominate the third sub-section (10) are therefore anticipated at the end of the first sub-section.[33]

The second sub-section (9) contains one long complex sentence in which Paul expresses his opinion (δοκῶ) about God's actions vis-à-vis the apostles and adduces a reason (ὅτι) in support of that opinion. The Corinthians are entirely absent from this sub-section, but reappear in the third sub-section (10), which contains three contrasts between the apostles and the Corinthians. The apostles are mentioned at the beginning of the first two contrasts but at the end of the third one. In this way Paul provides a smooth transition from the second sub-section (9), where only the apostles (and God) are mentioned, to the fourth sub-section (11–13), where again only the apostles are mentioned.

Both terms in the first contrast receive a Christological expansion (διὰ Χριστόν, ἐν Χριστῷ) that, while absent from the terms of the remaining two antitheses, is implied for them as well. The apostles are thus not only "fools" but also "weak" and "despised" for the sake of Christ. The rhetorical effectiveness of this entire sub-section is heightened by the irony of the antitheses, the absence of copulas, and the ABBA pattern of the second and third contrasts.

The fourth sub-section is devoted entirely to the apostles (11–13). That these verses form a separate sub-section is clear from the *inclusio* formed with ἄρτι (ἄχρι τῆς ἄρτι ὥρας: 11; ἕως ἄρτι: 13). Within this *inclusio* occur three units (as in the first sub-section). The first unit (11–12a) contains six verbs, all present tense and indicative mood. Five are in the active voice, one in the passive. They are all joined by καί, a connective used six times here but only once[34] in the first sub-section, twice in the second, and not at all in the third. The final verb in the catena (κοπιῶμεν) is expanded by means of a participle.[35] This expansion serves both to close the first unit and to provide a transition to the second unit (12b–13a), where participles play a key role. Moreover, this final verb and its

[33] Rhetorical features in the first sub-section include the anaphora with τίς/τί and ἤδη and the epistrophe, even epanadiplosis, with ἐβασιλεύσατε. For a rhetorical analysis of 1 Cor 4:6–13, cf. J. Weiss, "Beiträge zur Paulinischen Rhetorik," in *Theologische Studien. B. Weiss zu seinem 70. Geburtstage* (ed. C. R. Gregory; Göttingen: Vandenhoeck & Ruprecht, 1897) 165–247, esp. 209–10.

[34] Καί occurs two other times in 4:7–8, but not as a connective.

[35] Some, such as Barrett, *First Corinthians*, 111–12, treat "working with our own hands" as a separate, seventh item in the list of Paul's hardships and view κοπιῶμεν as a reference to the toil of preaching and pastoral care. But if this were the case, surely another finite verb would have been used, not a participle. Moreover, the amplification of items, esp. the final one, is extremely common in catalogues. Paul is not adding a new hardship but giving emphasis to the final one just mentioned (κοπιῶμεν). Cf. esp. the comparable formulation in Eph 4:28. Barrett's interpretation not only introduces a distinction between sacred and secular that is foreign to Paul but also posits a restrictive meaning for "toil" that it can scarely have in the other *peristasis* catalogues (2 Cor 6:5; 11:23,27).

accompanying participle serve as the AB part of a ABBA pattern of verb-participle-participle-verb. Thus we have κοπιῶμεν-ἐργαζόμενοι-λοιδορούμενοι-εὐλογοῦμεν.

The second unit (12b–13a) is comprised of three contrasts, each an oxymoron.[36] In this way it is very similar to the antitheses of the third sub-section. The difference from the preceding is that here the treatment accorded the apostles is contrasted with their reaction to that treatment. And while the third sub-section was without copulas, this unit is without connectives. This contrasts strongly with the three uses of δέ in verse 10 and the polysyndeton with καί in vv. 11–12a.

The third unit (13b–c) brings to a close the depiction of the apostles given in the fourth sub-section and also that begun in verse 9, the second sub-section. On the one hand, the ἕως ἄρτι is placed at the end, so that it corresponds to the ἄχρι τῆς ἄρτι ὥρας that began the sub-section. On the other hand, the τοῦ κόσμου ἐγενήθημεν of v. 13 corresponds to the ἐγενήθημεν τῷ κόσμῳ of v. 9. Thus this final unit contains the termination of two *inclusiones*, one begun in v. 11 and the other in v. 9. The use of ὡς with a plural noun (περικαθάρματα) in v. 13 recalls, moreover, the beginning of the depiction of the apostles in v. 9, ὡς ἐπιθανατίους.

As a result, the statement in verse 9 ("God has exhibited us apostles last") becomes the thesis sentence for all of verses 9–13.[37] That is, these verses function to provide support for Paul's opinion (δοκῶ) that the apostles appear as ἔσχατοι, utterly insignificant. Paul's hardships, therefore, provide backing for his interpretative claim.

The structure of this crucial fourth sub-section may be indicated in the following manner:

(1) ἄχρι τῆς ἄρτι ὥρας
        καὶ πεινῶμεν καὶ διψῶμεν καὶ γυμνιτεύομεν
        καὶ κολαφιζόμεθα καὶ ἀστατοῦμεν καὶ κοπιῶμεν
            ἐργαζόμενοι ταῖς ἰδίαις χερσίν·
(2)   λοιδορούμενοι εὐλογοῦμεν,
        διωκόμενοι ἀνεχόμεθα,
        δυσφημούμενοι παρακαλοῦμεν·
(3) ὡς περικαθάρματα τοῦ κόσμου ἐγενήθημεν,
        πάντων περίψημα
            ἕως ἄρτι.

The whole unit of vv. 9–13 is therefore highly symmetrical. It begins and ends with a statement of what the apostles have become in regard to the world (9,13). The movement through the passage is facilitated by two uses of chiasmus. The first concerns the shift from ἡμεῖς/ὑμεῖς to ὑμεῖς/ἡμεῖς in v. 10. The ἡμεῖς μωροί (10)

[36] Weiss, "Beiträge," 210, calls attention to the strong oxymora in 4:12b–13a.

[37] The thematic character of 4:9 is recognized also by Weiss, "Beiträge," 210.

provides continuity with the ἐγενήθημεν of 4:9. The concluding ἡμεῖς ἄτιμοι provides continuity with the πεινῶμεν, etc., of v. 11. In addition, it serves to close the contrast between the Corinthians and the apostles. The second use of chiasmus involves the movement from verb/participle to participle/verb. This structural shift serves both to close the series of indicative verbs and to introduce a second contrast, this one between the treatment of the apostles and their reaction to it.

There is, finally, a marked preference for triads in 4:7-13. There are three rhetorical questions (7), three exclamations (8), three ironic antitheses (10), and three hardships with accompanying response (12b-13a). In 4:9, moreover, the apostles are depicted in three ways, as ἔσχατοι, ἐπιθανάτιοι, and a θέατρον. Also, the division of the "world" into the categories of angels and men (9) is triadic in effect. The triadic tendency of this section thus makes likely what is preferable on internal grounds, viz., that the six items of 4:lla-12a are to be arranged primarily as triads rather than as pairs. They easily can be distributed on two lines, with the participial phrase amplifying κοπιῶμεν placed on a third line. In the final analysis, however, the multiple material links between the six items and the fact that each is joined to the others by the repeated use of καί are strong indications that the totality of the items and their interconnection are more important than their precise grouping.[38]

The Synkrisis of the Corinthians and the Apostles

The twin goals of exemplification and admonition are pursued by Paul chiefly through a *synkrisis* of the Corinthians and the apostles. This *synkrisis* is most obvious in 4:10, but it runs throughout 4:8-13. In this *synkrisis* Paul makes use of various traditions about the *sophos*, some of which have already been

[38] The lack of any clear structural break in the catalogue makes it difficult to arrange the items. A grouping by pairs is unlikely because the only well-established pair is "hunger and thirst." Items three and four could possibly be paired in the sense of "stripped and beaten." But this is unlikely, for there is no evidence that the verbs employed by Paul were used to express this idea (compare Luke 10:30; Acts 16:22; 19:16; Dio Chrys., *Or.* 4.67; Philo, *Flacc.* 75). Furthermore, since "nakedness" is more commonly associated with hunger and thirst as corporeal hardships necessitating food and clothing (Tob 1:17; 4:16; Matt 25:35-36,42-43; Rom 8:35; 2 Cor 11:27; Jas 2:15; Dio Chrys., *Or.* 7.55), it is better to join the third item with the first two to form a triad. Cf. esp. Deut 28:48: "in hunger, and in thirst, and in nakedness." A triadic arrangement, however, should not obscure the extent to which *all* the items are interconnected. The corporeal requirements of food, clothing, and shelter are stock items in the discussion of poverty and bodily necessities (Teles, II,7,4-8,5 Hense [=8,29-44 O'Neil]; IVA,41,3-12 Hense [=40,117-41,129 O'Neil]; Ps-Anacharsis, *Ep.* 5 [42,2-4 Malherbe]; Matt 6:25; 25:35-44; Jas 2:15-16) and establish conclusively the interconnection of items one, two, three, and five. For the affinity of items three, four, and five, cf. Dio Chrys., *Or.* 25.3. Again, items one and six (hunger and toil) are joined in Isa 40:31 and Sir 16:27; cf. also 2 Cor 6:5. On the catalogue as a whole, compare Dio Chrys., *Or.* 8.16.

discussed in chapter three. In regard to the apostolic *peristaseis*, the emphasis falls on the physical, bodily hardships suffered by the apostles and the lack of approbation accorded them. The apostles are depicted as the contemptible poor.

The first contrast is between the satiety of the Corinthians (8: κεκορεσμένοι ἐστέ) and the hunger and thirst of the apostles (11: πεινῶμεν καὶ διψῶμεν), with the former understood spiritually and the latter physically.[39] The concept of κόρος that Paul introduces here is important.[40] It was suggested by the term φυσιοῦσθε (4:6), which strongly conveys the idea of *hybris*.[41] The κόρος-ὕβρις connection is ancient, as is the idea that they lead to excessive deeds for which one must suffer retribution (*nemesis*) or ruin (*atē*).[42] This sequence is reflected here by Paul, for he moves from a statement of the Corinthians' inflated arrogance (4:18–19; 5:2) to the discussion of a case of extreme *porneia* (5:1) that demands the destruction of the flesh (5:5).[43] The Corinthians are a prime example of the human tendency to let an abundance of goods (1:7; 4:7–8) lead to a loss of restraint and perspective.[44]

Κόρος is not only traditionally connected with *hybris* but also typically contrasted with hunger and thirst.[45] Paul's *synkrisis* here, therefore, draws on a standard antithesis. And, while κόρος points back to the Corinthians' φυσίωσις (4:6), it points forward to the term ἐπλουτήσατε (4:8). It does so, for the connection of κόρος with πλοῦτος is equally well-established.[46]

[39] Hunger and thirst are frequently paired. Cf. Teles, II,7,8–10 Hense (=8,35–38 O'Neil); Dio Chrys., *Or.* 7.55; 8.16; *Soc.Ep.* 12 (250,11 Malherbe); Ps 106:5; Isa 5:13; Matt 5:6; 25:35–37, 42–44; John 6:35; Rom 12:20; 2 Cor 11:27; Rev 7:16; Ign., *Smyrn.* 6.2.

[40] The term *koros* appears in the discussion of *peristaseis* in Max. Tyr., *Or.* 34.6a,7a (397,7; 398,3–4 Hobein). Philo uses it as part of a *synkrisis* of the gloating rich and the dishonored, beaten poor (*Flacc.* 77).

[41] Cf., for example, Philo, *Virt.* 162. Boasting without any acknowledgement of indebtedness (4:7) is also a mark of self-reliant *hybris*.

[42] Solon 5.9 Diehl (=6.9 Edwards; cf. also 4.8–9,35 Edwards); Theog. 153–54; 1174; Pind., *Ol.* 13.10; Hdt. 3.80.3; 8.77; Diog. Laert. 1.59; Stob. 4.26.4–5; and compare Aesch., *Pers.* 821–22. Philo makes repeated use of this old pair. Cf. *Abr.* 228; *Agr.* 32, 48; *Flacc.* 91; *L.A.* 2.29, 70; *Mos.* 2.13, 164; *Op.* 169; *Post.* 98, 145; *Spec.* 3.43; *Virt.* 162. For surfeit and arrogance, cf. also Soph., *OT* 872–74; Ps-Heraclitus, *Ep.* 2 (188, 6–7 Malherbe). For the interconnection of *koros-hybris-atē*, cf. J. D. Denniston and Denys Page (eds.), *Aeschylus: Agamemnon* (Oxford: Clarendon, 1957) 136.

[43] For satiated arrogance leading to illicit sexual acts, cf. Philo, *Abr.* 135; *Spec.* 3.43.

[44] Cf. esp. Philo, *Abr.* 134–35, 228; *Conf.* 7; *Her.* 240; *Mos.* 2.13.

[45] For *koros* as the antonym of hunger (and thirst), Cf. Hom., *Il.* 19.166–67; Theog. 605; Heraclitus B 67, 111; Teles, IVB,45,7 Hense (=48,8–9 O'Neil); Max. Tyr., *Or.* 34.6a (397,7 Hobein); Joseph., *AJ* 10.260–62. Cf. also Matt 5:6; Luke 6:21,25; Phil 4:12; Dio Chrys., *Or.* 7.17; and Lucian, *Merc.Cond.* 8.

[46] For *koros* connected with wealth, cf. Theog. 153–54; Aesch., *Agam.* 382; Pind., *Isthm.* 3.2; *Ol.* 1.56; Democr. B 283 (cf. also 219); Max. Tyr., *Or.* 34.7a (398,3–4 Hobein); Diog. Laert. 1.59. For satiety and wealth, cf. also Luke 6:24–25. *Koros* is thus an antonym

The second contrast is thus between the spiritual wealth of the Corinthians and the physical poverty of the apostles.[47] Hunger and thirst are standard features of poverty, so that Paul's statement about the apostles' πεῖνα already indicates their πενία.[48] Their poverty is also reflected in the statement that γυμνιτεύομεν (4:11). The fact that the apostles are γυμνοί indicates, in the first place, the lightness and wretchedness of their clothing.[49] But this attire is, more fundamentally, the manifestation of the fact that they are destitute. Dio Chrysostom, for example, contrasts those who have money (ἀργύριον) with those who are γυμνοί (*Or.* 7.55). In a similar way, Apuleius describes Crates as "naked" after he has renounced his fortune (*Flor.* 14). The satiated, opulent Corinthians thus stand in vivid contrast to the hungry and destitute apostles.[50]

The fact that the apostles are not wealthy is also expressed by Paul's statement that ἀστατοῦμεν καὶ κοπιῶμεν ἐργαζόμενοι ταῖς ἰδίαις χερσίν (4:11–12a). The verb ἀστατεῖν is a frequentative verb that expresses incessant movement. It depicts the life of the wanderer, constantly moving from place to place. The theme of the poor wanderer appears already in the *Odyssey* and remains a stock item throughout ancient literature.[51] Its appropriateness in Paul's catalogue may be

---

of poverty and need (cf. Hes., *Th.* 593; Heraclitus B 65; Democr. B 283; Philo, *L.A.* 3.7; *Spec.* 1.208). For the arrogance of wealth, cf. Eur., frg. 438; Dem., *Or.* 21.98, 195; Dio Chrys., *Or.* 65.7; Diog. Laert. 6.24.

[47] Compare the combination of spiritual wealth and physical poverty in 2 Cor 6:10; Rev 2:9; *Diogn.* 5.13; *Herm.Sim.* 2.5. Cf. also the Stoic paradox of the needy but rich sage (e.g., Cic., *Mur.* 61; Philo, *Post.* 128; *Mos.* 1.156–57; *Plant.* 69).

[48] Cf., for example, Teles, II,7,8–10 Hense (=8,35–38 O'Neil) and Luke 6:20–21. The hungry are contrasted with the wealthy in Luke 1:53 and *Herm.Vis.* 3.9.5. To be hungry is to have need (Mark 2:25; *Barn.* 10.3), whereas the rich man claims to have no need (Rev 3:17).

[49] Cf. esp. Sen., *Ben.* 5.13.3: "one who has seen a man wretchedly clad and in rags says that the man he saw was 'naked' (*nudum*)."

[50] For poverty and nakedness, cf. Job 31:19–20 and Epict., *Diss.* 3.22.45; for "rich" contrasted with "poor and naked," cf. Rev 3:17. There are also other similarities between 1 Cor 4 and Rev 3:14–20. Both contain a wish with ὄφελον (1 Cor 4:8; Rev 3:15) and function as reproof offered out of love (1 Cor 4:14; Rev 3:19). In addition, both depict the false self-image held by the readers. The key difference between the two passages is that Paul contrasts the Corinthians with the apostles, whereas John opposes the true, pitiable picture of the Laodiceans to that which they themselves have painted. On the affinities between Paul and the Apocalypse, cf. esp. E. Schüssler Fiorenza, "Apocalyptic and Gnosis in the Book of Revelation and Paul," *JBL* 92 (1973) 565–81.

[51] Cf., for example, Hom., *Od.* 19.74; 21.327; Eur., *Med.* 515. The wanderer is, fundamentally, he who is not a permanent inhabitant of a city (Philo, *Mut.* 152). Exiles, for example, were often termed "wandrers" or "transients." This was the case, even if they became "resident aliens" in another place. Cf. D. L. Page, *Euripides: Medea* (Oxford: Clarendon, 1938) 172. For wandering and homelessness in a *peristasis* catalogue, cf. Sen., *Prov.* 4.14–15; Achilles Tatius 5.18.4; and Epict., *Diss.* 3.22.45,47; 4.8.30–31.

seen from Isa 58:7 Aq., where instructions are given to feed the hungry, clothe the naked, and provide lodging for the "homeless poor." Whereas the LXX translates the Hebrew (*mĕrûdîm*)[52] by "homeless" (ἀστέγους), Aquila does so with ἀστατεῖν. In both cases it modifies πτωχοί and the two translations are complementary, pointing out that the oppressed, wandering poor are those without shelter. Lodging, of course, belongs with food and clothing as a basic physical need.

Although the apostles are homeless wanderers, they do not beg, but "toil, working with their own hands."[53] The rich clearly do not work with their own hands, for it is a hardship to them simply to be without an attendant.[54] The stress on manual labor is in keeping with the poverty of the apostles, and also serves to distinguish them from the various mendicants of the ancient world and the beggar-missionaries of early Christianity.[55]

The Corinthians, on the other hand, are not merely proud and affluent spiritually; they are also kings (8: ἐβασιλεύσατε).[56] The designation of the sage as the wealthy king is common in Stoic circles and is here predicated of the Corinthian *sophoi.*[57] Kings and people of wealth are naturally the preeminent ones

[52] The Hebrew word occurs elsewhere in the MT only in Lam 1:7 and 3:19, both times in conjunction with "affliction."

[53] For the joint occurrence of "toil" and "work," cf. also 1 Cor 16:16; 1 Thess 1:3; 2:9; Eph 4:28; Rev 2:2; and compare 2 Cor 11:27; 1 Thess 2:9; 2 Thess 3:8; Col 1:29; 1 Tim 4:10. For working with one's hands, cf. also 1 Thess 4:11; Eph 4:28; Acts 20:34–35; *Barn.* 19.10.

[54] Cf. Teles, IVA,41,12–13 Hense (=42,130–31 O'Neil); Epict., *Diss.* 3.22.45,47; Dio Chrys., *Or.* 40.2: Sen., *Helv.* 12.4; Mar. Ant., *Med.* 6.30.2; and Apul., *Apol.* 17. The rich were not alone in their hostility to manual labor. Philosophers in general despised the trades. Cf. Hock, *Social Context,* 39, 87 n. 135.

[55] Poverty and working with one's hands are joined together by Dio Chrys., *Or.* 7.103, 125. The poverty of the artisan is emphasized by Hock, *Social Context,* 34–37, who stresses Paul's practice of a trade as a constant source of his *peristaseis.* On wandering charismatics in early Christianity, cf. now Gerd Theissen, *Sociology of Early Christianity* (Philadelphia: Fortress, 1978) esp. 8–16. For their pagan counterparts, cf. Walter Liefeld, "The Wandering Preacher as a Social Figure in the Roman Empire" (Ph.D. Diss., Columbia University, 1967).

[56] For the combination of kingship and satiety/arrogance, cf. Hdt. 3.80.3; 4.146; Soph., *OT* 872–74; Dio Chrys., *Or.* 1.67; 30.19. Happiness to the point of satiety within the royal circle is found in Psellus 175.21.

[57] For the sage as the rich man and ruler, cf. Cic., *Fin.* 3.22.75; *Mur.* 61; Hor., *Ep.* 1.1.106–07; *Sat.* 1.3.124–25; Sen., *Ben.* 7.10.6; Philo, *Sob.* 56–57; Plut., *Mor.* 472A; 1058B–D; Lucian, *Hermot.* 81. For the sage's wealth as the owner of all things, cf. also Pl., *Phdr.* 279B–C; Cic., *Paradoxa Stoic.* 6.42; Sen., *Ben.* 7.2.5; 3.2–3; 8.1; Philo, *Mos.* 1.156–57; *Plant.* 69; Plut., *Mor.* 1058C; Diog. Laert. 6.37, 72; 7.125; and the discussion of 1 Cor 3:21–22 by Weiss, *Korintherbrief,* 90, and Herbert Braun, "Exegetische Randglossen zum I. Korintherbrief," in his *Gesammelte Studien zum Neuen Testament und seiner Umwelt* (Tübingen: Mohr, 1962) 182–86. On the kingship of the sage, cf. also Hor., *Sat.* 1.3.133,136; Philo, *Abr.* 261; *Mig.* 197; *Mut.* 152; *Post.* 128; *Prob.* 20; *Som.* 2.44; Epict., *Diss.* 3.22.49,63,79; Diog. Laert. 7.122. The similarity of 1 Cor 4:8 to these affirmations

who stand at the top of the social order. The apostles, by contrast, are at the bottom of the social ladder. They are the ἔσχατοι, the least important, the most abject and insignificant of all (9).[58] As such, they are like the ἐλάχιστοι of Matt 25, who similarly are hungry, thirsty, and naked itinerants.[59] The contrast in rank

---

about the sage has long been noted. Cf., for example, E. L. Hicks, "St. Paul and Hellenism," *Studia Biblica et Ecclesiastica* 4 (1896) 1–14, esp. 9. What crystallizes in 4:8 is presupposed throughout 1 Corinthians. The "wealth" theme appears already in 1:5–7 and is restated in 3:21–22. The judicial assumptions of 4:3–5 and 6:3 belong to the kingship motif, as does the slogan "all things are permissible" (comp. Dio Chrys., *Or.* 3.10). The Corinthians' failure to mourn (5:2) also fits this theme (comp. Rev 18:7), and its importance is reflected in the fact that five of the eight occurrences of the word "kingdom" in the Pauline *homologoumena* are in 1 Cor (4:20; 6:9–10; 15:24,50). Finally, as we shall see, the affirmations about the Corinthians in 4:10 rest on the assertions of 4:8.

[58] There is a widespread exegetical tradition that links "last" to "condemned criminals" and sees Paul as comparing the apostles to gladiators who marched "last" in triumphal processions and/or were exhibited "at the end" of the show. This interpretation not only founders on an absence of supporting data (cf. Weiss, *Korintherbrief,* 109) but also overlooks the way in which "last" serves as the general rubric for the discussion of the apostles in 4:9–13. The comparison (ὡς) of the apostles to condemned criminals is but the first of the various ways in which Paul specifies and illustrates what it means for the apostles to be "last." Compare the way in which the general term *extremus* is particularized in Apul., *Met.* 4.31: "some perfect outcast of a man – someone who has lost rank, fortune, everything, someone who goes about in terror of his life and in such complete degradation that nobody viler can be found in the whole world" (trans. by R. Graves, *The Transformations of Lucius Otherwise Known as The Golden Ass* [New York: Farrar, Straus & Giroux, 1973] 98). The word "last" is used here to indicate the lowness of the apostles' worldly rank and status, in contrast to the exalted spiritual status of the Corinthians as affluent kings. Though "first" in the church (cf. 1 Cor 12:28), God reveals them to the world as "last." The "last" are typically those who are wronged, insulted, suffer drunken abuse, have their property confiscated, and, in short, are treated as fools (Dio Chrys., *Or.* 38.36–37). Neglected and despisd, they are shown no honor at all (Fronto, *Ep.* 2.130 Haines [119 Naber]). Poor, they live "a frugal and utterly miserable life" (Diod. Sic. 8.18.3), so that their only hope is to be enriched by the wealth of others (Cic., *Rosc.Am.* 47.137). The term "last" is tied to an absence of perceived worth (cf. Ign., *Rom.* 9:2; *Smyrn.* 11:1; *Trall.* 13:1), so that statements like "the lowest and basest of mankind" (*omnium nationum postremissimum nequissimumque*) are not uncommon (Gell., *NA* 15.12.3; comp. Cic., *Pis.* 27.66; 1 Cor 4:9,13). In the Synoptic tradition the designation is connected with the status of a servant or slave (Mark 9:35; cf. also 10:43–44), and in the *synkrisis* of the rich young man and the disciples (Matt 19:16–30), the "first" are the rich and the "last" are the wandering disciples who abandon all – homes, family, and fields – for Jesus' sake (comp. 1 Cor 4:10a). In their earthly way of life the apostles are thus, to borrow a phrase from 1 Cor 15:19, "the most pitiable of all persons."

[59] The equivalency of "least" and "last" is indicated by the way in which Ignatius (*Rom.* 9:2) substitutes "least" for "last" in drawing on 1 Cor 15:8–9. The similarities between Matt 25:31–46 and the *peristasis* catalogues in Paul and other Christian authors are treated illuminatingly by J. R. Michaels, "Apostolic Hardships and Righteous Gentiles," *JBL* 84

and status could not be more extreme.[60]

The use of Stoic *sophos*-imagery to depict the Corinthians continues in 4:10, with the affirmations of 4:8 serving as the basis of those made here. Thus, as affluent kings, the Corinthians are φρόνιμοι, ἰσχυροί, and ἔνδοξοι. The first of these is drawn from the sage's possession of φρόνησις, the chief of the four cardinal virtues.[61] The fact that the Corinthians are kings already implies their sagacity, for in the philosophical tradition the sage's kingship is equated with his wisdom (Philo, *Mig.* 197). Flatterers, moreover, typically proclaim that "kings and wealthy persons . . . rank first in understanding" (Plut., *Mor.* 58E). Paul, of course, is not using flattery here, but irony,[62] and his use of φρόνιμοι rather than σοφοί is deliberate.[63] The true sage always acts sensibly (φρονίμως),[64] for "he knows what he should and should not do" (Philo, *Mut.* 152). Φρόνησις, in other words, is especially concerned with conduct,[65] and "the wise (οἱ φρόνιμοι) are permitted to do anything whatsoever they wish" (Dio Chrys., *Or.* 14.17). Such an attitude is clearly in keeping with the Corinthians' self-understanding (1 Cor 6:12), and Paul ironically introduces the term here immediately prior to his

(1965) 27–37, esp. 32–36.

[60] Compare esp. Cass. Dio 42.5.5, where Pompey's death is said to be "like one of the lowest of the Egyptians." This statement is made more striking by the added comment that he was "the most powerful of the Romans" and was called "Agamemnon." Thus Pompey, "the king of kings" (Plut., *Pomp.* 67.3; *Caes.* 41.1), is compared to an abject Egyptian in the manner of his death.

The *synkrisis* with the kingship theme also implies comparisons with other items in the description of the apostles. As kings, for example, the Corinthians engage in judgment (4:3–5; 6:3), whereas the servant apostles (4:1) are those who are judged and condemned to death (4:9). The wealthy, luxurious life of a king involves a manifold contrast to the poverty of the apostles (comp. Tib. 3.3.23–24). Cf., for instance, the way in which the body of a manual laborer is compared to that of a king's son in Joseph., *AJ* 17.333. Cf. also the comparison of the wealthy Stoic king to poor, begging Odysseus in Plut., *Mor.* 1058D.

[61] Cf., for example, Philo, *L.A.* 1.66–67. For the sage as "prudent," cf. Sen., *Ep.* 85.2; Plut., *Mor.* 1043A–B; 1062A; *SVF* 2.41.14–15 (§131).

[62] For other ironical statements about the Corinthians' wisdom, cf. 1 Cor 6:5; 10:15; 2 Cor 11:19. Schmiedel, "Korinther," 114, correctly notes the ironic depiction of the Corinthians' self-understanding. The irony is missed completely by C. F. G. Heinrici, *Das erste Sendschreiben des Apostels Paulus an die Korinther* (Berlin: Hertz, 1880) 146, who holds that Paul speaks seriously here of their Christian wisdom. Of course, the Corinthians were not void of understanding; it was rather the case with them that "a little learning is a dangerous thing." For the presumption of wisdom, cf. also Philo, *Leg.* 64 and Rom 1:22.

[63] *Contra* Conzelmann, *1 Corinthians,* 89, the use of *phronimos* rather than *sophos* is not "merely a rhetorical variation without inherent meaning." The substitution is deliberate and done in anticipation of the discussion of conduct in chapters five and six.

[64] Cf. esp. Philo, *Prob.* 59, and also *SVF* 1.52.32 (§216) = 3.150.4 (§567); 3.149.16–17 (§563). Cf. also Plut., *Mor.* 1071B.

[65] Cf., for instance, *SVF* 3.63.23–35 (§262); 65.43–66.2 (§268); Philo, *L.A.* 1.65,74.

discussion in chapters five and six of their conduct, which is conspicuously lacking in true discernment. The Corinthians are not truly wise ἐν Χριστῷ, only παρ' ἑαυτοῖς (cf. Prov 3:7; Rom 11:25; 12:16). They are still children in their minds, not τέλειοι (1 Cor 14:20), and thus they continue to talk and act like children (cf. 1 Cor 13:11). Their behavior gives the lie to their pretensions of maturity and perfectionism.

The poor, abject apostles, by contrast, have become "fools for Christ" (4:10), a fact that paradoxically indicates their true wisdom (3:18). For Paul is in fact a wise architect (3:10), one whose work, unlike the fool's, will not collapse (Matt 7:24–27). Yet, from the world's point of view, the heralds of the "moronic message" appear as ludicrous as the crucified Christ whom they proclaim (1:18–25). It is the reality of that perception by the world and his readers' skewed self-perception that underlies the antithesis that Paul forms here between the sagacious Corinthians and the asinine apostles. The contrast between the sage and the fool is, of course, basic to the Stoic and Cynic view of humanity, and it is employed here with devastating effectiveness.[66]

The next contrast is between the Corinthians as ἰσχυροί and the apostles as ἀσθενεῖς.[67] The epithet "strong," since it was already sociologically associated with "kings" and "the rich,"[68] was naturally appropriated by Stoics to describe the *sophos*. As applied to the sage, ἰσχυροί indicated his moral power, the strength of his soul.[69] The result of *askēsis* (*SVF* 3.68.25–31 [§278]), it was that quality

[66] For the Cynic and Stoic contrast between the sage and the fool, cf. *SVF* 3.24.42–25.7 (§103); 25.24–34 (§106); Dio Chrys., *Or.* 69.4; Sext. Emp., *Math.* 11.207; and also *SVF* 2.223.20–21 (§809); 3.73.27 (§298); 158.23–29 (§615); 170.29–171.5 (§682); 241.35 (§117). This contrast is, of course, only a concretization of the basic contrast between *phronēsis* and *aphrosynē*; for the latter, cf. *SVF* 1.47.23 (§190); 2.49.36 (§173); 50.16–18 (§174); 3.17.19 (§70); 23.30–33 (§95); Diog. Laert. 7.92. The contrast is made more effective here by the ellipsis of copulas, which in rhetorical style was often almost obligatory. Cf. esp. G. Böhlig, *Untersuchungen zum rhetorischen Sprachgebrauch der Byzantier* (Berliner Byzantische Arbeiten 2; Berlin: Akademie-Verlag, 1956) 239. Needless to say, the contrast between wise man and fool is also a stock item in the OT sapiential tradition (Prov 11:12, 29; 15:21; 17:10; Sir 21:26; etc.). Cf. also Matt 7:24–27; 25:1–13.

[67] For these two words as antonyms, cf. 1 Cor 1:25,27; 2 Cor 10:10; Num 13:9; Ezek 34:20; Pl., *Euthd.* 281C; Philo, *Abr.* 216; *Ebr.* 186; *Som.* 1.155; *Aet.* 58; *1 Clem.* 38.2. Cf. also the contrast between Paul and the Corinthians in 2 Cor 13:9. For the sequence "wise . . . strong," cf. 1 Cor 1:24–27; 1 Sam 2:10 LXX; Jer 9:23; and comp. Philo, *Virt.* 174.

[68] Cf. Jer 9:23; Rev 6:15; 19:18; and the sociological analysis of the terms in 1 Cor 1:26–29 by Gerd Theissen, *The Social Setting of Pauline Christianity* (Philadelphia: Fortress, 1982) 70–73. His attempt to understand the three terms of 4:10 sociologically is, however, exegetically fallacious. It neglects the spiritualizing phrase "in Christ" and misses the way in which the epithets of 4:10 continue the imagery of 4:8. There is, of course, a social basis for this vocabulary, but the use of it in 4:10 is metaphorical rather than literal.

[69] Cf. esp. *SVF* 1.52.33–53.2 (§216). For the "strength of the soul," cf. *SVF* 3.23.24,28 (§95); 120.39–121.2 (§471); 123.1–5 (§473).

which manifested itself in virtuous conduct (Plut., *Mor.* 1034D–E) and which rendered him "unconquered and unconquerable" (*SVF* 1.53.1–2 [§216]). It will be recalled from chapter three that many moralists held that the person who had become a sage could not fall from that state, that virtue once gained could not be lost.[70] The Corinthians, confident of their knowledge and conquering spiritual power (compare 1 John 2:14), clearly see themselves as impregnable and secure. For that reason Paul has to remind them in chapter ten that their satiety of spiritual food and drink is no guarantee that they cannot fall (10:1–12). With biting irony he issues these unmistakable words of warning to "wise men" (10:15) who greatly overestimate their spiritual strength (10:22).

This is not the case with the "weak" apostles, who must reckon with the possibility of defeat in their *agōn* and thus exert themselves strenuously in order to avoid failure and attain their goal (1 Cor 9:26–27).[71] While the apostles know themselves to be weak, the world perceives them as such, but for a different reason. The world deems them as weak because of the way in which they respond to abuse. Their "weakness" is their failure to retaliate (1 Cor 4:12b–13a), their failure, either aggressively or defensively, to abuse others (contrast Wis 2:10–11). Unlike the Corinthians who powerfully assert their rights against each other (1 Cor 6:1–6; 8:1–13; 10:23–11:1), the apostles are willing to forgo their rights (1 Cor 9), suffer wrong, and be defrauded (1 Cor 6:7). Such conduct is, from the perspective of the world, already a mark of the ἀτιμία of which Paul will speak next.[72]

Whereas the apostles are ἄτιμοι, the Corinthians are ἔνδοξοι.[73] The latter term's association with kings and the rich is common,[74] and thus occurs in depictions

[70] Cf. chapter three, note 31.

[71] The word "weak" is used in the philosophical tradition in the description of those who have not become *sophoi* (cf. Cic., *Fin.* 4.28.77; Plut., *Mor.* 1057B; *SVF* 3.124.5 [§473]), that is, of those who especially require *askēsis.*

[72] Cf. esp. 2 Cor 11:20–21, where Paul refers to the "disgrace" that was his because he had been too "weak" to abuse the Corinthians in the same manner as the superapostles. Paul's personal demeanor was simply "weak" in the eyes of others (comp. 1 Cor 2:4; 2 Cor 10:10). By implication, then, the Corinthians' "strength" also alludes to the way in which they aggressively pursued the course that their "prudence" dictated. Thus, "strong," like "wise," anticipates the discussion of conduct that begins in chapter five. "Weak," on the other hand, since it was often associated with "poor" (Prov 22:22; 31:9; comp. Gal 4:9), may already contain a hint of the poverty that will be emphasized in 4:11–12a. This is especially the case if the "strong" of 4:10 is correlative with the "rich" of 4:8.

[73] The movement from a contrast of strong and weak to one involving honor and *atimia* occurs already in Pl., *Euthd.* 281C.

[74] For the use of the term in conjunction with kings and rulers, cf. Isa 23:8; 1 Macc 2:17; 7:26; Philo, *Jos.* 76; *Mig.* 161; Luke 7:25; Ael., *VH* 2.20. For its use with the rich, cf. Pl., *Soph.* 223D; Sir 10:22; Sus 4; Philo, *Fug.* 16; *Leg.* 13; *Prob.* 72; *Spec.* 4.172; *Virt.* 170. It is, of course, typical for kings to have glory, power, and great wealth. Cf. *Ep. Arist.* 211, 224.

of the sage.[75] The affluent Corinthians, having already assumed the eschatological reign, are thus seated in all their kingly splendor.[76] But just as their reign is not shared by the apostles (4:8), neither is their glory (4:10).[77]

It is the apostles' lack of honor and status that Paul emphasizes in the following catalogue, their ἀτιμία as the ἔσχατοι.[78] The poverty that is so conspicuous in the catalogue (4:11–12a) is, in and of itself, an open invitation to disparagement by the world. Furthermore, "like condemned criminals" (ὡς ἐπιθανατίους)[79] who are compelled to fight in the arena, the apostles constitute a spectacle (θέατρον)[80] to a rude, bloodthirsty and hostile cosmos of angels and men (4:9).[81]

[75] Cf. esp. Philo, *Sob.* 75, where even this term is not sufficient to describe the eminence of the affluent king-sage who has passed beyond the bounds of human happiness (cf. 1 Cor 4:8). Compare also Hor., *Ep.* 1.1.107: "the wise man is . . . honoured (*honoratus*)." Cf. also Sen., *Ep.* 81.13. In a similar way, the Stoics regard every φαῦλος as ἄτιμος, no matter how eminent he may be socially. Cf. *SVF* 3.149.24–25 (§563).

[76] The association of glory with the eschatological kingdom is common; cf., for instance, 1 Thess 2:12 and compare Matt 20:21 with Mark 10:27.

[77] Compare the contrast in Sir 40:3 between the one who sits on a glorious throne and the one who is humbled in dirt and ashes. For the basic contrast between the *endoxos* and the *tapeinos*, cf. also 1 Sam 18:23 LXX and Philo, *Post.* 109. Compare Philo, *Mos.* 1.160 and *Mut.* 232. The fact that the artisan Paul is not included in his converts' kingdom is somewhat comparable to the exclusion of artisans from Zeno's ideal state. For the latter, cf. H. C. Baldry, "Zeno's Ideal State," *JHS* 79 (1959) 3–25, esp. 10–11, and also Hock, *Social Context*, 36, 85 n. 113.

[78] That 4:9–13 expresses the multitude's *contempt* was observed already in the second century by Clement of Alexandria (*Str.* 4.7.51.2–3 [2.272.4–11 Stählin]). This contempt shows that the apostles' true identity "as servants of Christ and stewards of the mysteries of God" (1 Cor 4:1) remains as hidden from the unbelieving world as the gospel that they proclaim (2 Cor 4:4).

[79] That this is the meaning of this NT *hapax legomenon* is certain from its occurrence in Dion. Hal., *Ant.Rom.* 7.35.3–4. For the word, cf. also Bel 32. For the idea that the word expresses, cf. 2 Cor 1:9; 4:11; and esp. Ep Jer 17(18): "as though he were sentenced to death."

[80] The word "spectacle" is frequently applied to the gladiatorial games and sometimes to the combatant himself. Cf. Pliny, *Pan.* 33.3: "no spectator found himself turned spectacle (*spectaculum*), dragged off by the hook to satisfy grim pleasures, or else cast to the flames!" For the gruesome midday bouts of condemned criminals and the crowd's insatiable desire for blood, cf. esp. Sen., *Ep.* 7.2–5. Paul's statement in 4:11 that the apostles are "naked" may possibly contain an echo of this initial comparison to condemned criminals, for such fought "naked (*nudus*) and defenceless" (Sen., *Ep.* 95.33; cf. also 7.3). For noonday gladiatorial contests, cf. also Suet., *Claud.* 34.2. For gladiatorial shows in Corinth, cf. Dio Chrys., *Or.* 31.121 and C. P. Jones, *The Roman World of Dio Chrysostom* (Loeb Classical Mongraphs; Cambridge: Harvard, 1978) 32.

[81] The idea of the *kosmos* and men as spectators of human sufferings appears already in Jewish martyrology (4 Macc 17:14; cf. also 15:20). Similarly, in both Jewish (*1 Enoch* 9:1) and early Christian (cf. Ign., *Trall.* 9:1) thought, angels are witnesses of human sufferings. In view of the context and Paul's use of the word "world" and "angel" in the

In view of the *sophos*-imagery of this section, the term "spectacle" is especially ironic. The Stoic sage forms a worthy "sight" for both gods and men in that he evokes their admiration as they watch him struggle with adversity.[82] But the

---

Corinthian correspondence and elsewhere, there should be no doubt but that Paul has in mind here men and angels who are neither well-disposed nor neutral toward the apostles, but rather inimical toward them. Indeed, in Rom 8:38 angels are themselves part of the catalogue of forces that would "separate us from the love of God." They are linked there with the *archai*, the hostile powers responsible for the crucifixion of Jesus (cf. 1 Cor 2:6–8) who have been defeated by God (Col 2:15). The angels and men who witness the sufferings of the apostles do not, therefore, do so with admiration, but with the same bloodthirsty attitude as the spectators who watch the noonday gladiatorial contests of condemned criminals. For "evil spectators" and "unjust judges" watching the good man's *agōn* with an evil opponent, cf. Max. Tyr., *Or.* 12.9f (156,9–10 Hobein). Compare the eager expectation of the crowd in 3 Macc 5:24 as they await the "most pitiable spectacle" of the Jews being crushed by elephants. Note also the rejoicing at the "spectacle" of the bloody punishment of the oppressors in *1 Enoch* 62.11–12. For Paul's "negative" view of angels, cf. also 1 Cor 6:3; 11:10; 2 Cor 11:14; 12:7; Gal 1:8; and the discussions by W. Bousset, *Kyrios Christos* (1913; Nashville: Abingdon, 1970) 257–58; "Der erste Brief an die Korinther," *Die Schriften des Neuen Testaments* (ed. J. Weiss, W. Bousset, & W. Heitmüller; 3d ed.; Göttingen: Vandenhoeck & Ruprecht, 1917) 92; and Maurice Jones, "St. Paul and the Angels," *The Expositor*, Eighth Series, 15 (1918) 356–70, 412–25, esp. 361. The "world" is similarly viewed by Paul in a negative fashion (1 Cor 1:20–21; 3:19; 11:32; etc.), so that it is to be judged along with the angels (1 Cor 6:2–3).

[82] Cf. Sen., *Prov.* 2.9; Epict., *Diss.* 3.22.58–59; Min. Fel., *Oct.* 37; and also Synesius, *Prov.* 1, 10 p.100C (cited by BAGD 353). For the sage himself as a "spectacle," cf. Epict., *Diss.* 2.19.25 and compare Sen., *Ep.* 64.6. Since F. C. Baur it has been common to compare and contrast the "spectacle" presented by Seneca's sage with that given by the apostles. Cf. J. Kreyher, *L. Annaeus Seneca und seine Beziehungen zum Urchristentum* (Berlin: R. Gaertner, 1887) 107; Lietzmann, *Korinther*, 20; C. Clemen, *Religionsgeschichtliche Erklärung des Neuen Testaments* (Giessen: Töpelmann/Ricker, 1909) 49; Weiss, *Korintherbrief*, 110; A. Bonhöffer, *Epiktet und das Neue Testament* (Religionsgeschichtliche Versuche und Vorarbeiten 10; Giessen: Töpelmann, 1911) 170; P. Wendland, *Die urchristlichen Literaturformen* (HNT 1:3; Tübingen: Mohr, 1912) 357 n. 1; R. Knopf, "Paul and Hellenism," *AJT* 18 (1914) 497–520, esp. 509; R. Liechtenhan, *Die göttliche Vorherbestimmung bei Paulus und in der Posidonianischen Philosophie* (FRLANT 35; Göttingen: Vandenhoeck & Ruprecht, 1922) 127; A. Schweitzer, *The Mysticism of Paul the Apostle* (1931; 2d ed.; repr., New York: Seabury, 1968) 150 n. 1; G. Kittel, *TDNT* 3.42–43; Moffatt, *The First Epistle to the Corinthians*, 49; E.-B. Allo, *Saint Paul, Première Épître aux Corinthiens* (EBib; 2d ed.; Paris: Lecoffre-Gabalda, 1956) 75; Héring, *The First Epistle to the Corinthians*, 29 n. 4; Braun, *Gesammelte Studien*, 186–91; J. N. Sevenster, *Paul and Seneca* (NovTSup 4; Leiden: Brill, 1961) 115–16; V. C. Pfitzner, *Paul and the Agon Motif* (NovTSup 16; Leiden: Brill, 1967) 62 n. 4, 189–90; Conzelmann, *1 Corinthians*, 88; Barrett, *First Corinthians*, 110; and F. F. Bruce, *1 and 2 Corinthians* (New Century Bible Commentary; Grand Rapids: Eerdmans, 1971) 50. For the use of "spectacle" as an image in patristic literature, cf. E. Lucius, *Die Anfänge des Heiligenkults in der christlichen Kirche* (Tübingen: Mohr, 1904) 57 n. 11, and Pfitzner, *Paul and the Agon Motif*, 201.

"sight" presented by the apostles is "pathetic"[83] and evokes only the scornful abuse of the audience in the "theatre."[84] Consequently, they are δυσφημούμενοι (4:13),[85] regarded as περικαθάρματα and περίψημα (4:13),[86] and persecuted

[83] Compare the use of the word *spectaculum* in the appeal for pity in Sall., *Iug.* 14.23: "For when you lost your life it was not your throne you lost, but it was flight, exile, want, and all these troubles which weigh me down. While I, poor wretch, hurled from my father's throne into this sea of troubles, present a tragedy (*spectaculum*) of human vicissitude." Cf. also 14.7,9,11,15; 3 Macc 5:24; Achilles Tatius 13.2; and Philo, *Flacc.* 74.

[84] The theatre was infamous as a place of abuse. Cf., for example, Dio Chrys. *Or.* 33.9 and esp. Philo. *Leg.* 368: "theatre-like in the cackling of their hisses, their mockery and unbounded jeering." Cognates of "theatre" often express this. Cf. Heb 10:33; Polyb. 5.15.2; Diod. Sic. 34/35.2.46; Philo, *Flacc.* 72; and the texts of Achmes and Posidonius cited by BAGD 353.

[85] The verb occurs only here in the NT and its noun cognate only in 2 Cor 6:8, where the same connection with *atimia* is found (cf. also Soph., *El.* 1182–83). Closely allied with *loidoria* (Men. 715 Kock; Plut., *Luc.* 18.6; *Pel.* 8.5), it refers to the shameful way in which the apostles are insulted, derided, mocked, accused, cursed, taunted, and threatened (cf. Dion Hal., *Ant. Rom.* 6.48.3; Plut., *Mor.* 587F–588A; 1 Macc 7:34–38), so that their own good name and that of the cause they represent is tarnished (cf. Pind., *Nem.* 8.36–37; Philo, *Leg.* 101; 1 Tim 6:1; Tit 2:5). In short, it indicates the public defamation of their name and character (cf. also Rom 3:8; Acts 13:45; 18:6). It is placed last in the list of participles, not only because it is a more severe term than *loidoria* (cf. esp. Plut., *Pel.* 8.5) but also because it serves to introduce the two terms of reproach in 4:13. The latter serve to exemplify the consequences of the apostles' public ridicule and calumny. The use of this *dys*-word is a clear indication that the *atimoi* of 4:10 means that the apostles are not simply "unhonored," but actively denounced and "dishonored."

[86] The fundamentally opprobrious nature of these two virtually synonymous terms is indicated by the fact that they are introduced by δυσφημούμενοι (comp. Dem., *Or.* 21.185; Petron., *Sat.* 74; Lucian, *Pisc.* 34; *Symp.* 40) and occur as part of Paul's *synkrisis* of the apostles with the Corinthian *sophoi.* The latter consideration is of decisive significance in view of the use of similar epithets in ancient *synkriseis,* including those involving the sage. Cf. esp. Philo, *Virt.* 174; Lucian, *Hermot.* 81; and also Dem., *Or.* 21.198–99. The apostles are thus regarded as "the scum of the earth," "everyone's gunk" (cf. also Epict., *Diss.* 3.22.78; Dio Chrys., *Or.* 7.30; Julian, *Or.* 6.197C; Joseph., *BJ* 4.241; and esp. Philo, *Mos.* 1.30, where "scum" occurs with the reproach "vagabond" [comp. 1 Cor 4:11]). The apostles are, in short, the kind of people that one spits upon (Pollux 3.66). The juxtaposition of "scum" and "nobodies" in Dem., *Or.* 21.185 suggests, moreover, that περικαθάρματα τοῦ κόσμου . . . περίψημα is functionally equivalent to τὰ ἀγενῆ τοῦ κόσμου καὶ τὰ ἐξουθενήμενα (1 Cor 1:28). That Paul makes God responsible for the apostles' contemptible appearance to the world (4:9) rests on a firm OT basis. Cf. esp. Lam 3:45: "Thou hast made us offscouring and refuse among the peoples" (RSV) and the discussion by A. Hanson, "1 Corinthians 4:13b and Lamentations 3:45," *ExpTim* 93 (1982) 214–15. For a collection of Greek and Latin texts where the epithets of 1 Cor 4:13 are used as terms of abuse, cf. J. J. Wettstein, *Novum Testamentum Graecum* (1751; reprinted, Graz, Oesterreich: Akademische Druck-und Verlagsanstalt, 1962) 2.114–15. Κάθαρμα was a favorite Cynic *Schimpfwort* (cf. Diog. Laert. 6.32 and G. A. Gerhard, *Phoinix von Kolophon* [Leipzig/Berlin: Teubner, 1909] 38) and was used with great frequency by Lucian. For the latter's use of the term,

(διωκόμενοι),[87] both verbally (λοιδορούμενοι)[88] and physically (κολαφιζόμεθα).[89]

---

cf. the collection of texts in H. D. Betz, *Lukian von Samosata und das Neue Testament* (TU 76; Berlin: Akademie-Verlag, 1961) 67 n. 7. For equivalent expressions in Jewish texts, cf. Str-B 3.338–39; M. Jastrow, *A Dictionary of the Targumim, the Talmud Babli and Yerushalmi, and the Midrashic Literature* (2 vols.; New York: Padres, 1950) 2.971; and possibly IQH 5,21.

Finally, it is perhaps true, as many exegetes hold, that the epithets of 4:13 also serve to depict the apostles as the "scapegoats" through which the redemption of the world is effected. That is, the apostles may be depicted here not only as *purgamenta* but also as *piacula*. This is a possible, but by no means a necessary, implication of these terms. There is nothing in the context that requires this interpretation, and several major considerations have been raised against it by exegetes who reject this understanding of the passage. If, however, the cultic connotations of the terms are present in 4:13, they must be regarded as *secondary and ironic*, bringing to a climax the grand irony of the whole section. For the arguments in favor of the "scapegoat" interpretation, cf. the commentaries and also the discussion by H. Windisch, *Paulus und Christus* (UNT 24; Leipzig: Hinrichs, 1934) 240–41, 277, and G. Stählin, *TDNT* 6.84–93. For a *peristasis* catalogue with *katharmos* used in the sense of "expiatory offering," see Achilles Tatius 5.18.4.

87 "Persecution" appears also in the *peristasis* catalogues of Rom 8:35; 2 Cor 4:9; 12:10. Cf. also Gal 5:11; 2 Tim: 3:11; Acts 13:50. For the persecution of the "apostles," cf. Luke 11:49.

88 The reviling suffered by the philosopher is frequently the result of the severity with which he sometimes must speak (cf. esp. Dio Chrys., *Or.* 32.19). Of course, hardships themselves were a sufficient ground for abuse (cf., for instance, Teles, III, 29, 9–10 Hense = 30,159 O'Neil). For a host of words associated with *loidoria*, cf. Philo, *Flacc.* 32–34.

89 The two major discussions of this verb are both by K. L. Schmidt; cf. *TDNT* 3.818–21, and " Ἰησοῦς Χριστὸς κολαφιζόμενος und die 'colaphisation' der Juden," in *Aux sources de la tradition chrétienne* (Mélanges M. Goguel; Neuchâtel: Delachaux & Niestle, 1950) 218–27. Unfortunately, neither is particularly helpful in regard to 1 Cor 4:11, so that a fresh discussion is necessary. Basic to the meaning of the verb is the idea of striking with the fist or knuckles (κόλαφος = κόνδυλος). It should be regarded as the vernacular equivalent of κονδυλίζειν, which appears in the LXX (Amos 2:7; Mal 3:5; cf. also Zeph 2:8). The tendency of exegetes has been to treat the term as broadly as possible, so that it is taken to indicate the way in which the apostles were generally mistreated. Weiss, *Korintherbrief*, 111, for example, even points to the stoning of Acts 14:19 as the kind of rough and vulgar treatment included in κολαφιζόμεθα. In my judgment, this broad understanding of the term in regard to 1 Cor 4:11 is fallacious and arises from the tendency to mesh together the items in the various catalogues. It should be recalled that Paul in 1 Cor 4 is not stressing the *perils* of the apostles, but their *atimia*. The blows in mind are those offered as insults (cf. esp. Dem., *Or.* 21.72) and accompanied by verbal abuse. Cf. the combination of *loidoria* and hitting with the fist in Exod 21:18; Pol., *Phil.* 2:2; and compare Philo, *Som.* 2.168; *Spec.* 3.172. Both Socrates and Diogenes received their share of such blows (Diog. Laert. 2.21; 6.41; Ps-Diog., *Ep.* 20 [112,12 Malherbe]), and Crates was given a black eye on at least one occasion (Diog. Laert. 6.89). The "degrading (ἀτίμως) box on the ear" in Plato's *Gorgias* (527A–D; 486C) is another example of the kind of ignominious blow that Paul is referring to in 1 Cor 4:11, for it is precisely the *atimoi* who receive such (*Grg.* 508C–D). Furthermore,

The preceding analysis of 4:8–13 clearly demonstrates that Paul makes an extensive use of *sophos*-imagery in his depiction of the Corinthians. They are characterized as rich, kings, wise, strong, and illustrious, and each of these is a quality predicated of the sage. A similar appropriation of *sophos*-imagery is seen in Ben Zoma's list of questions in *'Abot* 4.1, where four of Paul's five items appear: "Who is wise? . . . Who is strong? . . . Who is rich? . . . Who is honored?"[90]

Unlike Ben Zoma, however, Paul uses these epithets ironically, and his irony indicates that in 1 Cor 1–6 he is dealing with those who, like certain Cynics, think they have achieved the ideal.[91] But they have not, and thus Paul denounces their attitude as "puffed up."[92] It is *hybris* that puffs itself up, says Philo (*Virt.* 172–74), sees itself as πλουσιώτατος, φρονιμώτατος, ἰσχυρότατος, and ἐντιμότατος, and looks down on others as poor, foolish (ἄφρονας), undistinguishd (ἀδόξους,

since Hesychius equates κολαφιζόμενος with ῥαπιζόμενος (BAGD 441), the various passages in the NT and elsewhere which deal with slapping someone in the face become relevant to Paul's statement here (cf. BAGD 734). Whether one slaps another with the palm or the knuckles, the person who is struck is clearly being maligned and accorded as little respect as a condemned criminal (Matt 26:66–67; Mark 14:64–65; cf. also John 18:22; 19:13; 1 Cor 4:9), a slave (1 Pet 2:20; "Longinus," *Subl.* 44.4; Philo, *Ebr.* 198; Ps-Sen., *Apocol.* 15), or a wanderer (1 Cor 4:11). For blows with the fist, cf. also Isa 58:4; Plut., *Alc.* 7.1; *Cat. Min.* 15; *Mor.* 439D.

[90] For a discussion of the use of Stoic *paradoxa* in this passage, cf. H. A. Fischel, *Rabbinic Literature and Greco-Roman Philosophy* (SPB 21; Leiden: Brill, 1973) 70–73, 147–51. Fischel correctly calls attention to Paul's use of these *paradoxa* in 2 Cor 6, but he fails to note the use in 1 Cor 4.

[91] This is not to argue that the Corinthians saw themselves as Cynics. It is rather to make the claim that their attitude is similar. Indeed, the similarity between the Corinthians and the Cynics in regard to certain points led Georg Hollmann, *Urchristentum in Korinth* (Leipzig: Hinrichs, 1903) 17, to advance the thesis that the Corinthians had been influenced by Cynic (and Stoic) philosophy. The crucial difference, however, is that the Corinthians themselves viewed their perfection in eschatological terms. Indeed, the ἤδη of 1 Cor 4:8 makes explicit what the term "satiety" already implies, viz., the sense of fullness and the loss of expectation. Κόρος dims or excludes ἐλπίς (cf. Pind., *Pyth.* 1.82–83), and it is for this reason that Paul in 1 Cor 1:7 ties the affirmation of their fullness of *charismata* to the expectation of the parousia. It is worth noting that the catalogue of what the Lamb is worthy to receive in Rev 5:12 corresponds in large part to Paul's description of the Corinthians. Kingly power, wealth, wisdom, strength, and glorious honor are all mentioned.

[92] "Puffed up" was a favorite designation that Cynics used to describe their opponents' conceit; cf. D. R. Dudley, *A History of Cynicism* (1937; reprinted, Hildesheim: Olms, 1967) 56 n. 8. There is, then, a certain irony in the fact that Paul chooses "puffed up" to reproach the Corinthians for their Cynic-like confidence that they have attained the ideal. The fact that they have not done so is not only said explicitly but also suggested by the perjorative term "surfeit." Cf. Solon 5.9–10 Diehl (=6.9–10 Edwards): "Surfeit breeds Pride when great prosperity follows those whose mind is *not perfect*" (emphasis mine; cf. also Theog. 153–54; 693–94).

ἀτίμους) scum (καθάρματα).[93] The Corinthians, quite simply, have forgotten that the sage's kingdom comes from God (cf. Philo, *Abr.* 261) and boast as though they themslves were responsible for their exalted status (1 Cor 4:7). In so doing they display a singular lack of gratitude to God (compare esp. Philo, *Sac.* 53–54; *Mut.* 220–21).

The apostles, on the other hand, are described in a severely derogatory way from the world's point of view (4:9,13). And yet, it must be emphasized, this description is not unrelated to the way in which the true sage is depicted in the philosophical traditions indicated in chapter three. To begin with, it must be remembered that all the affirmations about the sage's wealth and honor were *paradoxa,* "against public opinion." They were startling precisely because they clashed with the world's perception of things. The philosopher was in point of fact often poor and ridiculed. Thus the stress on poverty in the catalogue coincides with the especially Cynic thesis "that, in general, the poorest men are philosophers" (Teles, IVB,45,4–5 Hense = 48,5 O'Neil). The idea of the sage's poverty was clearly not unique to Cynics but had become a widespread motif among Greeks.[94] Even Philo, for example, depicts the lovers of virtue with a catalogue of hardships in much the same way that Paul does the apostles:

> The so-called lovers of virtue are almost without exception obscure people, looked down upon, of mean estate, destitute of the necessaries of life, not enjoying the privileges of subject peoples or even of slaves, filthy, sallow, reduced to skeletons, with a hungry look from want of food, the prey of disease, in training for dying (*Det.* 34).[95]

The lack of recognition accorded Philo's lover of virtue is a typical theme. That the apostles are called "scum" coincides with the fact that "the genuine disciples of Pythagoras and Plato and Aristotle" are called φαρμακεῖς (= καθάρματα: Julian, *Or.* 6.197E). The combination of poverty and obscurity is also frequent, especially in Cynic literature. For example, Dio Chrysostom in *Or.* 77/78 argues that the true philosopher is not only humble (26) but also marked by poverty and dishonor (28,33). Indeed, "he might himself be more inglorious than the beggars,

[93] Cf. also Philo, *Mos.* 1.30. The behavior of the rich at the Corinthian eucharist is also a sign of their *hybris,* for drunkenness and the shaming of others are typical manifestations of this attitude. Cf. D. M. MacDowell, "*Hybris* in Athens," *G & R* 23 (1976) 14–31, esp. 16, 21; N. R. E. Fisher, "*Hybris* and Dishonour: I," *G & R* 23 (1976) 177–93, esp. 185; and also Fisher's "*Hybris* and Dishonour: II," *G & R* 26 (1979) 32–47.

[94] Cf., for instance, Ael., *VH* 2.43; Apul., *Apol.* 18; and H. Leisegang, *Pneuma Hagion: Der Ursprung des Geistbegriffs der synoptischen Evangelien aus der griechischen Mystik* (Leipzig: Hinrichs, 1922) 135–40.

[95] This passage is part of a *synkrisis* of the lovers of virtue with those who take care of themselves. The latter are said to be both rich and glorious, "knowing nothing of labour." This last item implies the toil of the lover of virtue, which, of course, is a fact of life shared by the apostles (1 Cor 4:11b–12a).

more destitute than the wretches who lie prostrate in the streets, held worthy of no consideration at all by anybody" (33). Although "he trains his body, inuring it to labour," this very *askēsis* prompts ridicule (41; cf. also 72.8 and Philo, *Det.* 12). Thus, while the sage may offer a worthy sight to the gods, he, like the apostles, presents to the world a sad and rather inglorious spectacle.

The response that Dio's philosopher gives to this demeaning treatment is also what we have seen to be typical of the sage's demeanor.[96] In response to such abuse, "he is not enraged at them or vexed; on the contrary, I believe he is kinder to each one than even a father or brothers or friends" (42). It is precisely such a response that wins him honor in philosophical circles, but disdain among the masses. For the latter, he is the fool,[97] because he will not forsake justice and return evil for evil. It is the rash multitude who returns reviling for reviling (Epict., *Diss.* 2.12.13). The sage, like the apostles, is gentle with the one who reviles him (Epict., *Ench.* 42). Whether sage or apostle, to bless revilers, tolerate persecutors, and answer defamers with soft and gentle words (1 Cor 4:12b–13a)[98] are actions regarded by the common herd as indicative of an abject spirit. This non-virile response makes both even more despicable and foolish than they already appear. It is, of course, the lot of a "king" to do well but be reviled for it.[99] And yet, for the philosopher, such a response is not only right, but also a tactical necessity. Were a good man to attempt to retaliate, his effort would only end in disaster. "It is necessary," laments Maximus of Tyre, "that the depraved man should prevail when contending in a stadium of this kind, in which the depraved are spectators [cf. 1 Cor 4:9], and the judges are unjust" (*Or.* 12.9f [156,8–10 Hobein]).

Again, the connection that Hellenistic moralists make between God and the hardships of the sage or *proficiens* is made here by Paul as well. Epictetus compares God to a physical trainer (ἀλείπτης) and says that "when a difficulty befalls, remember that God, like a physical trainer, has matched you with a rugged young man" (*Diss.* 1.24.1). Like Epictetus, Paul in 1 Cor 4:9 draws his imagery from the *agōn*.[100] But Paul's formulation suggests that God is being depicted as the ἀγωνοθέτης, the exhibitor of the games,[101] and in this case, as the exhibitor of the apostles as a spectacle.

[96] Cf. the discussion of "The Philosopher's Demeanor" in chapter three.

[97] Cf. chapter three and the treatment of "The Righteous Sufferer as the 'Foolish' Wise Man."

[98] Theophylact's interpretation of παρακαλοῦμεν is correct. For his comment, cf. Heinrici, *Handbuch,* 130 n. 1.

[99] Cf. Dio Chrys., *Or.* 47.25; Epict., *Diss.* 4.6.20; Mar. Ant., *Med.* 7.36; Plut., *Alex.* 41.1; Diog. Laert. 6.3.

[100] Pfitzner, *Paul and the Agon Motif,* 189. For the connection that Hellenistic moralists make between God and adversity, cf. the discussion on "Fortune, God, and Free Will" in chapter three. It should be noted that their concern with humans conforming their will to that of the divine does not enter Paul's discussion here.

[101] For the term, see Dem., *Or.* 18.84; Andoc., *Or.* 4.26; and cf. also Htd. 6.127.

Paul's catalogue thus functions to specify the ways in which God exhibits him. Indeed, it is striking that there is no mention here of God *training* the apostles by means of their sufferings. The reference is solely to God's *exhibition* of the apostles in their sufferings. This use of a *peristasis* catalogue to depict the way in which God exhibits someone as a model is found also in Epictetus, who depicts God as exhibiting the sage in and through his hardships and contends that the service (ὑπηρεσία) which the sage renders to God is intimately connected with the hardships that he bears. "These are the terms," says the sage, "upon which now He brings me here, and again He sends me there; to mankind exhibits (δείκνυσι) me in poverty, without office, in sickness; sends me away to Gyara, brings me into prison" (*Diss.* 3.24.113–14). It is through poverty, death, and hardship that God exhibits the sage's virtue in a more brilliant way than he could otherwise, so that the sage becomes a spectacle (3.22.59). Similarly, Paul, who has just identified himself as the servant (ὑπηρέτης) of God (4:1), proceeds to speak of the way in which God has exhibited (ἀπέδειξεν) the apostles and made them a spectacle (4:9). In terms of its specific epideictic function, then, Paul's catalogue in 1 Cor 4 conforms to one of the ways in which the *peristasis* catalogue was used in the Hellenistic world.

Furthermore, the catalogue's more general functions of exemplification and admonition (see above on "The Hortatory Character of 1 Cor 1–4") also coincide with the functions of *peristasis* catalogues in other authors. As we saw repeatedly in chapter three, Hellenistic moralists made constant use of the figure of the suffering sage as a pedagogical and paraenetic device for depicting the ideal and exhorting and admonishing their hearers in regard to it. Paul's use of the catalogue for these purposes conforms to this standard practice, and his use of *synkrisis* serves to heighten the catalogue's admonitory function. Indeed, even outside the philosophical tradition the combined use of a *peristasis* catalogue and *synkrisis* was a powerful means of reproaching and persuading a reader whose more favorable circumstances presented a vivid contrast to the harsh situation and suffering of the author (see esp. Achilles Tatius 5.18.3–19.6 and cf. Chariton 4.3.10).

It is, moreover, not only the *functions* of the catalogues which are identical but also the *situations* in which they are sometimes used. The situation that evokes Paul's use of a *peristasis* catalogue in 1 Cor 4 is, for example, parallel to that for which Epictetus uses one. Paul uses a catalogue here when he is dealing with those who foolishly think they are already wise (3:18) and have already begun to reign (4:8). Similarly, it is when Epictetus is dealing with "those who hastily assume the guise of the philosophers" that he has recourse to the picture of the ideal Cynic (*Diss.* 4.8). These novices, though "being merely moved to philosophy," are at once "off to the sceptre, to the kingdom" (34) and arrogantly proclaim their freedom and tranquility (27). "Man, . . . you have grown insolently lush, you have leaped forward to occupy some petty reputation before its due time; you think that you are somebody, fool that you are among fools" (39). The model is provided by the ideal Cynic, who speaks without arrogance of the hardships of his life, and the service that he renders in so doing (31–32). He is recognized, not by the words that he speaks, but by his actions (20), which are in conformity to the witness that he bears in behalf of virtue (32). Indeed, it is because of his life that he invites others to listen to his words. Paul, too, as we have seen, sets forth the apostolic life as the paradigm for Christian existence and calls on the Corinthians to imitate him. He does so, furthermore, as part of his admonition and at the very point when he is ready to give specific instructions on how to live.

Paul's use of the catalogue in this situation is clearly fraught with irony, which is in keeping with the ironic depiction of the Corinthians as *sophoi.* Lucian, similarly, uses irony to depict the Stoic novice who thinks that if he learns his tenets properly, "there will be nothing to stop me being the only rich man, the only king, and the rest slaves and scum compared with me" (*Hermot.* 81). But Paul here moves beyond Lucian by ironically assuming the position of "scum" and treating the Corinthians as *sophoi* "filled with the truth" (cf. Max. Tyr. *Or.* 15.4e [168,13 Hobein]) in order to admonish them and rid them of their pretensions.

Paul's argument and admonition thus rest on the paradox that he creates of the exalted Corinthians and the abased apostles. If the apostles of whom the converts boast are still so lowly, how is it possible for the Corinthians, who received their privileges through the apostles' labors (3:5), to be so exalted?[102] For, whereas Epictetus' ideal Cynic shares in the reign of Zeus as his servant (*Diss.* 3.22.95), Paul as God's servant does not even share in his converts' reign (1 Cor 4:1,8). The irony is profound, and it is designed to prompt the Corinthians to make a radical reassessment of their present status. As 2 Corinthians indicates, however, any hopes that Paul may have entertained about the success of his admonition were soon to be dashed.

The Theme and Purpose of 2 Cor 1–7

Of the four catalogues of Paul's hardships that occur in 2 Corinthians, two are located in chapters 1-9. These catalogues (4:8–9; 6:3–10) are to be interpreted in light of the overall purpose of 2 Cor 1-9. Since, however, the chapters on the collection (8–9) contribute little, if anything, to the interpretation of the catalogues, attention here can be restricted to 2 Cor 1–7. As is well known, questions of unity have been raised in regard to this material. The section 6:14–7:1 is widely regarded as an interpolation and the remainder of 1:1–7:16 is increasingly viewed as a composite of two or more letters.[103] In view of the difficulties of reference and transition, it is indeed possible that 2 Cor 1–7 is a composite of several of Paul's letters. But this possibility should not deflect our vision from the *unity of theme and purpose* that underlines the present arrangement of the material. Whether the words stem from one of Paul's letters or from

[102] Cf. Massie, *Corinthians,* 160.

[103] Cf., for example, D. Georgi, "Second Letter to the Corinthians," *IDBSup* 183–86.

many, they have a basic coherence that is either the product of Paul's intention in penning them or the result of a redactor's activity. Concern with the issues of source criticism has obscured this basic unity, since it has posited various occasions and purposes for each of the fragments. Whatever specific and subsidiary functions the various sections of the present letter may once have had, these must now be seen in light of the overall purpose of 2 Cor 1-7.

The force of this claim is hardly diluted if the integrity of 2 Cor 1-7 is affirmed. Indeed, this solution is in many ways the least problematic, and certain aspects of chapters 1-7 are more readily explicable on the assumption that they are a unity. Therefore, while conceding the possibility of redactional activity, the following treatment assumes the unity of at least 1:1-6:13 and 7:2-16 as a working hypothesis[104] and commences with an examination of the two places in chapters 1-7 where Paul makes explicit statements about his intentions in writing.

The first of these comes in 1:12-14. These verses give what is in fact the theme and purpose of the *whole* of chapters 1-7.[105] The theme comes first, in verse 12, and is nothing other than Paul's boast about his personal conduct in general and toward the Corinthians in particular. It is perhaps at first surprising that Paul's theme in 2 Cor 1-7 concerns himself, but this insight is crucial to understanding what Paul is about in the material that follows. That 1:12 does indeed give the theme of the letter is clear from a comparison with other of Paul's letters.

In Romans, for example, Paul's salutation (1:1-7) is followed by a thanksgiving that ends with a statement concerning his desire to preach to the Romans (1:8-15). In 1:16-17 comes the theme of the letter, connected with the preceding introductory matters by γάρ. Similarly in Galatians, the salutation (1:1-3) and ironic rebuke (1:6-10) are followed in 1:11-12 by two thematic statements (the divine nature and the divine origin of Paul's gospel). These, too, are linked with the preceding by γάρ and in 1:13-2:21 Paul goes on to treat these two themes in reverse order.[106]

[104] 2 Cor 6:14-7:1 is clearly a non-Pauline fragment in origin. For the possibility, however, that Paul himself made use of this fragment and inserted it in its present context as a warning against associating with the superapostles, cf. the arguments mounted by N. A. Dahl, "A Fragment and Its Context: 2 Corinthians 6:14-7:1," *Studies in Paul* (Minneapolis: Augsburg, 1977) 62-69, and David Rensberger, "2 Corinthians 6:14-7:1—A Fresh Examination," *Studia Biblica et Theologica* 8 (1978) 25-49.

[105] The importance of 1:12-14 for the understanding of 2 Corinthians as a whole (including chapters 10-13) is emphasized by Karl Prümm, *Diakonia Pneumatos: Der zweite Korintherbrief als Zugang zur apostolischen Botschaft* (2 vols. in 3 parts; Rome: Herder, 1960-67) 1.36; 2/1.3; and Horst Baum, *Mut zum Schwachsein—in Christi Kraft* (Studia Instituti Missiologici Societatis Verbi Divini 17; St. Augustin: Steyler, 1977) 32.

[106] On Gal 1-2, cf. esp. N. A. Dahl, "Paul's Letter to the Galatians: Epistolary Genre, Content, and Structure" (unpublished 1973 SBL Paul Seminar Paper). Similarly in 1 Corinthians, the salutation (1:1-3) and thanksgiving (1:4-9) are followed in 1:10 by the opening of the *parakalô*—section, which urges the unity of the Corinthians. Unity is the concern

These examples show that Paul, especially in his lengthier letters, tends to move from the salutation, through a thanksgiving (or its substitute), to a thematic statement. 2 Corinthians fits within this pattern, with the benediction substituted for the thanksgiving. It is therefore about his own person that Paul will speak, and he indicates that he will do so in a boasting manner (καύχησις: 1:12). He hastens to add that this boasting will be the testimony of his conscience, for this assures his readers that what he says will be true (cf. Rom 9:1). The conduct of Paul, especially toward the Corinthians, is thus the subject of 2 Corinthians. His conduct, he assures them, has been upright, and this gives him a basis for boasting.

Following this introduction of his theme, Paul makes a somewhat optimistic statement about the clarity with which he writes (compare 2 Pet 3:15-16; 1 Cor 5:9-11) and proceeds to state what he hopes this letter will achieve. Reduced to its bare essentials, the statement is as follows: ἐλπίζω ὅτι ἐπιγνώσεσθε ὅτι καύχημα ὑμῶν ἐσμεν. "I hope that you will understand that we are your boast" (1:13-14; comp. 13:6).

Thus Paul says quite unmistakably that he will be writing about himself in a boasting manner and that his purpose in so doing is to reveal himself to them as one about whom they may boast. That is, ἡ καύχησις ἡμῶν is designed to bring the Corinthians to the knowldge that καύχημα ὑμῶν ἐσμεν. The movement is from καύχησις ἡμῶν to καύχημα ὑμῶν. Paul in 2 Cor 1-7 is therefore engaged in self-commendation, and throughout these chapters he is giving them reasons for being proud of him. 2 Cor 1-7 is therefore *a letter of recommendation, of self-commendation* and the longest example of this type that we possess.

But the goal is not simply this, and the argument does not move only in this direction. The boasting is to be mutual, so that the ultimate goal is that the Corinthians will understand that "we are your boast just as you are also ours." *The purpose of 2 Cor 1-9 is therefore to effect a mutuality of pride between Paul and the Corinthians.* Chapters 1-7 are primarily directed toward the establishment of Paul as a worthy object of boasting. Chapters 8-9 presuppose Paul's pride in the Corinthians and urge them to act in a manner that will justify Paul's confidence in them (cf. esp. 8:24; 9:2-4). Naturally there are elements of the other concern in both 1-7 and 8-9, but the main lineaments of these chapters are as indicated.

The fact that Paul presupposes his pride in the Corinthians (1:14; 7:4,14) and wishes to establish himself as worthy of their esteem (1:14) does not mean that he envisions his task as one of creating confidence in himself *de novo.* On the contrary, he presupposes a partial understanding of himself on the part of the Corinthians (καθὼς καὶ ἐπέγνωτε ἀπὸ μέρους) and writes with the conviction that a fuller understanding of himself by them (ἕως τέλους ἐπιγνώσεσθε) will achieve the desired end.

---

especially of 1:10-4:21 and continues to be of importance in other parts of the letter (cf. esp. chapters 6, 8, 10-12, 14).

In 5:11–12, as Paul is in the process of providing the Corinthians with this fuller understanding of himself, he returns to the theme that he announced in 1:14. Here he indicates that he is not so much commending himself as he is ἀφορμὴν διδόντες ὑμῖν καυχήματος ὑπὲρ ἡμῶν, "giving you a basis for boasting in our behalf," i.e., for being proud of us (5:12). This repetition indicates that the purpose uniting Paul's arguments has not changed from that given in 1:14, only the various arguments used to further that purpose. The links between 1:12–14 and 5:11–12 are clear. In 1:12–14, for example, the pride that Paul wants the Corinthians to have in him and his conduct is placed in an eschatological framework (ἐν τῇ ἡμέρᾳ τοῦ κυρίου ἡμῶν 'Ιησοῦ). In 4:16–5:10 Paul discusses his demeanor in light of the eschaton and in 5:11–12 indicates that in the preceding sections he has been providing them with grounds for pride in his behalf.

In 1:12 Paul's conscience bears witness to how he has conducted himself in the world. In 5:11 he expresses his hope that who he is has become manifest in their conscience. Just as the movement in 1:12–14 is from ἡ καύχησις ἡμῶν to καύχημα ὑμῶν ἐσμεν, so also here the movement is from τὸ μαρτύριον τῆς συνειδήσεως ἡμῶν (1:12) to a manifestation ἐν ταῖς συνειδήσεσιν ὑμῶν (5:11). From knowledge of himself to their knowledge of him, from boasting on his own behalf to their boasting on his, is the flow and purpose of Paul's argument.

There are other hints that 1:12–14 and 5:11–12 are linked. The ἐλπίζω δέ of 5:11 is a repetition from 1:13 and marks the first use of this verb since 1:13. Again, when Paul says that he speaks the testimony of his conscience, this is a way of indicating that he is speaking in the presence of God. Paul's boasting about himself is thus done with God as his witness. The frequent references in Paul to testimony in God's presence secure this inference (cf. 2 Cor 1:23; Rom 1:9; 9:1; Phil 1:8; 1 Thess 2:5,10). This idea is echoed in 5:11's θεῷ δὲ πεφανερώμεθα. Paul thus testifies to his conduct in the presence of God (2 Cor 1:12; 2:17; 4:2) and God knows both who and what Paul is (5:11). Known to God, he attempts to persuade men (5:11), not with fleshly wisdom, but by God's grace (1:12). 5:11–12 thus repeats and restates the initial disclosure of theme and purpose of 1:12–14.

And here, moreover, the necessity of the Corinthians having pride in Paul is made explicit. He is providing them with the resources from which they will be able to answer those who boast in the face and not the heart. In 2 Corinthians Paul is fighting for the Corinthians against braggarts whose boasting is misplaced. He is faced with the difficult and delicate task of reinstilling confidence in himself among the Corinthians, and yet doing so in a manner that is appropriate. It would be all too easy simply to match them vaunt for vaunt, but to do so would be false both to himself and to his Lord, who is the only final ground and object of boasting (1 Cor 1:31).

Paul's self-commendation in 2 Cor 1–7 is therefore not undertaken as an end in itself or as an exercise in self-glorification. The goal is rather that of preserving and strengthening his relationship with the Corinthians so that he can benefit them, and that is possible only if the Corinthians have confidence in him as a spiritual leader. This goal, however, places Paul in a dilemma—how does he praise himself in a manner that will be both inoffensive and congruent with the character and goals of his ministry?

It is this dilemma and the delicateness of his task that accounts for Paul's oscillating statements about the self-praise and self-commendation in which he is engaged. On the one hand, he explicitly says that he commends himself to every human conscience in the presence of God (4:2). In 4:2 he commends himself "by the manifestation of the truth" and in 6:4 he commends himself as a *diakonos* of God ἐν παντί. His conduct in various circumstances is thus a part of his self-commendation. At the conclusion of his *Narrenrede* (11:16–12:10), in which he has boasted of himself in various ways, he excuses this self-praise by saying that the Corinthians forced him to do it. Indeed, it was not properly his place to commend himself; such commendation of Paul was *their* obligation (12:11; cf. also 2:3). In these instances he is quite candid about what he is doing. In this same vein he can refer as well to the way in which the Corinthians have commended themselves (7:11).

There are, on the other hand, places where Paul eschews this candor. In 3:1 he asks whether he is again commending himself and whether he is in need of letters of recommendation. In 5:12 he denies that he is engaged in "self-commendation." Later, he characterizes the superapostles as those who commend themselves (10:12). It is not, he asserts, the self-commender but the God-commended who is approved (10:18).

Paul's oscillating statements are to be understood in light of several factors. First, as already indicated, there is the difficulty of his dilemma and the delicateness of his task. He *is*, on the one hand, engaged in self-praise in that he is providing the Corinthians with the data that will form a basis for pride in him. But, on the other hand, he is *not* engaged in self-commendation *as an end in and of itself.* His self-praise is not intended to make him a cult-hero. That sort of adulation he has already vigorously rejected in 1 Cor 1–4. He *does* preach himself to the Corinthians, and about that there can be no doubt. But it is as their slave, not their master, that he does so (2 Cor 4:5). Paul's self-commendation is thus a means to an end, not an end in itself. As such, it conforms to the standards of proper self-laudation that were delineated in chapter three (see above on "Praise and Self-Praise").

Second, Paul is acutely aware of the fact that God is the final judge of a person. In 1 Cor 1–4 he presents himself as a model and calls on the Corinthians to imitate him. Yet praise, he adds, comes from God (4:5). In 2 Cor 10:18 it is the approval of God that really counts. Paul may present himself as a model and commend himself as worthy of the Corinthians' boasting about him, but he recognizes that there are limits to this (2 Cor 10:13–18). The limits are set by Jer 9:23–24, twice quoted by Paul in his extant Corinthian correspondence (1 Cor 1:31; 2 Cor 10:17; cf. also 1 Cor 3:21). And, just as the Lord's approval is the only one that has ultimate reality, so also it is the Lord who is the only ultimate object of boasting.

Thus Paul's affirmative and negative statements on boasting and self-commendation are a system of checks and balances that is operative for him and the Corinthians alike. Paul wants the credit that is his due as their founding father as well as the confidence in him that his exemplary life inspires. This is what he wants, no more but no less. He will allow them, his children, neither to adore him nor to doubt his integrity, for their spiritual health is impaired by excess as well as deficiency. He knows his place, and he wants them to know theirs. He wishes to continue as their fellow-worker, so that they will not receive the grace of God in vain (6:1).

Third, there is the fact that Paul wishes to distinguish himself from his opponents, with their letters of recommendation (3:1), self-commendation (10:18), and misplaced boasting (5:12). Letters of commendation to (cf. Acts 18:27) or from (cf. Rom 16:1) Corinth he considers superfluous (cf. Ps-Diog., *Ep.* 18 [110,14–18 Malherbe]; Epict., *Diss.* 2.3.1–2), for "*you* are our letter of recommendation" (3:1–2). Since he must boast, however, he will do so in a manner that is appropriate and in matters that are legitimate.

2 Cor 1–7 is, therefore, truly a letter of commendation, written by Paul on his own behalf. It is a striking example of self-praise, written in order to secure and solidify his standing among the Christians at Corinth. The goal is a kind of "mutual admiration society" in which Paul and the Corinthians are fit objects of one another's praise. Two themes which flow through the letter are thus the integrity of Paul and the mutuality between Paul and the Corinthians. The brief analysis of the letter that follows will serve to indicate the presence of these themes and the encomiastic function of most of the sections.

Self-Commendation in 2 Cor 1–7

For the purposes of this brief analysis, 2 Cor 1–7 may be divided into the following sections: 1:1–2 (salutation), 1:3–11 (benediction), 1:12–14 (theme and purpose), 1:15–2:13, 2:14–7:4, and 7:5–16.

The Benediction (1:3–11)

As surprising as it at first may seem, Paul's self-praise begins already with his benediction, the very section in which the theme of his hardships is introduced. This section thus merits careful attention, and support for this claim needs to be given. To begin with, Nils A. Dahl has shown conclusively that a standard, indeed, traditional function of many *berakoth* is that of giving congratulations. Dahl notes that "the pure form of a congratulatory benediction follows a specific pattern: 'Blessed be YHWH (your God), who has done this to you.' "[107]

Congratulatory benedictions have a basic double function. God is praised as

[107] N. A. Dahl, "Benediction and Congratulation" (unpublished private paper, n.d.), 5. Naturally, there are also examples of congratulatory benedictions which do not exhibit this pure form.

the giver of the blessing and the recipient is congratulated on his reception of the gift. Both functions should be stressed. On the one hand, "to say *baruk YHWH* or εὐλογητὸς ὁ θεός is to praise God, not to state that he is praised or to wish that he might be praised."[108] It is a performative utterance whereby the speaker praises God. On the other hand, the congratulation offered the recipient of the blessing is no less real. For example, when Jethro joyfully exclaims to Moses, "Blessed be YHWH, who has delivered you out of the hand of the Egyptians and out of the hand of Pharaoh" (Exod 18:10), he is congratulating Moses on his escape no less than he is praising God for making it possible.

Congratulations may even fuse with commendation.[109] When Ignatius writes to the Ephesians (1:3), "For blessed be He who has granted you, who are worthy, to have obtained such a bishop," he is doing three things simultaneously. He is 1) praising God for his gracious gift, 2) congratulating the Ephesians on having secured Onesimus as their bishop and praising their worthiness to have such a man, and 3) praising and commending Onesimus to them.

Congratulations may be given to others (as in the above examples) or to oneself. Indeed, "as benedictions of God are normally expressions of gratitude and happiness, they often contain an element of self-congratulation."[110] Self-congratulation becomes especially explicit in Zech 11:5, "Blessed be YHWH, I have become rich!" In *Joseph and Asenath* 3:4 Pentephres, the priest of Heliopolis and father of Asenath, is told the news that Joseph is coming to see him and rest in his home. "And Pentephres heard and rejoiced with great joy and said, 'Blessed be the Lord, the God of Joseph, for my lord Joseph has thought me worthy.' "[111] The priest here congratulates himself on his coming good fortune, feeling himself flattered. Such self-congratulatory benedictions were not occasional matters. On the contrary, the morning benediction, "Blessed be He who has not made me a Gentile (or 'Who has made me an Israelite') . . . Who has not made me a slave . . . Who has not made me a woman" shows that such were a daily matter.[112]

There are two letters in the Pauline corpus that employ benedictions rather than thanksgivings, viz., 2 Corinthians and Ephesians. Dahl has argued, correctly in my judgment, that Ephesians is a letter of congratulations to Gentile Christians for having received the grace of God in Christ.[113] Prayers are offered on their behalf that they may fully appreciate and understand the richness of the gifts they have been given and so live in a manner appropriate to the great privileges given them.

The benediction that begins 2 Corinthians is also to be understood as

[108] Ibid., 6.

[109] Ibid., 19.

[110] Ibid., 7.

[111] The final clause is not in the Greek text edited by M. Philonenko, *Joseph et Aséneth* (Leiden: Brill, 1968) 138, but it does occur in the versions.

[112] Dahl, "Benediction and Congratulation," 11.

[113] Ibid., 24–25.

congratulatory in function. It differs from the benediction of Ephesians (and that of 1 Peter) by the fact that it is a self-congratulation. This does not imply, as has already been stressed, that God is not being praised. On the contrary, the section 1:3–11 both begins (εὐλογητός) and ends (εὐχαριστηθῇ) on the note of grateful praise to God. But the elements of self-congratulations are very strong. In the benediction Paul presents himself as "the comforted comforter." He begins by portraying himself not only as the one comforted by God but also as the one through whom God comforts others (1:3–4). To be precise, his vicissitudes of affliction and comfort convey the blessing of comfort to the Corinthians (1:5–6). That he has been delivered from certain death is, then, no inconsequential matter for them, and thus he invites them to join the chorus of those offering thanks to God for the gift given him (1:8–11). That is, he begins in v.3 by indirectly congratulating himself as blessed by God's comfort and as the conduit of that comfort to the Corinthians. He ends by explicitly asking them to bless God for him. The γάρ of 1:12 is thus highly appropriate, and 1:12–14 only make explicit the boasting and self-congratulations that have already appeared in 1:3–11.

Paul, therefore, begins with a benediction because it was a well-established vehicle for self-congratulations. It cannot be overstressed how quickly Paul moves from praise of the God who comforts to speaking of what he himself effects as a result of that comfort. Normally Paul gives thanks to God *for his readers,* for aspects of their lives and the grace given them. In 1 Thess 1:3, for instance, he thanks God for the Thessalonians' work of faith, endurance of hope, and labor of love (cf. also 2 Thess 1:3). In 1 Cor 1:7 he thanks God that the Corinthians do not lack any χάρισμα. But in 2 Corinthians all these items refer to Paul. It is Paul who has his hope set on God (1:10), and it is Paul's hope for the Corinthians that is firm (1:7). It is Paul's faith that is mentioned, how his trust is in God and not in himself (1:9). And, while he does not make it explicit, his sufferings for them testify to his love (cf. 1 Cor 13:3; 2 Cor 6:6). Furthermore, the χάρισμα that is mentioned and for which thanks is given is here the one that is bestowed on Paul (1:11). Again, Paul can speak in his letter openings of God's raising Jesus (Gal 1:1; 1 Thess 1:10) and use the idea of being delivered (1 Thess 1:10). Here, however, Paul refers to God's delivering him and likens it to a resurrection (1:9–10).

Everything that is normally affirmed of others becomes, therefore, self-referential in 2 Cor 1:3–11. The message communicated by this emphasis is clear: Paul is the one for whom the Corinthians should be very grateful, for it is through him that the blessings of God are channeled to them. Thus, the χάρισμα given to Paul (viz., his deliverance from death that makes the continuation of his ministry possible) is also a χάρισμα given to them. It should evoke thanksgiving to God and boasting about Paul for what God does to them through him.

But, as we have already seen, this self-emphasis occurs because Paul is seeking to establish a reciprocity of pride between the Corinthians and himself. Paradoxically, then, it is precisely because reciprocity is the goal that 2 Corinthians is so strikingly self-referential. The concern with mutuality and commonality begins already in the benediction. The very comfort Paul experiences is also experienced by the Corinthians (1:4). This is appropriate, for they are suffering the same hardships as Paul does (1:6). Thus they share in both hardships and comfort (1:7).

Throughout vv.3–10 Paul stresses his benefactions through Christ (1:5). He begins generally, saying he is able to comfort those in *any* affliction (1:4). At 1:6 he applies his vicissitudes to the Corinthians. His afflictions are for their comfort and salvation, his comfort for their comfort. Through 1:10 the benediction is all one way: God-Christ-Paul-the Corinthians. But in 1:11 his ὑπὲρ ὑμῶν changes to a two-fold ὑπὲρ ἡμῶν, as they are called upon to give aid by prayer and offer thanksgiving for Paul. The movement thus becomes two-way: we-you-you-we.

This same movement has already been seen in the thematic section (1:12–14) that follows. It begins with Paul's conduct toward the Corinthians (1:12) and ends by stating the goal of mutuality (1:14). This movement shows that it is wrong to believe that a benediction is used in 2 Corinthians because there is nothing in regard to the Corinthians for which *Paul* can be thankful. On the contrary, he affirms that they stand firm in the faith (1:24; cf. also 8:7), that his hope for them is firm (1:7), that they are his pride (7:4,14) and boast (1:14), and what one boasts about can certainly form the basis for giving thanks (2 Thess 1:3–4). It is much rather the case that Paul is trying to get the Corinthians to utter a thanksgiving *for him.* He wants them to see that there is something in him for which *they* can be grateful. He is confident that once they realize the full truth about him, they will see him as their real benefactor. The basic problem at Corinth, as Paul sees it, is a *lack of gratitude* on their part. He is grateful for them; they are his pride; he wants them to be grateful for him and proud of him. The whole correspondence is thus concerned with reciprocity, its basis, implications, and limitations.[114]

Finally, it is in the benediction that Paul introduces a number of themes that will be important in the remainder of the letter. It is here that he introduces the claim that he is able (δύνασθαι) to discharge the tasks of his ministry, a claim that he will advance more fully in 2:16ff in terms of his "sufficiency" as an apostle. Already in the benediction he makes clear what he will emphasize later (3:5–6), viz., that his capacity to perform his tasks does not derive from himself but from God (1:3–4). Even more than "the struggling sage" discussed in chapter three, he feels his hardships and harbors no illusions about his human limitations. The Asia-episode makes this explicit—he was burdened so excessively that it was beyond his power (ὑπὲρ δύναμιν) to endure his load of sorrow. It was God who

[114] Among the other Pauline letters it is Philippians that most shares 2 Corinthians' concern with reciprocity. Paul's repeated thanksgivings and assertions of gratitude reveal his concern that he not be thought guilty of ingratitude by the Philippians. Thus both letters address the issue of gratitude, which is a natural concern in communities and among friends. 2 Corinthians deals with the issue from one side of the apostle/church relationship, and Philippians from the other.

rescued and will rescue him (1:10–11), who comforts him so that he can comfort others (1:4). Paul does claim power, but it is not his own and it is not the sort that comes from reliance upon himself. Paul's weakness and God's power are thus the two emphases by which he seeks to keep his self-praise and self-congratulation in check and render it inoffensive.

From the benediction it is also clear that vicissitude will be an important emphasis of the letter. Here this theme is treated in terms of θλῖψις and παράκλησις. Later he will take up this theme again using other contrasts (cf., for example, the contrast of grief and joy in 1:24–2:4). But as the disclosure formula ("for we do not want you to be ignorant") of 1:8 makes clear, his hardships will be a major focus. He stresses that his sufferings are beneficial for both the Corinthians (1:6) and himself (1:9), a thesis to which he will return in chapter 4 (vv. 12,16).[115] He points as well to the endurance of hardships (1:6), a quality to which he will lay claim in 6:4.[116]

Again, already in the benediction Paul magnifies his hardships by speaking of "*all* our affliction" (1:4) and saying that the sufferings of Christ "overflow" to him (1:5). Out of the abundance of his sufferings Paul also does here what he does later in chapter 11, viz., he chooses one for greater and separate treatment. He describes his Asia experience—whatever it was—as a deliverance from death. Not just from "death" itself, but from "such a great death." By using such magnifying language in the benediction, by stressing the dangers and hardships of his life for the Corinthians' benefit, Paul is planting certain ideas that he will harvest in the remainder of the letter. First, he indicates that he is the kind of person who strives to benefit them at great personal cost to himself (= self-praise). Second, he shows that they are the recipients of the benefits of his sufferings and thus stand in his debt (= goal of mutuality). Third, he shows that the key to his accomplishments is not himself but God, who is thus deserving of praise and thanksgiving. Indeed, the more Paul stresses the danger and difficulty from which God delivers him, the greater the praise that is given to God and the fewer the grounds for taking offense at Paul's self-praise (= praise of God and a check against charges of offensive self-praise).

Apology and Self-Praise (1:12–14)

The thematic section 1:12–14 functions in the same way as an exordium does in a speech. In terms of Aristotle's *Rhetoric* (3.14.2, 1414b), vv. 12–14 show an

[115] Another link between chapter 4 and the benediction is the internalized "sentence of death" to which Paul refers in 1:9. This idea, which is clearly related to the depiction of the apostles as "men condemned to death" in 1 Cor 4:9, is taken up and developed in 2 Cor 4:10–11.

[116] The idea of endurance (1:6) is also used of the Corinthians' endurance of their hardships. The allusion here is to the mistreatment that they receive at the hands of the superapostles and thus anticipates the catalogue of their hardships in 11:20.

affinity to the exordia of epideictic speeches, in that the latter deal with praise (and/or blame). But inasmuch as eulogy is often a response to censure (Pl., *Grg.* 448E), it is not surprising that these verses also show an affinity to the exordia of forensic speeches, in which the exordium makes explicit the subject and purpose of the speech:

> But in speeches and epic poems the exordia provide a sample of the subject, in order that the hearers may know beforehand what it is about, and that the mind may not be kept in suspense, for that which is undefined leads astray; so then he who puts the beginning, so to say, into the hearer's hand enables him, if he holds fast to it, to follow the story. . . . So then the most essential and special function of the exordium is to make clear what is the end or purpose of the speech (3.14.6).

Verses 12–14 do this, and in a way that is more explicit than any other of Paul's letters. By doing so Paul gives his readers a thread by which they may follow the flow of his argument through its many disjunctures. He is this explicit, partly because his letter is to a certain degree apologetic, partly because of the importance of the task at hand.

An Apologetic Encomium (1:15–2:13; 7:5–16)

Aristotle also indicates that it is important for the defendant in a forensic speech to destroy any prejudice that the hearers might have. This is to be done at the outset: "The defendant, when about to introduce himself, must remove all obstacles, so that he must first clear away all prejudice" (3.14.7). Aristotle next indicates ways in which this removal of prejudice may be accomplished:

> One way of removing prejudice is to make use of the arguments by which one may clear oneself from disagreeable suspicion; for it makes no difference whether this suspicion has been openly expressed or not; and so this may be taken as a general rule. Another way consists in contesting the disputed points, either by denying the fact or its harmfulness, at least to the plaintiff (3.15.1).

Many other ways are indicated (3.15.1–10). Among these is the advice to maintain that one's actions, though injurious and painful, were honorable and beneficial (3.15.2). The motives of action are thus of crucial importance in such speeches (cf. 3.15.3,10).

This discussion by Aristotle is helpful in that it provides us with a perspective from which Paul's arguments may be better followed. After indicating his subject and purpose in 1:12–14, Paul turns in 1:15–2:13 to *the removal of prejudice.* He focuses on the suspicions created by his change in travel plans and his "severe" letter. Beginning with the former, he stresses the integrity with which he speaks (1:17–18) and the motives for his actions. He swears that his motive in not returning to Corinth was to spare them (1:23; cf. also 1 Cor 7:28 and contrast 2 Cor 13:2). A repetition of the painful experience of the previous visit (2:1) was in the best interests of neither the Corinthians nor himself (2:2–3).[117] Thus he wrote them instead, and his letter, he emphasizes, was *not* intended to cause them pain. On the contrary, it was, just as emphatically, to let them know his special love for them (2:4). Indeed, it is *for their sake* that he now forgives even the person who caused him pain (2:10).

In 1:15–2:13 Paul thus clarifies his moves and motives from the time of the painful visit to his arrival in Macedonia. He stresses that both his itinerary and his correspondence are to be understood in light of the affectionate motives that prompted them. He completes this clarification of his actions in 7:5–16, where he resumes the theme of his anxiety about the status of his relationship with the Corinthians (2:13; 7:5). He relates how the good news of their enthusiasm for him has brought him relief and comfort (7:6–7), and he justifies the severity of his letter by pointing to its beneficial results (7:8–10). This is, as we have seen, one of the methods suggested by Aristotle for the removal of prejudice (*Rhet.* 3.15.2), and its use here by Paul represents his final attempt to remove any prejudice against himself before turning to the matter of the collection. He thus pronounces his severe letter both justifiable and successful, for his goal in writing had been to reveal to the Corinthians not only *his* love for them (2:4) but also *their* zeal for him (7:12). The present letter of 2 Cor 1–9 represents Paul's attempt to capitalize on their positive response to his letter and Titus' mission by turning "your zeal for us" (7:12) into the insight that "we are your boast" (1:14).

The sections 1:15–2:13 and 7:5–16 are thus *an apologetic encomium* in which praise and apology are coordinated in service to each other. The removal of prejudice by a clarification of the motives for his actions is clearly apologetic, but it is also encomiastic in that it serves to place Paul in a positive light by removing the grounds for suspicion against him. The apologetic encomium was not new with Paul but had been employed as early as Gorgias in his famous "Encomium on Helen" (B 11 Diels-Kranz, *Vorsokr.*). The apologetic element in this encomium was in fact so dominant that Isocrates (*Helen* 14) criticized Gorgias for calling it an encomium rather than an apology. But since praise is a vital aspect even of Gorgias' apologies (cf. esp. B 11a.27–32 [2.301.3–302.16 Diels-Kranz]), it is clear that the "Encomium on Helen" is a mixed type, consisting of both praise and apology. As in 2 Cor 1–2 and 7, praise and apology go hand in hand and are justified by the forensic setting in which they are given.[118] And it is precisely to this forensic setting that Paul points by invoking

[117] His failure to return to Corinth not only spared them pain (1:23) but also Paul himself (2:2–3). His action was thus for their mutual benefit. Moreover, just as Paul works for their joy (1:24), so it is their obligation to make him rejoice (2:3a). Mutual pride in one another (1:14) is thus to be accompanied by mutual joy (2:3b; cf. also Rom 12:15; 1 Cor 12:26).

[118] For the appropriateness of self-praise within an apologetic context, cf. the discussion in chapter three on "Praise and Self-Praise." For an example of self-praise and defense in regard to a failure to come when expected, cf. Hor., *Ep.* 1.7, esp. lines 24–25.

God as witness to his testimony about the integrity of his behavior (1:12,18,23). 2 Cor 1–9 is thus at least quasi-apologetic and constitutes a middle stage between the stern admonition of 1 Cor 1–4 with its secondary apologetic function and the full apology of 2 Cor 10–13.

Finally, the connection of 2 Cor 1–2 and 7 with forensic speeches makes it difficult to maintain that this material is simply a "letter of reconciliation." Paul is only too aware that the reconciliation is tenuous at best and needs to be solidified both by assuring them of his confidence in them and by making them more confident of him as a person. Indeed, Paul's expressions of confidence in 2 Corinthians are not so much actual as potential. By using the language of confidence Paul hopes to create the very confidence of which he speaks.[119] The basis for that confidence is provided primarily in 2:14–7:4, the heart of 2 Cor 1–9.

Paul's Self-Depiction (2:14–7:4)[120]

From addressing the chief causes of any suspicion and prejudice against himself in 1:15–2:13, Paul turns in 2:14 to the positive presentation of himself as the one of whom the Corinthians can and should be proud (1:14). Like the preceding section, it is both encomiastic and apologetic, and the transition to this part of his self-depiction occurs when he moves from an expression of anxiety in 2:13 to an exclamation of gratitude in 2:14. Such a movement is in itself not strange, for there is a strong impulse in Paul to follow an expression of woe with one of thanksgiving. Such is the case, for example, in Rom 7:21–25, but whereas there the result of this move is a minor displacement of the conclusion of Paul's argument, in 2 Cor 2:14 his thanksgiving not only leads to a major displacement of the conclusion of his itinerary (2:11–12) but also serves to introduce a new train of thought that will be pursued in 2:14–7:4. The itinerary of 2:11–12 is resumed only in 7:5. What replaces the *specific* itinerary of Paul's movements from Troas to Macedonia is the *general* itinerary of his movements under God's direction. That Paul is now going to speak in general terms of the journey in which he is ever involved is made clear by the comprehensive temporal (πάντοτε) and spatial (ἐν παντὶ τόπῳ) terms that he adds.[121]

[119] On this topic, cf. esp. S. N. Olson "Confidence Expressions in Paul: Epistolary Conventions and the Purpose of 2 Corinthians," (Ph.D. Diss., Yale, 1976).

[120] The chief analysis of this section is that of J.-F. Collange, *Énigmes de la deuxième épître de Paul aux Corinthiens* (SNTSMS 18; Cambridge: University, 1972).

[121] It is typical of Paul that he should switch as well from the topic of what he has done or does, to what God does through him. The emphasis in 2 Corinthians ultimately falls upon the action of God upon Paul, upon his response to that action. This emphasis appeared already in the benediction, with the description of God as comforting Paul so that he can comfort others (1:3–4). And here, as in the benediction, it is God who acts on Paul, with Christ serving as the agent and locus of that action (1:5; 2:14; cf. also 2:17; 3:4; 4:6.)

Paul describes this journey as a triumphal procession, an image which also occurs in the discussion of hardship and vicissitude by moralists such as Seneca. For the latter, one should be the same, whether one rides in triumph or is "placed upon a foreign barrow to grace the procession of a proud and brutal victor." "No whit more humble shall I be," affirms Seneca, "when I am driven in front of the chariot of another than when I stood erect upon my own" (*V.B.* 25.4).[122]

It is as Paul participates in a constant triumphal procession that God makes manifest through him the knowledge of Christ (2:14).[123] But does Paul do so as a soldier of the One riding atop the victory chariot,[124] as a captive walking before the chariot,[125] or both?[126] The lexical evidence is crucial to this decision. The word that Paul employs here is θριαμβεύειν, which customarily describes a victory parade in which the vanquished enemy soldiers and generals are led about as prisoners.[127] It is in keeping with this significance of the term that the author of Colossians says that God stripped the defeated principalities and powers and exposed them to public ridicule by marching them about in a triumphal procession (2:15). Such usage strongly suggests that Paul is depicting himself in 2 Cor 2:14 as a *conquered captive* who walks before the chariot of the divine *Triumphator.* The opposite idea, that Paul participates in the procession as a conquering general or soldier in God's army, not only lacks lexical support but also fails to account for the mixed response of the crowd. The latter is possible *only* if Paul

[122] Cf. also Sen., *Ep.* 71.22; Epict., *Diss.* 3.24.85; and Fronto, *Ep.* (Vol. 2, p. 26 Haines).

[123] That "Christ" rather than "God" is the antecedent of αὐτοῦ in 2:14 is suggested by the explanatory statement in 2:15 that "we are the aroma of Christ." To shift from "smell of God" to "aroma of Christ" would be too sudden, especially in view of the ὅτι. That he speaks in 4:6 of the knowledge of "God" is not decisive for the interpretation of 2:14, since shifts between God and Christ occur elswhere in 2 Corinthians. In 4:7, for example, Paul attributes the power in his ministry to God, whereas in 12:9 he attributes it to Christ (the Lord). For the knowledge of Christ, cf. also Phil 3:8. This line of interpretation is also adopted, though for different reasons, by P. E. Hughes, *Paul's Second Epistle to the Corinthians* (NICNT; Grand Rapids: Eerdmans, 1962) 78–79, esp. n.11.

[124] The view that Paul is depicting himself as one of the soldiers of the victorious general is argued by C. K. Barrett, *A Commentary on The Second Epistle to the Corinthians* (HNTC; New York : Harper & Row, 1973) 97–98. Cf. also Jean Héring, *The Second Epistle of Saint Paul to the Corinthians* (London: Epworth, 1967) 18. This interpretation could appeal to 2 Cor 10:4–6, where Paul appears as God's soldier laying siege to the unredeemed intellect. See also 2 Cor 6:7 for Paul as the armed sage.

[125] Cf. esp. Wilhelm Bousset, *Kyrios Christos* (lst Ger. ed., 1913; Nashville: Abingdon, 1970) 153–54, and L. Williamson, Jr., "Led in Triumph," *Int* 22 (1968) 317–32.

[126] Cf. the discussion of R. H. Strachan, *The Second Epistle of Paul to the Corinthians* (MNTC; London: Hodder & Stoughton, 1935) 73.

[127] For the term itself, cf. Hans Windisch, *Der zweite Korintherbrief* (MeyerK 6; 9th ed.; Göttingen: Vandenhoeck & Ruprecht, 1924) 96–97, and Gerhard Delling, *TDNT* 3.159–60. On the Roman triumphal procession, cf. now H. S. Versnel, *Triumphus* (Leiden: Brill, 1970).

appears as a despised captive, a prisoner of war (Rom 16:7; Phlm 23; Col 4:10), not a garlanded hero.

Normally the captives in such processions were somber and sullen.[128] Joy resided with the victorious participants and spectators. A public thanksgiving (*supplicatio*) was customarily decreed by the senate prior to the procession,[129] so that the whole affair was a joyful celebration. Incense crackled and smoked on every altar (Ov., *Tr.* 4.2.4; Plut., *Aem.* 32) and was burned as well in front of the triumphal chariot (App., *Pun.* 66). At the head of the Roman procession came the magistrates and senators, with trumpeters following close behind. Then came the tangible proof of the victory, the various spoils. Boards with the names of vanquished countries and nations were carried in the procession, as well as pictures and models of the spoils that could not be physically carried back (Ov., *Pont.* 3.4.104–05). Fourth in line came the white oxen which were to be sacrificed. These sacrificial animals were attended by the Camilli, both groups bearing various instruments. Then came the chief captives, usually in chains or with ropes about their necks.[130] Following them came the lictors of the victorious general and a chorus of harpists and pipers. Only then came the general himself, riding in a circular chariot drawn by four horses. With him were members of his family and others. The army came last, bringing up the rear.[131]

The glory of the triumph went to the commander whose forces had conquered, but the display of material spoils and captives was the essence of the victory.[132] In such a procession, along with the customary incense (2:15) and thanksgiving (2:14), Paul places himself as the very showpiece of God's triumph. Such a circumstance was hardly glorious in and of itself. Thus, as in 1 Cor 4:9, Paul is once again a "spectacle," and the fact that he appears as such is again

[128] Cf. esp. Ov., *Tr.* 4.2.19–24, 29–34; Daremberg-Saglio, *Dictionnaire des antiquités grecques et romaines* 5.489, figure 7094. The plight of the war-slave was so severe that it was regarded as one of the circumstances in which suicide was justified (Plot., *Enn.* 1.4.7,32).

[129] Cf. Cic., *Sull.* 30.85; *Prov. Cons.* 11.27; *Pis.* 3.6; Caes., *BGall.* 4.38 *fin;* 7.90 *fin;* and LS (s.v. *supplicatio*).

[130] If the conquered enemy leader was not physically present in the procession, then his or her presence would be graphically depicted in some way (App., *Mith.* 117; Cass. Dio 51.21.8). It seems possible that the imagery of Gal 3:1 may be based on the objects carried in such processions.

[131] This discussion of the order of the processional is based on the treatments by R. Cagnat, "Triumphus," in Daremberg-Saglio, *Dictionnaire des antiquités grecques et romaines* 5.488–90; G. M. N. Rushford, "Triumphus," *A Dictionary of Greek and Roman Antiquities* (ed. W. Smith, W. Wayte, & G. E. Marindin; 2 vols.; London: J. Murray, 1891) 2.894–97; and W. Ehlers, "Triumphus," in PW, 2d Series, VIIA.1, 493–511. Compare the descriptions of triumphs in Joseph., *BJ* 7.123–57 and Plut., *Aem.* 32–34.

[132] Rushford, "Triumphus," 894.

attributed to God.[133] The distinctive aspect of the procession here is that its thanksgiving is uttered by "the prisoner of war," the very one who normally was in the depths of depression or bitter with resentment (cf., for example, Plut., *Aem.* 34.1-2). Paul does not grumble and curse his conqueror as a vanquished foe normally did, but rather expresses his gratitude as one who is exuberant over his defeat, for, though vanquished, he is no longer a foe. He is now "the sweet aroma of Christ to God" (2:15). It is thus Paul's *attitude* as an enslaved prisoner that transforms the imagery of 2 Cor 2:14 and makes it as powerful as it is paradoxical. And yet, as the use of triumphal imagery by Seneca indicates, Paul's joyful attitude in such an adverse and ignoble circumstance is a sign of his serenity, capacity, and worth. It is this very claim that he makes increasingly explicit as he proceeds.

Paul continues the imagery of a triumphal procession in 2:14b by introducing the term ὀσμή and affirming that it is through himself that God makes manifest "the smell that is the knowledge of Christ." As a participant in the procession Paul exudes a smell that is in reality a sweet, fragrant one (εὐωδία), but which meets with a mixed response. Some find it a smell of death, but others of life (2:15-16). The scenario of 2:15-16 recalls that found in 1 Cor 1. There Christ is in truth the wisdom of God (1:30), but the response to the message about the cross is mixed. While the ones being saved see it as the power of God, those perishing find it moronic and devoid of wisdom (1:18). The affinity between the two passages suggests that in 2 Cor 2:15-16 Paul is applying to himself the analysis given the message of the cross in 1 Cor 1. The message and the messenger are correlates, so that the response given the one matches that given the other. True knowledge is communicated by the Creator God through Paul (2 Cor 2:14), but this knowledge is perceived as folly (1 Cor 1:18) because the God of this world has blinded the minds of unbelievers so that they perish unenlightened (2 Cor 4:3-4). The message of a dead savior is thus perceived as moronic and its messenger as exuding a stench of death. The phrase ὀσμὴ ἐκ θανάτου suggests the putrid smell that comes from a corpse (cf. Soph., *Ant.* 408-13; *Phil.* 884-91; Joseph., *BJ* 6.2), and the immediate occasion for the concept of Paul exuding a death stench may be the imagery suggested by θριαμβεύειν. It could be that the captive Paul, coming from "battle," still has the stench of dead bodies about himself. Or, the idea may derive from the fact that captives were often executed following their forced march in the processional. Theirs was truly a march "from death unto death."

But it seems more likely that Paul is already thinking of an idea that he will express graphically in 4:10. That is, Paul exudes a "stench of death" because he

[133] For the captives and spoils as spectacles in the procession, cf. Joseph., *BJ* 7.132; Cass. Dio 51.21.8; and Plut., *Aem.* 33.4. Compare also Philo, *Flacc.* 74. Furthermore, it is striking that whereas Pliny (*HN* 7.43.135) speaks of *Fortune* having led Publius Ventidius captive in Pompey's triumph, Paul says that it is *God* who leads him captive in the processional.

carries about in his body τὴν νέκρωσιν τοῦ Ἰησοῦ. It should be noted that Paul affirms that God *always* leads him in a triumphal procession (2:14). This is the first use of the word πάντοτε in the letter. The next time he uses it is in 4:10, where he decribes his bearing around the *nekrōsis* of Jesus as something that he *always* does. 2:14 and 4:10 thus describe concomitant events. God is always leading Paul about as a grateful captive in his victory procession, and Paul is always in that procession bearing around the *nekrōsis* of Jesus.

It is ultimately Jesus' death that gives the offense, whether to the mind (1 Cor 1:18; 2 Cor 4:4) or to the senses (2 Cor 2:16; cf. Gal 3:1). The message about the crucified Jesus and him who embodies that message find the same rejection by those who do not believe. Those who reject the apostle and his crucified Messiah are repulsed and sickened by the fetidness that they experience in him and his message. But those who believe find in Paul the sweet fragrance of Christ, and in his message the power of God (1 Cor 1:18) that brings life (2 Cor 2:16). Paul thus takes his ministry with utter seriousness because he is convinced that a person's response to him leads to that person's life or death (2 Cor 2:15–16).

These assertions in 2:14–16b lead to the question that provides the theme of 2:14–7:4, viz., καὶ πρὸς ταῦτα τίς ἱκανός; (2:16c). What is at stake in the sections that follow is Paul's *sufficiency* as an apostle, with his authority[134] and legitimacy[135] grounded in his capacity to embody in his own person the paradoxical glory and suffering of Christ. To such sufficiency Paul lays claim here, for the answer to his question "Who is sufficient for this?" is clearly a boastful "*We are!*"[136] In 3:5–6 he will provide a check against the audacity of this claim by making clear that this sufficiency is a *charisma* and not a natural possession (cf.

[134] For this emphasis, cf. J. H. Schütz, *Paul and the Anatomy of Apostolic Authority* (SNTSMS 26; New York: Cambridge University Press, 1975).

[135] For this emphasis, cf. Ernst Käsemann, *Die Legitimität des Apostels: Eine Untersuchung zu II Korinther 10–13* (Darmstadt: Wissenschaftliche Buchgesellschaft, 1956), a study which appeared originally in *ZNW* 41 (1942) 33–71.

[136] The γάρ of 2:17 and Paul's distinction of himself from *hoi polloi* clearly imply this answer. The question of 3:1 recognizes Paul's self-praise without denying it, as a comparison with 4:2 makes clear. This understanding appears already in the Vulgate. As R. V. G. Tasker points out, the "Vulg. inserts the word 'so' before *sufficient* with the implication 'Who is so sufficient as myself?' " Cf. his *The Second Epistle of Paul to the Corinthians* (Tyndale NT Commentaries 8; Grand Rapids: Eerdmans, 1963) 58. It is unfortunate that Tasker himself misses both the point of Paul's question and the Vulgate's insertion, and thinks that the answer to Paul's question is "no one." Tasker is clearly trying to guard Paul from the charge of arrogance that could be leveled in response to the boast in 2:16c–17. But Paul provides his own explicative check against this deduction in 3:5–6. Indeed, it is precisely because of his boasting that such a check is necessary. For the recognition that the answer to Paul's question cannot be a negative one, cf. esp. R. C. H. Lenski, *The Interpretation of St. Paul's First and Second Epistles to the Corinthians* (Minneapolis: Augsburg, 1937) 902.

also 1 Cor 15:9). His ἱκανότης is not from himself, but from God, who has ἱκάνωσεν him to be a *diakonos* of the new covenant.[137] His ministry and his sufficiency for it are not the result of merit, but of mercy (4:1; contrast Xen., *Symp.* 8.38). But he *is* sufficient as a consequence, and it is this that he extols in 2:17–4:2. He does this in part by distinguishing himself both from those who peddle God's word and tamper with it (2:17; 4:2)[138] and from Moses (3:13). He is totally unlike the former, but distinct from Moses only in a particular way.

Indeed, Paul's thematic question in 2:16c recalls the statement by Moses in Exod 4:10 LXX: οὐχ ἱκανός εἰμί. Like Moses, Paul recognizes his incapacity for the task to which God appoints him (1 Cor 15:9; 2 Cor 3:5–6). This applies especially to his linguistic ability (2 Cor 10:10; 11:6), and in this respect he is fully like Moses (Exod 4:10 LXX). What sets him apart from Moses is thus not his own person or the fact that he has received capacity for his God-ordained task. It is rather the nature of the ministry and covenant entrusted to Paul which distinguishes him from Moses and sets him apart from the hero of the old covenant. It is in regard to this that Paul praises himself, in keeping with the ancient practice of praising oneself by bestowing praise on that in which one is involved or excels (cf. Pl., *Grg.* 485A).

Unlike Moses' ministry, Paul's is characterized by confident boldness (3:12–13). The absence of a veil in Paul's ministry is the sign of the boldness and freedom of the apostle vis-à-vis that of Moses (3:18). Those who abide in Moses wear the veil that Moses wore (3:13,15), but for those who with Paul turn to Christ, the veil is taken away (3:17). Moses' ministry of the letter ends in death and condemnation (3:7,9). That is, the result of death that the perishing see in Paul's ministry (2:16a) belongs in reality to that of Moses. Paul's ministry, on the other hand, ends in life, righteousness, and glory (3:6,9,11). Thus, for those who are being saved, Paul is truly "a fragrance from life unto life" (2:16). The confidence of Paul in his work is directly derivative from his call to be a *diakonos* of a new and better covenant (3:4,12; 4:1). This confidence reflects Paul's sufficiency as an apostle of the glorious gospel (4:4–6).

In 2:17–4:6 Paul thus praises himself and unfolds what he means by saying that he is "a fragrance from life unto life" (2:16). In 4:7 he will begin to discuss an aspect of his ministry that leads those who are perishing (2:15; 4:3) to see in him only "a stench of death unto death" (2:16). His sufficiency for this part of his ministry is seen especially in relation to the hardships that his ministry entails.

[137] For the possibility that Paul is deriving his "sufficiency" from El Shaddai as the "All-Sufficient One," cf. C. H. Dodd, *The Bible and the Greeks* (London: Hodder & Stoughton, 1935) 15–16.

[138] It is striking that Paul's depiction of himself in 2:14–16 as exuding a smell is followed in 2:17 by a polemical jab at charlatans who peddle and corrupt God's word. In contrast to such persons he characterizes himself as a person of "sincerity," a word that occurs with the term "straightforwardness" in 1:12. In his discussion of ἁπλότης Marcus Aurelius contrasts the charlatan who feigns this quality with the man who truly possesses it and affirms that "the simple and good man should in fact be like a man who has a strong smell about him" that makes him immediately recognizable (*Med.* 11.15).

2 Cor 4:7–12

This section contains the first of Paul's *peristasis* catalogues in 2 Corinthians. Whereas in 3:10 he characterizes the *diakonia* of the life-giving Spirit (3:6,8) in terms of its superlative splendor (τῆς ὑπερβαλλούσης δόξης), in 4:7 he points to the exceeding greatness of the power (ἡ ὑπερβολὴ τῆς δυνάμεως) that is displayed in the Lord's *diakonoi.* This power is shown above all in the triumph of Paul and his cohorts over adversity. Paul is just as emphatic as the Hellenistic moralists that *peristaseis* provide the occasion for the exhibition of *power* (cf., for example, Epict., *Diss.* 2.1.39; Sen., *Ep.* 71.26). Likewise, just as the moralists stress the sage's serenity in suffering, so also Paul emphasizes the failure of his adversities to crush him. Both before (4:1) and after (4:16) this section he affirms οὐκ ἐγκακοῦμεν, "we do not despair." The catalogue in 4:8–9 contains four more οὐκ-statements, two of which (4:8) point in the same direction: οὐ στενοχωρούμενοι ("we are not crushed") and οὐκ ἐξαπορούμενοι ("we are not despondent"). The climatic οὐκ-statement is, moreover, a resounding οὐκ ἀπολλύμενοι, "we are not destroyed" (4:9).

In all these respects Paul appears fully like the suffering sage who is triumphant over his hardships.[139] Indeed, his four-fold use of οὐ with the participle, rather than the customary μή, serves to make his assertions of victory all the more emphatic. Therefore, *the catalogue of 4:8–9 functions in part to demonstrate Paul's composure,* just as the catalogues of the sage's *peristaseis* serve to show his serenity. But Paul refuses here to claim credit for this achievement, insisting that the power at work in his ministry is God's and not his own (4:7).[140] Thus, whereas Seneca's sage "knows his own strength" (*Ep.* 71.26) and is full of self-confidence, Paul knows God's strength and is full of confidence in

[139] J. Weiss is correct in claiming that in 2 Cor 4:8–9 Paul expresses "the triumphant certainty that no suffering can destroy him." See his "Beiträge," 178. The criticism of Weiss by A. Fridrichsen, "Zum Thema 'Paulus und die Stoa'. Eine stoische Stilparallele zu 2. Kor. 4,8f.," *ConNT* 9 (1944) 30 n. 2, is thus unjustified. The feelings of triumph (Weiss) and defiance (Fridrichsen) are both, of course, characteristics of the sage. For the recognition that Paul is indeed drawing here on the theme of the sage, cf. esp. J. Dupont, ΣΥΝ ΧΡΙΣΤΩΙ: *L'union avec le Christ suivant Saint Paul* (Bruges, Belgium: Abbaye de Saint-André, 1952) 118–19; and also Windisch, *Korintherbrief,* 143–44, and Kümmel in the appendix to Lietzmann, *Korinther,* 201.

[140] The statement in 4:7 parallels that made in 3:4–6. In both cases Paul begins by affirming what he possesses (3:4: "we have such confidence"; 4:7a: "we have this treasure") and then quickly indicates his dependence upon the divine (3:5–6; 4:7b). Affirmations of Paul's servant status appear in both contexts as well (3:6: *diakonos;* 4:6: *doulos*). The idea of power deriving from God was introduced in 1:4, discussed in terms of "sufficiency" in 2:16c and 3:5–6, and is unfolded in 4:7–12. Furthermore, it is connected thematically with the depiction of God in 2:14 as the *triumphator.* As Versnel has convincingly demonstrated, the *triumphator* was understood as the bearer of extraordinary power. See his *Triumphus,* esp. chapter nine, pp. 356–97.

him (1:9). The fact that he credits God for his success rather than himself is, however, not unique, for, as we saw in the discussion of self-praise in chapter three, this is a recommended device of self-praise. For Paul, clearly, it is more than a device; it is an experiential and theological datum. But it is a device nonetheless, and it functions here both to render inoffensive his claims of composure and to acknowledge God as the source of the perceptible power in his ministry.

The designation of God as the real *dynamis* in Paul's life is facilitated by his derogatory self-characterization as an "earthen vessel" (4:7).[141] Earthen vessels were the disposable bottles of antiquity, as inexpensive as they were fragile. Vessels of bronze, for example, if they became unclean, could be purified by various procedures. But no such procedures existed for unclean earthen vessels; not only did their absorbency make it all but impossible to render them clean but they were also sufficiently inexpensive so as to be broken and discarded (cf. Lev 6:28; 11:32–33; 15:12). And, being made of clay, they were easily and irreparably broken (Isa 30:14 LXX; Jer 19:11; Dan 2:42; cf. also Ps 2:9; Jer 22:28; Sir 22:7). As an earthen vessel,[142] then, Paul is quintessentially

[141] On the derogatory character of "earthen vessels" as a term, compare the way in which contempt for the "precious sons of Zion" is expressed by likening them to earthen vessels in Lam 4:2 (cf. also Jer 22:28). Such vessels were normally used only for common or *ignoble* purposes (2 Tim 2:20; cf. also Rom 9:21). For earthen vessels in the OT, cf. esp. Lev 6:28; 11:33; 14:5,50; 15:12; Num 5:17; 2 Sam 17:28; Prov 26:23; Jer 32:14 (39:14 LXX); Ezek 4:9 LXX; and also *m. Kelim* 2:1–3.

[142] There has been considerable debate whether "earthen vessel" refers to the body alone or to the whole person. In Hellenistic literature the body is frequently compared to a vessel within which the soul or mind is contained (cf. Cic., *Tusc.* 1.22.52; Sen., *Marc.* 11.3; Dio Chrys., *Or.* 12.59; Mar. Ant., *Med.* 3.3.2; 8.27; 10.38; 12.2; cf. also 7.68; 10.1; 12.3; Epict., *Diss.* 1.1.11), even by Jewish writers (Philo, *Det.* 170; *Mig.* 193; *Som.* 1.26; 4 Ezra 7:88; cf. also Wis 9:15). On the other hand, persons as a whole can be compared to vessels (cf. Epict., *Diss.* 2.4.4–5; ps-Heraclitus, *Ep.* 8.4 [208,16–19 Malherbe]), a point which undercuts the contention of Collange, *Énigmes*, 146, that such is not the case. Moreover, 4 Ezra 4:11 even seems to use *vas* to denote the mind.

As for Paul's use of the expression "earthen vessel," the context of chapters 4–5 as a whole suggests that he has *primarily* the body (4:10–11; 5:6,8,10) in mind, the "outer man" (4:16), the "earthly tent" (5:1,4). But since he lists psychic (4:8) as well as physical distress, it seems clear that more than corporeality is intended by his metaphor. Indeed, the basic contrast in 4:7 is between divine power and human weakness, so that the power given "us" is both physical and psychic. Older commentators who adopt this position include C. F. G. Heinrici, *Das zweite Sendschreiben des Apostels Paulus an die Korinther* (Berlin: Hertz, 1887) 215, and *Der zweite Brief an die Korinther* (MeyerK 6; 7th ed.; Göttingen: Vandenhoeck & Ruprecht, 1890) 115–16; and James Denney, *The Second Epistle to the Corinthians* (The Expositors' Bible; New York: Hodder & Stoughton, 1894) 158–59. Cf. also Strachan, *Second Corinthians*, 93–94; Dupont, ΣΥΝ ΧΡΙΣΤΩΙ, 122–23, 129; and Prümm, *Diakonia Pneumatos*, 1.230–31.

fragile.[143] Consequently, there is a clear paradox in the placement of a valuable treasure (4:7) in a cheap, fragile container. A powerful paradox, and yet one that is fully consistent with the paradoxical nature of Paul's gospel in general and with the particular paradox that appears in 2:14.[144] That the knowledge of God in the face of Christ (4:6) is a treasure contained in an earthen vessel is no less paradoxical than the fact that that knowledge is disseminated by a spectacle in the divine processional.[145]

[143] The fact that "earthen vessel" connotes fragility was recognized already by John Chrysostom. Cf. J. Ashworth (trans.), *The Homilies of S. John Chrysostom on the Second Epistle of St. Paul the Apostle to the Corinthians* (Library of Fathers 27; Oxford: J. H. Parker, 1848) 112. This point, however, is not always recognized. Philipp Bachmann, *Der zweite Brief des Paulus an die Korinther* (Zahn's Kommentar zum Neuen Testament 8; lst & 2nd ed.; Leipzig: Deichert, 1909) 195, and Barrett, *Second Corinthians*, for example, deny that the fragility of earthen vessels is a primary aspect of Paul's figure. They do so because they see "earthen vessel" almost exclusively in contrast to "treasure." But the purpose clause of 4:7 makes abundantly clear that outside power is necessary precisely because of the inherent weakness and fragility of earthen containers. Cf. 1 Pet 3:7 and the weakness/power theme in 2 Cor 12:9. C. Spicq correctly recognizes the idea of fragility, but he commits the opposite error of restricting the image to this idea alone and not allowing it to serve also as a contrast to treasure. Cf. his "L'image sportive de II Corinthiens, IV, 7-9," *ETL* 14 (1937) 209-29, esp. 211-13.

[144] The paradox is grounded, of course, in the fact that valuable documents, metals, and coins were both temporarily and permanently placed in such containers (Jer 32:14; Plut., *Aem.* 32.5), so that the idea of "treasure in earthen vessels" was not unknown (cf. esp. Hdt. 3.96). And while 2 Cor 4:7 contains a striking Pauline paradox, it is clearly not unrelated to the Jewish paradox found in *b.Ned.* 50b and elsewhere about wisdom in an ugly vessel. It is also related to the Stoic paradox that only the wise man is beautiful, even when his true inner beauty is smothered by external unloveliness. Indeed, the fact that virtue is buried in a body that endures hardships like poverty, lowliness, and disgrace is one of the things that hinders its recognition (Sen., *Ep.* 115.6).

[145] The precise antecedent of "this treasure" is not clear. The suggestions most frequently made seek the explanation in 4:1-6 and include 1) "this ministry" (4:1), 2) "the word of God" (4:2), 3) "the truth" (4:2), 4) "the gospel of the glory of Christ" (4:3-4), and 5) all or part of the phrase "the illumination of the glory of God in the face of Christ" (4:6). Certainty on this matter is impossible, but if it is accepted that 4:7 begins a new discussion of themes contained in 2:14-17, viz., the power of the transcendent *triumphator* (2:14) and the "smell of death" (2:16), then the specific reference is likely to "knowledge" (4:6). This term has not been mentioned since 2:14, so that its repetition here seems deliberate. The imagery, however, is varied from "the smell of the knowledge of him" (2:14) to "the illumination of the knowledge of God" (4:6). Cf. also the repetition of other terms from 2:14-17 in 4:1-6, such as "manifestation" (2:14; 4:2), "the word of God" (2:17; 4:2), and "the perishing" (2:15; 4:3). This interpretation becomes even more compelling if the "earthen vessels" in which the treasure is contained can be taken as an allusion to the vessels carried in triumphal processions (Plut., *Aem.* 32.5), a suggestion made by Hughes, *Second Corinthians*, 136. At any rate, the association of "treasure" with "knowledge" is clearly Pauline (Col 2:3).

If a broader reference for "treasure" is preferred, it should be taken as a reference to both

By shifting the power that appears in his ministry from himself to God, Paul totally transforms part of the imagery in the catalogue that follows. In 4:9, for instance, Paul claims that he has not been shattered by his sufferings; he is, as it were, a vessel that is thrown to the ground yet remains unbroken (οὐκ ἀπολλύμενοι).[146] Without this attribution of power to God, the final antithesis in 4:9 would serve to depict Paul as a "man of steel," as one who, like the Stoic sage in Plut., *Mor.* 1057E, is still invincible even when he is thrown in wrestling (cf. also *Mor.* 541B). Again, he would be like Seneca's sage, who "even if he falls, . . . still fights upon his knees" (*Prov.* 2.6). The sage does so because "he has been downed in body but not in spirit" (*corpore nec proiecit animum proiectus*). Thus, "as often as he falls, (he) rises again with greater defiance than ever" and stands his ground all the more eagerly (Sen., *Ep.* 13.2-3).

But whereas such actions point to the strength and determination of the sage's will in the face of Fortune, Paul's statement points elsewhere. In light of the contrast between divine power and human frailty in 4:7 and the fact that Paul is only a "man of clay," a κεραμεὺς ἄνθρωπος,[147] his statement comes to mean that he as a mortal is "knocked down" (καταβαλλόμενοι)[148] by his hardships but

---

the ministry (4:1) and the gospel (4:3–4) through which the knowledge of the divine is transmitted, for the ministry and word of reconciliation are clearly inseparable for Paul (5:18–19). In this case, "treasure" could embrace all that was said in 3:1–4:6 (so Olson, "Confidence Expressions," 162–63). There is, finally, a remote possibility that "this treasure" is prospective rather than retrospective and refers to the dying and rising of Jesus that takes place in him (4:10–11).

[146] Contrast Ps 30:12 LXX, where the psalmist, likening himself to a dead person, says, "I have become like a broken vessel" (ὡσεὶ σκεῦος ἀπολωλός). For people compared to cracked or broken vessels, cf. Jer 22:28 (with Hos 8:8); Epict., *Diss.* 2.4.4–5; ps-Heraclitus, *Ep.* 8.4 (208,16–19 Malherbe); and also Ps 21:15 LXX.

[147] Diogenian. 5.98, cited by LSJ 940a as proverbial of frailty.

[148] The word καταβάλλω is a technical term for defeating one's opponent in both battle (Hdt. 4.64; 9.63; 2 Kgs 19:7 LXX; Jer 19:7 LXX; Ezek 23:25; 1 Macc 4:33) and the *agōn* (Pl., *Hp. Mi.* 374A; Philo, *Agr.* 120; Plut., *Per.* 8.4; *Mor.* 638D; Diog. Laert. 6.62; cf. also Hom., *Od.* 4.344). For this reason some have found in Paul's use of the word the image of the wounded warrior or of the defeated wrestler. That "knocked down" is contrasted with "perishing" could point to the battle motif, but only if "perishing" is taken literally and not metaphorically of Paul's spirit. In fact, either image is possible, since Paul is quite clearly drawing on Stoic depictions of the sage at this point, and in those depictions the sage's suffering is treated both as a war against Fortune and as a contest with an opponent. The sage is struck down and wounded by the darts of Fortune and thrown by the *peristasis* with which he wrestles. In any case, it should be stressed that Paul's use of the word need not imply physical hardships, as is almost always assumed. It can also indicate emotional turmoil, like ἀπορούμενοι in 4:8. One can be confused and thrown into distrust (Pl., *Phd.* 88C), ἀπορία (Pl., *Phlb.* 15E; cf. also *Euthd.* 277C with 275D and 278B), or into "an ocean of civil cares" (Philo, *Spec.* 3.6). Misfortune (Dio Chrys., *Or.* 11.139) as well as passion (Mar. Ant., *Med.* 3.4.3) may "overthrow" someone. Therefore, just as Paul's

because of God's power in him he is not "knocked out."[149] Neither he nor his spirit is destroyed![150] His human weakness is thus a foil for the glorification of God![151]

Indeed, this is precisely the intention (ἵνα) of the paradox (4:7). Paul's fragility serves to make inescapable the inference that he is not the powerhouse but only the place where the power appears. That Paul neither dies as a result of the abuse he suffers nor is fundamentally perturbed thereby is not ultimately a mark of his own capacity to endure pain but rather a reflection of the fact that God does not abandon him. In order to emphasize this point, Paul does not say, as he does in 1 Cor 4:12, διωκόμενοι ἀνεχόμεθα. That would emphasize here too much what he does. Rather he says διωκόμενοι ἀλλ' οὐκ ἐγκαταλειπόμενοι, i.e., by God. Thus

"despondency" in 4:8b can be seen as the result of his "affliction" in 4:8a, so also his being "cast down" or "downcast" in 4:9b may express the result of his being "persecuted" in 4:9a. Josephus, for example, can refer to being "downcast in adversity" (*BJ* 4.42). On the other hand, it could be a synonym for "persecuted," just as οἱ θλίβοντες can indicate "persecutors" (Ps 3:2 LXX; 12:4 LXX; 22:5 LXX). Ps 36:14 LXX uses it to indicate the persecution of the poor and needy, and combines this with the affirmation that God does not "abandon" the righteous (vv. 25, 28; cf. 2 Cor 4:9a).

[149] Philo's self-depiction in *Spec.* 3.3–6 is somewhat similar to Paul's. Philo says that he has been cast down (καταβάλλειν) into an ocean of civil cares, where he groans (στένων) and is not even able to keep his head above the water. Torrents of men and affairs pour in on him from all sides. "Yet," he says, "it is well for me to give thanks to God even for this, that though submerged I am not sucked down into the depths" (κατακλυζόμενος οὐκ ἐγκαταπίνομαι). Thus, he is "drowning, yet not drowned," and for that he gives thanks to God. Similarly, Paul is cast down and groans (5:2,4), but is not destroyed thereby, a fact for which there is nothing but gratitude (4:15).

[150] The phrase "not perishing" is taken in its literal sense almost unanimously by scholars. In support of this is the reference in the preceding contrast to the fact that Paul was not abandoned, viz., to death. That he does not perish is thus the result of the fact that he is not abandoned, even as his being knocked down is part and parcel of his being persecuted. Without denying this meaning of Paul's words, one can affirm that a metaphorical meaning is also quite likely to be found here. It is his "inner man" that is not crushed in the first antithesis, who is not desperate in the second (4:8). Paul's inner emotions are what he speaks of in 4:1,16 when he says "we do not despair." He is "always of good courage" (5:5), for he is constantly renewed (4:16). Thus, in light of the overall context of 2 Cor 4–5 and the statements in the first two antitheses, a "spiritual" understanding of his words is difficult to deny. This means that Paul, much like Seneca's (*Ep.* 13.2) sufferer, "has been downed in body," but he is not destroyed in spirit. For ἀπόλλυμι used to indicate the destruction of the spirit, cf. Soph., *El.* 26. This interpretation of the term makes the *peristasis* catalogue in Epict., *Diss.* 2.19.24, a much closer parallel, for there the sage is happy no matter what hardships he experiences. Indeed, even in terms of structure, *Diss.* 2.19.24 is very similar to 4:8–9.

[151] This point was made nearly a century ago by Heinrici, *Das zweite Sendschreiben,* 214. It is in keeping with this purpose that Paul speaks of "the glory of God" both before (4:6) and after (4:15) his *peristasis* catalogue.

the catalogue of Paul's hardships in 4:8–9 serves to show that the great power at work in him is divine rather than human.[152] *His catalogue of hardships is thus a catalogue of God's power at work in him.* Furthermore, this claim that God is active in him is part and parcel of the *boasting* in which he is engaged in this letter of self-commendation.

This use of a catalogue to point away from one possible conclusion to another is one that appears elsewhere. A catalogue of the Cynic's hardships can function, for instance, to show that his vibrant health cannot be attributed to his favorable circumstances but only to his judgments about what is good and evil (cf. Epict., *Diss.* 4.8.30–31 and pp. 111–12 above). More important, a catalogue of the Stoic sage's hardships can point, just like Paul's, to the divine power that makes endurance and victory over adversity possible. For example, since Seneca considers man "a vessel that the slightest shaking, the slightest toss will break" (*Marc.* 11.3), he can say:

> If you see a man who is unterrified in the midst of dangers, untouched by desires, happy in adversity, peaceful amid the storm, . . . will not a feeling of reverence for him steal over you? Will you not say: "This quality is too great and too lofty to be regarded as resembling this petty body in which it dwells? A divine power has descended upon that man." . . . A thing like this cannot stand upright unless it be propped by the divine (*Ep.* 41.4–5).

Again, Aelius Aristides in *Oration* 24 (303 Dindorf) compiles a catalogue of his illnesses "in order to make yet more evident the healing power of the god" Asclepius,[153] and, in keeping with this purpose, frames his catalogue with two references to Asclepius' "power and providence." His ἀσθένεια thus enables the observer to see more clearly the *god's* power (τοῦ τε θεοῦ τὴν δύναμιν . . . μειζόνως ὄψεται: 304 Dindorf).[154]

The idea that divine power or the divine source of something becomes conspicuous when it is revealed through a weak and lowly instrument is thus quite Greek. Indeed, it appears already in Plato, who says that "the god of set purpose sang the finest of songs through the meanest of poets," because he intended the poet "to be a sign to us that . . . these fine poems are not human

[152] Jacob Jervell correctly observes "dass nach Paulus Göttliches und Menschliches im Wirken des Apostels ohne Schwierigkeit zu unterscheiden waren." See his "Der schwache Charismatiker," *Rechtfertigung* (E. Käsemann Festschrift; ed. J. Friedrich; Tübingen: Mohr; Göttingen: Vandenhoeck & Ruprecht, 1976) 195.

[153] A.-J. Festugière, *Personal Religion Among the Greeks* (Berkeley/Los Angeles: University of California Press, 1954) 90.

[154] On the relevance of this point, see note 156 below. Aristides clearly sees his sufferings as a badge of honor and an occasion for rejoicing. He, like Paul (2 Cor 12:7–10), thus accepts his *astheneia* as the condition and means for experiencing the divine's *dynamis* and communion. On this point, cf. Festugière, *Personal Religion,* 86, and H. D. Betz, "Eine Christus-Aretalogie bei Paulus (2 Kor 12, 7–10)," *ZTK* 66 (1969) 301.

or the work of men, but divine and the work of gods." It is by this means that men may come to know "that it is God himself who speaks and addresses us through them" (*Ion* 534D–E).[155] In a similar way, Paul asserts that the treasure is in "earthen vessels" so that it may be seen that (ᾖ)[156] the power belongs to God and does not derive from him. This is one of the ways in which the Corinthians are to know that he has been commissioned by God and the word that he speaks comes from God. The appearance of divine power in his human weakness is thus a *proof* (δοκιμή) of the fact that he is a true apostle, that Christ speaks in him (13:3–4).[157]

The structure of 4:7–10 corresponds to this thesis that it is God's power that is revealed in him, and this structure may be depicted as follows:[158]

ἔχομεν δὲ τὸν θησαυρὸν τοῦτον ἐν ὀστρακίνοις σκεύεσιν,
    ἵνα ἡ ὑπερβολὴ τῆς δυνάμεως
        ᾖ τοῦ θεοῦ καὶ μὴ ἐξ ἡμῶν·
ἐν παντὶ θλιβόμενοι ἀλλ' οὐ στενοχωρούμενοι,
    ἀπορούμενοι ἀλλ' οὐκ ἐξαπορούμενοι,
    διωκόμενοι ἀλλ' οὐκ ἐγκαταλειπόμενοι,
    καταβαλλόμενοι ἀλλ' οὐκ ἀπολλύμενοι,
πάντοτε τὴν νέκρωσιν τοῦ Ἰησοῦ ἐν τῷ σώματι περιφέροντες,
    ἵνα καὶ ἡ ζωὴ τοῦ Ἰησοῦ ἐν τῷ σώματι ἡμῶν φανερωθῇ.

155 I owe this passage to Windisch, *Korintherbrief,* 143. The two texts are, of course, not complete parallels, as Bultmann points out. Cf. his *Der zweite Brief an die Korinther* (MeyerK 6; Sonderband; Göttingen: Vandenhoeck & Ruprecht, 1976) 115.

156 For this force of the verb, cf. John Chrysostom, *hom. 9.1 in 2 Cor.* (*PG* 10.459), who renders it with φανῇ; Schmiedel, "Korinther," 234; Lietzmann, *Korinther,* 114; Alfred Plummer, *A Critical and Exegetical Commentary on the Second Epistle of St. Paul to the Corinthians* (ICC; Edinburgh: Clark, 1915) 127; Spicq, "L'image sportive," 213 n. 12; and Mathias Rissi, *Studien zum zweiten Korintherbrief* (ATANT 56; Zürich: Zwingli, 1969) 46, esp. n. 96. Cf. also the use of *phaneroō* in 4:10–11. For the emphasis that the paradox of 4:7 is intended primarily for others (and not for Paul himself), cf. Lucien Cerfaux, "L'antinomie paulinienne de la vie apostolique," *RSR* 39 (1951) 229; Prümm, *Diakonia Pneumatos,* 231–32; and Schmithals, *Gnosticism,* 160.

157 The very fact that Paul as a vessel is tested by adversity can itself serve as a proof that he is righteous. "A potter does not test defective vessels, because he cannot give them a single blow without breaking them. Similarly the Holy One, blessed be He, does not test the wicked but only the righteous" (*Gen. Rab.* 32.3). The numerous blows that Paul receives without being broken thereby are thus a decisive proof of his integrity.

158 This particular depiction of the structure is essentially the same as that given by Weiss, "Beiträge," 177, and J. Zmijewski, *Der Stil der paulinischen "Narrenrede"* (BBB 52; Köln-Berlin: Hanstein, 1978) 308. Cf. also M. L. Barré, "Paul as 'Eschatologic Person': A New Look at 2 Cor 11:29," *CBQ* 37 (1975) 522. For the antithetic participial form of the catalogue, cf. esp. Epict., *Diss.* 2.19.24.

Several observations in regard to the catalogue in 4:8–9 are in order. The catalogue itself consists primarily of eight present tense participles, all either passive or middle as to voice.[159] The eight participles are divided into four contrasting pairs, with the contrast in each case made with ἀλλ' οὐ(κ). This asyndetic catalogue of contrasting participles is enclosed within two comprehensive phrases which serve to magnify the catalogue and give it the appearance of fullness, ἐν παντί at the beginning (4:8) and πάντοτε at the end (4:10). The latter, of course, is to be construed grammatically with περιφέροντες in 4:10. The ἐν παντί, on the other hand, not only modifies θλιβόμενοι but all the subsequent initial participles in 4:8–9.[160]

The first hardship that Paul lists is θλιβόμενοι, and it is placed first for two reasons. In the first place, it is the key term that he uses in this letter to express his hardships. In 2 Cor 1–8 he uses the terms θλίβειν and θλῖψις twelve times, far more frequently than he does any of the other words in 4:8–9. Its placement at the beginning of the catalogue thus reflects the importance of this concept for the document in which it appears. In the second place, it is the most comprehensive of the terms in the catalogue, expressing external as well as internal afflictions (7:5). Thus, as the most important and most comprehensive term in the catalogue, Paul places it first.

The final term in the catalogue is ἀπολλύμενοι, a term which Paul conceivably could have employed earlier in his list. It would have formed, for example, an appropriate contrast to διωκόμενοι. But Paul reserves it for the final position, and he does so for at least three reasons. First, since death is the ultimate *peristasis* (cf. 1 Cor 15:26), it is the strongest term in the catalogue. As such, it is appropriately reserved for the climactic position. Second, its placement at the end serves to highlight it, so that the contrast it forms to 2:15 and 4:3 becomes more conspicuous. That is, unbelievers may find in Paul a "stench of death," but it is *they* who are perishing (τοῖς ἀπολλυμένοις), *not* Paul (οὐκ ἀπολλύμενοι).

Third, as the final item in the catalogue, Paul's statement about "perishing" forms a smooth transition to the remark that he makes in 4:10 about carrying around the "dying" of Jesus and his two-fold use of the term "death" in 4:11–12. Yet, it is more than a transition, for 4:9b merges with 4:10a to form a paradox. It is the Paul who is *not perishing* who is constantly carrying around in his own

[159] The participles in the second antithesis are middles, and the remainder are passives.

[160] Most commentators agree that the phrase is intentionally comprehensive. Its connection with θλιβόμενοι suggests "squeezed on every side" (cf. also 7:5). Again, the same phrase clearly means "in everything" in 8:7. The connections already discerned between 2:14 and 4:10 make it likely that the phrase ἐν παντί is also equivalent to the ἐν παντὶ τόπῳ of 2:14. That is, just as in 2:14–16 Paul is always and everywhere manifesting a smell of death, so in 4:8–10 he is always carrying about the *nekrōsis* of Jesus and everywhere suffering affliction as he does so. That the phrase also suggests "always" is possible (cf. Bultmann, *Korinther,* 115) but the temporal idea may be a new one intended to balance the local and other senses of the phrase. Cf. 9:8.

body the *dying* of Jesus. Thus the catalogue of 4:8–10 is bracketed by two paradoxical statements, "treasure in earthen vessels" (4:7) and "not dying, yet carrying around the dying of Jesus" (4:9b–10a).

One final structural observation may be ventured. It is commonly recognized that the third contrast implies God. That is, though Paul is persecuted, he is not "abandoned," namely, by God![161] The implicit connection of God with the concluding participle of the third contrast suggests that the same connection is assumed with the concluding participle in the other contrasts as well. That is, the fact that Paul is not crushed, despondent, or destroyed is because of God. He himself, the fragile vessel, is afflicted, depressed, and downcast. If this is indeed the case, then Paul's move from 4:7 to 4:8 involves chiasmus. That is, in 4:7 the immense power belongs to and proceeds from God (A), not from Paul and his companions (B). In 4:8 the latter are "afflicted" (B), but they are not "crushed." That they are not, he implies, is due solely to the consoling and sustaining power of God (A). The pattern is thus ABBA, and the passive participles he uses serve to facilitate his claim that it is God's power which is at work in him and not his own![162]

As for the individual contrasts that comprise the catalogue, the items in each of the first two pairs are intimately connected. The term θλίβειν, which elsewhere in 2 Cor (1:6; 7:5) has the purely metaphorical meaning "to afflict, to oppress," trades in 4:7 on its literal meaning of "to press." That is, by virtue of its contrast with στενοχωρεῖν (literally, "to be or keep in a tight place"), the "press" in "op*press*" becomes clear. Thus, although Paul is "pressed hard," he is not pressed to the extent that he has little (στενός) or no room (χῶρος) to breathe. In short,

[161] Cf., for example, Lietzmann, *Korinther,* 115. That the Lord is a God of mercy (1:3) means that he will not abandon his own (Deut 4:31). Positively stated, it not only means that God will stand by and empower a person so that he can speak the Lord's word but also that he will ultimately deliver him (2 Tim 4:16–17). This happened to Paul in Asia (1:8–10), happens to him continually (4:9), and will continue to happen (1:10; cf. also 2 Tim 4:18). It is because of God's fidelity that Paul has faith and continues to speak (4:13). He knows that, even if he dies, God will not abandon him:, but raise him up (4:14; cf. also Ps 16:10 LXX; Acts 2:27). For the theme of God's refusal to abandon his elect, cf. also Gen 28:15; Deut 31:6,8; Josh 1:5; 1 Chr 28:20; Ps 16:10 LXX; 36:25,28 LXX; Jer 15:20; Sir 2:10; Heb 13:5. The agonistic interpretation of the third clause ("pursued but not overtaken") advocated especially by Spicq, "L'image sportive," 223–25, and Héring, *The Second Epistle to the Corinthians,* 31–32, shatters on the necessity of giving *diōkomenoi* a different sense than it has in Paul's other *peristasis* catalogues. For a convincing critique of the agonistic interpretation of 4:7–9 as a whole, see Dupont, ΣΥΝ ΧΡΙΣΤΩΙ, 118–23.

[162] Schmiedel, "Korinther," 234, correctly notes that the first member of each antithesis belongs to "us" the "earthen vessels" and the second to "the exceeding power of God." Cf. also Denney, *Second Corinthians,* 60, and Windisch, *Korintherbrief,* 143. That this interpretation involves chiasmus is a fact that none of these scholars makes explicit. With this interpretation, contrast that of Rissi, *Studien,* 48, who finds in 4:8–9 only a description of Paul's essence as an earthen vessel and not also a depiction of God's power at work.

he is "oppressed, yet not crushed."[163] The items in the second pair are even more closely related, for here Paul forms a pun[164] with the concept of ἀπορία. He and his cohorts are "perplexed (ἀπορούμενοι), yet not totally perplexed" (ἐξαπορούμενοι). That is, they may be distressed as a consequence of being oppressed (θλιβόμενοι) but they are not desperate or in despair.[165]

As Paul's perfective use of ἐξ in the second contrast makes clear, his serenity is relative. Like the struggling sage, Paul is willing in 4:8 to confess a certain degree of perturbation even while affirming his ultimate calm, though he makes it clear that his composure is derived from God. And yet elsewhere, completely unlike the sage and far more like the *proficiens* who has not yet attained the final goal (cf. Phil 3:12), Paul is willing to confess an occasional feeling of total despair. In 1:8, for example, he says explicitly that he was so burdened by his θλῖψις in Asia that he despaired (ἐξαπορηθῆναι) even of life itself. Here he confesses to the ἐξαπορία that he denies in 4:8.[166] But this "contradiction" only shows that the denial of ἐξαπορία in 4:8 has meaning only in relation to the term with which

[163] Since θλῖψις and στενοχωρία are normally paired as synonyms (Judg 16:16 LXX; Isa 8:22 LXX; Isa 30:6 LXX; 2 Cor 6:4; Rom 2:9; 8:35; Epict., *Diss* 1.25.26,28), the antithesis that Paul forms is somewhat contrived. But, *contra* scholars such as Plummer, *Second Corinthians,* 128, and F. V. Filson, "The Second Epistle to the Corinthians," *IB* 10 (1953) 319, Paul quite clearly is not speaking in the second member of *external* difficulties. The thought is not that he has been spared from "a plight from which extrication is impossible," that he is not tested beyond his ability to endure (so Plummer). That, he says, has in fact happened (2 Cor 1:8; contrast 1 Cor 10:13). Bultmann is thus quite right when he says that the antitheses of 4:8–9 do not mean "es geht uns schlimm, aber nicht ganz schlimm" but rather "in allem Schlimmen geht es uns letztlich und eigentlich nicht schlimm" (*Korinther,* 116). To be precise, he means that the burden of affliction (1:8; cf. also Epict., *Diss.* 1.25.17) that presses on him has not crushed him internally, that is, his "inner man" (4:16). He has bodily anguish, but his "inner man" or spirit is not gasping for breath (compare 4 Macc 4:11; Wis 5:3). Compare the internal constriction mentioned in 6:12 and see the comment of A. Bonhöffer, *Epiktet und das Neue Testament* (Religionsgeschichtliche Versuche und Vorarbeiten 10; Giessen: Töpelmann, 1911) 119.

[164] Depending on one's definition of terms, this pun involves either paronomasia (so BDF § 488 [1b]) or annominatio (so Winer & Lünemann, *Grammar,* 638, and A. T. Robertson, *A Grammar of the Greek New Testament in the Light of Historical Research* [2d ed.; New York: Doran, 1915] 1201). For other word plays in 2 Corinthians, cf. 1:13; 3:2; 6:10; 7:10; 10:5–6,12; 12:5. Compare the word play in the anecdote told of Diogenes the Cynic in Diog. Laert. 6.54, that he was "laughed at" but not "laughed down."

[165] Just as ἐξαπορία is the emotional consequence of θλῖψις in 1:8, so here ἀπορούμενοι is the result of θλιβόμενοι Cf. esp. Isa 8:22–23 LXX, where ἀπορία is the result of θλῖψις and στενοχωρία, and also Judg 16:16 LXX, where being "faint-hearted" is the result of being continually "pressed" (ἐξέθλιψεν) and "straitened" (ἐστενοχώρησεν). Cf. note 148 above for the suggestion that καταβαλλόμενοι is possibly the result of διωκόμενοι.

[166] Compare the affirmation of στενοχωρία in 6:4 with the denial of the same in 4:8. There is a conflict here, however, only if the term in 4:8 is taken to indicate external difficulties. There is no conflict if the participle in 4:8 indicates the lack of internal constriction. Paul could easily have said ἐν στενοχωρίαις ἀλλ' οὐ στενοχωρούμενοι.

it is contrasted. If it is taken out of tandem with its antithesis and individually compared elsewhere, its meaning is distorted.

Viewed as a whole, then, the hardships that Paul lists in his catalogue have, as it were, caused cracks in him as an earthen vessel, but the vessel itself remains intact. The vessel is held together by the power of divine adhesive, and the light that shines (4:5–6) through these cracks is none other than the light of the life of Jesus (4:10–11).

God's use of a fragile, cracked vessel such as himself is, in Paul's view, explicable only in the light of the divine folly displayed in the crucifixion. God's action vis-à-vis Paul is consonant with his action in Christ. Indeed, it is precisely because his ministry exhibits the paradox of the cross that Paul's own ministry is itself part of the message about Christ that he proclaims. It is for Jesus' sake that he not only runs the risk of death (4:11) but also proclaims himself the Corinthians' slave (4:5). "Consequently, death is at work in us, but life in you" (4:12), for his affliction is for their salvation (1:6). The Christ who abandoned equality with God, became a δοῦλος, and in humility suffered death (Phil 2:6–8) is clearly Paul's model. In keeping with that model he abandons preeminence and becomes the Corinthians' δοῦλος (4:5), in humility (7:6) experiences the sufferings of Christ (1:5), and, like him, undergoes a παράδοσις to death (4:11). It is because Jesus was a suffering Christ that Paul is a suffering apostle.

It is, moreover, precisely because Paul identifies with Jesus in his sufferings that he sees God's resurrection power at work in himself. It was through the weakness of a crucified Christ that the *dynamis* of God was demonstrated, viz., in the resurrection (13:4). So, too, in Paul's ministry the power of God is revealed in the weakness of the apostle. He thus serves as the locus for the dying and rising of Jesus. This thought he spells out in 4:10–12, the structure of which may be indicated as follows:

πάντοτε τὴν νέκρωσιν τοῦ Ἰησοῦ ἐν τῷ σώματι περιφέροντες,
  ἵνα καὶ ἡ ζωὴ τοῦ Ἰησοῦ ἐν τῷ σώματι ἡμῶν φανερωθῇ.
ἀεὶ γὰρ ἡμεῖς οἱ ζῶντες εἰς θάνατον παραδιδόμεθα διὰ Ἰησοῦν,
  ἵνα καὶ ἡ ζωὴ τοῦ Ἰησοῦ φανερωθῇ ἐν τῇ θνητῇ σαρκὶ ἡμῶν.
ὥστε ὁ θάνατος ἐν ἡμῖν ἐνεργεῖται,
  ἡ δὲ ζωὴ ἐν ὑμῖν.

This passage is marked by both repetition and variation of terms. On the one hand, the name "Jesus" occurs four times in the parallel lines of vv.10–11, a repetition that serves to emphasize the solidarity of Paul with Jesus in his experience. Again, the word "life" occurs three times, twice in the phrase "the life of Jesus" 4:10–11) and once by itself (4:12). This constancy in vocabulary for the one expression allows Paul to vary the other expressions without unduly confusing the reader. Some of these variations are slight, such as the switch from πάντοτε in 4:10 to ἀεί in 4:11. Others are more striking, such as the way in which οὐκ ἀπολλύμενοι (4:9) is transformed into a positive ἡμεῖς οἱ ζῶντες (4:11).[167] In addition, the phrase "in the body" in 4:10a is continually modified, first by the addition of "our" in 4:10b, then by the substitution of "in our mortal flesh" for "in our body" (4:11b). Finally, the phrase becomes a simple but comprehensive "in us" (4:12). Thus, just as "in earthen vessels" quickly turns into an unambiguous "us" in 4:7, so also in 4:10–12 the self-references terminate in a simple "us."

The crux in 4:10–12 concerns the meaning of two phrases, one that occurs in 4:10 and the other in 4:11. Paul says first that "we are always carrying about in our body the νέκρωσις of Jesus" (4:10), and then he explains (γάρ) his first statement by affirming that "we constantly, for Jesus' sake, εἰς θάνατον παραδιδόμεθα" (4:11). Attention may be focused first on the graphic word *nekrōsis*, whose precise import in 4:10 is open to debate. Since limitations of space preclude a full discussion of this term, a summary of the evidence must suffice.[168]

Nekrōsis is used by ancient Greeks predominantly in reference to dead and/or dying tissue. It is applied to both the incipient and the advanced stage of mortification, and to the postmortem period as well. In some instances the term is applied to death-like states such as hibernation, and in other instances it is used metaphorically. In most instances, however, it is used either of a person on the brink of death or of one who has already died.

According to ancient medical writers, the mortification of the body is accompanied by several processes and indicated by certain physical symptoms. When *nekrōsis* sets in, a person's vital power begins to drop, so that he becomes weak and sluggish. His vitality is like a flickering fire that is slowly dying out. As the body loses heat and energy, it becomes cold and livid, and the pulse grows fainter. The feet or other parts of the body may begin to swell. A hardening of the body eventually sets in, a hardening that continues and spreads in the postmortem period (rigor mortis).

[167] *Contra* M. Bouttier, "Le tesson: 2 Cor 4, 6–11," *AsSeign* 40 (1972) 41, the "we the living" of v.11 are identical to the "we" of vv.10 and 12. The phrase "the living" is added to heighten the paradox, not to enlarge the "we" to include all Christians. Again, *contra* Lenski, *Corinthians*, 982, "the living" certainly does not mean those who are "spiritually alive."

[168] The summary in the text is based on an analysis of the use of the word *nekrōsis* by the following authors: Aretaeus, *SA* 10.2 (=*CMG* II.32,14–17); Soranus, *Gynaecia* 4.3 (=*CMG* IV.140,2–9); Gal., *Comm. in Hippocratis prorrheticum* 1.13,65,77 (=*CMG* V.9,2.29,26–30,2; 78,33–34; 87,8–10); *Comm. in Hippocratis prognosticum* 2; 3; 13; 14; 17 (=*CMG* V.9,2.226,17–18; 230,1–3; 293,7–8; 297,15–17; 313,15–17); *Comm. in Hippocratis aph.* 7.50 (XVIII.1.156,7–13 Kühn); Philumenus, *Ven.* 25 (=*CMG* X.1,1.31,20–23); Vettius Valens, p.53,6–9 Kroll; "Astrampsychus," *Onir.* p.6 Rigalt; Porph., *Abst.* 4.20 (262,14–20 Nauck); Procl., *Comm. in Platonis rem publicam* 10.614B (II,117,7–19 Kroll); Phot., *Bibl.* 512b,27–38; 513a,32–37; *Suda* 3.446.4 Adler; *Herm. Sim.* 9.16.2–3; Iren., *Haer.* 3.18.3 (*PG* 7.933B); ps-Ath., *Apoll.* 1.18 (*PG* 26.1125B); Hipp., *Fr. 24 in Prov.* p.165,19 (*PG* 10.621D); Gregory of Nyssa, *Or. Catech.* 35 (p.132,10 = *PG* 45.88C); ps-Justin Martyr, *Qu. et resp.* 28 (*PG* 6.1276B).

As the body increasingly slumps, shivers, and swells, death grows more imminent. Even the sputum becomes foul smelling, for internal putrefaction has already set in. Putrefaction thus accompanies *nekrōsis*, as does decay. Indeed, *nekrōsis* is sometimes associated with gangrene and at other times identified with it and sphacelus. The body dies, being eaten away, and its decomposition renders one both weak and noxious. The postmortem period only continues and intensifies the processes and breakdowns that precede death.

When Paul employs the word *nekrōsis*, then, he is using one of the starkest words at his disposal. It is an immensely evocative word, for it brings to the reader's consciousness the full range of phenomena given above. Yet, precisely because of its broad meaning and connotational range, it is difficult to pinpoint a specific denotation that Paul may have in mind when he refers to the "*nekrōsis* of Jesus." On the basis of the use of the term indicated in the summary above, there are three basic possibilities.[169] The first is that Paul is using the term to denote Jesus in his passion, the dying Jesus. This is Jesus as he is crucified in weakness (13:4), devoid of all power. It is Jesus on the point of death, *in extremis*, the mortification of his body having already commenced and the "stench of death" already upon him. In support of this interpretation is the fact that 4:11 refers to a παράδοσις "to death," not death itself. In this case, Paul is affirming that he is constantly carrying about in his own body the dying, putrid body of Jesus.

The second possibility is that he means Jesus in the postmortem period, the dead and buried Jesus whose body has undergone considerable putrefaction. The stiffening of the body that began before death has now turned into rigor mortis. In this case, the "death of Jesus" into which Paul was baptized (Rom 6:3) and unto which he is being conformed (Phil 3:10) is also that which he constantly carries around in his own body. The Mortified is thus being carried about by the one being mortified for his sake.

In addition to arguments usually offered in support of this view,[170] a new one may be ventured. It *may* be significant that in 4:10 Paul uses the verb περιφέρω and not βαστάζω, as he does in the similar statement in Gal 6:17 (ἐγὼ γὰρ τὰ στίγματα τοῦ Ἰησοῦ ἐν τῷ σώματί μου βαστάζω). The reason may lie in the fact that the standard Greek term for "pallbearer" is νεκροφόρος, one who carries a corpse. Paul's use of *nekrōsis* with a compound of φέρω could be chosen deliberately to suggest that the Jesus carried in his body is a dead one. Indeed, Paul may even be suggesting that he is a "pallbearer" who not only proclaims to all the death

[169] The phrase has, of course, been understood in more than the three ways indicated here. For an orientation to and critique of various views, cf. the discussion of Erhardt Güttgemanns, *Der leidende Apostel und sein Herr* (FRLANT 90; Göttingen: Vandenhoeck & Ruprecht, 1966) 94–126. Cf. also R. C. Tannehill, *Dying and Rising with Christ* (BZNW 32; Berlin: Töpelmann, 1967) 84ff; and Rissi, *Studien*, 48–52.

[170] Cf., for example, Paul's use of the word in Rom 4:19, where the νέκρωσις of Sarah's womb is clearly equivalent to the νενεκρωμένον body of Abraham. Neither is "dying"; both are "dead."

of Jesus but even carries in his own body the dead one whom he proclaims![171]

The third possibility is that he is using the term broadly to refer to Jesus' "dying" as well as his "death." In this case Paul can be seen as identifying with Jesus from the inception of the passion up to the point of the resurrection. The term παραδίδωμι that occurs in 4:11 is intimately connected with the passion narrative in all the canonical gospels, a fact that supports the first option. Moreover, in Gal 2:20 Paul explicitly relates himself to the crucifixion of Jesus: "I have been crucified with Christ" (cf. also Rom 6:6)![172] The texts cited in support of the second option show that his identification with the fate of Jesus did not cease with the crucifixion itself but embraced its fatal consequence as well. On the whole, then, it seems preferable not to restrict the meaning of *nekrōsis* to either the "dying" of Jesus or his "death." *Nekrōsis* is likely intended to include both.

In any case, Paul carries the *nekrōsis* of Jesus in his own body (4:10). This suggests what 4:12 makes explicit, viz., that the *nekrōsis* of Jesus in his body entails his own mortification. Since death is at work in him, his own body is slowly deteriorating and decomposing. His "outer man" is being devastated (διαφθείρεται) by the affliction to which it is subjected (4:16). As death takes its toll on him and *nekrōsis* sets in, he loses even the bodily vitality that he once had. This is important for him, for it points to his own utter weakness and shows again why the power in his ministry must be seen as deriving from God and not from himself (4:7).

Again, as already suggested, the *nekrōsis* of Jesus that Paul carries in his own deteriorating body is what leads unbelievers to find in him the putrid smell (2:16) that is the product of putrefaction. Those who are being saved, however, find in Paul the "sweet aroma of Christ" (2:15), "a fragrance of life" (2:16), and they do so because "the life of Jesus" is manifested in his body (4:10), indeed, in the very mortal flesh (4:11) that is being mortified. That "the life of Jesus" appears precisely where "the *nekrōsis* of Jesus" does, is, of course, but another of the paradoxes with which Paul's theology is replete. Nor is this manifestation of Jesus' life in him a sporadic matter. It is clearly as constant in him as his carrying about the *nekrōsis* of Jesus, for the daily renewal of his "inner man" that he experiences (4:16) is the certain consequence of this manifestation.

Moreover, Paul not only bears in his body the *nekrōsis* "of Jesus" (4:10) but he also is exposed to death "for Jesus' sake" (4:11). This shift of terms most likely

[171] In this case Paul would be suggesting that he is constantly involved in two processionals, the *pompa triumphalis* (2:14) and the *pompa funebris* (4:10). For the intertwining of triumphal and funeral imagery, see Sen., *Marc.* 3.1 and Plut. *Philop.* 21.2. For the close relation of the two processionals, see Versnel, *Triumphus,* 115–29.

[172] The interpretation of the *skolops* of 2 Cor 12:7 in terms of a "cross" also deserves mention in this regard. Cf., for example, W. Bieder, "Paulus und seine Gegner in Korinth," *TZ* 17 (1961) 319–33; J. Bernard, "Lorsque je suis faible, c'est alors que je suis fort: 2 Cor 12, 7–10," *AsSeign* 45 (1974) 37–39; and H. Binder, "Die angebliche Krankheit des Paulus," *TZ* 32 (1976) 1–13, esp. 10–11.

indicates that Paul is identifying what he suffers *for* Jesus in the fulfillment of his apostolic commission as the sufferings *of* Jesus. The fact that he and Jesus suffered some of the same hardships (like flogging) doubtless enabled this identification and facilitated its extension to other hardships as well.

The final phrase that demands detailed discussion in this context is Paul's statement in 4:11 that εἰς θάνατον παραδιδόμεθα. The voice of the verb here is usually taken as passive, so that it is translated "we are always being given up to death" (as in the RSV). But the verb can also be middle, as is the deponent ἐνεργεῖται in 4:12. In view of the clear parallelism of 4:10–11 and the active participle περιφέροντες that παραδιδόμεθα replaces and is designed to explain, it is far more likely that the voice is middle. The meaning will thus be "we are always giving ourselves up to death for Jesus' sake," which in fact is precisely what Paul says that Jesus did for him (Gal 2:20; cf. also Eph 5:2,25). His giving himself up to death is thus part of his *imitatio Christi.*

Another implication of this interpretation of the verb as a middle is that it brings into prominence the *volitional* character of Paul's suffering. Just as Jesus willingly forfeited his life, so is Paul willing to do the same. As he says in another of his *peristasis* catalogues, he is "well pleased" with his hardships for Christ (12:10). The apostle's willingness to suffer, his consent to what he bears in the cause of Christ, thus coincides with that of the sage,[173] though it is quite clear that what prompts each's action is quite different. What the sage does out of reason, Paul does out of gratitude.

Verses 10–11 are thus fully parallel, with v.10a and v.11a giving Paul's action and vv.10b and 11b indicating the purpose that prompts it. In 4:12 Paul then draws the consequences of his action and purposes in terms of the beneficial result that it has for the Corinthians. In 4:13–15, moreover, Paul continues to speak of what he does and points once again to the way in which his actions benefit the Corinthians and are for their sake (4:15).[174] In 4:16 he will begin to speak at length of the personal benefits that he derives from his hardships and indicate additional reasons why his hardships leave him battered, but not broken.

2 Cor 4:13–6:2; 6:11–7:4[175]

Abraham J. Malherbe has convincingly demonstrated that Paul in 1 Thess 2 depicts himself in terms typically used to describe the ideal philosopher.[176]

[173] Cf. the discussion of volition in chapter three, in the section "Fortune, God, and Free Will." For the word *paradidōmi* in a *peristasis* catalogue, see Chariton 4.3.10; 6.6.4.

[174] Leucippe's brief letter to Cleitophon (in Achilles Tatius 5.18.3–6) contains *seven* statements of how she has suffered for his sake, and four of these occur in the *peristasis* catalogue itself. Cf. Chariton 4.4.10.

[175] On 2 Cor 4:12–5:10, cf. Norbert Baumert, *Täglich Sterben und Auferstehung* (SANT 34; München: Kösel-Verlag, 1973). A history of the interpretation of 5:1-10 is conveniently provided by F. G. Lang, *2. Korinther 5,1-10 in der neueren Forschung* (BGBE 16; Tübingen: Mohr, 1973).

[176] Abraham J. Malherbe, " 'Gentle as a Nurse': The Cynic Background to I Thess ii,"

According to Dio Chrysostom, for example, the true philosopher is the one who is willing to enter the *agōn* of life, speak with the boldness that is necessary to benefit his audience, and endure the abuse that his outspokenness generates. This separates him from resident philosophers who refuse to enter the fray, from sycophants who merely flatter their hearers, from sophists who only entertain them, and from harsh Cynics who severely berate them and make a hurried exit to escape the crowd's ridicule and uproar. Bold speech simply invites persecution (cf. Acts 9:26–29; 14:3–5). True courage, however, is not shown by a few bold words spoken merely for the sake of vituperation, but by a willingness to say what is necessary to do the hearers good, even at the cost of public abuse and scorn. Since it is good will and brotherly love that prompts the sage's bold speech, he does not cease to speak in this fashion when he must suffer for it but rather continues to speak words that are both appropriate and beneficial for his listeners. The true sage is thus a suffering sage, reaping "hatred, abuse, and reviling" (*Or.* 32.19) as his reward. Since his life is not particularly enviable, it is not surprising that few choose it. Indeed, Dio says of himself that he has chosen this role, not of his own volition, but only by the will of the divine (32.12). But his actions show that he is a man of courage and good will, and his endurance proves the reality of his divine call.

Paul's self-depiction in 1 Thess 2 clearly coincides with this portrait of the sage, for it is within the context of his *agōn* and sufferings that he refers to the courageous boldness of his speech (2:2). The situation in 2 Cor 4:7–6:10 is similar. The catalogue of his hardships in 4:7–12 is followed in 4:13 by a reference to his speaking. Again, the *peristasis* catalogue in 6:3–10 is preceded in 5:18–6:2 by a reference to the word of reconciliation that he has received and the appeal that he makes. His speech and his hardships thus go hand in hand. But whereas in 4:7–12 he indicates *how* he confidently endures his hardships, viz., by the power of God, he now begins in 4:13 to show *why* he does so, why he does not despair but continues to endure and to speak.

In 4:13–15 he gives two reasons why he continues to speak. The first (4:13) is that he has the same spirit of faith and steadfast assurance as that expressed by the psalmist of Ps 116:10. The second is that he knows that death, which is at work in him (4:12), does not have the final say. Once it has finished its task, God will raise him up (4:14), for the God who does not abandon him now (4:9) will not abandon him then (Ps 16:10). Thus, in view of the divine power that sustains him (4:7), the life of Jesus that is manifested in his body (4:10–11), the benefits that his ministry and sufferings bring the Corinthians (4:12,15), and his assurance and hope (4:13–14), he draws in 4:16 the only logical conclusion: "we, therefore, do not despair."

In support of this conclusion Paul then adds in 4:16–5:5 seven additional

---

NovT 12 (1970) 203–17.

reasons why his hardships do not leave him in despair.[177] He endures his hardships with confidence because, in the first place, his inner man is being renewed daily (4:16). Second, his affliction is slight in comparison to the greatness of the glory that awaits, and it is temporary, whereas the glory will be eternal (4:16; cf. also Rom 8:18). Third, his sufferings are the very instrument by which that glory is effected, for just as θλῖψις produces endurance (Rom 5:3), so does it also produce glory (4:17). Fourth, he has his eyes fixed on that which the eye cannot yet see (4:18). Fifth, he has an eternal home in the heavens (5:1). Sixth, the very fact of being weighed down and of groaning in this earthly tent serves to produce longing in him to put on the heavenly dwelling (5:2–4). Seventh, the resurrection of which he is confident (4:14) is guaranteed by the Spirit that God has given him (5:5).

Once again in 5:6 he draws the consequence of these considerations: "we, therefore, are always of good courage." At the same time he makes explicit that his real desire is to abandon his bodily home and be with the Lord (5:8), which is impossible as long as he is at home in the body (5:6–7). The fact that Paul prefers to be out of the body (5:8), that he yearns for his heavenly dwelling (5:2), that he wishes to be further clothed and to have the mortal swallowed up by life (5:4), is *not* disgraceful whining that belies his claims of courage and assurance. Rather, in full congruence with those claims it is both an expression of his desire to be with God and a recognition of his own mortality.

It is not without significance that Seneca follows a depiction of "that perfect man" (*vir ille perfectus*)—the sage whose hardships have not caused him to grieve or to bewail his lot—with a statement of that sage's readiness to depart this life. The sage's "heart is never more divine than when it reflects on its mortality" and recognizes that "the body is not a permanent dwelling, but a sort of inn (with a brief sojourn at that)." For the Stoic Seneca, "the greatest proof" of the soul's divine origin is when "it judges its present situation lowly and narrow, and is not afraid to depart" (*Ep.* 120.12–15).

For Seneca, then, the perfect sage is he who not only accepts his hardships without dismay but also is ready to depart his temporary dwelling. The statement of his triumph over adversity comes first, and this prevents the inference that the sage wishes to depart this life only because he despairs over the hardness and injustice of his lot. Paul's self-depiction proceeds in the same way. It is only after

[177] Against persistent attempts by scholars to isolate 4:16–18 from 5:1–10 and treat it as only an "Uebergangstück" to the latter, the essential unity of 4:16–5:5(10) must be maintained. It is above all Paul's five-fold use of γάρ in 4:16–5:5 that requires this interpretation. After the διό formed on the basis of 4:7–15 in 4:16, Paul links together his argument by using γάρ 5 times (4:17,18; 5:1,2,4) and a causal genitive absolute once (4:18) before reaching the οὖν of 5:6. The διό and the οὖν thus serve to bracket 4:16–5:5 as a special unit of thought. And, since οὖν is an inferential particle and much of the vocabulary of 5:1–5 continues in 5:6–10, it is quite clear that 5:6–10 is intrinsically related to 5:1–5. Moreover, the fact that 5:7 recalls 4:18 shows that 4:16–18 has not been forgotten even at this point in the argument. Thus, 4:16–5:10 stands as a basic unit of thought.

he has shown his triumph over adversity and his lack of despair that he expresses his desire to abandon the body altogether. It is only after he has spoken of the "weight of glory" (4:17) in comparison to the lightness of his affliction that he speaks of the way in which he is "weighed down" in this earthly tent (5:4). In both cases it is precisely the one who does not despair who *is* ready to depart. Paul's statements in 5:1–8 thus do not clash with Seneca's portrait of the sage but rather conform to it. As the similarity here between Seneca's depiction and Paul's self-depiction makes clear,[178] Paul's depiction of himself in terms of the ideal sage is not restricted to the *peristasis* catalogues of 4:8–9 and 6:3–10, but also occurs in the section found between them.

Paul may wish to abandon the body, but his real aspiration, whether in the body or out of the body, is to be pleasing to God (5:9). To be pleasing to the Lord is to receive a favorable verdict at the Lord's judgment seat, at which all must appear in order to receive recompense for their actions (5:10). This future judgment is another reason why he does not abandon his ministry but rather attempts to persuade men (5:11) to live no longer for themselves but for the Christ who died for them (5:15), who indeed was made sin for them (5:21). Paul, grateful for the reconciliation that he himself has experienced with God through Christ (5:18), thus persists in his ministry because he is constrained by the love of Christ (5:14) to be the ambassador through whom God offers to others that same reconciliation (5:18–20).

In referring to the judgment in 1 Cor 4:3–5 Paul stressed its futurity. It is at the parousia that the Lord "will bring to light the things now hidden in darkness and will make manifest (φανερώσει) the purposes of the heart," bestowing praise where it is due (4:5). But in 2 Cor 5:11 he claims that the judgment in his own case has been proleptically realized. "But we *have* been made manifest (πεφανερώμεθα) to God." The repetition of the verb φανερόω from 5:10 makes his meaning clear, viz., that what he does *is* pleasing to the Lord and therefore good (5:9–10).[179] Of God's approval he is thus completely confident. His hope is that the Corinthians, on the basis of all that he has made manifest about himself in this letter, will now see him as God does (5:11). It is by the manifestation of the truth about himself that Paul commends himself (4:2; cf. Plut., *Mor.* 539E), and the Corinthians should now grant him the approval of their conscience (5:11),[180] become proud of him, and defend him against those whose boasting is misplaced (5:12).

[178] Compare also 2 Cor 4:12 with *Ep.* 120.18 and also 2 Cor 5:13 with *Ep.* 120.15.

[179] Cf. Olson, "Confidence Expressions," 177–78. For reference to one's actions and character in praising oneself inoffensively, cf. Plut., *Mor.* 539E. By claiming that God approves his actions Paul is appealing to the only one who is truly qualified to judge and whose judgment is the only one that really matters (1 Cor 4:4–5). It functions here like the testimony of the "expert" in Hellenistic tradition.

[180] M. E. Thrall, "The Pauline Use of συνείδησις," *NTS* 14 (1967) 118–25, esp. 123, argues convincingly that "conscience" in both 4:2 and 5:11 conveys the idea of positive evaluation of behavior.

In 5:13–6:2 he then presents himself as one who is constrained by the love of Christ (5:14), who looks at no one from a *sarkic* perspective (5:16), who is a new creation (5:17), and who has been both reconciled to God and entrusted with the ministry and word of reconciliation (5:18–19).[181] As the διάκονος δικαιοσύνης (cf. 11:15) entrusted with the διακονία τῆς δικαιοσύνης (3:9), he is necessarily the δικαιοσύνη θεοῦ in Christ (5:21). Hence he works together with God (6:1), and it is through him that God makes his appeal (5:20). His appeal both in general (5:20: "Be reconciled to God!") and to the Corinthians in particular (6:1: "Do not receive God's grace in vain!") is thus simultaneously *God's* appeal as well.

In light of this claim and the correlation of the messenger with his message, there is a clear implication in his two appeals. To "be reconciled to God" is also to be reconciled to the messenger through whom that appeal is made. To fail to be reconciled to that messenger is tantamount to receiving the grace of God in vain. In short, to reject Paul as Christ's ambassador is to reject Christ himself (cf. also Gal 4:14; Matt 10:40; John 12:44; 13:20; Acts 16:15). "Be reconciled to us!" is thus the corollary of "Be reconciled to God!" and the time for that reconciliation is the present. Now, today, is the "acceptable" time to "accept" Paul, now is the day of salvation (6:2).[182]

No barrier to that reconciliation is to be found in the way in which he conducts his ministry (6:3). On the contrary, his conduct both commends him and provides proof of his divine commission, as his *peristasis* catalogue confirms (6:4–10; cf. Epict., *Diss.* 4.8.30–32). Hence, the only thing that remains is for the Corinthians to receive him as the *diakonos* of God that he is. His mouth is open and he would give them the kiss of peace (cf. 1 Cor 16:20). His heart and arms are open for a reconciling embrace. They have only to reciprocate by accepting his embrace (6:11–13) and by distancing themselves from the superapostles (6:14–7:1). And Paul expresses every confidence that they will do so (7:2–4).

2 Cor 6:3–10[183]

As the preceding sketch of 2 Cor 4:13–7:4 is intended to suggest, 6:3–10 has a definite role and place within its literary context. It is necessary to stress this

[181] On the idea of reconciliation, cf. Ernst Käsemann, "Erwägungen zum Stichwort 'Versöhnungslehre' im Neuen Testament," *Zeit und Geschichte: Dankesgabe an R. Bultmann zum 80. Geburtstag* (eds. E. Dinkler, et al.; Tübingen: Mohr, 1964) 47–59. For this context in particular, cf. F. Hahn, " 'Siehe, jetzt ist der Tag des Heils', Neuschöpfung und Versöhnung nach 2 Kor 5,14–6,2" *EvT* 33 (1973) 244–53.

[182] Cf. Dahl, "Fragment," 67: "The exhortations to be reconciled to God (5:20) and not to receive the grace of God in vain (6:1) are narrowed down to the request that the Corinthians should be open to Paul as his heart is open to them. The three appeals are not identical in content, yet the sequence suggests that it would be difficult to conform to the former injunctions without also accepting the last one."

[183] On this section, cf. G. Friedrich, *Amt und Lebensführung. Eine Auslegung von 2 Kor. 6,1–10* (Biblische Studien 39; Neukirchen-Vluyn: Verlag des Erziehungsvereins, 1963), and Baum, *Mut,* 143–78. On the relationship of Dio Chrys., *Or.* 8.15–16 and 2 Cor 6:3–10, cf. Ragnar Höistad, "Eine hellenistische Parallele zu 2. Kor. 6.3ff," *ConNT* 9 (1944) 22–27.

fact, since many scholars have failed to discern its function and contextual connections.[184] The grammatical roughness of the transition from 6:1–2 to 6:3 should not cause one to miss the thematic connections,[185] three of which need to be indicated.

First, the διακονία in 6:3 that is not to suffer blame is the διακονία τῆς καταλλαγῆς mentioned in 5:18. Since God gave it to him (5:18), it is ἡ διακονία τοῦ θεοῦ, just as he is the θεοῦ διάκονος (6:4).[186] But it is also the ministry of *reconciliation.* Paul mentions reconciliation five times in 5:18–20, and he does so precisely because there is need for reconciliation between himself and the Corinthians. If the *diakonos* of reconciliation is estranged from the very community that he founded, if the father of the church is at odds with his children (6:13), then this can only result in the ministry itself being ridiculed (6:3).

The need for reconciliation is thus urgent, and it is for this reason that Paul quotes Isa 49:8. It should not be overlooked that Paul has begun his exhortation already in 5:20 with the petition δεόμεθα, "we beseech you." In 6:1 he follows this with παρακαλοῦμεν ("we exhort you"), which resumes the exhortation (παρακαλοῦντος) that God makes through him in 5:20. It is in keeping with this paraenesis that Paul urges the necessity of acting now (νῦν), emphasizing also that the time is right (6:2).

The concern with the appropriate time for speech and action was a Hellenistic *topos.*[187] Philosophers were especially concerned with the *kairos* being appropriate when they engaged in bold speech. This was necessarily the case when they dared to speak on the subject of concord and reconciliation. Dio Chrysostom, for instance, shows his boldness in *Or.* 38 by daring to speak to the Nicomedians about the enmity and strife they have with the Nicaeans. Conscious of the dangers that his *parrēsia* entails, he asks his audience to bear with him and not make an uproar (6). He emphasizes that he speaks out of good will (9), expresses his confidence that they will be persuaded by what he says (4), and mentions the difficulty of getting them to see that his remarks will not be *akairos,* untimely. He then proceeds to praise concord and stress the need for reconciliation

[184] Cf. esp. Windisch, *Korintherbrief,* 202–03; and also Lietzmann, *Korinther,* 127; Strachan, *Second Corinthians,* 123; Martin Dibelius, *A Fresh Approach to the New Testament and Early Christian Literature* (New York: Scribners, 1936) 157; and Höistad, "Parallele," 22. Cf. also Collange, *Énigmes,* 282–83, who conjectures that 6:3–13 and 6:14–7:4 were originally alternate endings to 2:14–6:2.

[185] Cf. Bachmann, *Der zweite Brief,* 277, and Kümmel in Lietzmann, *Korinther,* 205. Those who stress the coherence of 6:3–10 to its context include R. Bultmann, *Exegetische Probleme des zweiten Korintherbriefes* (SymBU 9; Uppsala: Wretmans Boktryckeri, 1947) 14 n. 17, 20; *Korinther,* 169; Prümm, *Diakonia Pneumatos,* 1.360; 2/1.73; Güttgemanns, *Der leidende Apostel,* 316–17; and Baum, *Mut,* 147.

[186] Cf. Bultmann, *Korinther,* 171.

[187] Cf. A. J. Malherbe, " 'In Season and Out of Season': 2 Timothy 4:2," (unpublished private paper, n.d.).

(καταλλαγή: 9,11) between the two cities. Paul, too, in showing *parrēsia* toward the Corinthians and expressing confident pride in them (7:4), is conscious of the need for right timing (6:2) in seeking a reconciliation with them.

Second, Paul refers to himself and his cohorts in 6:4 as θεοῦ διάκονοι (cf. also 1 Thess 3:2 v.l.). Although he has not used the noun *diakonos* since 3:6, he has just referred to himself in 5:20 as an "ambassador" (πρεσβεύομεν). These two terms are related, each conveying the idea of "messenger." Pollux (*Onom.* 8.137), for example, defines πρεσβευτής as ἄγγελος καὶ διάκονος.[188] Even the verb πρεσβεύειν can have the meaning "to be a messenger."[189] Since the messenger often delivered the message orally, Pollux also defines the πρεσβευτής as a κῆρυξ another function that Paul sees himself as fulfilling (4:5; cf. also 1 Tim 2:7; 2 Tim 1:11). That Paul substitutes διάκονος for πρεσβευτής indicates not only that the two terms are related for him, but also that διάκονοι in 6:4 means "messengers of God." In short, since he is the κῆρυξ announcing Jesus Christ as Lord (4:5) and the πρεσβευτής for Christ through whom God makes his appeal (5:20), he is in both cases the "messenger" of God (6:4) who proclaims that now is the right time for salvation (6:2). What is common to all three words is the idea of "messenger."

This same interconnection of terms appears in the oration by Dio Chrysostom that was just mentioned. He first mentions "heralds (κηρυκές) sent by the gods" and then proceeds to give an illustration. He says that those "ambassadors" (πρεσβεύουσιν) who go unarmed into armed camps are not touched, owing to the belief that "all messengers (ἀγγέλους) in behalf of friendship are servants of the gods" (*Or.* 38.18). Similarly, Philo refers to the Logos as God's "chief messenger" (ἀρχαγγέλῳ) and "ambassador" (πρεσβυτάτῳ), who "acts as ambassador (πρεσβευτής) of the ruler to the subject." Like Paul, he is "the harbinger of peace to creation from that God whose will is to bring wars to an end, who is ever the guardian of peace." It is in keeping with such an important function that the Logos, like Paul, "glories in this prerogative (δωρεᾷ) and proudly describes it" (*Her.* 205–06).

Again, Paul moves from the verb πρεσβεύομεν to δεόμεθα, and then calls himself a *diakonos.* Lucian, similarly, has Moon begin by requesting that Menippus διακόνησαι something for her to Zeus. She then clarifies her meaning by asking him to carry a simple πρεσβεία and δέησις from her to Zeus (*Icar.* 20). By delivering her intercession and request, Menippus, therefore, will function as Moon's *diakonos.*[190]

[188] The following treatment is informed by the discussion offered by Dieter Georgi, *Die Gegner des Paulus im 2. Korintherbrief* (WMANT 11; Neukirchen-Vluyn: Neukirchener Verlag, 1964) 31–38, and the critique by J. N. Collins, "Georgi's 'Envoys' in 2 Cor 11:23," *JBL* 93 (1974) 88–96.

[189] G. Bornkamm, *TDNT* 6.682 n. 9.

[190] On the connection of *presbeutēs* and *diakonos,* cf. also Dem., *Or.* 18.311; 19.68–69; Plut., *Mor.* 794A; Ign., *Phld.* 10.1.

Third, 6:3–4 is a restatement of 5:12. The latter is preceded by the statement of Paul that he attempts to persuade men, and in 6:1–2 Paul is engaged in persuasion. In 5:12 he says that he is trying to give (διδόντες) them cause for being proud of him. The next time that Paul uses the verb δίδωμι is in 6:3, where he says he tries to give no cause for offense in anything (μηδεμίαν ἐν μηδενὶ διδόντες προσκοπήν),[191] so that the *diakonia* will not be blamed. The two goals coincide, with the avoidance of blame serving as the prelude for pride and praise. Even what appears at first glance as a striking contradiction turns out not to be one at all. In 5:12 he says: οὐ ἑαυτοὺς συνιστάνομεν. In 6:4, on the other hand, he says: συνιστάνοντες ἑαυτούς. The difference in the placement of the pronoun is crucial. Every time in 2 Corinthians that Paul wishes to make a negative comment about self-commendation he places the pronoun before the verb (3:1; 5:12 10:12,18; compare 4:5: ἑαυτοὺς κηρύσσομεν). When he speaks positively, either of the Corinthians' self-commendation (7:11) or of his own (4:2; 6:4), he places it after the verb. *Self*-commendation is castigated, self-*commendation* is approved. One may boast "in the heart," but not "in the face" (5:12).[192] Paul does boast in what follows, but he does so as *God's* messenger, as the word order shows (θεοῦ διάκονοι).

In view of these and other connections that will become apparent as the discussion proceeds,[193] 6:3–10 can be affirmed as integrally tied to its context. But even those who have recognized some of the thematic links have not normally seen the pericope's literary function. The standard view is that the passage is totally apologetic, with differences among scholars emerging only in the extent to which thy see polemical and apologetic remarks underlying Paul's statements. But the links that have been discerned between 5:18–6:2 and 6:3–10 already suggest the dubiousness of this interpretation. It has already been observed that Paul's exhortation begins in 5:20 and resumes in 6:1, following the delayed conclusion to 5:17–19 in 5:21.[194] There is every reason to think that he is continuing that exhortation in 6:3–10. Indeed, the *communis opinio* is that the participles in

[191] Paul's formulation is equivalent to διδόναι προσκοπῆς ἀφορμάς. For the latter, cf. Polyb. 27.7.10. Compare esp. 1 Tim 5:14 and Dio Chrys., *Or.* 33.38: "Are you not aware that such conduct has provided occasion for slander against you, with the result that those who are ill-disposed toward you are supplied with material wherewith to defame you as a people?" Cf. also Ign., *Trall.* 8.2.

[192] For a different view, cf. Bultmann, *Korinther,* 149. The observation on the placement of the reflexive pronoun is that of H. Alford, *The Greek New Testament* (4 vols; rev. ed.; 1871–75; repr., Grand Rapids: Baker, 1980) 2.688.

[193] There is merit in the suggestion of Prümm, *Diakonia Pneumatos,* 2/1.66 79, 156, 382, that 6:3–10 is to be connectd with the "love of Christ" mentioned in 5:14. The life that Paul describes in 6:3–10 is a manifestation of how he is constrained by the love of Christ, with his love (6.6) a response to that love. For the necessity of bearing *peristaseis* out of love, cf. 1 Cor 13:3. The coherence of 6:3–10 to its context allows the observation that the catalogues in chapters 4 and 6 are both preceded by references to "creation" (4:6; 5:17).

[194] Dahl, "Fragment," 66 n. 10.

6:3-4 are dependent on παρακαλοῦμεν in 6:1, that is, on a word of exhortation. This strongly suggests that 6:3-10 is primarily *paraenetic* in function, and that the apologetic aim is only secondary![195] It occurs between the appeals of 5:20-6:2 and that of 6:11-13, and provides the *character basis* on which the appeals are made.

Exhortation is a vital part of persuasion, and the centrality of character to the art of persuasion had long been recognized by the time of Paul. According to Aristotle, character is the most powerful means of persuasion (*Rhet.* 1.2 [1356a]). Isocrates is but one who shares this perspective, affirming that "the argument which is made by a man's life is of more weight than that which is furnished by words" and that the "stronger a man's desire to persuade his hearers, the more zealously will he strive to be honourable and to have the esteem of his fellow-citizens" (*Or.* 15.278). As we have seen in the previous chapter (in the section on "Praise and Self-Praise"), a speaker's self-praise serves to create confidence in his listeners so that they will heed his words. Since, moreover, character is revealed most conspicuously in adversity (see above, chapter two), it is not surprising that Paul has recourse to his own hardships as part of his attempt to create confidence in himself so that he can persuade both men in general (5:12) and the Corinthians in particular.

Indeed, Paul's recognition of the decisive role of his own character in the paraenesis that he gives is reflected at the very beginning of 6:3-10. According to his statement in 6:3, Paul's goal is a πανάμωμος διακονία. To that end he tries to provide no προσκοπή that would result in ridicule and carping criticism (μωμηθῇ)[196] being directed at the *diakonia.* Since he has been given a glorious *diakonia* (2 Cor 3), he strives by his conduct not to stain or tarnish it (cf. Sir 33:22; 47:20; and also Wis 10:14). His statement in 6:3 is essentially the same as one he had already made in 1 Cor 9:12. There he refuses the right to support and burdens himself by working, for, he explains, "we bear all things in order that we may put no obstacle (ἐγκοπὴν δῶμεν) in the way of the gospel of Christ." Again, in 1 Cor 10:32-33 he urges the Corinthians to become ἀπρόκοποι and adduces himself as an example of such behavior. "I try to please all men in all

[195] One of the few scholars to refer to 6:3-10 as an *Ermahnung* in which Paul presents himself as a model is Otto Schmitz, *Apostolische Seelsorge: Eine Einführung in den zweiten Korintherbrief* (Die urchristliche Botschaft 8; Berlin: Furche-Verlag, 1940) 77. For an assessment of 6:1-7:1 in terms of paraenesis, cf. also Prümm, *Diakonia Pneumatos,* 1.360-81; 2/1.66, who argues that the emphasis in the catalogue falls on Paul's "*Haltungen als solche*" (2/2.344) and that the catalogue functions to allow Paul to address the Corinthians more powerfully (2/1.156). Zmijewski, *Stil,* 310, also sees the paraenetic implications of 6:3-10 in its canonical context, but he rejects this view by placing 6:3-10 immediately after 5:1 and interpreting it as part of Paul's so-called "first letter of apology" (2:14-5:13; 6:3-10). He thus joins the *communis opinio* that the pericope has an apologetic function. For advocates of this view, cf. Güttgemanns, *Der leidende Apostel,* 303 n. 132.

[196] On the word μῶμος and related words from Hesiod to the Hellenistic period, cf. A. A. Parry, *Blameless Aegisthus* (Mnemosyne Suppl. 26; Leiden: Brill, 1973) esp. 253-84.

things, not seeking my own advantage but that of the many, that they may be saved." This goal of salvation coincides with the fact that in 2 Cor 6:2 "now is the day of salvation." It is in keeping with his goal of avoiding the attachment of any blame to the *diakonia* (6:3) or to himself as he is involved in that *diakonia* (8:20), that he takes thought for (προνοοῦμεν) what is noble in the sight of both God and men (8:21). This endeavor on his part to act irreproachably befits one who is the "righteousness of God" (5:21) and it serves as well to show that he is worthy of pride and praise![197] His self-commendation in this secion thus does not begin first in 6:4, but already in 6:3.

Paul's sentiments here place him on one side of a debate among philosophers and others as to whether one should care about public opinion. Since a good reputation was considered by both Stoics and Cynics to be something indifferent, some chose to disregard it completely. According to a Cynic speech of Dio Chrysostom, Diogenes always "held to the same line of conduct, not changing his ways nor caring whether anyone of his audience commended or criticized him" (*Or.* 9.7; cf. also Plut., *Mor.* 227E). But others felt that the sage should guard his reputation. According to Epicurus, the sage "will pay so much regard (προνοήσεσθαι) to his reputation as not to be looked down upon" (Diog. Laert. 10.120). Cicero argues that one should have reverence toward all people, even for the ignorant masses, "for indifference to public opinion implies not merely self-sufficiency, but even total lack of principle," that is, arrogance (*arrogantis: Off.* 1.28.99). The sage who takes utterly no account of public opinion and praise is perceived only as arrogant and self-righteous. Thus, even ridiculous slanders sometimes receive a response. Apuleius, for example, justifies his response to such charges with the argument that his most earnest effort "is to avoid incurring the slightest spot or blemish to my fair fame" (*Apol.* 3). For many, to scorn fame is simply to scorn virtue itself (Tac., *Ann.* 4.38). Such is clearly Fronto's opinion: "Certain it is that he who cares not to be thought virtuous does not care to be virtuous either" (II,182 Haines).

This concern with public opinion is often coupled with a desire, *whatever* people may think, to do nothing that would offend others or invite criticism. Marcus Aurelius knows that he cannot prevent others from scorning him, yet his task is "not to be found doing or saying anything worthy of scorn" (*Med.* 13.1). The philosopher Areus praises Livia because "you have taken pains that no one should find anything at all in you to criticize" (Sen., *Marc.* 4.3). Epictetus argues, clearly against certain Cynics, that one should bathe and brush one's teeth. This is appropriate, not only because it befits a human being but also "so as not to offend those whom you meet" (*Diss.* 4.11.14).

[197] 2 Cor 6:3 is therefore linked with 5:2 through the connection of "blameless" and "righteousness." Cf. Phil 3:6; 1 Thess 2:10; Luke 1:6; Mus. Ruf., III,11,1-3 Hense = 40,25-26 Lutz. Cf. also Phil 2:15-16, where being "blameless" and "without blemish" are qualities in the Philippians that provide Paul with a boast.

Significantly, this attitude can also be extended to include a concern and a determination not to let one's actions sully the divine enterprise in which one is engaged. According to Epictetus' Stoic version of the ideal Cynic, the true Cynic is the "messenger" (ἄγγελος) and the "herald" (κῆρυξ) of the gods (*Diss.* 3.22.69), sent by God to show men the true nature of good and evil (3.22.23), and set them a proper example (4.8.31). He performs both tasks simultaneously by taking upon himself hardships and bearing them with *ataraxia.* His cheerful endurance of poverty and adversity not only provides a model for imitation but also proves the Cynic dogma that hardships are not evils and that possessions are not goods vital for happiness (3.22.45–56). It is, moreover, precisely because it is "the work of Zeus" in which he is engaged that the ideal Cynic takes care "that he shall never lay bare to the multitudes anything whereby he shall himself invalidate the testimony which it is his to give in behalf of virtue, and against externals" (4.8.32).

Paul's desire not to bring reproach on the *diakonia* is clearly analogous to the attitude of the ideal Cynic. Even the literary context in which the two statements occur is similar. Paul's statement precedes his catalogue of hardships, while the Cynic's declaration follows his *peristasis* catalogue. For Paul, the offense is clearly to lie in the message (1 Cor 1:23), not in a messenger whose life is incongruent with that message![198] The message itself is regarded as ridiculous by men, but only because their minds have been blinded (2 Cor 4:4). And yet the philosophical evaluation of "goods and evils" is likewise perceived as folly by the masses. The Stoic *paradoxa* were especially viewed as inane. Philo, for example, notes that the paradox that "every good man is rich" is regarded by men with bedimmed and blinded minds as absurd, irrational, shamelessly impudent and mad (*Prob.* 6,8,11,55). Both the Pauline and the philosophical kerygma are paradoxes, and so it is not surprising that Paul at the end of this section draws on several of the Stoic *paradoxa* to describe his own person.

There is yet another similarity that merits notice in regard to the relation of 6:3–4 to this Graeco-Roman material. Epictetus says that Diogenes "gladly took upon himself all those troubles and physical hardships for the sake of the common weal" (3.24.64). What is interesting is the statement that he did so as the *diakonos* of Zeus (3.24.65). Both Diogenes and Paul suffer in the capacity of a *diakonos* of the divine.

In this Stoic depiction of the ideal Cynic, the sage bears witness above all by his actions. It is through his hardships that his message is delivered, that he fulfills his function as God's *diakonos.* And yet, the true Cynic is no mute messenger. In the midst of deprivation he proclaims, "Make trial of me, and if you see that I am free from turmoil, hear (ἀκούσατε) my remedies and the treatment which cured me" (4.8.31). Paul, too, issues a call to experience the reconciliation with God that he himself has experienced (5:18,20), and it is as one who

[198] On the congruence and incongruence of profession and practice, cf. Diog. Laert. 7.10–11; Lucian, *Nec.* 5; Plut., *Mor.* 1033A–B; Matt 23:3.

is experiencing adversity that he issues this call. That Paul commends himself as God's messenger by his endurance of adversity shows that it is not incidental to his fulfillment of that function.

It is with the notion of his "much endurance" (ἐν ὑπομονῇ πολλῇ) that the catalogue begins![199] Paul's self-praise is focused above all on his endurance of adversity, the very virtue so frequently extolled in the material examined in chapter three. Just as *peristasis* catalogues functioned there as literary foils to depict the magnitude of the sage's endurance, so here Paul compiles a catalogue of hardships in order to extol his own endurance of adversity.[200] The next nine items he mentions are *peristaseis* in which his endurance is shown, and the number of items is intended to prove and to illustrate his claim that his endurance is "great."

Paul's praise of his own endurance is in keeping with the way in which he praises others for this same virtue. In 2 Thess 1:3–4 he gives thanks for the abundant growth of the Thessalonians' faith and for the increase of their love for one another. As a result, "we ourselves boast (ἐγκαυχᾶσθαι) of you in the churches of God for your endurance (ὑπομονῆς) and faith(fulness) in all your persecutions and in the afflictions which you are withstanding." The single article (τῆς) that is used with ὑπομονή and πίστις serves to bind the two items together. Theirs is a faith-filled and thus faithful endurance of afflictions and persecutions, and for this reason he boasts of them among the churches, thereby commending them to their fellow-Christians.

Paul's boasting in regard to the endurance of hardships is thus not something new with him, not something that owes its inception to the boasting of his opponents at Corinth. On the contrary, it is basic to him and represents only an application to himself of what he practices in regard to the churches under his care. His endurance of affliction is but the counterpart to his assertion that he does not lose heart in those same afflictions (4:1,16; cf. esp. Eph 3:13). This praise of endurance is basic to his paraenesis as a whole (Rom 12:12; cf. also 5:3).

199 On the basis of the initial term that Paul employs for introducing each item, the catalogue may be divided into three sections. In the first section all the items are introduced by the preposition ἐν (6:4b–7b). In the second section all the items are introduced by the preposition διά (6:7c–8). Ὡς serves to introduce the items in the final section (6:9–10). As a result, the items in the first section are in the dative case, the items in the second are in the genitive, and the items in the third are in the nominative. There are 18 items in the first section, all introduced by ἐν. On the basis of both form and content, the section may be divided into two sub-sections of 9 items each. The first sub-section consists of hardships, the second primarily of virtues. All of the hardship items are in the plural, while all the items in the second sub-section are in the singular. None of the hardship items receives a qualifying or descriptive term. More than half of the items in the second sub-section have a second term, either in the dative or in the genitive.

200 See above, "The Serene and Steadfast Sage." That *hypomonē* for Paul has a christological and eschatological dimension that separates it from typical Greek usage hardly diminishes the force of the analogy. The *literary* function is identical. For Josephus'

As is generally recognized,[201] the nine hardships that comprise this part of Paul's catalogue are arranged in three groups of three items each:

ἐν θλίψεσιν, ἐν ἀνάγκαις, ἐν στενοχωρίαις,
ἐν πληγαῖς, ἐν φυλακαῖς, ἐν ἀκαταστασίαις,
ἐν κόποις, ἐν ἀγρυπνίαις, ἐν νηστείαις.

The first triad is composed of hardships that are closely associated in Paul's mind. θλῖψις occurs first, just as θλιβόμενοι occupies the initial position in the catalogue of 2 Cor 4, so that there is in effect a repetition of the initial item from the former catalogue. The repetition of items from a previous catalogue is traditionally for *emphasis,* and Paul's repetition of θλῖψις serves both to increase the significance of this term in the initial catalogue of 2 Cor 4 and to heighten its importance here in the second. Furthermore, by the repetition of items from a previous catalogue and the introduction of new ones, an author not only reminds his readers of the previous catalogue but suggests to them that what follows is to be understood as a *supplement* to that initial list. Paul clearly does this in the present case, so that *the catalogue of 2 Cor 6 both assumes and supplements the catalogue of 2 Cor 4.*[202] This supplementation begins immediately with ἀνάγκη, a term that occurs with θλῖψις in 1 Thess 3:7 (cf. also Job 15:24; Ps 118 [119]:143; Zeph 1:15; *T.Jos.* 2:4). This is followed by στενοχωρία, which occurs together with θλῖψις in the *peristasis* catalogue in Rom 8:35 and also in Rom 2:9 (cf. also 2 Cor 4:8; LXX Deut 28:53,55,57; Judg 16:16; Esth 1:1g; Isa 8:22; 30:6). The placement of στενοχωρία at the end of the triad creates a crescendo rhetorically in that this is the longest word in the line.[203] More important is the fact that it is the most severe *peristasis* in this triad, as the formulation in 4:8 suggests and the placement of στενοχωρία as the final, climactic item in the catalogue of 12:10 confirms. All three words are generic terms intended to indicate the multiplicity of the various circumstances in which Paul's endurance is manifested.[204] ἀνάγκη, for example, is used by Leucippe to summarize the catalogue of her hardships, several of which were experienced by Paul:

---

use of a *peristasis* catalogue to praise the Essenes and depict their endurance of hardships on both philosophical and eschatological grounds, see *BJ* 2.151–53.

[201] For a different arrangement, see Baum, *Mut,* 159–60.

[202] For the use of multiple catalogues for emphasis and supplementation, cf. Károly Maróti, *Die Anfänge der griechischen Literatur: Vorfragen* (Budapest: Verlag der Ungarischen Akademie der Wissenschaften, 1960) 396, 469 n. 189.

[203] Cf. esp. Fridrichsen, "Paulus und die Stoa," 28, who argues for a strictly rhetorical arrangement of items.

[204] *Contra* Fridrichsen, "Paulus und die Stoa," 29, who argues that the first triad depicts the "Stimmungslage" of the apostle rather than the *peristaseis* which beset him. This involves interpreting both ἀνάγκαι and στενοχωρίαι in a different sense from that which he admits they have in 12:10, and this is simply intolerable. The internal impact of the

For you I left my mother and took up the life of a wanderer; for you I suffered shipwreck and fell into the hands of pirates; for you I became a victim for sacrifice and an expiatory offering (καθαρμός) and twice entered the valley of the shadow of death; for you I was sold and fettered, I carried a hoe, I tilled the ground, I underwent the scourge. . . . I, through all these trials (ἀνάγκαις), have persevered to the end (Achilles Tatius 5.18.4–5).

Whereas Leucippe itemizes and then summarizes, Paul reverses this procedure. In the second triad he narrows the broad scope of the first triad by focusing on specific hardships that are illustrative of the items mentioned in the first. The first item, πληγαί, for example, occurs in Diod. Sic. 4.43.3 in reference to the blows of a whip that some youths were receiving. In 4.43.5 these youths are referred to as those ἐν ταῖς ἀνάγκαις, those "who were suffering these tortures." In the catalogue in chapter 11 Paul refers to the excessive number of blows that he has received (11:23), and specifies this by reference to his synagogue floggings and his beatings with a rod (11:24–25; cf. Philo, *Flacc.* 75). That "imprisonment" is placed next is natural in light of the sequence in Acts 16:22–23, where Paul and Silas are beaten with rods and then placed in prison (cf. also Acts 16:37; Heb 11:36). The first two items thus point to this triad as a *catalogue of punishments* (see above, "The Variety of *Peristasis* Catalogues"). The third item, ἀκαταστασία, occurs in a catalogue of punishments in *Herm. Sim.* 6.3.4, but in 2 Cor 6:4 it is probably not a punishment *per se.* It seems added to the first two items by general association, for riots often led to scourging and incarceration (cf. Acts 16:19–23; 21:30–22:29). All three items thus point to concrete situations in which Paul and his associates were persecuted, and ἀκαταστασία (linked with διωγμός in *1 Clem.* 3.2) is placed last as the longest item in the line and the one that perhaps most clearly encompasses the possibility of death (cf. Acts 14:19).

The third triad is a catalogue of Paul's *occupational hardships* (see above, "The Variety of *Peristasis* Catalogues"), both as apostle and artisan. His tentmaking trade involved him in exhausting toil, loss of sleep, and lack of food.[205] That he worked from dawn till dusk (1 Thess 2:9; 2 Thess 3:8) meant that any evening hours spent in evangelism would only result in greater weariness and loss of sleep (cf. Acts 20:31).[206] His steadfast refusal to accept support condemned him to a life of poverty with few provisions. This poverty is explicitly mentioned twice at the end of this section (6:10), but it is already anticipated in the items mentioned in the first triad, both ἀνάγκη (Ael., *VH* 14.24; Plut., *Solon* 14.1; cf. also 1 Sam 22:2) and στενοχωρία (cf. Sir 10:26; Dio Chrys., *Or.* 31.114–15).

---

hardships may not be excluded from his meaning, but Barrett, *Second Corinthians,* 186, 188, captures the primary meaning when he says they are "external circumstances."

[205] Cf. Hock, *Social Context,* esp. 34–35,60,64,84–85,101. The same sequence of κόπος, ἀγρυπνία, and νηστεία occurs also in 2 Cor 11:27, though here there are some intervening items.

[206] Paul's praise of his κόπος is comparable to the praise of Epaphras' πόνος in Col 4:12–13.

Many commentators claim that the hardships mentioned in the third triad are distinct from those of the first two triads in that they are voluntary in nature. This interpretation goes back at least to John Chrysostom and Theodoret and owes its popularity to Bengel. As already seen in connection with 2 Cor 4:11, Paul's suffering in general is marked by its volitional character. He not only hands himself over to death (4:11) but is well pleased with his hardships (12:10), exulting in the instrumental value of his afflictions (Rom 5:3). Yet there is a sense in which this old claim may be particularly true for this third triad. His κόπος as an artisan was certainly voluntary, and it is clear that many artisans lost sleep as a result of the pursuit of their trade (Sir 38:27–30; cf. also Dio Chrys., *Or.* 77/78.7). Paul's selection of νηστεία as the final item in the line points in the same direction. It breaks the pattern of placing the longest word of the triad at the end of the line and leads into the catalogue of virtues, which were universally regarded as volitional. It is, moreover, the standard word used for voluntary abstinence from food, and lack of food was certainly the consequence of his voluntary life as an artisan. That he also voluntarily forwent sleep as well as food in the pursuit of his freely chosen life as an artisan-apostle is equally certain (cf. Xen., *Mem.* 2.1.17; Epict., *Diss.* 3.15.11; *Ench.* 29.6). A volitional emphasis in the third triad is thus likely, and this emphasis makes the discussion of free will in chapter three all the more relevant (see above, "Fortune, God, and Free Will").

The catalogue of virtues that follows these three triads is not without significance for the understanding of the *peristasis* catalogue itself. Paul mentions a total of nine hardships and nine virtues and gifts. The first item in the list of virtues is "endurance," which has been separated from the rest and placed at the head of the catalogue. As a result of this placement, the *peristasis* catalogue is enclosed by a catalogue of virtues, with ὑπομονή and ἁγνότης serving as the frames. This frame gives the catalogue a qualitative character, so that it demonstrates that Paul has done more than simply endure his toils and afflictions. It shows that he has endured with purity, out of knowledge, with patience and kindness. There is thus a character and an integrity to Paul's endurance that distinguishes it from a mere withstanding, and makes it like that of the Thessalonians (2 Thess 1:3–4).

To be concrete, it means that he has not endured his adversities out of avarice (see above, chapter three, notes 8, 41–42), but with the purest of motives and the truest of words (cf. Philo, *Prob.* 84). Like the sage, he does not endure with the obstinacy of an ass, but with knowledge, though the source and the content of that knowledge is different in the two cases (see above, "The Crucial Role of Philosophy and Reason"). His demeanor toward his persecutors (as in the second triad) is marked by patience, kindness, and unfeigned love, just like the sage (see above, "The Philosopher's Demeanor"). But just as his virtues are fruits of the Spirit (Gal 5:22), so is his endurance the result of "the power of God" (2 Cor 6:6; cf. also Col 1:11).[207]

[207] For ἀνάγκη and incapacity, cf. Job 36:19. The interpretation of the items in the catalogue of virtues in terms of Paul's adversities is not intended to imply that this is their

The catalogue of virtues that surrounds the catalogue of hardships thus serves to indicate the manner and means by which Paul deals with his hardships and persecutors. The catalogue of hardships, in turn, gives substance to the catalogue of virtues. The reference to the "power of God" in 6:6 is a conscious cross-reference to the catalogue of 4:7-12. As we have just seen to be the case with multiple catalogues in works, the later catalogues frequently assume the previous ones and build upon them. Thus the fact that Paul does not provide as many checks against his self-praise in 6:3-10 as he does in the preceding catalogue is because he now assumes them. By referring to the divine power in 6:6 he is reminding his readers of those previous assertions and their continuing foundational validity for what he asserts here.

Paul's catalogues of hardships and virtues comprise the two units of the first section of 6:3-10. The beginning of the second section is marked by a change in the preposition used to introduce the terms. From using ἐν with each of the 18 items in 6:4-7a, Paul switches now to διά. This section contains a short catalogue of vicissitudes (6:8a-b), and the items that appear in it serve to indicate the varying responses that Paul and his way of life elicit. The picture that he gives of himself here as the "armed soldier" is in keeping with the military imagery that is prominent in the depictions of the sage in his battle with Fortune (see above, "Fortune, God, and Free Will," and also Dio Chrys., *Or.* 16.6). The function of this section is transitional. It is linked with the preceding catalogue of virtues by the word δικαιοσύνη (cf. also 5:21), particularly with "purity" (cf. *CIG* 1133,15: δικαιοσύνης ἕνεκεν καὶ ἁγνότητος), and the chiasmus that ends this section (δόξα—ἀτιμία—δυσφημία—εὐφημία) serves to introduce the third section in which the perception of Paul as a "deceiver" exemplifies the δυσφημία that he as a just man endures.[208]

The third section consists of seven antithetic clauses, each introduced by ὡς. The initial item in each instance presents the external impression that Paul and his cohorts give. In the first case, this impression is blatantly false, viz., the impression that they are πλάνοι. In the other cases, this impression is not so much false as it is inadequate, for Paul's claim is that he is much more than he

---

only meaning. It is, however, to insist that the two catalogues interlock and are intended to be interpreted in light of each other. As was seen in both chapters two and three, there is an intimate connection between *aretē* and adversity, so that the coherence of a *Peristasenkatalog* and a *Tugendkatalog* in Paul is not at all surprising. See also 1 Cor 4:12b-13a.

[208] The line from *CIG* is cited from T. Nägeli, *Der Wortschatz des Apostels Paulus* (Göttingen: Vandenhoeck & Ruprecht, 1905) 16, 38. As 2 Cor 10:4 suggests, "weapons" looks back to "the power of God" and thus provides another link with the preceding section. For the Cynic's cloak and wallet as "the weapons of the gods," cf. Ps-Crates, *Ep.* 16 (66,4-5 Malherbe).

externally appears to be. Over against this false or deficient external appearance Paul then sets the truth and the greater reality.[209]

The perception of πλάνη contrasts with what Paul has already asserted about himself in the catalogue of virtues. He is no deceiver, for he speaks "the word of truth" (6:7), that is, veraciously,[210] and is characterized by purity and moral integrity (6:6). What is true is closely tied to what is pure (Phil 4:8), just as deceit is closely linked with impurity (1 Thess 2:3). The hypocrisy that is part and parcel of deceit is not found in one who acts and speaks with unfeigned, unhypocritical (ἀνυποκρίτῳ) love (6:6), a trait common to both apostle and sage (see above, "The Philosopher's Demeanor"). This first hardship thus concerns the misperception concerning Paul's δικαιοσύνη (5:21; 6:7). This recalls the situation of the righteous sufferer, who is everywhere perceived as unjust. In 11:13–15 Paul completes this picture by depicting his opponents as those who appear ὡς διάκονοι δικαιοσύνης, but are in fact ἐργάται δόλιοι. This, too, recalls the *synkrisis* of the righteous sufferer with his unjust counterpart, for the latter presents himself to all as just and is mistakenly perceived as such (see above, "The Righteous Sufferer as the 'Foolish' Wise Man," and also Philo, *Mig.* 86).

Whereas the first item concerns Paul's character and illustrates the δυσφημία to which he is subjected, the second deals with his status and exemplifies his ἀτιμία, his lack of honor. He and his associates appear ὡς ἀγνοούμενοι, and yet are ἐπιγινωσκόμενοι. Obscurity was a much dreaded hardship in the ancient world. According to Dio Chrysostom, "most men are so completely corrupted at heart by opinion that they would rather be notorious for the greatest calamities than suffer ill and be unknown" (*Or.* 11.6). Herodian (1.9.5) refers to an unknown and obscure Cynic philosopher trying to obtain δόξα, reputation (cf. 2 Cor 6:8). But the true sage is free from vanity, for he is indifferent to both good and bad repute (Diog. Laert. 7.117). Obscurity, insignificance, and unpopularity do not prevent the wise man from being happy (Cic., *Tusc.* 5.36.103). Indeed, Democritus despised fame and boasted that when he was in Athens he knew of Socrates, but that he was unknown to Socrates and everyone else (Diog. Laert. 9.36). This is one example of someone boasting of his hardships, his "weaknesses" as it were. And yet Cicero comments, "What dignified firmness for a man to glory in having no glory!" (*Tusc.* 5.36.104).

That Paul is "unknown" does not mean that he is not a sage or a *diakonos* of God, for "it is very possible to be a θεῖος ἀνήρ and yet not to be recognized by any one" (Mar. Ant., *Med.* 7.67). But Paul is not ultimately unknown, for he is "well known" (6:9a), that is, to God. This fact marks him as the messenger of

[209] The basic antithesis is thus that of *Schein* versus *Sein*. For other assessments, cf. esp. Lietzmann, *Korinther*, 128; Windisch, *Korintherbrief*, 207; Allo, *Seconde Épître*, 177; and Bultmann, *Korinther*, 175.

[210] Cf esp. J. Murphy-O'Connor, "Truth: Paul and Qumran," *Paul and Qumran* (ed. J. Murphy-O'Connor; London: G. Chapman, 1968) 195.

God that he claims to be (6:4), and, indeed, as a *sophos*. For, according to Porphyry, "the wise man is known by few, and if he wishes, unknown (ἀγνοούμενος) even to all, yet is known by God" (γινώσκεται ὑπὸ θεοῦ).[211]

The third and fourth paradoxical antitheses are formed on the basis of Ps 117(118):18. The psalm he quotes is a thanksgiving celebrating the king's deliverance from death and military victory, and it likely has furnished part of the imagery of 2 Cor 6:7. As in the preceding paradox, God is implied rather than mentioned explicitly. In the psalm Yahweh chastens the speaker sorely, yet does not give him over to death. Paul formulates his antitheses so as to emphasize that he is not killed (μὴ θανατούμενοι) but continues to live (ἰδοὺ ζῶμεν), as in 1:8–10. But it is not only his deliverance that he owes to God, but his very sufferings themselves, as the psalm clearly shows. That his sufferings are a means of God's *paideia* (παιδευόμενοι) recalls the fact that the good man's hardships come from the divine and function as the discipline and *askēsis* by which he achieves virtue (see above, "Fortune, God, and Free Will").[212] What is striking here, however, is the fact that Paul sets God's discipline over against his deliverance and emphasizes the latter. As the use of the OT already suggests, Paul's thought draws here on an ancient biblical idea in which there is an intimate connection between God's discipline and his deliverance (cf., for example, Ps 94:12–15). Paul's conviction is that his constant deliverance from death shows that he is righteous (5:21; 6:7), that he is a good man whose sufferings point to God's love (Prov 3:11–12; cf. also Heb 12:5–6) rather than his wrath. God does not discipline him in his wrath (Pss 6:1; 38:1), for that would annihilate him (cf. Jer 10:24; Job 16:6–10). On the contrary, that God leaves him among the living means that God is only testing him (Ps 66:9–10). Since there is no ἀδικία in his heart, God listens to his prayer and delivers him (Ps 66:17–19).[213] His

[211] Porph., *Marc.* 13, cited by A. S. L. Farquharson, *The Meditations of the Emperor Marcus Antonius* (2 vols.; Oxford: Clarendon, 1944) 2.752. This is an important text which apparently never before has been cited in connection with 2 Cor 6:9. It should settle the old debate whether Paul is presenting himself as well known to men or to God. The former is the majority viewpoint, but it clearly can no longer be maintained in light of Porphyry's comment about the sage. For the conviction that true virtue, though it may long remain unknown, will eventually become famous, cf. Sen., *Ep.* 79.13–16, who lists Democritus, Socrates, Cato, and Epicurus as examples of virtuous men who were obscure for much or all of their lives. For both the name and the reality of virtue, cf. Philo, *Mig.* 88.

[212] For a rabbinic treatment of Ps 118:18 and the connection of the sufferings of the righteous with God's *paideia* and love, see E. P. Sanders, "R. Akiba's View of Suffering," *JQR* 64 (1973) 332–51.

[213] Cf. Pss 4:2–3; 7:1–11; 17:1–15; 18:20–27; 22:1–31; 26:1–12; 31:1–24; 35:7,9–10; 119:92; Isa 1:15; 38:1–6; 59:1–3. For God's testing of the righteous, cf. also Ps 26:1–3 and Jer 20:12. According to a widespread rabbinic interpretation of Ps 11:5, moreover, God tests *only* the righteous. See *Gen. Rab.* 32.3; *Midr.Ps.* 11.4; and note 157 above. For the confidence of the pure in heart, cf. also 1 John 3:21. For the occurrence of a catalogue of calamities in connection with the idea of discipline, see Job 5:17–22. Finally, it should be added that the references to dying and living in Paul's paradoxes are perhaps additional cross-

sufferings only lead him to cleave closer to the God whose *diakonos* he is (1:9).

God's deliverance of Paul from his perils thus serves here to support his claims and to establish him as righteous. It is not without significance that Paul quotes Ps 44:22 in conjunction with the *peristasis* catalogue of Rom 8:35. This psalm contains a plea for God to deliver Israel, and one of the bases for this plea is the fidelity of suffering Israel. "All this has come upon us, though we have not forgotten thee, or been false to thy covenant" (Ps 44:17, RSV). Since it is "for thy sake" (Rom 8:36) that Paul suffers the *peristaseis* of Rom 8:35, he has reason both to expect divine deliverance and to see in that deliverance a confirmation of his claims.

The *peristasis* catalogue that provides the best commentary on Paul's third and fourth paradoxes, however, is probably the one found in *T. Jos.* 1:3–7. The catalogue there both proves and illustrates the thesis that "the Lord doth not forsake them that fear Him, neither in darkness, nor in bonds, nor in tribulations (θλίψεσιν), nor in necessities (ἀνάγκαις)" (2:4). God may, however, withdraw for a brief period in order to test (δοκιμάσαι) a person. Such was the case with Joseph:

> In ten temptations He showed me approved (δόκιμόν με ἀνέδειξε),
> And in all of them I endured;
> For endurance (μακροθυμία) is a mighty charm,
> And patience (ὑπομονή) giveth many good things (2:7).

Thus Joseph's *peristasis* catalogue, like Paul's, provides proof of both his endurance and his approval by God. The catalogue merits quotation in full:

> I have seen in my life envy and death,
> Yet I went not astray, but persevered in the truth of the Lord.
> These my brethren hated me, but the Lord loved me:
> They wished to slay me, but the God of my fathers guarded me:
> They let me down into a pit, and the Most High brought me up again.
> I was sold into slavery, and the Lord of all made me free:
> I was taken into captivity, and His strong hand succoured me.
> I was beset with hunger, and the Lord Himself nourished me.
> I was alone, and God comforted me:
> I was sick, and the Lord visited me:
> I was in prison, and my God showed favour unto me;
> In bonds, and He released me;
> Slandered, and He pleaded my cause;
> Bitterly spoken against by the Egyptians, and He delivered me;
> Envied by my fellow-slaves, and He exalted me. (*T. Jos.* 1:3–7).[214]

---

references to the catalogue of 4:7–12. Cf. esp. 4:9–11.

[214] The translations of *The Testament of Joseph* are those of Charles in *APOT* 2.346–47. For the text, cf. now M. De Jonge (ed.), *The Testaments of the Twelve Patriarchs* (Leiden: Brill, 1978) 144–46. For an orientation to this document, cf. esp. G. W. E.

Thus, as with Paul, the assertions of human endurance and divine deliverance go hand-in-hand. Furthermore, both are "fathers" speaking to their children (*T.Jos.* 1:2; 2 Cor 6:13), commending themselves as models by means of their behavior. This part of Paul's catalogue thus conforms in important ways to the catalogue in the *The Testament of Joseph,* and this shows that Paul's use of the *peristasis* catalogue is not unrelated to its use in the Jewish world.

Now, whereas the third and fourth items deal with Paul's physical sufferings and point back to the *peristaseis* of 6:4b–5, the fifth item expresses the psychic hardship of λύπη. By definition, it was impossible in strict Stoic circles for the sage to experience grief and sorrow. But, as we have seen, significant concessions to the demands of nature were made within those branches of milder Stoicism as represented by Seneca, so that the sage's experience of *dolor* was affirmed. This concession coincided with the position taken in other philosophical traditions that grief is natural and thus appropriate for the sage (see above, "The Struggling Sage"). Paul unabashedly confesses his grief (2 Cor 2:1–3; Rom 9:1; Phil 2:27), for it, no less than his physical hardships, is the consequence of his *diakonia.* But he couples this confession here with an affirmation of his constant (ἀεί) joy, a joy that overflows in all his afflictions (7:4) and forms the basis for his exhortation "rejoice always" (Phil 4:4; 1 Thess 5:16). Nothing, not even λύπη, can shake Paul's constant joy, and the latter, as we have seen in the discussion of "The *Sapiens* and the *Proficiens,*" is a sign of the sage.[215]

The last two items in this final section refer to the paradox that Paul is simultaneously poor and wealthy.[216] The first of these points to Paul as spiritual benefactor, and, as is typical of the Stoic *paradoxa,* the explanation of this paradox is left unstated. But the logic is clearly christological and represents part of Paul's *imitatio Christi.* "Although Christ was rich, for your sake he became poor, so that you by his poverty might become rich" (8:9). As an

Nickelsburg, Jr. (ed.), *Studies on the Testament of Joseph* (SBLSCS 5; Missoula: Scholars, 1975). For a treatment of *T.Jos.* 1:3–7, cf. H. W. Hollander, *Joseph as an Ethical Model in the Testaments of the Twelve Patriarchs* (SVTP 6; Leiden: Brill, 1981) 17–21.

[215] This is not to deny that there are important differences between Paul's understanding of joy and that of the Stoics and Cynics. On the difference between the Cynic's paradoxical joy and that of Paul, cf., for example, Höistad, "Parallele," 26–27. One can, however, overstate the differences, which is an error committed by Baum, *Mut,* 174–75 n. 88.

[216] The attempt by Collange, *Énigmes,* 299, to interpret this paradox apologetically results in his impossible suggestion that the poverty to which Paul refers is spiritual rather than material. Extreme caution should be used in trying to relate items in the *peristasis* catalogues to specific situations. Indeed, the very typicality of the hardships referred to in 6:8–10 should lead scholars to exercise the same restraint in dealing with the *Peristasenkataloge* as they do with the catalogues of vices. In both cases the individual items may have particular relevance to the church to which they are addressed, but it is precarious to assume either that all are equally relevant or are occasioned by a particular situation in that church.

ambassador for Christ (5:20) and the *diakonos* of God and Christ (6:4; 11:23), Paul does continually what Christ once did. Thus, just as the Corinthians are the beneficiaries of Paul's sufferings in general (1:6; 4:12,15), so are Paul's poverty and lowliness a means of their enrichment.[217]

It is the christological rationale that distinguishes Paul's paradox from somewhat similar Stoic *paradoxa* and their theological rationales. For Seneca, the divine has nothing (*deus nihil habet*), neither money nor clothing, and remains unknown to all and is held in low esteem by many (*Ep.* 31.10). The gods "have neither manors nor gardens nor costly estates farmed by a foreign tenant, nor a huge yield of interest in the forum." In short, upon close examination it turns out that the gods are "quite needy, giving all and having nothing (*omnia dantis, nihil habentis*)." The person who strips himself of his property and becomes poor is thus like the gods (*Tranq.* 8.5). Such a person was the Cynic Crates, who divested himself of all resources and became the material benefactor of others by giving away his wealth (Diog. Laert. 6.87; Apul., *Apol.* 22). In Cynic eyes this divestiture served to render him paradoxically both rich and poor. In Ps-Crates, *Ep.* 7 (58,6–8 Malherbe), the author has Crates say, "But as for us, we observe complete peace since we have been freed from every evil by Diogenes of Sinope, and although we possess nothing, we have everything" (ἔχοντες μηδὲν πάντ' ἔχομεν; compare 2 Cor 6:10c).[218]

Paul, like Crates, is paradoxically the poor man who is also rich and serves as the benefactor of others. But there is an important difference. Whereas Crates bestowed his material wealth on others, Paul is the spiritual benefactor of the many. And whereas Crates did this once, Paul draws continually on the treasure (4:7) at his disposal in order to enrich others. In functioning as a spiritual benefactor Paul is closer to Antisthenes, who prized spiritual wealth over material prosperity and argued that "wealth of this kind makes people generous." He had been enriched by Socrates, and he says of himself that, "I am now niggardly to no one, but make an open display of my abundance to all my friends and share my spiritual wealth with any one of them that desires it" (Xen., *Symp.* 4.43).

In the final paradox Paul presents himself "as having nothing and yet owning everything" (6:10c). As the quotation of Ps-Crates, *Epistle* 7, already indicates, Paul's sentiment is not unique. As has long been recognized, Paul is drawing here on the Cynic and Stoic idea that "all things belong to the wise" (Cic., *Fin.* 3.22.75; Philo, *Plant.* 69). This idea was often stated paradoxically, viz., that the sage is rich, however needy he may be.[219] Different explanations

[217] The similarity of 2 Cor 6:10 and 8:9 leads Windisch, *Paulus und Christus*, 166, 239, to refer to Paul as "ein zweiter Christus."

[218] On the similarity of this Cynic sentiment to Paul's, cf. Windisch, *Korintherbrief*, 209, and D. L. Mealand, " 'As having nothing, and yet possessing everything': 2 Kor 6:10c," *ZNW* 67 (1976) 277–79. On what "having nothing" entails in the Cynic tradition, see esp. Epict., *Diss.* 3.22.45 and chapter three, note 95 above.

[219] Cf. Cic., *Fin.* 5.28.84; *Mur.* 61; Sen., *Ep.* 66.22; Plut., *Mor.* 1058C. For Cynic texts, cf. Ps-Crates, *Ep.* 7 (58,6–8 Malherbe) and compare *Soc.Ep.* 21.3 (270,22–24 Malherbe); 22.1

were provided for this claim, some involving legal distinctions (cf. Sen., *Ben.* 7.5.1; 6.3; comp. Diog. Laert. 7.125) and some giving a theological justification. In the latter case, the true ownership of all things is attributed to the gods, and the sage is said to share in their bounty because he is their friend (Diog. Laert. 6.37, 72; Philo, *Mos.* 1.156–57). The unstated basis of Paul's claim is that he has a "treasure" (4:7) in himself that has been bestowed by God, so that he has "all things" (cf. 1 Cor 3:21-22), including confidence toward God (3:4), hope (3:12), his *diakonia* (4:1), God's promises (7:1), and ultimately a building from God (5:1).

In short, Paul places at the end of his catalogue the most famous of all the ancient paradoxes about the sage, and he does so to make clear that the one who is exhorting them to receive him and his message is none other than the poor but virtuous *sophos* who enriches others with the goods at his disposal. His paraenesis could not claim a greater character basis. And yet, it is as God's *diakonos* that he makes this claim, clearly suggesting that the reason why he can do so is that he has God's approval and confidence.

Therefore, in the final section Paul makes use of several paradoxes that are intended to suggest to the Corinthians that God has sent him to them as his messenger. He is known by God, disciplined by God, and delivered by God. As one who has been made rich by God's act in Christ (8:9), he now possesses all things and enriches others with spiritual wealth. It is thus on the basis of what he has affirmed about himself in 6:3–10 that he seeks to be accepted by the Corinthians and reconciled to them. His character and his endurance of adversity give substance to his claim to be a divine emissary and suggest what the paradoxes make explicit, viz., that he is much more than his physical appearance suggests. "Man looks on the outward appearance (πρόσωπον), but God looks on the heart" (καρδία: 1 Sam 16:7 LXX). The Corinthians should look where God looks and accept Paul as one who, unlike his opponents, boasts in the καρδία and not the πρόσωπον (2 Cor 5:12). His heart is open wide (6:13) and he invites them to look beyond his appearance and into his heart. Only then will they see him for who he truly is.

(272,2–4 Malherbe). The same basic idea occurs in other texts as well; cf. Philo, *Prob.* 77; Plut., *Mor.* 101D; Philostr., *VA* 3.15; Quint. Curtius 4.1.25. Cf. also Ath. 3.124A; Ter., *Eun.* 2.2.12; and *T.Gad* 7.6.

Conclusion

The chief points in the preceding discussion may now be summarized and the major conclusions drawn. It has been shown that *peristasis* catalogues are essentially "catalogues of circumstances," with the circumstancs envisioned either "good" or "bad" or both. The catalogues that contain several of both kinds of circumstances are the most comprehensive and constitute the basic category. Since they envision the changing circumstances that are part and parcel of human existence, they are "catalogues of vicissitudes." The catalogue that occurs in Phil 4:12 is an example of this basic type (cf. also 2 Cor 6:8a–b). Other catalogues emphasize or concern only one set of circumstances, usually those of an adverse nature. Indeed, the word *peristasis* often means "adverse circumstance," "difficulty," or "hardship," and when lists of such *peristaseis* are given, these are "catalogues of hardships." All of the catalogues in Paul's Corinthian correspondence are examples of this subset of the basic type.

These catalogues of hardships are of various kinds. They include (1) catalogues of human hardships, (2) hardships of national groups, (3) catalogues of occupational hardships, (4) catalogues of punishments, (5) hardships of the passions, (6) the vicissitudes of particular individuals, and (7) the hardships of various types, such as those of the wise man. It is the last of these that has received extensive treatment in this investigation.

The sage was an immensely popular figure in Graeco-Roman philosophy. As the embodiment of reason and virtue, he played a central role in both the propaganda and the pedagogy of philosophy. Moralists and philosophers were especially fond of discussing him in terms of his hardships, and they often did so by means of *peristasis* catalogues. The latter are thus a prominent feature of descriptions of the wise man as the "suffering sage," for the amplification of the sage's sufferings serves to magnify him as a person and establish him as a reliable guide for those who aspire to the life of virtue. *Peristasis* catalogues thus function as rhetorical and literary foils for the depiction and demonstration of the sage's various qualities as the ideal philosopher.

Peristasis catalogues serve to legitimate the claims made about a person and show him to be virtuous because *peristaseis* have a revelatory and probative function in regard to character. Since it is axiomatic in the ancient world that adversity is the litmus test of character, a person's virtuous attitude and action while under duress furnish the proof that he is a man of genuine worth and/or a true philosopher. They distinguish him from the person who owes his high standing to Fortune as well as from the person who feigns virtue and knowledge.

Plutarch, for example, makes reference to Alexander's many hardships in an attempt to argue that the Macedonian's success is to be attributed to his virtue rather than to lady luck (*Mor.* 326D–33C). As for the true philosopher, Epictetus says that the true Stoic is the "man who though sick is happy, though in danger is happy, though dying is happy, though condemned to exile is happy, though in disrepute is happy" (*Diss.* 2.19.24). It is his serenity that serves to distinguish him from the one who merely puts on the guise (σχῆμα) of being a philosopher (2.19.28). The latter merely utters brave words but collapses under the threat of hardship. To such a one Epictetus says pointedly, "But yet, philosopher, tell me, why are you trembling? Is not the danger death, or prison, or bodily pain, or exile, or disrepute?" (2.19.18; cf. also Gell., *NA* 1.2.6–7; 17.19.3; Sen., *Ep.* 71.30).

As we have seen in chapter four, Paul in 1 and 2 Corinthians frequently depicts himself in terms typically used to describe the ideal philosopher, and his use of *peristasis* catalogues is an integral part of this *Selbstdarstellung.* His catalogues, moreover, have many of the same literary functions as those of the sage.

The sage's sufferings, for example, serve to show both his serenity and his endurance. The catalogues in 2 Cor 4 and 6 clearly function in these two standard ways. In 2 Cor 6:4–5 Paul enumerates nine hardships in order to magnify and prove the greatness of his endurance (cf. also 2 Cor 11:23–28). Similarly, the catalogue in 2 Cor 4:8–9 attests his assertions in 4:1 and 4:16 that he does not despair. In both cases, the emphasis falls on Paul's superiority to suffering and his triumph over it.

Again, Hellenistic philosophers use the figure of the suffering sage in order to admonish their students and set before them the proper model for their conduct. Similarly, in 1 Cor 4 Paul presents himself as a model and admonishes his young converts by means of the catalogue that he compiles. Like the philosophers, then, he uses *peristasis* catalogues as part of his paraenesis and pedagogy. A second example of the paraenetic use of a *peristasis* catalogue occurs in 2 Cor 6. As we have seen, the catalogue there is not primarily apologetic in nature, but provides the character basis on which his exhortation rests.

Furthermore, like some Hellenistic moralists, Paul in his catalogues attributes his hardships to God (1 Cor 4:9; 2 Cor 6:9). Just as the sage's suffering plays a role in the divine plan, so does Paul's. The suffering of both is inseparable from the mission to which they have been called, and, in the case of both these suffering *diakonoi,* the divine is said to exhibit them as a model. The sage accepts the hardships of his life because they are part of the divine will, and this assent is expressed by means of catalogues that list the *peristaseis* to which he assents. Paul, for his part, not only states that he gives himself up to death for Jesus' sake (2 Cor 4:11) but also in 2 Cor 12:10 uses a catalogue to express his willing, even joyful, acceptance of all that his ministry entails. Indeed, he affirms that he is "well pleased with," "takes delight in" (εὐδοκῶ) his various sufferings: "I delight in weaknesses, in insults, in hardships, in persecutions, in difficulties" (NIV).

There are other similarities between the sage and the apostle that appear in connection with Paul's catalogues. The demeanor that the sage was expected to display toward his adversaries is given in the catalogue of 1 Cor 4:12–13. The sage's *autarkeia* was a result of his *askēsis,* and Paul in Phil 4:11–12 not only lays claim to this quality but also says that this is something that he has "learned," viz., by *askēsis.* As we have seen, the sage's victory and invincibility were repeatedly celebrated by rehearsing the hardships over which he triumphed and the forces against which he was invincible. In Paul's case, not only does the catalogue of 2 Cor 4:8–9 ring with "the triumphant certainty that no suffering can destroy him" (J. Weiss) but also he follows the *peristasis* catalogue of Rom 8:35 with the triumphant shout that "in all these things we are more than conquerors through him that loved us" (8:37, RSV).

For both Paul and the sage, what enables this victory over adversity is power. *Peristaseis* provide the occasion for displaying this power, and with this display comes the victory and the vaunting that goes with it. In the case of the sage, what is shown is the power of his mind, the strength of his will. It is he who triumphs, and he does so by his own power. But for him to boast of his accomplishment as a purely personal one, however, struck most moralists as a vain and vulgar exercise in self-glorification. They argued that proper self-laudation acknowledges a debt outside itself and aims at a benefit beyond itself. In the case of the sage, it was usually felt that he owed his victory above all to philosophy, and, since that was the case, it was appropriate for him to glorify philosophy and vaunt himself in its name. It was still the power of the mind that triumphed, but it was the philosophically informed mind that did so. It is in keeping with this perspective and philosophy's own propaganda that one finds catalogues of the evils against which philosophy provides protection.

To the extent that hardships were seen as signs of the divine's loving esteem and the divinely appointed means of achieving and displaying virtue, the sage's triumph over adversity could also be attributed to God. The actual role that the divine played in this triumph depended, of course, on the moralist's understanding of God, but it is significant that the divine was in some way linked to the attainment of the ideal. It is also significant that one finds catalogues that point to the exhibition of divine power in human weakness and that these catalogues are intended to point the reader or observer beyond the frailty to the divine source of the power.

Although he has a quite different understanding of God from that found in the various Hellenistic philosophers, Paul is like some of them in that he attributes his accomplishments to God. In Phil 4:13 he concludes his catalogue with the claims of power and that power's origin: "I can do all things in him who gives me strength." Likewise in Rom 8:37, the calamities over which he triumphs are "through him who loved us." The hardships and forces that are powerless to separate him from "the love of Christ" and "the love of God in Christ" (Rom 8:35,39) are thus, more fundamentally, catalogues of the evils over which divine love triumphs and against which the divine provides protection. As such, they are comparable to those catalogues that celebrate the power of philosophy in regard to suffering. What Seneca affirms of philosophy, Paul thus affirms of God.

It is in 2 Cor 4, however, that Paul points to the appearance of divine power in his human frailty. As a consequence, the catalogue of his hardships serves both to show the power of God at work in him and to demonstrate at the same time his own weakness (cf. also 2 Cor 11:30; 12:10). His serenity and endurance are thus the work of God, and, for this reason his boasting of his hardships in 2 Corinthians is "boasting of the Lord" (1 Cor 1:31). His self-praise places him in the third of the three levels of perception distinguished in chapter three, viz., the religious level. He stands in radical contrast to those of the first level who saw in their triumph the demonstration of their own power and thus boasted of their victory as their own achievement.

Paul's depiction of himself in 2 Corinthians in terms typically used to describe the ideal philosopher and his extensive use, in that connection, of *peristasis* catalogues as part of his self-commendation, are grounded in the fact that he is concerned with showing the Corinthians that he is a person of integrity in whom they may have both confidence and pride. Since *peristasis* catalogues were a traditional means of demonstrating virtue, it was natural that he should choose to employ them for this purpose. Furthermore, since the *peristasis* catalogue was an established device for distinguishing true philosophers from false ones, it provided him with a tool in his task of establishing himself as a true apostle and distancing himself from the superapostles. His situation in 2 Corinthians is in fact very similar to that envisioned for the "foolish" righteous sufferer (6:8c; 11–12). He is perceived as the devious one, while his opponents put on the guise (μετασχηματίζονται) of being *diakonoi* of righteousness (11:13–15). Since his catalogues depict his serene (4:8–9) endurance (6:4–5) of a truly excessive number of hardships (11:23–28), they establish that it is he who is the truly righteous one, armed with the weapons of righteousness (6:7).

While Paul asserts in one of his catalogues that his joy is constant (6:10), it is clear from his other catalogues and his letters as a whole that the experience of grief was not foreign to him. By no means was he absolutely unperturbed by adversity, for, as 4:8–9 make clear, his serenity was only relative. Indeed, one gets the distinct impression that his greatest hardships were provided by the churches to whose care he devoted himself, and that his experience of grief was largely the product of his involvement with them. They were his Achilles' heel, for as long as his relationship with his churches was good and the churches themselves were at peace, all was well. When there was strife within a church or he himself was at odds with his "children," then his "fears within" made his "fightings without" all the more fierce (7:5). In any case, he not only depicts himself by means of *peristasis* catalogues and in terms typically used to describe the ideal wise man, but he also does the same in depicting the Corinthians. We have seen this to be the case in 1 Cor 4, but this use of *sophos*-imagery occurs also in 2 Cor 11:19–20. In fact, 11:20 contains a catalogue of the Corinthians' sufferings in which their endurance is ironically presented as that of the φρόνιμοι (11:19). As in 1 Cor 4, then, Paul once again resorts to irony in the depiction of the Corinthians as "wise men." The catalogue here serves the dual function of castigating his opponents by describing their abusive acts and of shaming the Corinthians by mock praise. This vilification of the opponents by means of a *peristasis* catalogue recalls the use of catalogues to describe Fortune's ruthless assaults. Again, Paul's use of an ironic *peristasis* catalogue is not unique, for it recalls the speech of Ananus in book four of Josephus' *Bellum Judaicum,* where the "endurance" of atrocities is likewise mocked (4.165,171,174).

In conclusion, Paul's use of *sophos*-imagery and *peristasis* catalogues clearly shows that he is familiar with the traditions about the sage and the means used to depict him. In his Corinthian correspondence he adopts and adapts these traditions for his own purposes and uses them in the ways that have been indicated. Such adoption and adaption of these traditions are not unique to Paul but occur as well in other authors (cf., for example, Philo and *T. 12 Patr.*). But Paul's own use of these traditions and the catalogues associated with them is highly creative. It is informed by OT traditions about the afflicted righteous man and suffering prophet, and it is transformed by his fixation on the cross of Christ. His *peristasis* catalogues thus represent the convergence of several traditions and reflect his own personal experiences of suffering and divine power. They take us to the center of Paul's understanding of God and his own self-understanding, yet anchor him in the culture and conventions of his time.

This investigation is now complete. It is obvious that many questions about the *peristasis* catalogue remain. Only one of the various kinds of catalogues has been treated at length, and a detailed analysis of only three of Paul's catalogues has been attempted. Much work still needs to be done, not only on Paul's other catalogues but also on the *peristasis* catalogues and catalogues of righteous sufferers in Jewish and other early Christian documents (cf. esp. 4 Macc 16:20–21; Heb 11:35–38; *1 Clem.* 5.3–7; 45.4; *Diogn.* 5.12–15; 7.7–9; *Acts John* 103; *Acts Thom.* 145; and *Ap. Const.* 2.56.3). In addition, the toils and tribulations of various individuals need examination, not only those in the Greek tradition but also those in the Jewish tradition, such as the trials of Abraham (*'Abot* 5.2; *'Abot R. Nat.* 33; *Pirqe R. El.* 26–31). The use of *peristasis* catalogues in particular encomia likewise merits examination, as does the use of catalogues of hardships to persuade an audience or to evoke sympathy. It is hoped that the present treatment will prompt such investigations, so that our understanding of this ancient literary phenomenon can be further sharpened.

Select Bibliography

Texts and Translations

I. Lexica and Tools

Bauer, Walter. *A Greek-English Lexicon of the New Testament and Other Early Christian Literature.* Translated, adapted, revised, and augmented by W. F. Arndt, F. W. Gingrich, & F. W. Danker. 2d ed.; Chicago: University Press, 1979.

Blass, F. and A. Debrunner. *A Greek Grammar of the New Testament and Other Early Christian Literature.* Trans./rev. R. W. Funk. Chicago: University Press, 1961.

Glare, P. G. W., ed. *Oxford Latin Dictionary.* Oxford: Clarendon, 1982.

van Herwerden, H. *Lexicon Graecum suppletorium et dialecticum.* Leiden: Sijthoff, 1910.

Jastrow, M. *A Dictionary of the Targumim, The Talmud Babli and Yerushalmi, and the Midrashic Literature.* 2 vols.; New York: Padres, 1950.

Lampe, G. W. H., ed. *A Patristic Greek Lexicon.* Oxford: Clarendon, 1961.

Lewis, C. T. and C. Short. *A New Latin Dictionary.* New York: American, 1907.

Liddell, H. G. and R. Scott. *A Greek-English Lexicon.* Rev. H. S. Jones & R. McKenzie. 9th ed.; Oxford: Clarendon, 1940.

Mauersberger, Arno, ed. *Polybios-Lexicon.* Berlin: Akademie, 1956– .

Moule, C. F. D. *An Idiom-Book of New Testament Greek.* 2d ed.; Cambridge: University, 1959.

Moulton, J. H., W. F. Howard and N. Turner. *A Grammar of New Testament Greek.* 4 vols.; Edinburgh: T. & T. Clark, 1906–76.

Rengstorf, K. H., ed. *A Complete Concordance to Flavius Josephus.* 3 vols.; Leiden: Brill, 1973–79.

Robertson, A. T. *A Grammar of the Greek New Testament in the Light of Historical Research.* 2d ed.; New York: Doran, 1915.

—— *Word Pictures in the New Testament.* 1930–33; 6 vols.; reprinted, Grand Rapids: Baker, 1980.

Schweighäuser, J., ed. *Lexicon Polybianum.* Oxford: Baxter, 1822.

Smyth, H. W. and G. M. Messing. *Greek Grammar.* Harvard: Cambridge, 1956.

Souter, Alexander. *A Glossary of Later Latin to 600 A.D.* Oxford: Clarendon, 1949.

Winer, G. B. and G. Lünemann. *A Grammar of the Idiom of the New Testament.* 7th ed.; Andover: Draper, 1893.

II. Collected Texts and Translations

Adler, Ada, ed. *Suidae Lexicon.* 4 vols.; Leipzig: Teubner, 1928–35.

von Arnim, H., ed. *Stoicorum Veterum Fragmenta.* 4 vols.; Leipzig: Teubner, 1921–24.

Charles, R. H., ed. *The Apocrypha and Pseudepigrapha of the Old Testament.* 2 vols.; Oxford: Clarendon, 1913.

Diels, H. and W. Kranz, eds. *Die Fragmente der Vorsokratiker.* 3 vols.; 7th ed.; Berlin: Weidman, 1954.

Dittenberger, W., ed. *Orientis Graeci Inscriptiones Selectae.* 2 vols.; Leipzig: Hirzel, 1903–05.

—— *Sylloge Inscriptionum Graecarum.* 4 vols.; 4th ed.; Leipzig: Hirzel, 1915–24.

Edmonds, J. M., ed./trans. *The Fragments of Attic Comedy.* 3 vols.; Leiden: Brill, 1957–61.

——. *Greek Elegy and Iambus.* 2 vols.; LCL; Cambridge: Harvard, 1931.

—— *Lyra Graeca.* 3 vols.; LCL; Cambridge: Harvard, 1922–27.

Halm, Karl, ed. *Rhetores Latini Minores.* Leipzig: Teubner, 1863.

Heiberg, I. L. et al., eds. *Corpus Medicorum Graecorum.* Leipzig/Berlin: Teubner, 1908– .

Kern, O., ed. *Orphicorum fragmenta.* Berlin: Weidmann, 1922.

Kock. T., ed. *Comicorum Atticorum Fragmenta.* 3 vols.; Leipzig: Teubner, 1880–88.

Kühn, K. G., ed. *Medicorum Graecorum Opera.* 20 vols.; Leipzig: Cnoblochii, 1821–33.

Lake, Kirsopp, trans. *The Apostolic Fathers.* 2 vols.; LCL; Cambridge: Harvard, 1912–13.

Malherbe, Abraham J. "Ancient Epistolary Theorists." *Ohio Journal of Religious Studies* 5 (1977) 3–77.

—— *The Cynic Epistles: A Study Edition.* SBLSBS 12; Missoula: Scholars, 1977.

Nauck, A. and B. Snell, eds. *Tragicorum Graecorum Fragmenta.* Hildesheim: G. Olms, 1964.

Roberts, A. and J. Donaldson, eds. *The Ante-Nicene Fathers.* 10 vols.; repr., Grand Rapids: Eerdmans, 1978.

Schaff, P., ed. *A Select Library of the Nicene and Post-Nicene Fathers of the Christian Church.* First Series; 14 vols.; repr., Grand Rapids; Eerdmans, 1978–79.

—— and H. Wace, eds. *A Select Library of the Nicene and Post-Nicene Fathers of the Christian Church.* Second Series; 14 vols.; repr., Grand Rapids: Eerdmans, 1979.

Spengel, L., ed. *Rhetores Graeci.* 3 vols.; Leipzig: Teubner, 1856–94.

Walz, C., ed. *Rhetores Graeci.* 9 vols.; Tübingen: Cotta, 1832–36.

Warmington, E. H., trans. *Remains of Old Latin.* 4 vols.; LCL; Cambridge: Harvard, 1935–40.

III. Major and Other Sources Cited from Multiple Editions, and/or Translations

Aeschylus:

Aeschylus. Trans. H. W. Smyth. 2 vols.; LCL; Cambridge: Harvard, 1922–26, 1957.

Aeschylus: Agamemnon. Ed. J. D. Denniston and D. Page. Oxford: Clarendon, 1957.

Apuleius:

The Apologia and Florida of Apuleius of Madaura. Trans. H. E. Butler. Oxford: Clarendon, 1909.

Apuleius: The Golden Ass. Trans. W. Adlington and rev. by S. Gaselee. LCL; Cambridge: Harvard, 1915.

The Transformations of Lucius Otherwise Known as the Golden Ass. Trans. Robert Graves. New York: Farrar, Straus & Giroux, 1973.

Aristotle:

Aristotle. Trans. H. P. Cooke, et al. 23 vols.; LCL; Cambridge: Harvard, 1926–70.

Aristotle, Nicomachean Ethics. Trans. Martin Ostwald. Indianapolis/New York: Bobbs-Merrill, 1962.

The Nicomachean Ethics of Aristotle. Trans. R. W. Browne. Bohn's Classical Library; London: Bohn, 1850.

The Rhetoric of Aristotle. Trans. Lane Cooper. New York: Appleton-Century-Crofts, 1960.

Augustus:

Res Gestae Divi Augusti. Ed. P. A. Brunt & J. M. Moore. Oxford: University Press, 1967.

Res Gestae Divi Augusti. Ed. Jean Gagé. 3d ed.; Paris: Les Belles Lettres, 1977.

Chariton:

Charitonis Aphrodisiensis. Ed. W. E. Blake. Oxford: Clarendon, 1938.
Chariton's Chaereas and Callirhoe. Trans. W. E. Blake. Ann Arbor: University of Michigan Press, 1939.

Cicero:

Cicero. Trans. H. Caplan, et al. 28 vols.; LCL; Cambridge: Harvard, 1912–77.
On the Commonwealth: Marcus Tullius Cicero. Trans. G. H. Sabine and S. B. Smith. Columbus: Ohio State University, 1929.

Dio Chrysostom:

Dio Chrysostom. Trans. J. W. Cohoon and H. L. Crosby. 5 vols.; LCL; Cambridge: Harvard, 1932–51.
Dio von Prusa. Ed. H. von Arnim. Leipzig: Teubner, 1893–96.

Epictetus:

Epicteti dissertationes ab Arriani digestae. Ed. H. Schenkl. 2d ed.; Leipzig: Teubner, 1916.
Epictetus. Trans. W. A. Oldfather. 2 vols.; LCL; Cambridge: Harvard, 1925–28.

Epicurus:

Epicurea. Ed. H. Usener. Leipzig: Teubner, 1887.
Epicuro. Ed. E. Bignone. Studia Philologica 4; ed. anast.; Rome: "L'Erma" di Bretschneider, 1964.
Epicurus: The Extant Remains. Ed. Cyril Bailey. Oxford: Clarendon, 1926.

Euripides:

Euripides. Trans. A. S. Way. 4 vols.; LCL; Cambridge: Harvard, 1912.
Euripides: Medea. Ed. D. L. Page. Oxford: Clarendon, 1938.

Hesiod, Homer and the Homeric Hymns:

Hesiod, The Homeric Hymns, and Homerica. Trans. H. G. Evelyn-White. LCL 57; 1914; rev. ed.; London: Heinemann, 1936.
Homer: The Iliad. Trans. A. T. Murray. 2 vols.; LCL; Cambridge: Harvard, 1924–25.
Homer: The Odyssey. Trans. A. T. Murray. 2 vols.; LCL; Cambridge: Harvard, 1919.
The Homeric Hymn to Demeter. Ed. N. J. Richardson. Oxford: Clarendon, 1974.

Horace:

Horace: Odes and Epodes. Ed. C. E. Bennett and rev. by J. C. Rolfe. Boston: Allyn and Bacon, 1957.

Horace: Satires, Epistles, Ars Poetica. Trans. H. R. Fairclough. LCL 194; Cambridge: Harvard, 1926.

Marcus Aurelius:

The Communings with Himself of Marcus Aurelius Antoninus. Trans. C. R. Haines. LCL 58; rev. ed.; Cambridge: Harvard, 1930.

Marci Aurelii Antonini. Ad se ipsum libri XII. Ed. J. Dalfen. Leipzig: Teubner, 1979.

The Meditations of the Emperor Marcus Antoninus. Ed./trans. A. S. L. Farquharson. 2 vols.; Oxford: Clarendon, 1944.

Maximus of Tyre:

The Dissertations of Maximus Tyrius. Trans. Thomas Taylor. 2 vols.; London: C. Whittingham, 1804.

Maximus Tyrius philosophumena. Ed. H. Hobein. Leipzig: Teubner, 1910.

Musonius Rufus:

C. Musonii Rufi reliquiae. Ed. O. Hense. Leipzig; Teubner, 1905.

Musonius Rufus: "The Roman Socrates." Ed./trans. C. Lutz. Yale Classical Studies 10; New Haven: Yale, 1947.

Ovid:

Ovid. Trans. G. P. Goold, et al. 6 vols.; LCL; Cambridge: Harvard, 1916–79.

P. Ovidius Naso, Tristia. Ed./trans. Georg Luck. 2 vols.; Heidelberg: C. Winter, 1967–77.

Publii Ovidi Nasonis Tristium Liber IV. Ed. T. J. De Jonge. Groningen: De Waal, 1951.

Philo:

Philo. Trans. F. H. Colson, G. H. Whitaker, and R. Marcus. 12 vols.; LCL; Cambridge: Harvard, 1929–62.

Philonis Alexandrini opera quae supersunt. Ed. L. Cohn and P. Wendland. 7 vols.; Berlin: G. Reimer, 1896–1930.

Plato and Platonica:

Plato. Trans. H. N. Fowler, P. Shorey, et al. 12 vols.; LCL; Cambridge: Harvard, 1914–35.

The Republic of Plato. Trans. F. M. Cornford. New York/London: Oxford, 1966.
The Works of Plato. Trans. Henry Cary. Bohn's Classical Library 6; London: Bell, 1881.

Plutarch:

Plutarchi Moralia. Ed. M. Pohlenz, C. Hubert, H. Drexler, et al. 5 vols.; Leipzig: Teubner, 1925–67.
Plutarch's Lives. Trans. B. Perrin. 11 vols.; LCL; Cambridge: Harvard, 1914–26.
Plutarch's Moralia. Trans. F. C. Babbitt, W. C. Helmbold, H. Cherniss, et al. 16 vols.; LCL; Cambridge: Harvard, 1927–69.

Proclus:

The Commentaries of Proclus on the Timaeus of Plato. Trans. T. Taylor. 2 vols.; London: the translator, 1820.
Proclus, Commentaire sur le Timée. Trans. A. J. Festugière. 5 vols.; Paris: Vrin, 1966–68.

Seneca:

L. Annaei Senecae, De Constantia Sapientis. Ed./trans. Francesca Minissale. Messina: EDAS, 1977.
L. Annaei Senecae opera quae supersunt. Ed. E. Hermes, O. Hense, et al. 4 vols.; Leipzig: Teubner, 1898–1907.
L. Anneo Seneca, La Provvidenza. Ed. E. Andreoni. Rome: Edizioni dell' Ateneo, 1971.
Select Letters of Seneca. Ed. W. C. Summers. London: Macmillan, 1910.
Seneca: Apocolocyntosis. Trans. E. H. Warmington. LCL 15; Cambridge: Harvard, 1969.
Seneca: Epistulae Morales. Trans. R. M. Gummere. 3 vols.; LCL; Cambridge: Harvard, 1917–25.
Seneca: Moral Essays. Trans. J. W. Basore. 3 vols.; LCL; Cambridge: Harvard, 1928–35.
Seneca: Naturales Quaestiones. Trans. T. H. Corcoran. 2 vols.; LCL; Cambridge: Harvard, 1971–72.
Seneca: Tragedies. Trans. F. J. Miller. 2 vols.; LCL; Cambridge: Harvard, 1917.
Sénèque, De Constantia Sapientis, Commentaire. Ed./trans. Pierre Grimal. Paris: Société d' Edition "Les Belles Lettres," 1953.

Teles:

Teles (The Cynic Teacher). Ed./trans. Edward N. O'Neil. SBLTT 11; Missoula: Scholars, 1977.
Teletis reliquiae. Ed. O. Hense. 2d ed.; Tübingen: Mohr, 1909.

IV. Other Sources Frequently Cited or Quoted

Achilles Tatius. Trans. S. Gaselee. LCL 45; Cambridge: Harvard, 1917.

Aristides. Ed. W. Dindorf. 3 vols.; Leipzig: Reimer, 1829; reprinted, Hildesheim: Olms, 1964.

Athenaeus: The Deipnosophists. Trans. C. B. Gulick. 7 vols.; LCL; Cambridge: Harvard, 1927–41.

The Babylonian Talmud. Ed. I. Epstein. 18 vols.; London: Soncino, 1935–48.

Bacchylides: The Poems and Fragments. Ed./trans. R. C. Jebb. Cambridge: University Press, 1905; reprinted, Hildesheim: Olms, 1967.

Cyril of Jerusalem and Nemesius of Emesa. Trans. W. Telfer. LCC 4; Philadelphia: Westminister, 1955.

Demosthenes. Trans. J. H. Vince, et al. 7 vols.; LCL; Cambridge: Harvard, 1926–49.

Diogenes Laertius: Lives of Eminent Philosophers. Trans. R. D. Hicks. 2 vols.; LCL; Cambridge: Harvard, 1925–38.

Fronto: Correspondence. Trans. C. R. Haines. 2 vols.; LCL; Cambridge: Harvard, 1919–20.

Gellius: Attic Nights. Trans. John C. Rolfe. 3 vols.; LCL; Cambridge: Harvard, 1927.

Herodotus. Trans. A. D. Godley. 4 vols.; LCL; Cambridge: Harvard, 1920–24.

Hippocrates. Trans. W. H. S. Jones and E. T. Withington. 4 vols.; LCL; Cambridge: Harvard, 1923–31.

Isocrates. Trans. G. Norlin and La Rue Van Hook. 3 vols.; LCL; Cambridge: Harvard, 1928–45.

The Homilies of S. John Chrysostom on the Second Epistle of St. Paul the Apostle to the Corinthians. Trans. J. Ashworth. Library of Fathers 27; Oxford: J. H. Parker, 1848.

Saint John of Damascus: Writings. Trans. F. H. Chase, Jr. FC 37; New York: Fathers of the Church, 1958.

Joseph et Aséneth. Ed. M. Philonenko. Leiden: Brill, 1968.

Josephus. Trans. H. St. J. Thackeray, et al. 9 vols.; LCL; Cambridge: Harvard, 1926–65.

Julian. Trans. W. C. Wright. 3 vols.; LCL; Cambridge: Harvard, 1913–23.

Juvenal and Persius. Trans. G. G. Ramsay. LCL 91; London: Heinemann, 1918.

Livy. Trans. B. O. Foster, et al. 14 vols.; LCL; Cambridge: Harvard, 1919–67.

"Longinus" on the Sublime. Ed. D. A. Russell. Oxford: Clarendon, 1964.

Lucan: The Civil War (Pharsalia). Trans. J. D. Duff. LCL 220; Cambridge: Harvard, 1928.

Lucian. Trans. A. M. Harmon, et al. 8 vols.; LCL; Cambridge: Harvard, 1913–67.

Lucretius: De Rerum Natura. Trans. W. H. D. Rouse and rev. by M. E. Smith. LCL 181; Cambridge: Harvard, 1975.

Mekilta de-Rabbi Ishmael. Ed./trans. J. L. Lauterbach. 3 vols.; Philadelphia: Jewish Publication Society, 1933–35.

Menander Rhetor. Ed./trans. D. A. Russell and N. G. Wilson. Oxford: Clarendon, 1981.

Metrodori Epicurei fragmenta. Ed. A. Körte. Leipzig: Teubner, 1890.

Midrash Rabbah. Ed. H. Freedman and M. Simon. 10 vols.; 3d ed.; London/New York: Soncino, 1983.

The Mishnah. Trans. H. Danby. London: Oxford, 1933.

Novum Testamentum Graece. 26th ed. rev. by K. Aland, et al. Stuttgart: Deutsche Bibelstiftung, 1979.

Petronius. Trans. M. Heseltine. LCL 15; Cambridge: Harvard, 1969.

Philostratus and Eunapius. Trans. W. C. Wright. LCL 134; Cambridge: Harvard, 1968.

Philostratus: The Life of Apollonius of Tyana. Trans. F. C. Coneybeare. 2 vols.; LCL; Cambridge: Harvard, 1912.

The New Phrynichus. Ed. W. G. Rutherford. London: Macmillan, 1881.

Pindar. Trans. J. E. Sandys. LCL 56; Cambridge: Harvard, 1915.

Pliny The Younger: Letter and Panegyricus. Trans. B. Radice. 2 vols.; LCL; Harvard: Cambridge, 1969.

Plotinus. Trans. A. H. Armstrong. 3 vols.; LCL; Cambridge: Harvard, 1966–67.

Polybius: The Histories. Trans. W. R. Paton. 6 vols.; LCL; Cambridge: Harvard, 1922–27.

Quintilian: Institutio Oratoria. Trans. H. E. Butler. 4 vols.; LCL; Cambridge: Harvard, 1920–22.

Sextus Empiricus. Trans. R. G. Bury. 4 vols.; LCL; Cambridge: Harvard, 1933–49.

Sophocles. Trans. F. Storr. 2 vols.; LCL; Cambridge: Harvard, 1912–13.

Ioannis Stobaei Anthologium. Ed. C. Wachsmuth and O. Hense. 5 vols.; Berlin: Weidmann, 1884–1912.

Suetonius. Trans. J. C. Rolfe. 2 vols.; LCL; Cambridge: Harvard, 1914.

The Tabula of Cebes. Trans. J. T. Fitzgerald and L. M. White. SBLTT 24; Chico: Scholars, 1983.

Tacitus. Trans. R. M. Ogilvie, et al. 5 vols.; LCL; Cambridge: Harvard, 1925–70.

The Testaments of the Twelve Patriarchs. Ed. M. De Jonge. Leiden: Brill, 1978.

Thucydides: History of the Peloponnesian War. Trans. C. F. Smith. 4 vols.; LCL; Cambridge: Harvard, 1919–23.

Xenophon. Trans. C. L. Brownson, E. C. Marchant, et al. 7 vols.; LCL; Cambridge: Harvard, 1914–68.

Other Works

Albrektson, Bertil. *History and the Gods.* ConB: OT Series 1; Lund: Gleerup, 1967.

Alford, H. *The Greek New Testament.* 4 vols.; rev. ed.; 1871–75; repr., Grand Rapids: Baker, 1980.

Almquist, Helge. *Plutarch und das Neue Testament.* ASNU 15; Uppsala: Appelberg, 1946.

Allo, E.-B. *Saint Paul, Première Épître aux Corinthiens.* EBib; 2d ed.; Paris: Lecoffre-Gabalda, 1956.

—— *Saint Paul, Seconde Épître aux Corinthiens.* EBib; 2d ed.; Paris: Lecoffre-Gabalda, 1937.

Amand, David. *Fatalisme et liberté dans l'antiquité grecque.* Louvan: 1945; reprinted, Amsterdam: Hakkert, 1973.

Armstrong, A. H. *An Introduction to Ancient Philosophy.* 3d ed.; Boston: Beacon, 1967.

von Arnim, H. "Entstehung und Anordnung der Schriftensammulung Dios von Prusa." *Hermes* 26 (1891) 366–407.

—— *Leben und Werke des Dio von Prusa.* Berlin: Weidmann, 1898.

Arnold, E. V. *Roman Stoicism.* Cambridge: University Press, 1911.

Austin, J. N. H. "Catalogues and the Catalogue of Ships in the *Iliad.*" Ph.D Diss., Berkeley, 1965.

Bachmann, Philipp. *Der zweite Brief des Paulus an die Korinther.* Zahn's Kommentar zum Neuen Testament 8; lst & 2d ed.; Leipzig: Deichert, 1909.

Balch, David L. "1 Cor 7:32–35 and Stoic Debates about Marriage, Anxiety, and Distraction." *JBL* 102 (1983) 429–39.

Baldry, H. C. "Zeno's Ideal State." *JHS* 79 (1959) 3–25.

Barré, M. L. "Paul as 'Eschatologic Person': A New Look at 2 Cor 11:29." *CBQ* 37 (1975) 500–26.

—— "Qumran and the 'Weakness' of Paul." *CBQ* 42 (1980) 216–27.

Barrett, C. K. *A Commentary on The First Epistle to the Corinthians.* HNTC; New York: Harper & Row, 1968.

—— *A Commentary on The Second Epistle to the Corinthians.* HNTC; New York: Harper & Row, 1973.

Barrow, R. H. *The Romans.* 1949; repr., Baltimore: Penguin, 1965.

Barth, Paul. *Die Stoa.* 3d ed.; Stuttgart: Frommann, 1922.

Bauer, Bruno. *Christus und die Caesaren.* Berlin: Grosser, 1877.

Baum, Horst. *Mut zum Schwachsein—in Christi Kraft.* Studia Instituti Missiologici Societatis Verbi Divini 17; St. Augustin: Steyler, 1977.

Baumert, Norbert. *Täglich Sterben und Auferstehen.* SANT 34; München: Kösel-Verlag 1973.

Benz, Ernst. "Der gekreuzigte Gerechte bei Plato, im Neuen Testament und in der alten Kirche." *Akademie der Wissenschaften und der Literatur.* Abhandl. d. Geistes—u. Sozial wiss. Klasse; Mainz: Verlag d. Akademie d. Wissensch. u.d. Lit., 1950. 1029–74.

Berger, Klaus. *Die Griechische Daniel-Diegese.* SPB 27; Leiden: Brill, 1976.

Bernard, J. "Lorsque je suis faible, c'est alors que je suis fort: 2 Cor 12,7–10." *AsSeign* 45 (1974) 34–39.

Betz, Hans Dieter. *Der Apostel Paulus und die sokratische Tradition.* BHT 45; Tübingen: Mohr, 1972.

—— "Eine Christus-Aretalogie bei Paulus (2 Kor 12,7–10)." *ZTK* 66 (1969) 288–305.

—— "De Laude Ipsius (Moralia 539A–547F)." *Plutarch's Ethical Writings and Early Christian Literature.* Ed. H. D. Betz; Studia ad Corpus Hellenisticum Novi Tetamenti 4; Leiden: Brill, 1978. 367–93.

—— "The Delphic Maxim 'ΓΝΩΘΙ ΣΑΥΤΟΝ' in Hermetic Interpretation." *HTR* 63 (1970) 465–84.

—— *Lukian von Samosata und das Neue Testament.* TU 76; Berlin: Akademie-Verlag, 1961.

Bevan, E. "Hellenistic Popular Philosophy." *The Hellenistic Age.* Ed. J. D. Bury. Cambridge: University Press, 1923. 79–107.

—— *Stoics and Sceptics.* Oxford: Clarendon, 1913.

Bieder, W. "Paulus und seine Gegner in Korinth." *TZ* 17 (1961) 319–33.

Billerbeck, Margarethe. *Epiktet: Von Kynismus.* Leiden: Brill, 1978.

Binder, H. "Die angebliche Krankheit des Paulus." *TZ* 32 (1976) 1–13.

Bjerkelund, C. J. *Parakalô: Form, Funktion und Sinn der paraklô-Sätzen in den paulinischen Briefen.* Oslo: Universitetsforlaget, 1967.

Böhlig, G. *Untersuchungen zum rhetorischen Sprachgebrauch der Byzantier.* Berliner Byzantische Arbeiten 2; Berlin: Akademie-Verlag, 1956.

Boll, Franz. *Aus der Offenbarung Johannis: Hellenistische Studien zum Weltbild der Apokalypse.* Stoicheia 1; Leipzig/Berlin: Teubner, 1914.

Bonhöffer, Adolf. *Epictet und die Stoa.* Stuttgart: F. Enke, 1890.

—— *Epiktet und das Neue Testament.* Religionsgeschichtliche Versuche und Vorarbeiten 10; Giessen: Töpelmann, 1911.

—— "Epiktet und das Neue Testament." *ZNW* 13 (1912) 281–92.

—— *Die Ethik des Stoikers Epictet.* Stuttgart: F. Enke, 1894.

Bonwetsch, N. *Das slavische Henochbuch.* Berlin: Weidmann, 1896.

Bornkamm, Günther. *Paul.* New York: Harper & Row, 1969.

—— "πρέσβυς, κτλ." *TDNT* 6 (1968) 651–83.

Bousset, Wilhelm. "Der erste Brief an die Korinther." *Die Schriften des Neuen Testaments.* Ed. W. Bousset & W. Heitmüller. 3d ed.; 4 vols.; Göttingen: Vandenhoeck & Ruprecht, 1917–18. Vol. 2, 74–167.

—— *Kyrios Christos.* 1st Ger. ed., 1913; Nashville: Abingdon, 1970.

Bouttier, M. "Le tesson: 2 Cor 4,6–11." *AsSeign* 40 (1972) 37–42.

Braun Herbert. "Exegtische Randglossen zum I. Korintherbrief." *Gesammelte Studien zum Neuen Testament und seiner Umwelt.* Tübingen: Mohr, 1962.

Bréhier, É. *The History of Philosophy: The Hellenistic and Roman Age.* Chicago: University Press, 1965.

—— Les idées philosophiques et religieuses de Philon d' Alexandrie. Études de philosophie médiévale 8; 3d ed.; Paris: J. Vrin, 1950.

Bridoux, A. *Le Stoicisme et son influence.* Paris: Librairie philosophique J. Vrin, 1966.

Bruce F. F. *1 and 2 Corinthians.* New Century Bible Commentary; Grand Rapids: Eerdmans, 1971.

Brun, L. "Noch einmal die Schriftnorm I Kor. 4, 6." *TSK* 103 (1931) 453–56.

Bultmann, Rudolf. *Exegetische Probleme des zweiten Korintherbriefes.* SymBU 9; Uppsala: Wretmans Boktryckeri, 1947.

—— "Neueste Paulusforschung." *TRu,* N.F. 6 (1934) 229–46; 8 (1936) 1–22.

—— *Primitive Christianity.* Cleveland/New York: World, 1956.

—— "Das religiöse Moment in der ethischen Unterweisung des Epiktet und das Neue Testament." *ZNW* 13 (1912) 97–110, 177–91.

—— *Der Stil der paulinischen Predigt und die kynisch-stoische Diatribe.* FRLANT 13; Göttingen: Vandenhoeck & Ruprecht, 1910.

—— *Der zweite Brief an die Korinther.* Ed. E. Dinkler; MeyerK 6; Sonderband; Göttingen: Vandenhoeck & Ruprecht, 1976.

Cagnat, R. "Triumphus." In Daremberg-Saglio, *Dictionnaire des antiquités grecques et romaines* 5 (1912) 487–91.

Cancik, Hildegard. *Untersuchungen zu Senecas epistulae morales.* Spudasmata 18; Hildesheim: Olms, 1976.

Cerfaux, Lucien. "L'antinomie paulinienne de la vie apostolique." *RSR* 39 (1951) 221–35.

Christensen, J. *An Essay on the Unity of Stoic Philosophy.* Copenhagen: Munksgaard, 1962.

Chroust, A. H. "The Meaning of Philosophy in the Hellenistic Roman World." *Thomist* 17 (1954) 196–253.

Clemen, C. *Religionsgeschichtliche Erklärung des Neuen Testaments.* Giessen: Töpelmann/Ricker, 1909; 2d ed., 1924.

Collange, J.-F. *Énigmes de la deuxième épître de Paul aux Corinthiens.* SNTSMS 18; Cambridge: University, 1972.

Collins, J. N. "Georgi's 'Envoys' in 2 Cor 11:23." *JBL* 93 (1974) 88–96.

Colson, F. H. "Μετεσχημάτισα: I Cor. IV.6." *JTS* 17 (1916) 379–84.

Conzelmann, Hans. *1 Corinthians.* Hermeneia; Philadelphia: Fortress, 1975.

Craig, C. T. "The First Epistle to the Corinthians." *IB* 10 (1953) 3–262.

Crotty, Kevin. *Song and Action: The Victory Odes of Pindar.* Baltimore/London: Johns Hopkins, 1982.

Dahl, Nils Alstrup. "Benediction and Congratulation." Unpublished Private Paper, n.d.

—— "A Fragment and Its Context: 2 Corinthians 6:14–7:1." *Studies in Paul.* Minneapolis: Augsburg, 1977. 62–69.

—— "The Neglected Factor in New Testament Theology." *Reflection* 73 (1975) 5–8.

—— "Paul and the Church at Corinth according to 1 Corinthians 1:10–4:21." *Studies in Paul.* Minneapolis: Augsburg, 1977. 40–61.

—— "Paul's Letter to the Galatians: Epistolary Genre, Content, and Structure." Unpublished SBL Paul Seminar Paper, 1973.

Dalfen, J. "Formgeschichtliche Untersuchungen zu den Selbstbetrachtungen Marc Aurels." Ph.D. Diss., Ludwig-Maximilians-Universität zu München, 1967.

Daniélou, Jean. *Philon d'Alexandrie.* Paris: A. Fayard, 1958.

Daube, David. "Paul a Hellenistic Schoolmaster?" *Studies in Rationalism, Judaism and Universalism.* L. Roth Festschrift; ed. R. Loewe; London: Routledge and Kegan Paul, 1966. 67–71.

Deissmann, Adolf. *Paul: A Study in Social and Religious History.* 1st Ger. ed., 1911; 2d ed.; London: Hodder & Stoughton, 1926.

Deissner, Kurt. *Das Idealbild des stoischen Weisen.* Greifswalder Universitätsreden 24; Greifswald: Bamberg, 1930.

—— *Paulus und Seneca.* BFCT 21.2; Güttersloh: Bertelsmann, 1917.

—— "Das Sendungsbewusstsein der Urchristenheit." *ZST* 7 (1930) 772–90.

De Lacy, P. H. "The Four Stoic *Personae.*" *ICS* 2 (1977) 163–72.

Delling, Gerhard. "θριαμβεύω." *TDNT* 3 (1965) 159–60.

Denney, James. *The Second Epistle to the Corinthians.* The Expositors' Bible; New York: Hodder & Stoughton, 1894.

Dibelius, Martin. *A Fresh Approach to the New Testament and Early Christian Literature.* New York: Scribners, 1936.

—— "Zur Formgeschichte des Neuen Testaments (ausserhalb der Evangelien)." *TRu,* N.F. 3 (1931) 207–42.

Dihle, Albrecht. *Die goldene Regel: Eine Einführung in die Geschichte der antiken und frühchristlichen Vulgärethik.* Göttingen: Vandenhoeck & Ruprecht, 1962.

—— *The Theory of Will in Classical Antiquity.* Sather Classical Lectures 48; Berkeley: University of California, 1982.

Dill, Samuel. *Roman Society From Nero to Marcus Aurelius.* 1904; repr., Cleveland/New York: World, 1956.

Dion, H.-M. "Le genre littéraire sumérien de l' 'hymne à soi-même' et quelques passages du Deutéro-Isaïe." *RB* 74 (1967) 215–34.

Dodd, C. H. *The Bible and the Greeks.* London: Hodder & Stoughton, 1935.

Donlan, W. "Simonides, Fr. 4D and *P.Oxy.* 2432." *TAPhA* 100 (1969) 71–95.

Dressler, H. *The Usage of* Ἀσκέω *and its Cognates in Greek Documents to 100 A.D.* Washington, D.C.: The Catholic Univ. of America Press, 1947.

Dudley, D. R. *A History of Cynicism.* 1937; reprinted, Hildesheim: Olms, 1967.

Dumézil, Georges. *Servius et la Fortune: Essai sur la fonction sociale de louange et de blâme sur les éléments indo-européens du cens romain.* Paris: Gallimard, 1943.

Dupont, Jacques. ΣΥΝ ΧΡΙΣΤΩΙ: *L'union avec le Christ suivant Saint Paul.* Bruges, Belgium: Abbaye de Saint-André, 1952.

Edelstein, Ludwig. *The Meaning of Stoicism.* Cambridge: Harvard, 1966.

Ehlers, W. "Triumphus." PW, 2d Series, V11A. 1 (1939) 493–511.

Eucken, R. *Geschichte der philosophischen Terminologie.* Leipzig: Veit, 1879.

Fascher Erich. *Der erste Brief des Paulus an die Korinther.* THKNT 7.1; 2d ed.; Berlin: Evangelische Verlagsanstalt, 1980.

Feine, Paul. *Der Apostel Paulus.* BFCT, 2. Reihe, 12; Gütersloh: Bertelsmann, 1927.

—— "Stoizismus und Christentum." *Theologisches Literaturblatt* 26 (1905) 65–69, 73–80, 89–91.

Feldman, L. H. Review of *A Complete Concordance to Flavius Josephus* by K. H. Rengstorf. *JBL* 100 (1981) 151–54.

Festugière, A.-J. *Personal Religion Among the Greeks.* Berkeley/Los Angeles: University of California Press, 1954.

Fiedler, Peter. "Röm 8:31–39 als Brennpunkt paulinischer Frohbotschaft." *ZNW* 68 (1977) 23–34.

Filson, F. V. "The Second Epistle to the Corinthians." *IB* 10 (1953) 263–425.

Findlay, G. G. "St. Paul's First Epistle to the Corinthians." *The Expositor's Greek Testament.* Ed. W. R. Nicoll. 5 vols.; 1897–1910; reprinted, Grand Rapids: Eerdmans, 1980. Vol. 2, 729–953.

Fiore, Benjamin. "The Function of Personal Example in the Socratic and Pastoral Epistles." Ph.D. Diss., Yale, 1982.

Fischel, H. A. *Rabbinic Literature and Greco-Roman Philosophy.* SPB 21; Leiden: Brill, 1973.

Fischer, K. M. "Die Bedeutung des Leidens in der Theologie des Paulus." Ph.D. Diss., Humboldt-Universität zu Berlin, 1967.

Fischer, Ulrich. *Eschatologie und Jenseitserwartung im hellenistischen Diasporajudentum.* BZNW 44; Berlin/New York: de Gruyter, 1978.

Fisher, N. R. E. "Hybris and Dishonour: I." *G & R* 23 (1976) 177–93, and "Hybris and Dishonour: II." *G & R* 26 (1979) 32–47.

Fleury, Amédée. *Saint Paul et Sénèque.* 2 vols.; Paris: Landrange, 1853.

Fränkel, Eduard. *Horace.* Oxford: Clarendon, 1957.

Fränkel, H. *Early Greek Poetry and Philosophy.* Oxford: Blackwell, 1975.

Fraikin, Daniel. "Romains 8:31–39. La position des églises de la Gentilité." Ph.D. Diss., Harvard, 1974.

Fridrichsen, Anton. "Peristasenkatalog und Res Gestae." *SO* 8 (1929) 78–82.

—— "Sprachliches und Stilistisches zum Neuen Testament." *Kungliga Humaniska Vetenskapssamfundet I* (Uppsala, *Årsbok,* 1943) 24–36.

—— "Zum Stil des paulinischen Peristasenkatalogs 2 Cor. 11:23ff." *SO* 7 (1928) 25–29.

—— "Zum Thema 'Paulus und die Stoa'. Eine stoische Stilparallele zu 2. Kor. 4,8f." *ConNT* 9 (1944) 27–31.

Friedrich, Gerhard. *Amt und Lebensführung. Eine Auslegung von 2 Kor. 6, 1–10.* Biblische Studien 39; Neukirchen-Vluyn: Verlag des Erziehungsvereins, 1963.

—— "Die Gegner des Paulus im 2. Korintherbrief." *Abraham unser Vater.* O. Michel Festschrift; ed. O. Betz, et al.; Leiden: Brill, 1963. 181–215.

von Fritz, Kurt. "Stoa." *OCD*² (1970) 1015–16.

Gagé, Jean. "Le genre littéraire des '*res gestae*' triomphales et ses thèmes." Summary in *REL* 17 (1939) 33–34.

Ganss, Wilhelm. *Das Bild des Weisen bei Seneca.* Freiburg, Schweiz: Buchdruckerei Gutenberg, Schaan, 1952.

Gardner, Percy. *The Religious Experience of Saint Paul.* Crown Theological Library 34; 2d ed.; London: Williams & Norgate, 1913.

Georgi, Dieter. *Die Gegner des Paulus im 2. Korintherbrief.* WMANT 11; Neukirchen-Vluyn: Neukirchener Verlag, 1964.

—— "Second Letter to the Corinthians." *IDBSup* (1976) 183–86.

Gerhard, G. A. *Phoinix von Kolophon.* Leipzig/Berlin: Teubner, 1909.

—— "Zur Legende vom Kyniker Diogenes." *ARW* 15 (1912) 388–408.

Gerstenberger, E. S. and W. Schrage. *Suffering.* Biblical Encounters Series; Nashville: Abingdon, 1980.

Graff, Jürgen. *Ciceros Selbstdarstellung.* Heidelberg: C. Winter, 1963.

Greene, W. C. *Moira.* Cambridge: Harvard, 1944.

Grimal, P. *Sénèque, sa vie, son oeuvre, sa philosophie.* 2d ed.; Paris: Presses universitaires de France, 1957.

Grube, G. M. A. *A Greek Critic: Demetrius On Style.* Phoenix Supplementary Volumes 4; Toronto: University Press, 1961.

Guillemin, A. "Sénèque directeur d'âmes, I: L'idéal." *REL* 30 (1952) 202–19.

Güttgemanns, Erhardt. *Der leidende Apostel und sein Herr.* FRLANT 90; Göttingen: Vandenhoeck & Ruprecht, 1966.

Hadot, I. *Seneca und die griechisch-römische Tradition der Seelenleitung.* Berlin: de Gruyter, 1969.

Hahn, F. " 'Siehe, jetzt ist der Tag des Heils', Neuschöpfung und Versöhnung nach 2. Kor 5,14–6,2." *EvT* 33 (1973) 244–53.

Halbauer, Otto. *De Diatribis Epicteti.* Leipzig: Robert Norske Bornen, 1911.

Hammond, N. G. L. and H. H. Scullard, eds. *The Oxford Classical Dictionary.* 2d ed.; Oxford: Clarendon, 1970.

Hanson, A. "1 Corinthians 4:13b and Lamentations 3:45." *ExpTim* 93 (1982) 214–15.

Hatch, E. *The Influence of Greek Ideas on Christianity.* 1889; reprinted, New York: Harper & Row, 1957.

Hausleiter, J. Review of *Das Idealbild des stoischen Weisen* by K. Deissner. *DLZ* 36 (1930) 1688–91.

Heinrici, C. F. Georg. *Das erste Sendschreiben des Apostels Paulus an die Korinther.* Berlin: Hertz, 1880.

—— *Hellenismus und Christentum.* Biblische Zeit-und Streitfragen V.8; Gr. Lichterfelde-Berlin: Edwin Runge, 1909.

—— *Kritisch exegetisches Handbuch über den ersten Brief an die Korinther.* MeyerK 5; 7th ed.; Göttingen: Vandenhoeck & Ruprecht, 1888.

—— *Der literarische Charakter der Neutestamentlichen Schriften.* Leipzig: Dürr'sche Buchhandlung, 1908.

—— *Der zweite Brief an die Korinther.* MeyerK 6; 7th ed.; Göttingen: Vandenhoeck & Ruprecht, 1890; 8th ed., 1900.

—— *Das zweite Sendschreiben des Apostels Paulus an die Korinther.* Berlin: Hertz, 1887.

Heinze, R. *De Horatio Bionis imitatore.* Diss., Bonn; Leipzig: Fock, 1899.

Helm, Rudolf. *Lucian und Menipp.* Leipzig/Berlin: Teubner, 1906.

Hengel, Martin. *Crucifixion.* Philadelphia: Fortress, 1977.

Héring, Jean. *The First Epistle of Saint Paul to the Corinthians.* London: Epworth, 1962.

—— *The Second Epistle of Saint Paul to the Corinthians.* London: Epworth, 1967.

Herter, H. "Zur ersten Satire des Horaz." *RhM* 94 (1951) 1–42.

Hicks, E. L. "St. Paul and Hellenism." *Studia Biblica et Ecclesiastica* 4 (1896) 1–14.

Hicks, R. D. *Stoic and Epicurean.* 1910; repr., New York: Russell & Russell, 1962.

Hijmans, B. L., Jr. "ΑΣΚΗΣΙΣ: *Notes on Epictetus' Educational System.* Assen: Van Gorcum, 1959.

Hirzel, Rudolf. *Untersuchungen zu Cicero's philosophischen Schriften.* 3 vols.; Leipzig: Hirzel, 1877–83.

Hock, R. H. "Simon the Shoemaker as an Ideal Cynic." *GRBS* 17 (1976) 41–53.

—— *The Social Context of Paul's Ministry.* Philadelphia: Fortress, 1980.

Hodgson, Robert. "Paul the Apostle and First Century Tribulation Lists." *ZNW* 74 (1983) 59–80.

Höistad, Ragnar. *Cynic Hero and Cynic King.* Lund: C. Blom, 1948.

—— "Eine hellenistische Parallele zu 2. Kor. 6.3ff." *ConNT* 9 (1944) 22–27.

Holl, Karl. "Die schriftstellerische Form des griechischen Heiligenlebens." *Neue Jahrbücher für das klassische Altertum* 29 (1912) 407–27.

Holladay, C. R. *The First Letter of Paul to the Corinthians.* The Living Word Commentary 8; Austin: Sweet, 1979.

Hollander, H. W. *Joseph as an Ethical Model in the Testaments of the Twelve Patriarchs.* SVTP 6; Leiden: Brill, 1981.

Hollmann, Georg. *Urchristentum in Korinth.* Leipzig: Hinrichs, 1903.

Hommel, Hildebrecht. *Schöpfer und Erhalter.* Berlin: Lettner, 1956.

Hooker, M. D. " 'Beyond the Things Which Are Written': An Examination of I Cor. IV.6." *NTS* 10 (1963–64) 127–32.

Howard, W. F. "I Corinthians IV.6 (Exegesis or Emendation?)." *ExpTim* 33 (1921–22) 479–80.

Hughes, P. E. *Paul's Second Epistle to the Corinthians.* NICNT; Grand Rapids: Eerdmans, 1962.

Jervell, Jacob. "Der schwache Charismatiker." *Rechtfertigung.* E. Käsemann Festschrift; ed. J. Friedrich, et al.; Tübingen: Mohr; Göttingen: Vandenhoeck & Ruprecht, 1976. 185–98.

Jones, C. P. *The Roman World of Dio Chrysostom.* Cambridge: Harvard, 1978.

Jones, Maurice. "St. Paul and the Angels." *The Expositor,* Eighth Series, 15 (1918) 356–70, 412–25.

—— "The Style of St. Paul's Preaching." *The Expositor,* Eighth Series, 14 (1917) 241–58, 330–47.

Juhnke, Johannes. *Das Persönlichkeitsideal in der Stoa im Lichte der paulinischen Erlösungslehre.* Greifswalder Theologische Forschungen 5; Greifswald: Bamberg, 1934.

Käsemann, Ernst. *An die Römer.* HNT 8a; 3d rev. ed.; Tübingen: Mohr, 1974.

—— "Erwägungen zum Stichwort 'Versöhnungslehre' im Neuen Testament." *Zeit und Geschichte: Dankesgabe an R. Bultmann zum 80. Geburtstag.* Ed. E. Dinkler, et al. Tübingen: Mohr, 1964. 47–59.

—— *Die Legitimität des Apostels: Eine Untersuchung zu II Korinther 10–13.* Darmstadt: Wissenschaftliche Buchhandlung, 1956. A Reprint from *ZNW* 41 (1942) 33–71.

Kamlah, E. *Die Form der katalogischen Paränese im Neuen Testament.* WUNT 7; Tübingen: Mohr, 1964.

—— "Wie beurteilt Paulus sein Leiden?" *ZNW* 54 (1963) 217–32.

Karris, R. J. "The Function and Sitz im Leben of the Paraenetic Elements in the Pastoral Epistles." Th.D. Diss. Harvard, 1971.

Kim, Chan-Hie. *Form and Structure of the Familiar Greek Letter of Recommendation.* SBLDS 4; Missoula: SBL, 1972.

Kirkwood, G. M. "*Nemean* 7 and the Theme of Vicissitude in Pindar." *Poetry and Poetics from Ancient Greece to the Renaissance.* Ed. G. M. Kirkwood. Cornell Studies in Classical Philology 38; Ithaca/London: Cornell, 1975. 56–90.

Kittel, G. "Θέατρον, κτλ." *TDNT* 3 (1965) 42–43.

Klek, J. *Symbouleutici qui dicitur sermonis historiam criticam per quattuor saecula continuatam.* Rhetorische Studien 8; Paderborn: Schöningh, 1919.

Knopf, R. "Paul and Hellenism." *AJT* 18 (1914) 497–520.

Kornemann, E. *Mausoleum und Tatenbericht des Augustus.* Leipzig: Teubner, 1921.

Kreyher, Johannes. *L. Annaeus Seneca und seine Beziehungen zum Urchristentum.* Berlin: Gaertner, 1887.

Kroll, W. "Rhetorik." *PWSup* 7 (1940) 1039–1138.

Kümmel, W. G. Review of "Der gekreuzigte Gerechte bei Plato, im Neuen Testament und in der Alten Kirche" by E. Benz. *TLZ* 77 (1952) 423–25.

Lang, F. G. *2. Korinther 5,1–10 in der neueren Forschung.* BGBE 16; Tübingen: Mohr, 1973.

Laqueur, R. "Formen geschichtlichen Denkens im alten Orient und Okzident." *Neue Jahrbücher für Wissenschaft und Jugendbildung* 7 (1931) 489–506.

Lausberg, H. *Handbuch der literarischen Rhetorik.* 2 vols.; München: Hueber, 1973.

Legault, A. " 'Beyond the Things Which are Written' (I Cor. IV.6)." *NTS* 18 (1971–72) 227–31.

Leisegang, H. *Pneuma Hagion: Der Ursprung des Geistbegriffs der synoptischen Evangelien aus der griechischen Mystik.* Leipzig: Hinrichs, 1922.

Lenski, R. C. H. *The Interpretation of St. Paul's First and Second Epistles to the Corinthians.* Minneapolis: Augsburg, 1937.

Levy, F. Review of *Symbouleutici* by J. Klek. *BPhW* 40 (1920) 577–87.

Liechtenhan, Rudolf. *Die göttliche Vorherbestimmung bei Paulus und in der Posidonianischen Philosophie.* FRLANT 35; Göttingen: Vandenhoeck & Ruprecht, 1922.

—— "Die Ueberwindung des Leides bei Paulus und in der zeitgenössischen Stoa." *ZTK* 30 (1922) 368–99.

Liefeld, Walter. "The Wandering Preacher as a Social Figure in the Roman Empire." Ph.D. Diss., Columbia University, 1967.

Lietzmann, Hans. *An die Korinther I/II.* Appendix by W. G. Kümmel. HNT 9; 5th ed.; Tübingen: Mohr, 1969.

Lightfoot, John. *A Commentary on the New Testament from the Talmud and Hebraica.* 1658–74 (Latin); 4 vols.; reprint of the 1859 English translation, Grand Rapids: Baker, 1979.

Lightfoot, Joseph B. *Notes on the Epistles of St. Paul.* 1895; reprinted, Grand Rapids: Zondervan, 1957.

—— *St. Paul's Epistle to the Philippians.* London: Macmillan, 1891.

Linton, O. " 'Nicht über das hinaus, was geschrieben steht' (1 Kor. 4,6)." *TSK* 102 (1930) 425–37.

Long, A. A. *Hellenistic Philosophy: Stoics, Epicureans, Sceptics.* New York: Scribners, 1974.

—— ed. *Problems in Stoicism.* London: Athlone, 1971.

Lucius, E. *Die Anfänge des Heiligenkults in der christlichen Kirche.* Tübingen: Mohr, 1904.

Lütgert, W. *Freiheitspredigt und Schwarmgeister in Korinth.* BFCT 12.3; Gütersloh: Bertelsmann, 1908.

Luz, Ulrich. *Das Geschichtsverständnis des Paulus.* BEvT 49; Munich: Kaiser, 1968.

MacDowell, D. M. "*Hybris* in Athens." *G & R* 23 (1976) 14–31.

Malherbe, Abraham J. "Antisthenes and Odysseus, and Paul at War." *HTR* 76 (1983) 143–73.

—— "The Beasts at Ephesus." *JBL* 87 (1968) 71–80.

—— "Cynics." *IDBSup* (1976) 201–03.

—— "Epictetus." *IDBSup* (1976) 271.

—— "1 Thessalonians as a Paraenetic Letter." Paper delivered at the 1972 SBL Seminar on the Form and Function of the Pauline Letters. Incorporated in "Hellenistic Moralists and the New Testament." *Aufstieg und Niedergang der römischen Welt.* Ed. H. Temporini; Berlin: Forthcoming. Vol. 2, Pt. 3.

—— " 'Gentle as a Nurse': The Cynic Background to I Thess ii." *NovT* 12 (1970) 203–17.

—— " 'In Season and Out of Season': 2 Timothy 4:2." Unpublished private paper, n.d.

—— "Pseudo-Heraclitus, Epistle 4: The Divinization of the Wise Man." *JAC* 21 (1978) 42–64.

—— "Self-Definition among Epicureans and Cynics." *Jewish and Christian Self-Definition.* Vol. III: *Self-Definition in the Greco-Roman World.* Ed. B. F. Meyer and E. P. Sanders. Philadelphia: Fortress, 1982. 46–59.

Marót, Károly. *Die Anfänge der griechischen Literatur: Vorfragen.* Budapest: Verlag der ungarischen Akademie der Wissenschaften, 1960.

Marrou, H. I. *A History of Education in Antiquity.* Mentor Books; New York: The New American Library, 1964.

Martha, Constant. *Les Moralistes sous l'empire romain.* 1865; 7th ed.; Paris: Hachette, 1900.

Marti, Berthe. "Seneca's Tragedies. A New Interpretation." *TAPhA* 76 (1945) 216–45.

Massie, J. *Corinthians.* The New-Century Bible; New York: Frowde, 1902.

Mates, Benson. *Stoic Logic.* Berkeley: University of California Press, 1973.

Matthes, D. "Hermagoras von Temnos 1904–1955." *Lustrum* 3 (1958) 58–214.

Maurach, Gregor, ed. *Seneca als Philosoph.* Wege der Forschung 414; Darmstadt: Wissenschaftliche Buchgesellschaft, 1975.

Mealand, D. L. " 'As having nothing, and yet possessing everything': 2 Kor 6:10c." *ZNW* 67 (1976) 277–79.

Meeks, Wayne A. *The First Urban Christians.* New York/London: Yale, 1983.

—— ed. *The Writings of St. Paul.* New York: Norton, 1972.

Merlan, P. "Greek Philosophy From Plato to Plotinus." *The Cambridge History of Later Greek and Early Medieval Philosophy.* Ed. A. H. Armtrong. Cambridge: University Press, 1967. 11–132.

Michaels, J. R. "Apostolic Hardships and Righteous Gentiles." *JBL* 84 (1965) 27–37.

Milik, J. T. *The Books of Enoch.* Oxford: Clarendon, 1976.

Moffatt, James. *The First Epistle of Paul to the Corinthians.* MNTC; London: Hodder & Stoughton, 1938.

Momigliano, Arnaldo. "Monumentum Ancyranum." *OCD*² (1970) 700.

Montée, P. *Le stoïcisme à Rome.* Paris: A. Durand, 1895.

More, P. E. *Hellenistic Philosophies.* Princeton: University Press, 1923.

Morfield, W. R. and R. H. Charles. *The Book of the Secrets of Enoch.* Oxford: Clarendon, 1896.

Morris, Leon. *The First Epistle of Paul to the Corinthians.* Tyndale New Testament Commentaries, NT Series 8; Grand Rapids: Eerdmans, 1958.

Mowinckel, S. "Die vorderasiatischen Königs- und Fürsteninschriften. Eine stilistische Studie." ΕΥΧΑΡΙΣΤΗΡΙΟΝ. *Studien zur Religion und Literatur des Alten und Neuen Testaments Hermann Gunkel . . . dargebracht. . . .* Ed. H. Schmidt. FRLANT N.F. 19; Göttingen: Vandenhoeck & Ruprecht, 1923. 278–322.

Murphy-O'Connor, J. "Truth: Paul and Qumran." *Paul and Qumran.* Ed. J. Murphy-O'Connor. London: G. Chapman, 1968. 179–230.

Murray, Gilbert. *Five Stages of Greek Religion.* 3d ed., 1951; repr., Garden City: Doubleday, 1955.

Nägeli, T. *Der Wortschatz des Apostels Paulus.* Göttingen: Vandenhoeck & Ruprecht, 1905.

Nickelsburg, G. W. E., ed. *Studies on the Testament of Joseph.* SBLSCS 5; Missoula: Scholars, 1975.

Nilsson, M. P. *Geschichte der griechischen Religion.* 2 vols., Munich: Beck, 1967.

Nock, A. D. *St. Paul.* New York: Harper, 1938.

Norden, Eduard. *Die antike Kunstprosa.* 2 vols.; Leipzig: Teubner, 1898; 3d ed. with Nachträge, 1915.

North, Helen. *Sophrosyne: Self-Knowledge and Self-Restraint in Greek Literature.* Cornell Studies in Classical Philology 35; Ithaca: Cornell, 1966.

Oepke, A. "Plato Resp II 5, 361e eine unbewusste Weissagung auf Christi Passion?" *TLZ* 78 (1953) 639–40.

Olson, S. N. "Confidence Expressions in Paul: Epistolary Conventions and the Purpose of 2 Corinthians." Ph.D. Diss., Yale, 1976.

Parry, A. A. *Blameless Aegisthus.* Mnemosyne Suppl. 26; Leiden: Brill, 1973.

Pears, David. "Courage as a Mean." *Essays on Aristotle's Ethics.* Ed. A. O. Rorty. Berkeley: University of California, 1980. 171–87.

Pfitzner, V. C. *Paul and the Agon Motif.* NovTSup 16; Leiden: Brill, 1967.

Plummer, Alfred. *A Critical and Exegetical Commentary on the Second Epistle of St. Paul to the Corinthians.* ICC; Edinburgh: Clark, 1915.

Pohlenz, Max. "Paulus und die Stoa." *ZNW* 42 (1949) 69–104.

—— Review of *De Senecae philosophi dicendi genere Bioneo* by H. Weber. *BPhW* 17 (1897) 1064–66.

—— *Die Stoa.* 2 vols.; 3d ed.; Göttingen: Vandenhoeck & Ruprecht, 1964.

Pratt, N. T., Jr. "The Stoic Base of Senecan Drama." *TAPhA* 79 (1948) 1–11.

Price, E. J. "Paul and Plato." *HibJ* 16 (1917–18) 263–82.

Prümm, Karl. *Diakonia Pneumatos: Der zweite Korintherbrief als Zugang zur apostolischen Botschaft.* 2 vols. in 3 parts; Rome: Herder, 1960–67.

Pucci, Pietro. *Hesiod and the Language of Poetry.* Baltimore: Johns Hopkins, 1977.

Rabbow, Paul. *Seelenführung: Methodik der Exerzitien in der Antike.* München: Kösel, 1954.

Radermacher, L. "Plutarchs Schrift de ipso citra invidiam laudando." *RhM* 52 (1897) 419–24.

Rensberger, David. "2 Corinthians 6:14–7:1—A Fresh Examination." *Studia Biblica et Theologica* 8 (1978) 25–49.

Rich, A. N. M. "The Cynic Conception of AYTAPKEIA." *Mnemosyne,* Ser. IV. 9 (1956) 23–29.

Rissi, Mathias. *Studien zum zweiten Korintherbrief.* ATANT 56; Zürich: Zwingli, 1969.

Rist, J. M. *Stoic Philosophy.* Cambridge: University Press, 1969.

Robertson, A. and A. Plummer. *A Critical and Exegetical Commentary on the First Epistle of St. Paul to the Corinthians.* ICC; 2d ed.; Edinburgh: T. & T. Clark, 1914.

Ross, J. M. "Not Above What is Written: A Note on 1 Cor. 4:6." *ExpTim* 82 (1970–71) 215–17.

Rouwet, J. "De Lijdende Rechtvaardige bij Plato." *Studia Catholica* 30 (1955) 105–18.

Rubinstein, Arie. "Observations on the Slavonic Book of Enoch." *JJS* 13 (1962) 1–21.

Rudberg, Gunnar. *Hellas och Nya Testament.* Stockholm: Uppsala Svensk Kyrk. diak. Bokförlag, 1929.

Rushford, G. M. N. "Triumphus." *A Dictionary of Greek and Roman Antiquities.* Ed. W. Smith, W. Wayte, & G. E. Marindin. 2 vols.; London: J. Murray, 1891. 894–99.

Sambursky, S. *Physics of the Stoics.* London: Routledge and Kegan Paul, 1959.

Sandbach, F. H. *The Stoics.* New York: Norton, 1975.

Sanders, E. P. "R. Akiba's View of Suffering." *JQR* 64 (1973) 332–51.

Sandmel, Samuel. *Philo of Alexandria.* New York: Oxford, 1979.

Schlatter, A. *Die Korinthische Theologie.* BFCT 18.2; Gütersloh: Bertelsmann, 1914.

—— *Paulus der Bote Jesu.* 1934; Stuttgart: Calwer, 1962.

Schmid, W. "Epikur." *RAC* 5 (1962) 681–819.

Schmidt, K. L. "'Ιησοῦς Χριστός κολαφιζόμενος und die 'colaphisation' der Juden." *Aux sources de la tradition chrétienne.* Mélanges M. Goguel; Neuchâtel: Delachaux & Niestle, 1950. 218–27.

—— "Nicht über das hinaus, was geschrieben steht!" *In Memoriam E. Lohmeyer.* Ed. W. Schmauch; Stuttgart: Evangelisches Verlag, 1951. 101–09.

Schmiedel, P. W. "Die Briefe an die Thessalonicher und an die Korinther." *Hand-Commentar zum Neuen Testament.* Ed. H. J. Holtzmann, et al. 2d ed.; Freiberg/Leipzig: Mohr, 1893.

Schmithals, Walter. *Gnosticism in Corinth.* Nashville: Abingdon, 1971.

—— *The Office of Apostle in the Early Church.* Nashville: Abingdon, 1969.

Schmitz, Otto. *Apostolische Seelsorge: Eine Einführung in den zweiten Korintherbrief.* Die urchristliche Botschaft 8; Berlin: Furche-Verlag, 1940.

—— *Der Freiheitsgedanke bei Epiktet und das Freiheitszeugnis des Paulus.* NTF 1; Gütersloh: Bertelsmann, 1923.

—— *Das Lebensgefühl des Paulus.* München: Beck, 1922.

Schneider, J. "σχῆμα, μετασχηματίζω." *TDNT* 7 (1971) 954–58.

Schneider, R. *Christliche Klänge aus den griechischen und römischen Klassikern.* Gotha: F. A. Perthes, 1865.

Schrage, Wolfgang. "Leid, Kreuz und Eschaton. Die Peristasenkataloge als Merkmale paulinischer theologia crucis und Eschatologie." *EvT* 34 (1974) 141–75.

Schreiner, T. *Seneca im Gegensatz zu Paulus: Ein Vergleich ihrer Welt-und Lebensanschauung.* Ph.D. Diss., Basel; Tübingen: E. Göbel, 1936.

Schrenk, G. "γράφω, κτλ." *TDNT* 1 (1964) 742–73.

Schüssler Fiorenza, E. "Apocalyptic and Gnosis in the Book of Revelation and Paul." *JBL* 92 (1973) 565–81.

Schütz, J. H. *Paul and the Anatomy of Apostolic Authority.* SNTSMS 26; New York: Cambridge University Press, 1975.

Schweitzer, Albert. *The Mysticism of Paul the Apostle.* 1931; 2d ed.; reprinted, New York: Seabury, 1968.

Scultetus, Abraham. *Deliciae evangelicae pragenses.* Hanoviae: Typis Wechelianus, apud D. & D. Aubrios & C. Schleichium, 1620.

Sevenster, J. N. *Paul and Seneca.* NovTSup 4; Leiden: Brill, 1961.

Snell, Bruno. *The Discovery of the Mind.* Cambridge: Harvard, 1953.

Sorabji, Richard. "Aristotle on the Role of Intellect in Virtue." *Essays on Aristotle's Ethics.* Ed. A. O. Rorty. Berkeley: University of California, 1980. 201–19.

Spicq, C. "L'image sportive de II Corinthiens,IV,7–9." *ETL* 14 (1937) 209–29.

Spiess, Edmund. *Logos Spermaticós: Parallelstellen zum Neuen Testament aus den Schriften der alten Griechen.* Leipzig: Engelmann, 1871.

von Staden, Heinrich. "The Stoic Theory of Perception and Its 'Platonic' Critics." *Studies in Perception.* Ed. P. K. Machamer and R. G. Turnbull; Columbus: Ohio State, 1978. 96–136.

Stählin, G. "περίψημα." *TDNT* 6 (1968) 84–93.

Steck, Rudolf. *Der Galaterbrief nach seiner Echtheit untersucht, nebst kritischen Bemerkungen zu den paulinischen Hauptbriefen.* Berlin: Reimer, 1888.

Stelzenberger, Johannes. *Die Beziehungen der frühchristlichen Sittenlehre zur Ethik der Stoa.* Munich: Hueber, 1933.

Stock, St. George. *Stoicism.* New York: Dodge, 1909.

Stowers, S. K. *The Diatribe and Paul's Letter to the Romans.* SBLDS 57; Chico: Scholars, 1981.

Strachan, R. H. *The Second Epistle of Paul to the Corinthians.* MNTC; London: Hodder & Stoughton, 1935.

Strachan-Davidson, J. L. *Selections from Polybius.* Oxford: Clarendon, 1888.

Strack, H. L. and Paul Billerbeck. *Kommentar zum Neuen Testament aus Talmud und Midrasch.* 6 vols.; München: Beck, 1924–61.

Striller, F. *De Stoicorum studiis rhetoricis.* Breslauer philologische Abhandlungen I. 2; Breslau: Köbner, 1886.

Strugnell J. "A Plea for Conjectural Emendation in the New Testament, with a Coda on 1 Cor. 4:6." *CBQ* 36 (1974) 543–58.

Stuart, D. R. *Epochs of Greek and Roman Biography.* Sather Classical Lectures 4; Berkeley: University of California Press, 1928.

Täubler, E. "Die Anfänge der Geschichtschreibung." *Tyche. Historische Studien.* Leipzig/Berlin: Teubner, 1926. 17–74.

Tannehill, R. C. *Dying and Rising with Christ.* BZNW 32; Berlin: Töpelmann, 1967.

Tasker, R. V. G. *The Second Epistle of Paul to the Corinthians.* Tyndale NT Commentaries 8; Grand Rapids: Eerdmans, 1963.

Taylor, A. E. *Plato: The Man and His Work.* 1926; reprinted, New York: Meridian, 1956.

Theissen, Gerd. *The Social Setting of Pauline Christianity.* Philadelphia: Fortress, 1982.

Thévenaz, Pierre. "L'intériorité chez Sénèque." *Melanges offerts à M. Niedermann.* Neuchâtel: Univ. de Neuchâtel, 1944. 189–94.

Thrall, M. E. "The Pauline Use of συνείδησις." *NTS* 14 (1967) 118–25.

Thyen, Hartwig. *Der Stil der Jüdisch-Hellenistischen Homilie.* FRLANT 65; Göttingen: Vandenhoeck & Ruprecht, 1955.

Timothy, H. B. *The Tenets of Stoicism, Assembled and Systematized, from the Works of L. Annaeus Seneca.* Amsterdam: Hakkert, 1973.

Toussaint, Constant. *L'hellénisme et l'Apôtre Paul.* Paris: Nourry, 1921.

Trillitzsch, Winfried. *Senecas Beweisführung.* DAWB; Berlin: Akademie Vlg., 1962.

Tsekourakis, D. *Studies in the Terminology of Early Stoic Ethics.* Wiesbaden: Steiner, 1974.

Turowski, Edmund. *Die Widerspiegelung des stoischen Systems bei Philon von Alexandria.* Borna-Leipzig: Universitätsverlag von R. Norske, 1927.

Ueberweg, F. and K. Praechter. *Grundriss der Geschichte der Philosophie.* Vol. I: *Die Philosophie des Altertums.* 12th rev. ed.; Berlin: Mittler, 1926.

Vaillant A. *Le Livre de Secrets d'Hénoch.* Paris: Institut d'études slaves, 1952.

Vallette, Paul. *L'Apologie d' Apulée.* Paris: C. Klincksieck, 1908.

Versnel, H. S. *Triumphus.* Leiden: Brill, 1970.

Vischer, Rüdiger. *Das einfache Leben.* Göttingen: Vandenhoeck & Ruprecht, 1965.

Vögtle, A. *Die Tugend- und Lasterkataloge im Neuen Testament.* NTAbh 16, 4/5; Münster: W. Aschendorff, 1936.

Volkmann, H. "Monumentum Ancyranum." *Kl. Pauly* 3 (1969) 1419–20.

Volkmann, Richard. *Die Rhetorik der Griechen und Römer.* 1885; Hildesheim: G. Olms, 1963.

Walbank, F. W. *A Historical Commentary on Polybius.* 3 vols.; Oxford: Clarendon, 1957–79.

Wallis, P. "Ein neuer Auslegungsversuch der Stelle I Kor. 4,6." *TLZ* 75 (1950) 506–08.

Watson, Gerard. *Stoic Theory of Knowledge.* Belfast: The Queen's University, 1966.

Weber, H. *De Senecae philosophi dicendi genere Bioneo.* Marburg: F. Soemmerling, 1895.

Weiss, Johannes. *Die Aufgaben der neutestamentlichen Wissenschaft in der Gegenwart.* Göttingen: Vandenhoeck & Ruprecht, 1908.

—— "Beiträge zur Paulinischen Rhetorik." *Theologische Studien. B. Weiss zu seinem 70. Geburtstage.* Ed. C. R. Gregory. Göttingen: Vandenhoeck & Ruprecht, 1897. 165–247.

—— *Die christliche Freiheit nach der Verkündigung des Apostels Paulus.* Göttingen: Vandenhoeck & Ruprecht, 1902.

—— *Der erste Korintherbrief.* MeyerK 5; 9th ed.; Göttingen: Vandenhoeck & Ruprecht, 1910.

—— and R. Knopf. *The History of Primitive Christianity.* 2 vols.; New York: Wilson-Erickson, 1937.

Wendland, H.-D. *Die Briefe an die Korinther.* NTD 7; 12th ed.; Göttingen: Vandenhoeck & Ruprecht, 1968.

Wendland, Paul. *Die hellenistisch-römische Kultur in ihren Beziehungen zu Judentum und Christentum.* HNT 1:2; 2d and 3d ed.; Tübingen: Mohr, 1912.

—— "Philo und die kynisch-stoische Diatribe." *Beiträge zur Geschichte der griechischen Philosophie und Religion.* Ed. P. Wendland and O. Kern. Berlin: Georg Reimer, 1895.

—— *Quaestiones Musonianae.* Berlin: Mayer und Müller, 1886.

—— Review of *De Stoicorum studiis rhetoricis* by F. Striller. *BPhW* 7 (1887) 367–70.

—— *Die urchristlichen Literaturformen.* HNT 1:3; Tübingen: Mohr, 1912.

Wenley, R. M. *Stoicism and Its Influence.* Boston: Marshall Jones, 1924.

Westcott, B. F. *The Epistle to the Hebrews.* 3d ed.; London: Macmillan, 1914.

Wetmore, J. H. L. *Seneca's Conception of the Stoic Sage as Shown in His Prose Works.* Alberta, Canada: University of Alberta, 1936.

Wettstein, J. J. *Novum Testamentum Graecum.* 1751; 2 vols.; reprinted, Graz, Oesterreich: Akademische Druck-und Verlagsanstalt, 1962.

Wibbing, S. *Die Tugend-und Lasterkataloge im Neuen Testament und ihre Traditionsgeschichte unter besonderer Berücksichtigung der Qumran-Texte.* BZNW 25; Berlin: Töpelmann, 1959.

Williamson, L., Jr. "Led in Triumph." *Int* 22 (1968) 317–32.

Wimmel, Walter. *Zur Form der horazischen Diatribensatire.* Frankfurt am Main: Klostermann, 1962.

Windelband, Wilhelm. *History of Ancient Philosophy.* New York: Scribners, 1899.

Windisch, Hans. "Literature on the New Testament in Germany, Austria, Switzerland, Holland, and the Scandinavian Countries, 1914–1920." *HTR* 15 (1922) 115–216.

—— *Paulus und Christus.* UNT 24; Leipzig: Hinrichs, 1934.

—— *Der zweite Korintherbrief.* MeyerK 6; 9th ed.; Göttingen: Vandenhoeck & Ruprecht, 1924.

Wischmeyer, Oda. *Der höchste Weg.* SNT 13; Gütersloh: Mohn, 1981.

Wolfson, H. A. *Philo.* 2 vols.; Cambridge: Harvard, 1947.

Zeller E. *Die Philosophie der Griechen in ihrer geschichtlichen Entwicklung.* Vol. III. 1: *Die nacharistotelische Philosophie.* 2 vols.; 6th ed.; Darmstadt: Wissenschaftliche Buchgesellschaft, 1963.

—— *The Stoics, Epicureans, and Sceptics.* Rev. ed.; London: Longmans, Green, and Co., 1892.

Zmijewski, Josef. *Der Stil der paulinischen "Narrenrede."* BBB 52; Köln/Berlin: Hanstein, 1978.

Indexes

NOTE: n = footnote(s). If the same page of this monograph contains a reference in both the text and the footnotes to the same passage or author, only the reference in the text will be indicated in the following index. Pseudonymous works are listed under the supposed author; e.g., for Pseudo-Plutarch, see "Plutarch." In general, the index contains citations from only one edition of an ancient author. In the case of certain authors (such as Musonius Rufus), citations from alternative editions are given in the text and footnotes.

I. ANCIENT TEXTS AND AUTHORS

A. Old Testament (Without Apocrypha)

B. Apocrypha and Pseudepigrapha

C. Josephus and Philo

D. The Dead Sea Scrolls and Rabbinica

E. New Testament

F. Non-Biblical Early Christian Literature

G. Other Ancient Texts and Authors

II. MODERN SCHOLARS

1. Attacks on Paul (opponents & "some")
2. Doubts about Paul ("many")
3. What Paul wants in the relationship
   - mutual pride   - acknowledgement of his role
   - Full understanding
4. The need for defense & self-promotion
5. The need for a shared "measure" by which to evaluate the effectiveness of his leadership

Purpose statements – 149-50
Purpose of self-commendation – 151-153
Ambiguity about boasting – 152-153

Printed in the United States
28192LVS00002B/234